The Changing Canadian Population

Edited by

BARRY EDMONSTON AND ERIC FONG

McGill-Queen's University Press
Montreal & Kingston • London • Ithaca

© McGill-Queen's University Press 2011
ISBN 978-0-7735-3793-4 (cloth)
ISBN 978-0-7735-3794-1 (paper)

Legal deposit first quarter 2011
Bibliothèque nationale du Québec

Printed in Canada on acid-free paper that is 100% ancient forest free
(100% post-consumer recycled), processed chlorine free

Publication of this book was made possible by financial support from
the Population Change and Lifecourse Cluster, Strategic Knowledge
Cluster, which is funded by Canada's Social Sciences and Humanities
Research Council.

McGill-Queen's University Press acknowledges the support of the Canada
Council for the Arts for our publishing program. We also acknowledge the
financial support of the Government of Canada through the Canada Book
Fund for our publishing activities.

Library and Archives Canada Cataloguing in Publication

The changing Canadian population / edited by Barry Edmonston and Eric Fong.

Includes bibliographical references.
ISBN 978-0-7735-3793-4 (bound). – ISBN 978-0-7735-3794-1 (pbk.)

1. Canada – Population. 2. Population geography – Canada. I. Edmonston, Barry
II. Fong, Eric, 1960–

HB3529.C425 2011   304.60971   C2010-903975-0

This book was typeset by Interscript in 10/13 Sabon.

Contents

Contributors

RODERIC BEAUJOT, professor, Department of Sociology University of Western Ontario

MONICA BOYD, Canada Research Chair and professor, Department of Sociology, University of Toronto

ELIC CHAN, graduate student, Department of Sociology, University of Toronto

BARRY EDMONSTON, research professor, Department of Sociology, University of Victoria

ERIC FONG, professor, Department of Sociology, University of Toronto

ERIN GIBBS VAN BRUNSCHOT, vice dean, Faculty of Arts, and associate professor, Department of Sociology, University of Calgary

GUSTAVE GOLDMANN, senior fellow, Faculty of Social Sciences, University of Ottawa and adjunct professor, School of Public Policy and Administration, Carleton University

MADELINE A. KALBACH, professor emeritus, Department of Sociology, University of Calgary

DON KERR, associate professor, Department of Sociology, King's University College at University of Western Ontario

RÉJEAN LACHAPELLE, visiting researcher, Centre Urbanisation, Culture, Société (Montreal), Institut national de la recherche scientifique

SHARON M. LEE, research professor, Department of Sociology, University of Victoria

JIANYE LIU, associate professor, Department of Sociology Lakehead University

BILL MARR, professor emeritus, Department of Economics, Wilfrid Laurier University

KEVIN MCQUILLAN, dean, Faculty of Arts, and professor, Department of Sociology, University of Calgary

K. BRUCE NEWBOLD, professor, School of Geography and Earth Science, McMaster University

FERNANDO RAJULTON, professor emeritus, Population Studies Centre, University of Western Ontario

CHRISTOPH M. SCHIMMELE, graduate student, Department of Sociology, University of Victoria

ALAN SIMMONS, professor, Department of Sociology, York University

ZONGLI TANG, associate professor, Department of Sociology, Auburn University at Montgomery

FRANK TROVATO, professor, Department of Sociology and Population Research Laboratory, University of Alberta

RICHARD A. WANNER, professor, Department of Sociology, University of Calgary

RIMA WILKES, associate professor, Department of Sociology, University of British Columbia

ZHENG WU, professor and chair, Department of Sociology, University of Victoria

THE CHANGING CANADIAN POPULATION

Introduction

BARRY EDMONSTON AND ERIC FONG

Most countries conduct periodic population censuses to serve electoral and legislative needs, such as assigning the number of parliamentary seats for each province and setting the boundaries for legislative members. Population censuses also assist government in important policy and program functions, such as coordinating and planning education, health, labour force, and other public policies. Canada has conducted regular population censuses since 1851 and, since 1951, has taken population censuses every five years.

In addition to functions directly related to government, Canada's population censuses have other important uses. Businesses rely on census data to understand the market potential for their products and for information about local employment markets. Non-profit and service organizations need the census for information about their client populations, such as the location and number of low-income or disabled people. The population census also provides a critical element, in conjunction with other demographic data, for the scientific study of population. Demographers and other social scientists rely to a great extent on periodic Canadian census data for their study of social and economic changes in the Canadian population.

BACKGROUND

The study of demographic dynamics relies on two key sources of data. The first are population censuses, typically conducted every ten or five years in most industrialized nations. Population censuses provide a snapshot, at one point in time, of the national population and its numbers, location, and characteristics. With data from two censuses, demographers are able to provide information about rates of population growth, migration, and changes in a variety of important social and economic measures, such as differences in families and households, educational attainment, the proportion married, and family income levels. Population census data, either in tabulations prepared by national statistical agencies such as Statistics Canada, or public-use microdata files (sample data files for individuals, families, or households that are made available for public use and, for confidential reasons, do not include personal information about names, addresses, or other personal identifiers) are a major data source for specialized demographic research.

The second main source of demographic data is records of vital events, including births, deaths, marriages, and divorces. These data provide information about population events over time: how many births occurred, how many deaths occurred, and the difference in the number of births and the number of deaths. Demographers use data on these vital events to calculate a variety of important measures, such as the average number of children born to a women over her lifetime (the total fertility rate), the probability of dying by age and the number of years of life expectancy at birth, and rates of population change (the difference between the birth rate and the death rate is referred to as the rate of natural increase). This volume is primarily devoted to the analysis of population census data. Some chapters refer to vital statistics, however, in order to support their analysis.

In addition to population censuses and vital statistics, demographers also use data from other sources, such as sample surveys, in order to study specific topics for which data are appropriate. Many countries, for example, have conducted surveys of the elderly in order to collect more detailed information about their health, access to medical care, and retirement income.

This volume includes eighteen chapters written by many of Canada's leading population scholars. The purpose of this volume is to understand the current population situation and future population-related challenges through an analysis of data from Canada's 2001 census.

We have grouped the eighteen chapters in this volume in the following five sections: an overview of Canada's population context; social stratification; population distribution and migration; families, children and the elderly; and ethnicity, religion, and language. The following chapters explicate in greater details the main themes of this volume.

DEMOGRAPHIC PROCESSES

Demographic processes play an important role in broader changes of Canada. The eminent Canadian historian Robert Bothwell (2006) notes in his concluding chapter that there have been several great constants in Canadian history. One constant has been external: that Canada has always been concerned with relationships with a larger political power, which was Great Britain for several centuries and has been the United States more recently. Three historical constants are primarily internal and all have strong demographic aspects: English-French, native-non-native, and East-West relationships. English-French relationships are affected by the relative growth of the population, especially as it changes the numbers and proportions of English and French speakers. Growth rates, in turn, are a reflection of differences in fertility rates (which do not vary greatly at present for language groups) and migration. In recent years, the movement of people to English-speaking provinces and the large-scale arrival of immigrants have affected the language composition of the population. This volume includes discussion of language (Chapter 18) as well as chapters on the spatial distribution of the Canadian population (Chapter 8).

Native-non-native relationships have been an important feature of Canadian society since the arrival of Europeans to a land inhabited by about 200,000 native peoples. In the early period, the higher fertility and lower mortality of Europeans, supplemented by new arrivals, led to a predominance of European-origin residents within a few decades. By the mid-1900s, there were fewer native peoples than when European settlers first arrived (Kalbach and McVey 1979,176). In recent decades, there has been a demographic revival of the native peoples (described in Chapter 16), as well as dramatic increases in the number of Canadian residents who report themselves as Métis. Mortality improvements as well as higher average fertility levels helped Aboriginal populations recover from the drastic reductions of the early colonial period. In spite of the demographic revival of the Aboriginal population, their numbers remain relatively small.

East-West relationships are a recurrent topic on Canada's national political scene. Barely a month goes by without some mention in the national press about which provinces contribute the most (or the least) to the federal budget, taxation of national resources (especially if they occur in Alberta), and the provincial voting pattern of parliamentary members. The East-West relationships have a demographic aspect to them because population movements have changed the provincial distribution of population over the past century. If everyone lived primarily in Ontario and Quebec, as was the case in the early 1900s, there would probably still be national concerns with the West, but they would not be a pressing national issue. Indeed, the settlement of the Prairies and the continued recent growth of Alberta and British Columbia – the result of both internal and international migration – have redefined the role of western Canada in the national political debate and the East-West relationship.

CANADA'S POPULATION CONTEXT

The first section of this volume includes three chapters that place the Canadian population in a historical and comparative perspective and include overviews of the age and sex composition, and of households and families.

Canada's population, seen from a global perspective, is quite small, constituting less than one percent (actually, 0.5 percent) of the world's population. And, given the immense size of the Canadian land mass, it is not a surprise that Canada ranks as one of the least densely settled countries. In spite of its small population, Canada has been among the main destinations for immigrants and has had relatively higher population growth rates than other industrialized nations. Alan B. Simmons' chapter, "The Population of Canada," provides a comprehensive description and interpretation of Canada's historical population change in a global context.

Seen through a historical lens, Canada's population growth from 2.5 million in 1851 to slightly more than 31 million in 2001 suggests why Canadians have become accustomed to the idea of population increase. A more careful study of historical population change, however, reveals that there have been substantial variations, with slower rates of growth in the Great Depression of the 1930s, for instance. In recent years, Canada's rate of population growth has diminished as a result of lower fertility levels that decreased the rate of natural increase (the excess of births minus deaths).

Simmons' chapter argues that Canada is entering a period of slower population change and could even experience population decreases in the near future if fertility were to decrease to European levels. If current trends continue for fertility and net immigration (the difference between the number of international arrivals and departures) – assuming continued mortality improvements – Canada's population would peak at about 42 million in the mid-2050s and then slowly decrease. For a country that has long assumed continued population increases, the notion of population decrease may seem controversial. Other countries, particularly Japan and Europe, have been debating the consequences of population shrinkage for several years. Canadians should be interested in this debate, including policy options for affecting and dealing with the possibility of population shrinkage.

The most fundamental feature of populations is their age and sex structure. The age and sex composition of a population is largely a consequence of earlier patterns of fertility, mortality, and migration. If fertility has been relatively high in the past, for example, then there will be a larger population of younger persons compared to the number of older persons. If mortality is substantially higher for males, then there will be an excess of elderly females compared to elderly males. The age and sex composition of migrants also affects a population's structure. The age and sex composition of a population, in turn, affects vital rates themselves. A population with a larger number of women in the childbearing ages is generally associated with greater numbers of births. A population's age and sex structure, therefore, is both a determinant and consequence of other population processes. Frank Trovato discusses Canada's age and sex composition in his chapter.

Trovato demonstrates that Canada, like other low fertility countries, will experience demographic aging over the next two to three decades. For Canada, which experienced a large baby boom during the first two decades after World War II, the greatest increase in the elderly population will occur roughly between 2011 and 2036. It is during this period that the greatest demographic pressures will occur on the public pension system and, in later years, on the public health system. As Trovato notes, pressures on the public pension system are accentuated by the tendency of older workers to retire at earlier ages.

Every individual is faced with decisions about whom to live with (or to live alone) and to find some sort of housing. Such decisions, of course, are made in the context of personal circumstances, available choices, and local housing markets. For many years, the modal or most common choice seemed to be a married couple with several children living in a single housing unit that they owned. Such a modal choice no longer adequately describes the Canadian population today. Household arrangements are considerably more diverse, ranging from a large proportion of individuals who live alone to complex households that include several related families and, perhaps, several unrelated individuals. Housing is also varied, including rental as well as owned units, mobile homes, tents, shelters for transient persons, and no permanent housing for the homeless. This topic is the subject of Fernando Rajulton's chapter, "Households and Housing in Canada."

Studying households and housing at one point in time, using 2001 census data, may hide the social, economic, and political processes that are changing Canada's household structure and the type of housing for households. The main processes affecting households, Rajulton argues, include international migration and population aging. In recent years, the housing market has changed in several ways, with some Canadians seeking larger housing and with some younger persons and those with part-time employment experiencing difficulties buying homes because of inadequate income for increasing housing prices.

SOCIAL STRATIFICATION

Canadians are differentiated by several dimensions of social status. Census data provides useful information about various important measures of social status, including educational attainment, income, employment, and occupation. The second part of this volume includes four chapters dealing with specific measures of social status.

By the mid-1800s, several provinces offered free public education to their residents. The British North America Act of 1867 enshrined these practices by stating that provinces would be responsible for the education of their residents with the exception of Native Peoples or people living outside the ten provinces, who would be the responsibility of the federal government. In the years following Confederation, each province formed its educational department, devised taxation and funding schemes for public education, and enacted legislation for compulsory education. From these early beginnings, the educational system has expanded to more than 15,500 public elementary and secondary schools and more than 90 places of higher education. In addition, there are about 1,700 private elementary and secondary schools. As a consequence of the tremendous expansion of educational institutions over the past 150 years, adult illiteracy has become rare (although there are still concerns about functional literacy in a more demanding technological economy) and virtually all younger persons attend and complete elementary school. What has become more important is the amount of advanced education completed by Canadians. This is a topic covered by Kevin McQuillan in his chapter "The Educational Attainment of Canadians."

The evolving economies of the industrialized world have witnessed decreases in manual employment and the expansion of knowledge workers. As a result, governments direct large amounts of public funds toward education and programs to advance the training and education of adults. Parents also are willing to spend considerable sums to make sure that their children have a high-quality education. McQuillan's examination of recent census data on educational attainment highlights the great success of women and children of recent immigrants. Women's attendance in college and university now exceeds that of men, and the gap seems to be increasing. Despite the challenge that some recent immigrants may have experienced in the labour market, their children have been remarkably successful in formal education, and this encourages hopes that children of immigrants will do well in the labour market due to their educational attainment.

The concept of low income was developed in the 1960s in Canada as a way to measure and describe families who are economically worse off than the average household. The measure of low income was developed for analysis of 1961 Canadian census data, based on a definition of low income by Statistics Canada. In the chapter on "Low Income Status by Population Groups," Roderic Beaujot, Jianye Liu, and Don Kerr examine low income groups for the past forty years.

The analysis of Beaujot, Liu, and Kerr suggests that there has been an overall downward trend in the proportion of families in the low income category. The generally improving downward trend, however, has been interrupted by higher rates of low income families during the 1982–84 and 1993–96 recessions. Not all family types have experienced improvements: two parent families with children and one-earner families have witnessed increases in the proportion that are in the low income category. Researchers have distinguished several processes associated with low income, and this chapter presents useful discussion of these processes. The elderly are no longer an important pocket of low income, for example, although divorce continues to remain an important determinant of low income families. In terms of policy challenges for the future, the authors argue that youth and younger families present the greatest needs for attention with programs and policies to alleviate their low income status.

Census data provides valuable information about the numbers and types of economically productive work of Canadians. The types of activities of workers reveal much about the changing economy. As previously noted, census data are collected in Canada every five years. The timing of the census, however, is not frequent enough for analysis of cyclical changes in the economy. Rather, census data are more useful for describing the longer-term structural changes in the Canadian labour force. To understand recent changes in the labour force, Bill Marr prepared a chapter entitled "Labour Force" for this volume.

Using data from the 1991 and 2001 censuses, Marr reports on changes in labour force participation rates, full-time and part-time employment, and weeks worked. The chapter also includes discussion of three structural dimensions of the labour force – industry, occupation, and class of worker – and the foreign-born.

Occupation is a central aspect of social status. Occupation is affected to a considerable extent by education and, in turn, is an important determinant of income. The Canadian economy sets the conditions for employment and the type of occupations, but individual occupations are largely a matter of personal choice and attainment. Over the past century, urbanization and industrialization have profoundly altered Canada's occupational structure. As late as 1871, more than one-half of workers were classified as farmers or directly involved in agriculture. The proportion of the labour force engaged in agricultural activities has declined to only 3 percent in 2001. In recent years, there have been gains in the share of workers employed in trade, finance, insurance, and real estate, and public administration. Richard A. Wanner's chapter on "Occupation and Industry" presents a clear description of changes in the national occupational structure.

Along with the momentous changes that have occurred over the past century in Canada's industry and occupational structures, equally important changes have been occurring in the composition of the labour force. In particular, there has been a surge in employment of women during the past fifty years, coupled with decreases in male employment rates, especially at the older ages. As a result, women have become a much more critical part of the labour force, and have changed the sex composition for many occupations. Wanner's chapter also includes a discussion of how immigrants, visible minorities, and population aging are changing Canada's occupational structure.

POPULATION DISTRIBUTION AND MIGRATION

Where Canadians live and where they move is the subject of the third part of this volume. It includes four chapters dealing with the spatial distribution of the population, internal migration, and international migration.

The first chapter in this section looks at the spatial distribution of racial and ethnic groups. The geographic distribution of population varies among groups. In the last century, immigrant groups settled in different parts of the country when they arrived. Current settlement patterns reflect the economic opportunities and developments that were present in different periods. Despite the arrival of new immigrants and the change in the source of immigrants from European to non-European countries at the second half of the last century, this multicultural regionalism still persists. In their chapter on the spatial distribution of racial and ethnic groups in Canada, Eric Fong and Elic Chan show that of the Charter groups, French are still overwhelming represented in Quebec, and British in Ontario and British Columbia at the beginning of the 21st century. At the same time, new immigrant groups, such as southern Europeans and visible minorities, have higher proportions in Ontario and British Columbia. Although they have settled in various cities, recent immigrant groups are mainly found in major cities like Montreal, Toronto, and Vancouver.

Fong and Chan also explore the racial and ethnic composition of neighbourhoods. This information indicates the spatial interaction among some groups may be limited, even if they reside in the same city. Using 2001 census data from the four largest Canadian cities, they document that most neighbourhoods are diverse in their racial and ethnic composition. Despite the multiethnic composition of neighbourhoods, English and old European immigrant groups, such as German, Scottish, and Dutch, are more likely to share their neighbourhoods with their own groups and less likely to share them with visible minority groups. At the same time, more recent European immigrant groups, such as Italians and Portuguese, reside in ethnic neighbourhoods, while visible minority groups are more likely to reside in neighbourhoods with other visible minority groups. The high ethnic clustering of more recent European immigrant groups and visible minority groups may reflect their recent arrival, which draws members together. In short, Fong and Chan suggest that not only are racial and ethnic groups unevenly distributed in provinces and cities, they share neighbourhoods unevenly with other groups, even in multiethnic cities.

The chapter by Bruce Newbold examines the urban population in Canada. He finds that the population of Canada has become more concentrated in urban areas, particularly in large urban areas. At the beginning of the last century, only 40 percent of the population was living in urban areas. The pace of urbanization was still slow in the middle of the century, when less than 60 percent of the population resided in urban areas. However, urbanization accelerated in the second half of the 20th century. By 2001, only 2.4 percent of Canada's population was living in rural areas.

At the beginning of the 21st century, not only do Canadians overwhelming reside in urban areas, they are concentrated in three major cities. For example, in 2001, the population of Toronto, Montreal, and Vancouver accounted for 35 percent of the total Canadian population. The growth of these cities has led to population decline in some smaller urban areas. Using census data, Newbold found that seven CMAs experienced decline in their total population between 1996 and 2001. Newbold explains that rapid urbanization and concentration of population in major cities were the consequences of a net gain in internal migration and international immigration. People moved to cities because of economic conditions and attractive amenities.

Internal migration is one of the major factors contributing to urbanization and concentration of population in a few major cities as suggested by Newbold, and it is also one of the major components of population change. Internal migration refers to movement of population within a country, whereas as international migration is movement across countries. Using 2001 Canadian census, Barry Edmonston reports in his chapter that internal migration rates differ among provinces. Ontario's rate of non-movers (i.e., individuals whose residence remains the same as five year ago) is similar to the national average. Alberta and British Columbia, and the combined populations of Yukon, Northwest Territories, and Nunavut have considerably lower rates of non-movers than the national average. In other words, these provinces/territories have a higher rate of people moving in or out. To explain these differences, Edmonston studied the in and out migration rates of provinces/territories. Census data shows that between 1996 and 2001 there was net out-migration from the Atlantic provinces, Quebec, Manitoba, and Saskatchewan. These findings echo Newbold's explanation of the concentration of population in a few major cities. Alberta has experienced considerable in-migration. Internal migration patterns are varied by a set of demographic and socioeconomic factors. Individuals who are in their late teens, twenties, and early thirties, who have higher education levels, holding managerial and professional occupations, or with lower income are more likely to move. However, these patterns vary among provinces.

International migration, as demonstrated in earlier chapters in this section, has a profound effect on the Canadian population. International migration makes major contributions to Canada's population growth, as well as affecting its economic development and its demographic and social diversity. In a chapter on "Immigrants in Canada," Monica Boyd discusses the enduring and defining qualities of international migration. She observes that net migration now is the most important factor fuelling population growth and soon is likely to account for Canada's net labour force growth.

Canada's immigrants are a diverse group. Boyd's chapter demonstrates that the overall immigrant population is a composite of different entry cohorts that come from all countries of the world and vary greatly in their age, family characteristics, religions, languages, and education, occupations and earnings. In recent years, a high proportion of immigrants are visible minorities. Boyd's chapter confirms that recent visible minority immigrants have not been doing as well economically as earlier arrivals. The children of immigrants, however, are doing better. Compared to the non-visible minority third-plus generation adults (the Canadian-born with Canadian-born parents), those who are Canadian-born visible minorities but have immigrant parents are more likely to still be attending school and, as noted in McQuillan's chapter, they have higher educational attainment. In combination with results for occupations and earnings, these findings suggest that the difficulties faced by recent visible minority immigrants in the labour market may not extend to the next generations.

The chapters in this section have revealed the unique spatial distribution of the population in Canada. The population is increasingly concentrated. Racial and ethnic groups are continuing to disperse unevenly in different parts of the country, and visible minority groups are heavily concentrated in major cities. Part of the existing geographic distribution is due to the internal and international migration of groups with selective demographic and social characteristics.

FAMILIES, CHILDREN, AND THE ELDERLY

The fourth section of the volume focuses on families, children and youth, and the elderly. It includes three chapters dealing with these important demographic aspects.

Childbearing is an important element that affects population growth, while the family is one of the major institutions of society. In the first chapter of this section, Zheng Wu and Christoph Schimmele provide a detailed description of the status of Canadian families at the beginning of the 21st century. They warn that trying to understand current family patterns, including fertility patterns and family structure, by contrasting them to family patterns in the 1950s can be misleading and also exaggerate the claims of "family in crisis" proponents in today's society. Therefore, their analysis compares census data from 1981 and 2001.

Their findings suggest that the nuclear family remains the dominant family structure among Canadians. In 2001, the two major household types in Canada were couple-family households with children, comprising 31 percent of all private households, and couple-family households without children, comprising 28 percent of all private households. Together they account for about 60 percent of all private Canadian households.

Given that couple-family households are the dominant family structure, Wu and Schimmele explore marriage patterns. They document a number of important patterns: fewer men and women are married, despite couple-family households being the dominant structure; the average age at first marriage for both men and women has been further delayed; cohabitation among Canadians has drastically increased (Wu and Schimmele argue that cohabitation is only a short term arrangement and most cohabitation transits to long term marital union); divorce has drastically increased; the remarriage rate has increased considerably; and the percentage of households with children has dropped. Without doubt, Canadian family life in the 21st century is significantly different from the last century.

The study of childbearing and family patterns is not complete without the discussion of children. The chapter by Jianye Liu, Don Kerr, and Rod Beaujot on the demography of children and youth in Canada echoes the findings of Wu and Schimmele. It documents the decline in the number of children (persons aged 0 to 14 years), youth (persons aged 15 to 24 years) and number of siblings in Canadian families today. A larger percentage of children and youth live with single parents than was the case twenty years ago. Most youths, however, still live with two-parent families – a pattern which the authors suggest reflects the delay in youths leaving home.

The economic well-being of children and youth varies according to their family structure. Children and youth are more likely to live in poverty in one-parent families and less likely to live in poverty in married couple families. The situation of children is better than previous decades regarding school attendance; this is an important improvement because educational attainment is a key determinant of occupation success and higher lifetime income. More youth are in school now compared to twenty years ago. The number of young women in school has increased more than the number of young men. As more youth are in school, their labour force participation is lower than it was twenty years ago.

Zongli Tang's chapter documents the elderly population. He reports that about 13 percent of Canadians were aged 65 and over in 2001. Five years earlier, the percentage was only 10 percent. These older Canadians have a lower level of education than younger generations and, as expected, lower income than younger Canadians. However, the income level does not fully reflect their economic condition, as most of them have paid their home mortgages, and their children have usually left home and are financially independent. Older women have lower income than older men. Most seniors have retired by age 65. Of persons aged 65 and older, only about 13 percent of men and 5 percent of women are still working. Most of them reside with their spouses, which implies that most of them enjoy companionship and support.

ETHNICITY, RELIGION, AND LANGUAGE

The fifth and final section of the volume focuses on the ethnic origin, the Aboriginal peoples of Canada, religious affiliation, and language of Canadians. This section includes four chapters.

Canada is increasingly diverse as it enters the 21st century. Most of our knowledge of racial and ethnic groups in Canada is drawn from census data. However, Sharon Lee's chapter cautions against comparing data about racial and ethnic origin from different census years, because over time there have been changes in the format of questions, and changes in respondents' understanding of their ethnic origins. At the same time, data collection has become more complicated, as the population has become more ethnically diverse and has a higher proportion of immigrants. There can be confusion in answering overlapping and separate questions about nativity, ethnic origin, and visible minority status.

Focusing on the population in 2001, Lee shows that the diverse ethnic composition of Canada is related to immigration. This was first evident in the 1981 census, after changes in immigration policies resulted in a shift in the country-of-origin of immigrants: in the 1970s and after, most Canadian immigrants arrived from non-European countries. As she compares ages among ethnic groups, Lee notes that ethnic groups with large proportions of foreign-born population, such as African and Latin American groups, are younger. She also shows that the multiple ethnic origin group is younger, reflecting recent increases in ethnic intermarriage among Canadians.

The comparison of the geographic distribution of ethnic groups suggests that they are not evenly distributed. The two largest groups, "Canadian" and "multiple origins," are mainly in Quebec and the Eastern provinces. The ethnic composition differs among the three largest metropolitan areas, Montreal, Toronto, and Vancouver, are quite different, reflecting historical and recent demographic, social, and economic developments. The growing ethnic diversity in Canada (largely due to immigration) means greater language diversity. However, only a few Canadians do not know either English or French. About 12 percent of respondents report that their home language is other than English or French, and groups with a large representation of immigrants have a higher percentage of respondents who do so.

The census also shows that there are substantial variations among ethnic groups in education, income, and rates of homeownership, with particularly lower educational and income achievements among the Aboriginal population.

In her chapter, Rima Wilkes analyzed census data on the aboriginal population. Based on the 2001 census, her paper provides updated information on the aboriginal population. In addition, her analysis explores national patterns instead of the conventional approach of comparing urban and rural differences. She focuses on the socioeconomic resources of the aboriginal population. Aboriginals are more likely than non-Aboriginals to be occupied in sales, trades, and primary industries. There is a wide disparity in income between Aboriginals and non-Aboriginals. Over 50 percent of the Aboriginal population is considered to be low income as compared to 30 percent to 45 percent of the non-Aboriginal population. The lower income of Aboriginals is partly related to their lower rate of participation in the labour force, and partly related to their educational level. Although there are provincial differences, a lower percentage of Aboriginals have completed

university, and a much higher percentage have less than high school education, in comparison with the non-Aboriginal average. In short, Aboriginals
truly are the disadvantaged group in Canada.

To add to the discussion of the ethno-cultural contour of Canada,
Madeline Kalbach discusses religious affiliation among Canadians. She reports that Roman Catholicism has been the major identified religious affiliation among Canadians since 1871, and a large proportion of those identified
as Roman Catholic are located in Quebec. However, the traditional main-
stream Christian religion has been declining over recent decades, and there
is a growing diversity of religious affiliation because of recent immigration
from non-European countries. According to Kalbach, new immigrants are
less likely to identify themselves as Roman Catholic, Jewish, or other main-
stream Christian denominations such as Lutheran.

This section concludes with a chapter on the important topic of language
in Canada, co-authored by Réjean Lachapelle and Gustave Goldmann. The
linguistic duality of Canada is important because, while Aboriginal languages
and the languages of immigrant groups are widely spoken, French and English
hold a special place – both have equal status at the federal level by law. This
chapter uses available census data to trace the evolution of Canada's linguistic
duality, including trends in French and English as mother tongues and the self-
reported language behaviour of individuals and families. The chapter discusses the situation of Aboriginal languages and their current and potential users,
especially recent trends concerning the persistence and revitalization of these
languages. The chapter describes changes in groups whose language is associated with immigration from non-English and non-French speaking countries.
While the major languages from earlier waves of immigration – including
German, Ukrainian and Italian – are declining, there is a strong upswing in
the languages of more recent immigrant groups – especially Chinese, Punjabi
and Arabic. For Canada's recent immigrants, there are many interesting questions about language. Are almost all the people who speak these languages
speaking them as a mother tongue or are others acquiring these languages?
Do the languages survive beyond the second or third generation as the main
languages spoken at home? When immigrants acquire new home languages,
do they learn French, English, or both?

CENSUS INFORMATION

Statistics Canada conducts a census of the Canadian population every five
years, in years ending in "1" and "6." The most recent census was conducted
in 2006. Statistics Canada releases numerous data products as soon as pos-

sible after census data has been processed and tabulated. Several products are helpful for learning more about recent changes in the Canadian population. The Statistics Canada's website address for the 2006 census is http://www12. statcan.ca/census-recensement/index-eng.cfm for English language materials. The website also includes French language materials.

Among the most useful Statistics Canada census products are the following:

- Highlight Tables present information topics for key indicators for various levels of geography. They present, for example, the percent distribution by age as well as the percentage change between 2001 and 2006. Users can also get data shown for simple functions, such as ranked from the highest to lowest percentage change in the elderly population for Canada's metropolitan areas.
- Topic-based Tabulations are available for aboriginal peoples, age and sex, education, ethnic origin and visible minorities, families and households, housing and shelter costs, immigration and citizenship, income and earnings, labour force status, language, marital status, mobility and migration, and place of work and commuting to work.
- Community Profiles from the 2006 census provide useful tabulations for Canada, its provinces and territories, and for 5,418 communities, 288 counties (or their equivalents), and 33 large and 111 smaller metropolitan areas. Each profile reports several tabulations, including the total number of persons and households, as well as the distribution of population for such variables as age, marital status, family and household characteristics, home language, immigrant status, education, occupation, and income.
- Census Trends presents a series of summary data trends for three censuses: 2006, 2001, and 1996. Users can request analysis and comparisons for 85 key data indicators, such as the percent of the population of recent immigrants for Canada's provinces and territories.

Readers will find recent information from the 2006 census for many topics discussed in this volume. Chapters in this volume provide more detailed analysis of census data, however, than can be found in tabulations available from the Statistics Canada website. Results reported in this volume were usually obtained from analysis of census microdata files. Census microdata files are an anonymous sample of actual individuals, families, or households from the complete census records. Statistics Canada removes all names, addresses, and identifying information from the original data files so that they are completely anonymous. The sample files, for instance, report age, sex, marital status, and other information for someone living in Saskatchewan.

But, the sample would not provide the name, address, or other information that could identify an actual person.

Statistics Canada releases two types of census microdata files. The most common files are public-use microdata files that include samples of individuals, families, and households. These files are usually released about four years after the census. Public-use census microdata files from the 2006 census will probably be released in 2010. Public-use microdata census files are widely analyzed by social science researchers for the study of population trends.

A second type of census microdata file is restricted data files that provide more detailed variable categories and geographic information from the census. These data files are restricted to Statistics Canada's Research Data Centres. Research Data Centres provide researchers in a secure university setting with access to microdata from population censuses as well as household surveys. The centres are staffed by Statistics Canada employees and are operated under the provisions of the Statistics Act in accordance with all the confidentiality rules. Research Data Centres are accessible only to researchers with approved projects who have been sworn in under the Statistics Act as 'deemed employees.' There are currently fifteen Research Data Centres located throughout Canada.

Microdata files are especially useful for researchers because they provide access to non-aggregated individual-level data. Researchers can tabulate and manipulate variables to suit their data and research requirements – as illustrated in the tables and figures in this volume. Tabulations that are not presented in Statistics Canada's other census products can be created, relationships between variables can be analysed using different statistical tests, and more sophisticated analysis can be undertaken.

MAJOR THEMES

Several common ideas cross-cut the chapters in this volume. First, the fertility rate of the Canadian population has been relatively low for several decades and, like other developing countries, has led to the aging of the population.

Second, Canada ranks among the largest recipients of international migration. Since 1960, Canada has received about 8 million immigrants. In recent years, about 250,000 immigrants settle in Canada each year, contributing about two-thirds of Canada's annual population increase of 1 percent. Besides adding to Canada's population growth, immigrants have been diversifying the population and changing the ethnic composition in new ways. Large-scale immigration has been changing Canada's society, government, and attitudes of residents. Canada's two most recent governor-generals have been Hong Kong-born Adrienne Clarkson and Haiti-born Michaëlle Jean, symbolizing the significant changes that immigration has brought to Canada. Although the Canadian population was historically distinctive in terms of native and non-natives and French and English-speakers, immigration is changing the population, creating a more multi-ethnic society.

Third, the Canadian population continues to reshape society through internal migration (that is, through the domestic geographical mobility of people). Two long-term population movements persist: migration from rural areas and small towns to larger towns and cities, and movement from province to province. During recent years, most migrants have settled in Alberta, British Columbia, and Ontario – a pattern of movement that has prevailed for several decades.

REFERENCES

Bothwell, Robert. 2006. *The Penguin History of Canada*. Toronto: Penguin Canada

Kalbach, Warren, and Wayne W. McVey. 1979. *The Demographic Bases of Canadian Society*. 2nd edition. Toronto: McGraw-Hill Ryerson

Trovato, Frank, and Carl F. Grindstaff, eds. 1994. *Perspectives on Canada's Population*. Toronto: Oxford University Press.

PART ONE

Canada's Population Context

1

Population Growth:
From Fast Growth to Possible Decline

Canada's population grew rapidly over the period from the 1850s to 1960. Since then, the pace of growth has gradually slowed. At present the total population of the country is somewhat more than 33 million people, a number that will increase slowly compared with the past if the current growth trajectory continues. This chapter concerns the reasons why Canada's population grew quickly in the past and why it is growing slowly now, future population growth scenarios, the challenges that slow population growth will create for the well-being of Canadians, and how these challenges can be addressed. These issues are examined within a "nation building" framework covering the relationship of population growth to Canada's political-economic opportunities and strategies.

I EXPLAINING PAST PATTERNS

In 1851 the area that now comprises Canada had a population of two and one-half million (figure 1.1). A hundred and sixty years later, in 2010, Canada had a population of slightly more than 33 million – an increase of more than twelve times over. In a graph showing Canada's population size over this long historical period, the trend is steadily upward with no readily apparent indication that the population growth of the past may be coming to an end (figure 1.1). Yet a more careful examination of the numbers reveals that the percent increase in the Canadian population from one census to another has been extremely variable in the past and has been decreasing steadily since the 1960s (figure 1.2). Canada's population growth over the period 2001–2006 was less than 1 percent per year, the lowest ever recorded. If current trends continue, Canada will enter a period of increasingly slower population growth. If population growth drops further, Canada would be vulnerable to population decline within the foreseeable future.

Figure 1.1
Canadian Population (in thousands) 1851 to 2001

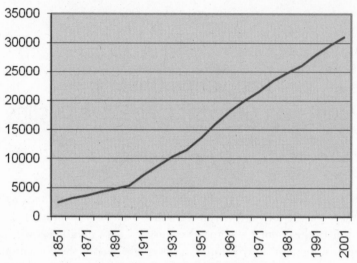

Source: http://www.statcan.ca/english/freepub/98-187-XIE/pop.htm.

Figure 1.2
Percent Growth in the Canadian Population by Decade, 1851 to 2001

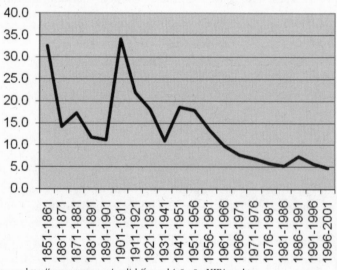

Source: http://www.statcan.ca/english/freepub/98-187-XIE/pop.htm.

Describing trends in Canadian population growth is relatively simple. Explaining these trends is a much more demanding task. The goal in this section is to provide a "big picture" that examines the broad historical and structural forces that have shaped Canadian population trends. The analysis draws on three interdependent theoretical frameworks. The first is the *Demographic Transition Model*; this provides insights into the role of natural increase (births less deaths) in population growth (Weeks 2008: 89–107; Trovato 2009: 55–69). The second is the *International Migration Systems Framework*; this helps us to understand immigration and emigration patterns over time (Kritz, Lim, and Zlotnik 1992; Massey et al 1998, ch. 3; Simmons 2010, ch. 2). The third is a *Canadian Nation Building Model*; it provides a macro-framework for understanding both the Canadian demographic transition and the Canadian experience with international migration (Simmons 1997; 1999; 2010, ch. 3, 10).

To begin, we may note that Canada has undergone a particular pattern of *demographic transition* from high mortality and fertility to low mortality and fertility. The Canadian demographic transition pattern falls into the Northwestern (Northwestern Europe and North America) variant of the generic demographic transition model (Weeks 2008, 89). In the Northwestern variant, the transition process begins early and unfolds over a long period. It becomes evident in a long-term decline in mortality that is brought about initially by gradual improvements in living conditions (food supply, housing, sanitation, etc.) and later by innovations in disease control (vaccinations, etc.). Either somewhat after mortality begins to decline or at the same time but more slowly, fertility also begins to gradually fall due to a mix of factors associated with economic growth: urbanization, industrialization, and "modernization," more generally. These developments include rising schooling standards, increased costs of raising children, declining economic benefits to parents of having children, and assurances based on emerging low mortality that existing children will survive and that having more children "for insurance" is not required. In this process, births outnumber deaths, resulting in moderate to high rates of natural increase over a fairly long period of time. Eventually fertility levels drop to low levels and population growth declines to a variable point between slow increase and incipient decline.

Figure 1.3 presents estimates of Canadian birth and death rates over the period from 1750 to the present. The trends fit well within the Northwestern model of the demographic transition. Death rates had already fallen from higher levels by 1801–11, the first estimates shown. Death rates continued to fall gradually until they achieved very low levels around 1960. Subsequent

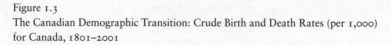

Figure 1.3
The Canadian Demographic Transition: Crude Birth and Death Rates (per 1,000)
for Canada, 1801–2001

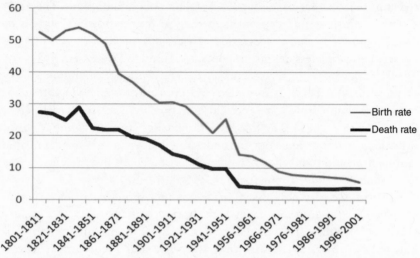

Sources: The rates for 1861 to 2001 are based on births, deaths, and on population figures estimated from census data. See Statistics Canada (2006) estimates of the components of population growth for Canada. http://www40.statcan.ca/l01/cst01/demo03.htm. The rates for 1801 to 1861 are from Henripin and Peron (1962, 224) and are for New France-Quebec only.

declines have been modest. Around 1820 or shortly thereafter, birth rates also began a steady long-term decline. The trend line for the decline in birth rates is smoothly downward except at two points. There is a short unexpected downward dip over the period 1930 to around 1945, covering the Depression and World War II. Through this period, couples delayed marriage and childbearing. Then the downward trend is interrupted by a shift to much higher than expected birth rates during the "baby boom" from the late 1940s to the mid 1960s. The baby boom came about due to a resumption of marriage, catch-up fertility (bearing children that would otherwise have been born earlier), and a temporary upward shift in the number of children born per couple, all within the context of an affluent post-War economic recovery. From a broad historical perspective, these deviations are relatively minor fluctuations in a long-term trend toward low fertility. Continuing the analysis, we next turn to the dynamics of international migration. Canadian population growth has been significantly shaped by international migration. However, the process reveals major historical variations in immigrant numbers and emigration over time (figure 1.4). These variations reflect changes

Figure 1.4
Immigration and Emigration Rates, 1851–2001

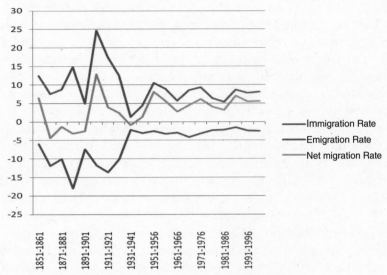

Source: Statistics Canada, 2006. http://www.statcan.ca/l01/cst01/demo03.htm.

in Canadian nation building circumstances and strategies. We may usefully view the combined circumstances and strategies as being part of a historical sequence of larger transnational political-economic systems, each of which had a major international migration component.

1 The first was *the early colonial system* operating over the period from the early 1600s to the late 1700s. This political economic system promoted very limited immigration to Canada and made it difficult for early Canadian nation-builders to attract settlers. Over the period from the early 1600s through to the late 1700s, European nations that laid claim to territories in Canada had very little interest in investing money in large overseas settlements (Knowles 1992, 4). The resources that the European countries sought to extract from Canada could be obtained far less expensively without large settlements. Fish could be caught by fishermen who came annually in boats from Europe. Furs could be obtained by trade with native peoples. Moreover, living conditions in Canada were harsh and settlers were reluctant to accept invitations from those in Canada who wanted greater immigration (Knowles 1992, ch. 1). Living conditions improved gradually, and by the 1850s Canada was receiving large numbers of European immigrants, but this took place under new political-economic conditions, as examined next.

2 The second transnational system was the *North Atlantic System,* a trading system within which Canadian leaders in the period from around 1800 to 1962 found more scope for nation building through attracting investments, bringing in immigrants, and expanding exports (Simmons 2010, ch. 2). The industrial revolution centred in Europe created a huge demand for raw materials for manufacturing and foods for an increasingly urban population. Europe also had many displaced workers as large industries forced the closure of small less efficient artisanal shops, and as cheap food imports from abroad led to the abandonment of farm lands or their redeployment as sheep grazing estates by rich land owners (Polanyi 2001). Canada and the United States had rich resources and unsettled land for producing food. North America needed capital and settlers. These complementary needs led to large movements of European immigrants to North America, expanded trade between North America and Europe, and economic growth for all countries involved. The United States was a particularly powerful player in the North Atlantic economic trade bloc and the corresponding international migration system (Thomas 1972). It drew far more immigrants from Europe. In certain periods, the United States also attracted large numbers of Canadian residents. Figure 1.4 reveals migration outcomes for Canada arising from its position in the North Atlantic economy. Prior to the 1930s, very large numbers of immigrants, nearly all from Europe, entered Canada (the notable exception is the period 1891 to 1901 when a recession led to a cut back in immigrant entries). At the same time, however, very large numbers of emigrants left Canada for the United States. In some periods, such as from the 1870s to the 1890s, emigrants outnumbered immigrants. From 1901 on to the present, immigrants have outnumbered emigrants, with the result that net international migration over this long period has contributed positively to national population growth, with the exception of the 1930s and early 1940s, namely the years of the Great Depression and the Second World War, when immigration was closed down to protect Canadian jobs and later for security reasons as well.

3 The *Contemporary Global System* is a complex world-wide economic trade system with a significant international migration component. Canadian governments have taken several steps over the period from the 1960s to the present to incorporate Canada more fully into the Global System (Simmons 2010, ch. 2, 3). They did so with the expectation that greater incorporation would strengthen the nation. Perhaps the first step was the 1962 decision to drop the White Canada policies that privileged European immigrants and virtually excluded immigrants from other parts of the world. This decision was made in significant part because Europe was drying up as a source of the

skilled immigrants Canada, as an industrializing nation, wanted. The post-World War II economic recovery in Europe had advanced to the point where skilled Europeans could find good jobs in their home countries. Another factor was that anti-racist sentiment was building in Canada, leading to a strong desire to remove racist immigration provisions. Still another reason was the fact that newly emerging nations around the world had large populations containing many individuals with the kinds of skills that Canada was seeking. For all these reasons, in 1962 Canada opened its doors to immigrants from all parts of the world. A few years later, in 1967, the points system was developed to improve skill selection.

Over time, Canada became deeply embedded in the Global System by entering into international free-trade agreements, such as the North American Free Trade Agreement (1989) and by signing onto trade rules established by the World Trade Organization. Canada had a previous long-standing concern with increasing worker productivity in order to be able to boost exports and protect national industry from lower priced imports. Entering into free trade increased the pressure to raise productivity by various means, including improving the educational levels of workers. This led Canada to place greater emphasis on selecting immigrants with very high levels of education. Individuals who meet these criteria have come from all around the globe, making Canada a far more multicultural nation.

From the above we can conclude that Canada's natural increase and net international migration patterns have both been deeply shaped by nation-building opportunities, constraints, and strategies. In the pre-national stage, Canada was a peripheral colony linked to Europe, and as such it experienced difficulty encouraging immigration. It also experienced low rates of natural increase due to high death rates in the larger system. Later, shifting circumstances allowed Canada to become a more central player in an emerging North Atlantic System. The new system brought additional economic growth to Europe and North America, reinforcing a Western model demographic transition and leading to high rates of natural increase. It also promoted immigration to Canada from Europe, although initially this was not always sufficient to cover the losses through emigration that Canada experienced as many Canadian residents moved to the United States, a more wealthy and powerful player in the system. Throughout the period in which Canada was embedded in the North Atlantic system, Canadian immigration remained Euro-centric and racist, reflecting values widespread in the system as a whole. Finally, Canada's shift to incorporate itself more fully in the Contemporary Global System has brought about significant changes in immigration. Due to Canada's high level of social and economic development, combined with ample supplies of potential immigrants in less developed nations throughout the world, the numbers of immigrants entering Canada have remained relatively high since the 1960s (figure 1.4). These levels correspond to those targeted by Canada. At the same time, the skill levels of the immigrants sought have increased, and the number of countries from which immigrants come has expanded enormously.

With respect to fertility trends, the Global System tends to accentuate trade competition between nations. Canada and other nations around the world therefore seek to increase their economic efficiency through promoting higher levels of education. These priorities tend to reinforce the trend toward low fertility. A competitive society will seek to increase the schooling, job skills, and employment of all adults, both men and women. This provides an additional incentive for two-career households, and further constrains the desire to have large families. Arguably, the competitive and individualistic values associated with the contemporary Global System tend to encourage the individuation of lives, weaker family ties, delayed marriage, and reduced commitments to child-bearing and rearing.

II FUTURE POPULATION GROWTH SCENARIOS

We turn in this section to briefly examine future population growth scenarios. These scenarios are created by developing models of future population growth based on different assumptions about trends in mortality, fertility, and international migration. For example, figure 1.5 shows the projected population of Canada from 2003 to 2031 under the assumption that current levels of low fertility in Canada will continue over this period. Specifically, the model assumes a total fertility rate (an estimate of the number of children born per woman over her reproductive years) of 1.6, well below the 2.1 required for a population to replace itself over time. Net international-migration is also assumed to be about the same as it has been recently. If these assumptions turn out to be correct, the contribution of natural increase to Canadian population growth will fall to zero around 2029. From that point on, international migration will begin to cover the deficit arising from below-replacement natural increase. International migration will also provide the additional numbers required to ensure continuing population growth, but at a low and slowing rate of increase (figure 1.5).

Figure 1.6 compares the outcome of using three different "plausible" sets of assumptions: a low growth scenario, a middle growth scenario (identical to that used for figure 1.5), and a high growth scenario. The low growth scenario assumes a Total Fertility Rate (total number of children born per

Figure 1.5
Observed (1981–2004) and Projected (2005–2056) Natural and Migratory Increase
in Canada according to Scenario 3 (medium growth)

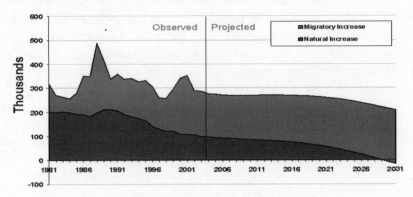

Figure 1.6
Population Observed (1981 to 2005) and Projected (2006–2056) according to
Three Scenarios, Canada

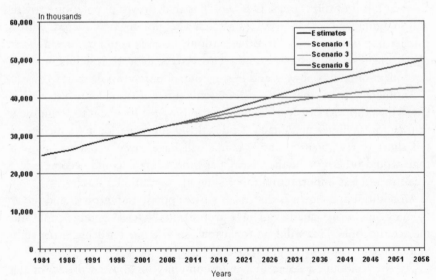

Source: Statistics Canada, 2006. http://www.statcan.ca/english/ads/91-520-XPB/about.htm.

mother) of 1.3. This is *very* low fertility of the kind that has been evident throughout many parts of Europe since the late 20th century. Under this scenario, Canada's population will peak around 2040 and gradually begin to decline after this date. This may be contrasted with the high growth scenario that assumes replacement level fertility and a continuing positive net migration pattern somewhat higher than the current level. In the high growth projection, the population of Canada will continue to grow at about one percent per year (in effect, the same rate of growth evident from 1981 to 2001) indefinitely into the future. At this rate of growth, Canada's population would double every 70 years. The middle scenario, based on a continuation of current levels of natural increase and net international migration, lies between these two extremes.

In the next section we examine the challenges that would arise most strongly under the medium and slow growth scenarios.

III CONCERNS ABOUT SLOW POPULATION GROWTH

Concerns about slower and possibly negative future population growth in Canada fall into three areas. One worry is that slower population growth will marginalize Canada in world affairs. The gloomy view is that, with a smaller population relative to other nations, Canada could become a weak player in global trade, finance, and security arrangements. It would be more dependent on major powers and less in control of its own destiny.

Another worry is that the economy will suffer if business investors discover that shortages of workers make it impossible for them to set up new production facilities in Canada. Under this grim scenario, investment will fall short of its potential and Canada will have lower economic growth than would otherwise be the case. Over time, Canada could become a less wealthy and less important nation, falling in international stature.

An additional concern is that, with slower population growth and fewer babies being born, Canada will have proportionally fewer young people and more old people. This will lead to various unwelcome burdens on the state and on those who work and pay taxes.

The very gloomiest scenario would combine the above worries. In the most dismal case, labour shortages would reduce business investment and the generation of new, better paid jobs just when a relatively small working-age population will need increased incomes to support the high costs of maintaining an elderly population. Such extremely negative future scenarios, referred to by Ellen Gee (2000) as "Voodoo Demographics," are founded on questionable and distorted assumptions. Consider the following points.

Table 1.1
Population of the World and Selected Countries

	Population (in millions)			% Growth		% Distribution		
	1950	2000	2050	1950-2000	2000-2050	1950	2000	2050
World	2,595	6,124	9,191	136.0	50.1	100.0	100.0	100.0
MDCs	813	1,215	1,245	49.4	2.5	31.3	19.8	13.5
LDCs	1,721	4,929	7,946	186.4	61.2	66.3	80.5	86.5
Two Largest LDCs								
China	554	1,269	1,408	129.1	11.0	21.3	20.7	15.3
India	371	1,046	1,658	181.9	58.5	14.3	17.1	18.0
G-8 Countries	561	844	917	50.4	8.6	21.6	13.8	10.0
Canada	13	30	42	130.8	40.0	0.5	0.5	0.5
France	41	59	68	43.9	15.3	1.6	1.0	0.7
Germany	68	82	74	20.6	-9.8	2.6	1.3	0.8
Italy	47	57	54	21.3	-5.3	1.8	0.9	0.6
Japan	83	127	102	53.0	-19.7	3.2	2.1	1.1
Russia	102	147	107	44.1	-27.2	3.9	2.4	1.2
United Kingdom	50	58	68	16.0	17.2	1.9	0.9	0.7
United States	157	284	402	80.9	41.5	6.1	4.6	4.4
Selected Other MDCs								
Sweden	7	9	10	28.6	11.1	0.3	0.1	0.1
Finland	4	5	5	25.0	0.0	0.2	0.1	0.1

Source: United Nations, 2007. Source: http://esa.un.org/unpp/index.asp?panel=2.

The geo-political concerns in the gloomy scenario above appear to be exaggerated and out of context. Canada is a medium nation in terms of population size. As such it has a very small share of the world's population: about one-half of one percent, a proportion that has held constant from 1950 to the present and which is projected to hold constant until 2050 (table 1.1). Canada's current status and autonomy in the international system depends, not on its population size, but on the strengths of its social, economic and political institutions. Like other nations, the main source of international influence and autonomy arises from a skilled work force, high levels of investment in advanced technology, transparent and efficient government, and agreements on trade, security, and human rights negotiated with other like-minded nations.

Canada has the smallest population of the current G8 nations that form the grouping of industrially advanced countries whose leaders meet to coordinate international economic, security, and other policies (table 1.1). Very small yet wealthy industrialized nations such as Sweden and Finland (and many others) have considerable autonomy and world leadership, even if they are not part of the G-8 association. Sweden and Finland each have only about one tenth of one percent of the world's population. Moreover, the G-8 countries taken together are home to an increasingly smaller proportion of the world's population: in 1950 about 22 percent of the world's population lived in these countries, while by 2050 it is projected that they will have less than one half this proportion.

In sum, population size is not irrelevant to national power and autonomy. The most powerful countries in the world, such as the United States and the European Union, are both populous and wealthy while very large, and poor countries with fast-growing economies such as China and India are soon to join the club of dominant geo-political players. Yet, nations with small populations can garner and retain power and autonomy through advanced social-economic development and participating in international trade and security accords.

Corresponding to the anticipated gradual slowing of the Canadian population, future shifts in its age composition are also projected to be relatively moderate under the "medium" population projection examined earlier. Figure 1.7 shows the proportions (in percent) of the Canadian population in three broad age groups (0–14, 15–64, and 65 and over) over the period from 1950 to 2050, with the projection to the future being based on middle range assumptions about fertility and international migration. The projection also points to the anticipated rise in the proportion aged 65 and over. This rise is gradual over time, starting around 1980, then accelerating after 2010. Similarly the proportion in the main working ages, 15 to 64 years of age, begins to decline from a high around 70 percent in 2010–2015 to less than 60 percent of the total in 2050.

Combining these two trends – the rise in the proportion who are elderly and the drop in the proportion in the main working ages – suggests that Canada may indeed soon face a new, serious, and unprecedented challenge. Yet, another perspective is to think of children and the elderly as together comprising the dependent (largely non-working) population. From this viewpoint, the long term shift in dependency ratios (the young and the old together as a proportion of the working-age population) is much less dramatic. The reason is that initially, in the period under consideration, there were relatively many children and few elderly, while at the end of this period there are relatively many elderly people and few children. As a result, total dependency levels do not change as much as the elderly dependency ratio alone (figure 1.8). In fact, the total dependency ratio in Canada was high (about .7 dependents per person aged 15–64) in the 1960s due to the post-War baby boom. It then fell to about .5 around 1980 and is expected to remain at this low level until around 2020. Then it is expected to rise back up to .7 again

Figure 1.7
Percent of Canadian Population in Selected Age Groups, 1950 to 2006, and Projected Percent in the Same Age Groups 2006–2050 under Medium Growth Assumptions

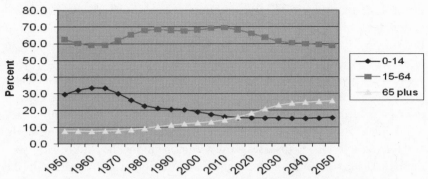

Source: United Nations, 2007: The 2006 Revision and World Urbanization Prospects: The 2005 Revision, http://esa.un.org/unpp, Monday, June 18, 2007.

Figure 1.8
Dependency Ratios for Canada 1950–2006 and Projected Dependency Ratios 2006 to 2050 under Medium Growth Assumptions

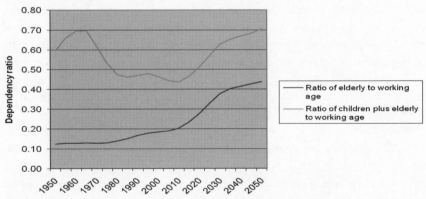

Source: United Nations, 2007: The 2006 Revision and World Urbanization Prospects: The 2005 Revision, http://esa.un.org/unpp, Monday, June 18, 2007.

by 2050. Managing the costs of a dependency ratio that Canada was able to cope with in the 1960s will require effort but should not be overwhelming. In the 1960s the need was to build more schools, colleges, and universities, while by 2050 there will be a need to build more retirement housing, elder-friendly transport, and care facilities that will respond to the needs of seniors. Perhaps the most difficult challenge will be addressing the health costs of an aging population. The challenges here are complex. The population is not only aging, but people are living longer. At older ages they are at risk for diseases, such as arthritis and dementia, that increase health care costs.

Finally, it is not correct to assume that all the elderly are poor and dependent, or that they need large amounts of health care. Many elderly individuals have accumulated savings, generate revenues from pensions and investments, pay significant taxes, are healthy, and look after themselves in all respects well into their advanced years (Gee 2000).

In sum, slower population growth and aging will bring serious challenges to well-being in Canadian society. These challenges include filling gaps in the labour force, strengthening pension funds to enhance the self-sufficiency of all older Canadians, providing more institutional support for the elderly, and finding solutions to diseases more common among the elderly. However, these challenges should not be exaggerated into doomsday scenarios. In the next section we examine various possible responses to address the concerns of a more slowly growing population.

IV POSSIBLE POLICY RESPONSES

Two population-focused solutions have been proposed to address the challenges of slower population growth and aging. The first is to encourage higher fertility. The second is to increase immigration levels. The first of these may be difficult to implement, while the second may help solve gaps in the labour force but will not solve problems of aging. As a result, a third option may be the most important one: it is to adjust to slower population growth while at the same time protecting and improving the well-being of all Canadians. These three options are examined in more detail below:

More babies? In the period 1966 to 1989 Romania, under the authoritarian Ceauscescu government, instituted coercive and punitive policies to restrict contraceptive use and prohibit abortion in all circumstances. These ethically unacceptable policies raised birth rates from 14 to 27 per thousand but at a high cost to parents, children, and society, evident for example in high maternal deaths resulting from botched illegal abortions (Serbanescu et al. 1995). In 1987 Singapore instituted "positive" incentive polices in the form of more subsidized child-care facilities and tax incentives for working mothers to increase fertility from two children or less per family to three children per family: these measures improved the well-being of mothers and their children, but the overall impact on fertility was very limited. Some women who had postponed childbearing had children when the new measures were adopted, leading to an increase in birth rates. However, this initial "blip" disappeared and birth rates returned to their previous levels (Saywell 2003). Similar policies were adopted in Quebec; the results were also similar. European nations such as France have very strong family support policies that may play some role in preventing fertility from falling from low to very low levels (Bergman 1996). All mothers in France have access to nursery schools; single mothers get special monthly allowances. While France still has a birth rate slightly below replacement, its fertility level (a Total Fertility Rate around 1.9) is higher than most other countries in Europe. In sum, what works in one country may not work in another. Measures to increase fertility which are ethically acceptable, affordable, and effective at least in some measure in the Canadian context have not yet been found, but that is not to say that they cannot be discovered.

More immigrants? Policies to increase immigration levels above those currently in place in Canada would necessarily have to solve many problems. Would the Canadian public be prepared to accept a significant rise in immigration, given that Canada already has one of the world's highest immigration rates? Will highly skilled immigrants continue to come? This last question arises because other wealthy nations also seek such immigrants, and because skilled immigrants to Canada often find it difficult to find jobs for which they have training (Picot, Hou, and Coulombe 2007; Simmons 2010, ch. 7; Sweetman and Warman 2008).

Even if all the above questions could be answered positively and immigration levels were to double, for example, Canada would still face slowing population growth and an increase in the proportion of elderly citizens. This conclusion may seem counterintuitive, yet it is based on careful modeling for Canada (Beaujot 2003) and for other countries (McDonald and Kippen 2001, United Nations 2000). The reasoning, is straightforward: individuals who apply and are accepted as immigrants are mostly well-educated young adults from towns and cities in their countries of origin. Even if they come from countries with higher fertility, their own fertility tends to be low before arrival (reflecting their schooling and urban background) and tends to stay low or fall further after settling in Canada. In other words, immigrants to Canada have below-replacement fertility and replicate the existing age structure of Canadian society. Their presence adds temporarily (until they die) to the number of people in Canada, but their low reproduction rates also tend to reinforce population aging. In sum, there are good economic reasons (and additional social and political reasons) for maintaining a pro-immigration policy in Canada. These include postponement of population decline under conditions of below-replacement fertility, filling selected job skill gaps in the labour market, and creating a vibrant multicultural society. However, the reasons should not include reversing the aging processes, because immigration at plausible levels does not have this effect.

Adapt to slow population growth? Canada can adapt by pursuing some mix of the following steps.

a) Increase levels of productivity. Policies that support job training, new technology, and better economic infrastructure can be implemented in order to allow each new worker to produce more than before. More robots, computers, and just-in-time production techniques can employ fewer well-trained workers to generate more products and services to support an aging population.

b) Exploit under-utilized labour pools. Much of the enormous expansion of employment in Canada and other more developed countries in the second half of the 20th century was achieved by encouraging large numbers of previously under-employed women to enter the work force (see Li 1996, ch. 3). A remaining under-utilized labour pool is that of retired workers. Some nations facing population decline are now contemplating legislation to increase the age at retirement in order to solve labour force shortages and in order to allow workers to accumulate more pension funds. Subsequently, these workers will have a shorter period from retirement to death. This logic is pushing more provinces in Canada to adopt legislation that removes the right of employers to demand retirement at age sixty-five.

c) Exporting jobs. Instead of importing labour as immigrants, additional workers for certain jobs can be found by employing them in their home countries. Wealthy contemporary nations do this by allowing their firms to set up industrial and assembly production in low-wage developing nations. Unfortunately, many of these operations are "sweat shops" with unacceptable wages and health risks for workers. Some low-wage countries with well-developed medical systems now provide surgery and other medical treatments to foreign visitors. If more industrial production and medical and other services are to be transferred overseas, the main challenge will be to establish quality standards for the work provided and for the workers employed.

CONCLUSIONS

Based on the analysis in this chapter, we may conclude that Canada's population seems destined to grow in the future at a level much lower than it did over most of its past history. At least this seems likely in the absence of major changes in Canadian nation-building strategies or the international system that sets the opportunities and constraints in which these strategies are developed.

How the Canadian population will grow is unknown. Plausible scenarios provide a fairly wide range. The middle growth scenario on which our analysis has focused suggests that population growth will continue to slow but remain positive long into the future. Labour force gaps and aging trends will be moderate and capable of being addressed through various policies well known to Canadians: maintaining immigration at current levels at least, increasing productivity, delaying retirement, improving pensions, exporting jobs, and finding solutions to health care costs. If, in contrast, rate of population growth falls further and population decline sets in, the challenges will be greater, but hopefully not insurmountable if these same strategies are adopted.

REFERENCES

Beaujot, Roderick. 2000. *Earning and Caring in Canadian Families.* Peterborough: Broadview Press

– 2003. "Effect of Immigration on the Canadian Population: Replacement Migration?" Discussion paper no. 03–03. Department of Sociology, University of Western Ontario. www.sociology.uwo.ca/popstudies/dp/dp03–03.pdf

Bergman, Barbara. 1996. *Saving our Children from Poverty: What the United States Can Learn from France.* New York: Russell Sage Foundation

Gee, Ellen M. 2000. "Voodoo Demography, Population Aging, and Social Policy." Chapter 1 in *The Overselling of Population Aging,* eds. Ellen Gee and Gloria Gutman. Don Mills: Oxford University Press

Knowles, Valerie. 1992. *Stranger at Our Gates: Canadian Immigration and Immigration Policy, 1540–1990.* Toronto and Oxford: Dundurn Press

Kritz, Mary M., Lin L. Lim and Hania Zlotnik, eds. 1992. *International Migration Systems: A Global Approach.* Oxford: Clarendon Press

Li, Peter. 1996. *The Making of Post-War Canada.* Don Mills: Oxford University Press

Massey, Douglas S., Joaquin Arrango, Graeme Hugo, Ali Kouaouci, Adela Pellegrino, and J.E. Taylor. 1998. *Worlds in Motion: Understanding International Migration at the End of the Millennium.* Oxford, New York: Clarendon Press

McDonald, Peter, and Rebecca Kippen. 2001. "Labor Supply Prospects in 16 Developed Countries, 2000–2050." *Population and Development Review* 27 (1): 1–32

Picot, Garnett, Feng Hou, and Simon Coulombe. 2007. *Chronic Low Income and Low-Income Dynamics among Recent Immigrants.* Ottawa: Statistics Canada, Analytical Studies Branch Research Paper Series. Cat. no. 11F0019MIE – No. 294

Polanyi, Karl, 2001. *The Great Transformation: The Political and Economic Origins of Our Time.* Foreword by Joseph E. Stiglitz, introduction by Fred Block. 2nd Beacon Paperback ed. Boston, MA: Beacon Press

Saywell. Trish. 2003. "Cupid the Bureaucrat? Singapore Tries to Play Matchmaker." *The Wall Street Journal* (30 January): A8

Serbanescu, F., L. Morris, P. Stupp, and A. Stanescu. 1995. "The Impact of Recent Policy Changes on Fertility, Abortion, and Contraceptive Use in Romania." *Studies in Family Planning* 26 (2): 76–87

Simmons, Alan. 1997. "Canadian Immigration and Nation Building: Social and Political Implications of Recent Trends." In *Re(Defining) Canada: A Prospective Look at our Country in the 21st Century*, eds. R. Hebert and R. Theberger, 43–70. Winnipeg: Presses Universitaires de Saint-Boniface

– 1999. "Immigration Policy: Imagined Futures." Chapter 2 in *Immigrant Canada*, eds. S. Halli and L. Driedger. Toronto: University of Toronto Press

– 2010. *Immigration and Canada: Global and Transnational Perspectives*. Toronto: Canadian Scholars Press

Sweetman, Arthur, and Casey Warman. 2008. "Integration, Impact and Responsibility: An Economic Perspective on Canadian Immigration Policy." Chapter 1 in *Immigration and Integration in Canada in the Twenty-first Century*, eds. John Biles, Meyer Burstein, and James Frideres. Montreal: McGill-Queen's University Press

Thomas, Brinley. 1972. *Migration and Economic Growth*. London: Cambridge University

Trovato, Frank. 2009. *Canada's Population in a Global Context*. Toronto: Oxford University Press

United Nations. 2000. *Replacement Migration: Is it a Solution to Declining and Ageing Populations?* United Nations Population Division. www.un.org/esa/population/publications/migration/execsum.htm

Weeks, John R. 2008. *Population: An Introduction to Concepts and Issues*. 10th ed. Belmont: Wadsworth/Thompson.

2

Canada's Age and Sex Composition

FRANK TROVATO

INTRODUCTION

This chapter is devoted to an examination of age and sex composition, with special reference to Canada based on the data from the 2001 census. The term "composition" is used to mean the distribution of the population in accordance with the intersecting characteristics of age and sex. In some aspects of the ensuing discussion, age and sex are treated together, as when one speaks of a population's age-sex distribution, or of age-specific sex ratios. In other places, emphasis is on age composition without direct reference to sex.

Besides their obvious biological dimensions, age and sex are undoubtedly two of the most important variables in social science research. It would be difficult to envision any meaningful social phenomenon transpiring independently of age and sex. For example, in contemporary North America, church attendance has been observed to increase with age (in general young adults are less inclined to attend religious services than are older adults); and as compared to males, females are more likely to attend church on regular basis and to believe in life after death (Pryor and Norris 1988; Hout, Greeley, and Wilde 2001) Another example from the sociological literature is the distinct age differential in violent crime rates, these being disproportionately high among young adult males (Hirschi and Gottfredson 1983). At a more general level, the significance of these two variables is clearly reflected in society's constant preoccupation with gathering varied types of information, based on people's age and sex, through surveys, censuses, vital registration systems, and other legal documentation, including income tax, earnings, and health records.

It should be unambiguously clear that the processes of birth, death, and migration are strongly conditioned by age and sex. This is also true in connection with other demographic events such as cohabitation, marriage, divorce, remarriage, widowhood, labour force entry, and unemployment. In empirical research the statistical association between age and these other variables is generally nonlinear. For instance, across populations the probability of death is relatively high in infancy, drops substantially in childhood, and rises thereafter with increasing age (gradually throughout adulthood and faster at the older ages). In the case of fertility, birth rates tend to be highest among women between the ages of twenty and thirty and relatively low at younger and older ages. In virtually all populations the geographical mobility propensities of young adults generally exceed those of other age categories.

DEMOGRAPHIC DETERMINANTS OF AGE COMPOSITION

Coale (1957, 1964, 1972) has conducted comprehensive analyses of the demographic dynamics of age composition. Coale determined that change in fertility is the major determinant of change in age composition, and that the effect of mortality change is relatively minor. Thus, a young population results mainly from sustained high fertility rates. Under this demographic condition there will be proportionately more people below age 15, and the median age of population will be relatively young. (The median age of a population is the age that divides the distribution in half, such that 50 percent of the people are above the median, and 50 percent are below that value.)[1] Declining fertility would have the opposite effect on the age structure: proportionately fewer people below age 15 and an increasing proportion of elderly, thus accounting for an older median age.[2]

AGE PYRAMID

Table 2.1 (see also figure 2.1) displays absolute and percentage distributions of Canada's population in 2001 in accordance with age and sex. The percentages in this table were graphed to obtain a population age pyramid (a graphical representation of the age-sex distribution).[3] For each age-sex intersection, percentages are based on the overall total population. To illustrate, the 2001 census counted 1,051,455 males aged 10–14, and the total size of the population was 30,007,090. The corresponding percentage for males aged 10–14 is therefore 3.50 (i.e., 1,051,455/30,007,090 x 100). There were 1,001,665 females aged 10–14, and the percentage is calculated as: 1,001,665/30,007,090 x 100 = 3.34 percent. These computations were executed independently for all age-sex categories, starting with age 0–4 through 80–84 and finally 85+.[4]

Table 2.1

Age and Sex Distribution of the Canadian Population in 2001 and Associated Summary Measures of Age Composition

	Number of persons			Percent		
Age group	males	females	total	males	females	total
0–4	868 075	828 205	1 696 280	2.9	2.8	5.7
5–9	1 011 460	964 670	1 976 130	3.4	3.2	6.6
10–14	1 051 455	1 001 665	2 053 120	3.5	3.3	6.8
15–19	1052145	1 001 180	2 053 325	3.5	3.3	6.8
20–24	982 285	973 530	1 955 815	3.3	3.2	6.5
25–29	935 510	962 690	1 898 200	3.1	3.2	6.3
30–34	1 031 255	1 065 490	2 096 745	3.4	3.6	7.0
35–39	1 244 995	1 277 860	2 522 855	4.2	4.3	8.4
40–44	1 271 725	1 307 040	2 578 765	4.2	4.4	8.6
45–49	1 151 155	1 182 375	2 333 530	3.8	3.9	7.8
50–54	1 033 365	1 052 395	2 085 760	3.4	3.5	7.0
55–59	789 205	805 035	1 594 240	2.6	2.7	5.3
60–64	621 570	652 210	1 273 780	2.1	2.2	4.2
65–69	543 830	589 800	1 133 630	1.8	2.0	3.8
70–74	461 780	547 430	1 009 210	1.5	1.8	3.4
75–79	338 820	474 850	813 670	1.1	1.6	2.7
80–84	192 645	323 495	516 140	0.6	1.1	1.7
85+	125 580	290 325	415 905	0.4	1.0	1.4
Total	14 706 855	15 300 245	30 007 100	49.0	51.0	100.0
Broad age groups						
<15	2 930 990	2 794 540	5 725 530	9.8	9.3	19.1
15–64	10 113 210	10 279 805	20 393 015	33.7	34.3	68.0
65+	1 662 655	2 225 900	3 888 555	5.5	7.4	13.0
Total	14 706 855	15 300 245	30 007 100	49.0	51.0	100.0
Summary measures						
Youth dependency ratio			28.08			
Old age dependency ratio			19.07			
Total Dependency Ratio			47.15			
Median age			37.52			
Sex ratio			96.00			

Source: Statistics Canada. 2002. *Age and Sex for the Population of Canada. 2001 Census.* Ottawa (July 16). Catalogue no. 95F0300XCB01004.

The age-sex composition for the Canadian population in 2001 does not conform to a true pyramidal form because the base is quite narrow, there is a pronounced bulge in the ages between 35 and 55, and the top of the distribution is fairly wide. These features reflect the following facts about Canada's demographic patterns: (1) fertility has declined over roughly the past four decades, as indicated by the reduced percentages of the age categories below age group 40–44; (2) fertility is currently low, as suggested

Figure 2.1
Population Age and Sex Composition of Canada, 2001

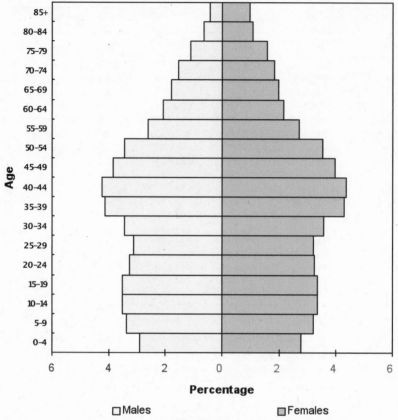

Source: Author's computations based on data from Statistics Canada. 2002. *Age and Sex for the Population of Canada*. 2001 Census. Ottawa (July 16). Catalogue no. 95F0300XCB01004.

by the narrowness of the base (i.e., age group 0–4); in the past there occurred a significant rise in fertility, as indicated by the large bulge in the pyramid between ages 30–34 and 55–59 (i.e., the baby boom cohorts born between 1946 and 1966); (3) mortality is low, as demonstrated by the relatively wide top of the age pyramid (i.e., favourable survival probabilities in the older ages).

CHANGE IN AGE COMPOSITION

Figure 2.2 shows age-sex pyramids of Canada at different points in history and also projected to the years 2016 and 2041. The two pyramids for 1881 and 1911 are reflective of a youthful population, a period in Canada's

Figure 2.2

Age-sex Pyramids for the Population of Canada at Different Points in History and Projected to the Future, Showing the Birth Cohorts of Associated Age Groups

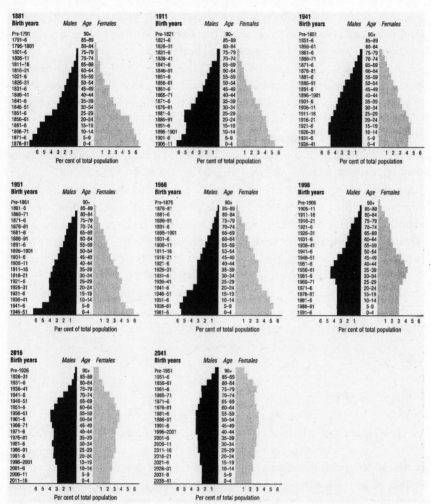

Sources: Adapted from the following: Carl F. Grindstaff. 1981. *Population and Society: A Sociological Perspective*. West Hanover, MA: The Christopher Publishing House (Figure 6, 134–5; M.V. George et al. 2001. Population Projections for Canada, Provinces and Territories, 2000–2026. Ottawa: Ministry of Industry, Cat. No. 91–520 (Table A3, 179, 181); Frank T. Denton, Christine H. Feaver, and Byron G. Spencer. 2000. "The Future Population of Canada and its Age Distribution." Pp. 27–56 in Frank T. Denton, Deborah Fretz, and Byron G. Spencer (Eds.), *Independence and Economic Security in Old Age*. Vancouver: UBC Press (Figure 3.1: 48–9).

past when fertility rates were by today's standards high, and consequently these early age pyramids exhibited a wide base. Indeed, as noted by McVey and Kalbach (1995, 60), in 1881, the median age of the Canadian population was 20.1 years. However, as birth rates fell, by the early 1940s this parameter had risen to almost 28 years. The trend toward an increasingly older median age would have continued had it not been for the baby boom phenomenon following World War II.[5] Thus, in 1951, the median age had dropped to 25 years. But subsequent to the baby boom phenomenon, fertility rates embarked on a long term pattern of decline, reaching the current below-replacement levels. (In recent years the total fertility rate has fluctuated around 1.5 children per woman; at the peak of the baby boom, in 1959, this rate was nearly 4.0). Accordingly, the median age has been increasing steadily, reaching almost 28 in 1976, and nearly 38 by 2001.

Another important feature of figure 2.2 concerns the large baby boom cohorts, identified earlier as the large bulge in the age pyramid of 2001. The beginning of this phenomenon is clearly visible in the large base of the 1951 pyramid. In subsequent periods, these cohorts are seen as moving upward through the age structure, and by midway into the 21st century this feature of the Canadian age structure will have virtually disappeared due to the natural roles of aging and mortality. The projected age pyramid for 2041 differs substantially from those of previous periods. This is the shape of the future: a substantially older population.

DEPENDENCY RATIOS

An appropriate starting point in the analysis of age distributions is the subdivision of the population into three broad age segments: (1) the youth (ages 0–15), who are typically not engaged in full-time economic activity; (2) the labour force population (ages 15–64); (3) the post-retirement population (ages 65 and older), who throughout their working lives contributed to the maintenance of their society, and in retirement are being supported by the working population. These three broad age designations can be thought of as rough approximations to the reality they purport to reflect, for it is well understood that not all persons aged 65 and older, for example, are completely retired from the labour force; nor are all individuals aged 15–64 necessarily employed.

The Total (i.e., overall) Dependency Ratio for a population is usually expressed as $(P_{0-14} + P_{65+}/P_{15-64}) \times 100$. This can be broken down into its two component parts: the Youth Dependency Ratio $(P_{0-14}/P_{15-64}) \times 100$; and the Old Age Dependency Ratio $(P_{65+}/P_{15-64}) \times 100$, where the letter "P" stands for population.[6] An overall dependency ratio greater than 100 indicates the

Table 2.2
Percentage Distribution of Population by Three Broad Age Categories, Dependency Ratios, and Median Age in 2000; the World, Development Regions, and Selected Countries

Country	Age group (%)			Dependency ratio (per 100)			Median age (years)
	<15	15-59	60+	Youth	Old age	Total	
World	30.0	60.0	10.0	47.5	10.9	58.4	26.5
More Developed Regions	18.3	62.3	19.4	27.1	21.2	48.3	37.4
Less Developed Regions	32.8	59.5	7.7	52.9	8.2	61.1	24.3
Least Developed Countries	43.1	52.0	4.9	80.2	5.8	86.0	18.2
Selected countries							
China	24.8	65.0	10.1	36.4	10.0	46.4	30.0
Nigeria	45.1	50.2	4.8	86.8	5.9	92.7	17.2
Brazil	28.8	63.4	7.8	43.6	7.8	51.4	25.8
Occupied Palestinian Tertry.	46.4	48.7	4.9	92.8	7.1	99.9	16.8
India	35.5	58.9	7.6	54.4	8.1	62.5	23.7
Mexico	33.1	59.9	6.9	53.3	7.6	60.9	23.3
United States	21.7	62.1	16.1	32.9	18.6	51.5	35.5
Canada	19.1	64.2	16.7	28.0	18.5	46.5	36.9
Sweden	18.2	59.4	22.4	28.3	27.1	55.3	39.7
Russian Federation	18.0	63.5	18.5	25.8	18.0	43.8	36.8
Japan	14.7	62.1	23.2	21.6	25.2	46.8	41.2
Italy	14.3	61.7	24.1	21.1	26.7	47.8	40.2
Spain	14.7	63.5	21.8	21.5	24.8	46.4	37.7
France	18.7	60.7	20.5	28.7	24.5	53.2	37.6
Germany	15.5	61.2	23.0	22.8	24.1	46.9	40.1
United Kingdom	19.0	60.4	20.6	29.1	24.1	53.2	37.7

Source: United Nations Department of Economic and Social Affairs Population Division. 2002. World Population Ageing: 1950–2050. New York: United Nations (ST/ESA/SER.A/207).

presence of more dependants (youth and seniors combined) than workers in the population, thus the greater the ratio, the greater the dependency "burden" on the working age population. A ratio below 100 would mean the opposite – more workers than dependants, and a ratio of 100 would be indicative of an equal balance between dependants and workers.

In some cases these ratios are calculated with slightly different cut-off points for the working age and old age components. Table 2.2, taken from a United Nations report for the year 2000, shows these three ratios for the world, the developing and developed countries, and a number of selected nations, calculated with the age group 15–59 as the denominator, rather than 15–64 (United Nations Economic and Social Affairs Population Division 2002).

In developing countries, youth dependency ratios are in general substantially larger than the old age dependency ratios. Contrastingly, the more developed countries have long passed through the demographic transition and have reached a state of demographic maturity. In such countries old, age dependency ratios have been increasing steadily, accompanied by gradual declines in youth dependency.

Populations with young median ages generally have a relatively large proportion of persons below age 15 and therefore high youth dependency ratios. This can be illustrated with some of the information in table 2.2. In Nigeria, for instance, the median age is 17.2, and almost half of the population is comprised of youths below age 15 (45.1 percent). In the Occupied Palestinian Territory, the proportion of the population below age 15 is even higher (46.4 percent), and the median age is lower, at 16.8 years. The population over age 60 in these two populations are only 4.8 and 4.9 percent, respectively.

High old age dependency ratios imply aging populations and an older median age. Contrast for example, the cases of Nigeria and the Occupied Palestinian Territory with demographically mature countries such as Canada, United States, Japan, Italy, and Sweden. In the latter group of countries, the old-age dependency ratios range between nearly 19 (USA and Canada) and 27 per 100 (Sweden). Consequently, the median age of these countries will be much older than that of the developing countries. Consider for example the median ages of Canada (36.9), Italy (40.2), and Japan (41).

CHANGE IN DEPENDENCY RATIOS

In table 2.1, the dependency ratios for Canada in 2001 have been worked out as being 28.1 (Youth), and 19.1 (Old Age). The sum of these ratios equals the total dependency ratio, 47.2 per 100. McVey and Kalbach (1995, 73) have calculated these three measures for Canada, stretching back to 1881 (see figure 2.3). The youth dependency ratio declined from 67.7 per 100 in 1881 to 42.4 in 1941. It increased during the baby boom period, peaking at 57.6 in 1961, and has declined thereafter. The old age dependency has been rising gradually, from 7.2 per 100 in the late 1800s to 17.3 in 1991 and to 19.1 in 2001.

Thus, historically, the Youth Dependency Ratio has been the more important component of Canada's overall dependency burden. It is important to note, however, that as the population gets increasingly older the long-term picture will change: Old Age Dependency will get increasingly larger and is expected to account for an increasing portion of Canada's dependency ratio overall in the future. The crossover point, when the graphs of the Youth and Old Age Dependency Ratios meet and then diverge, is expected to occur around 2016, when the population aged 65 and above is envisioned to outnumber those aged 15 and under (Denton, Feaver, and Spencer 2000).

Figure 2.3
Youth (YDR), Old Age (OADR) and Total Dependency ratio (TDR) for Canada, 1881 to 2001

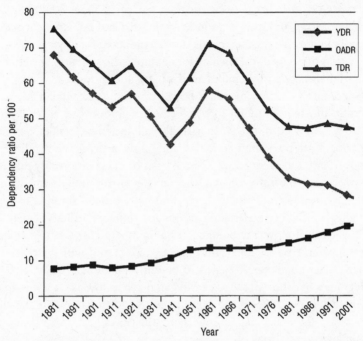

Sources: Wayne McVey and Warren E. Kalbach. 1995. *Canadian Population*, 73. Toronto: Nelson;
Source: Statistics Canada. 2002. *Age and Sex for the Population of Canada. 2001 Census*. Ottawa (July 16). Catalogue no. 95F0300XCB01004.

SEX RATIO

The sex ratio of a population refers to the balance of males to females (number of males/number of females) x 100).[7] The 2001 census of Canada enumerated 14,706,850 males and 15,300,245 females. The resultant sex ratio was therefore 96.1 males for every 100 females.[8] In human populations, the sex ratio is seldom exactly 100 (an equal balance of males and females). In most cases, especially in the more developed countries, the value of this index is a little below 100 (females outnumber males).

Why is this so? In order to answer this question let us first distinguish between three types of sex ratios. The *primary sex ratio* is the sex ratio of conceptions – the number of male conceptions to the number of female conceptions. In general, more males are conceived, but the intrauterine mortality of male fetuses is much greater than that for females, such that at birth the imbalance favouring male infants reduces to about 105 boys for every 100 girls (Perls and Frets 2002). This is the *secondary sex ratio*, the sex ratio of live births.[9] The *tertiary sex ratio* is the sex ratio at ages beyond infancy. As indicated by Teitelbaum (1972, 90), this is an indeterminate measure because it covers so many possibilities. That is, sex ratios can be computed for any age category or combination of age groups, such as for example, the sex ratio at ages 20–24, or that of males 20–29 to females aged 15–24, and so forth.

Age-specific sex ratios in adulthood are mainly determined by sex differences in mortality, though in some cases migration can also play a role (Guttentag and Secord 1983). In virtually all societies, females have lower age-specific death rates than do males, and on the average women live longer than men (Perls and Frets 2002). On the basis of the sex mortality differential alone, therefore, the ratio of males to females in the population would be expected to decline gradually with age, and more rapidly among the elderly.

In industrialized countries such as Canada, Japan, and Italy, where death rates are relatively low, the balance in the numbers of males to females begins to approach parity at around age 25 or 30; and with increasing age, especially after about 60, it begins to favour females disproportionately. In the older ages beyond 60, the sex ratio can reach as low as 25 males to every 100 females, depending on the population. Sex differentials in age-specific mortality are the main reason underlying the overall sex ratio being below 100 in many populations.

CHANGE IN SEX RATIOS

Until fairly recently in Canadian history, the overall sex ratio for the population has favoured males. For example, in 1911 the value of this measure was 112.9 (figure 2.4). After 1971, this ratio has been declining: It was 98.3 in 1981, 97.2 in 1991, and as already noted, in 2001 it had dropped to 96.1. The high sex ratios around the turn of the century can be explained by sex-selective migration to Canada, which was predominantly male. The declines of this measure below 100 in recent decades may relate in part to the changing nature of immigration, as since the early 1970s there has been increasingly more female migration to Canada than in past times. However, the more important factor, as already described, is the relative survival advantage of women over men.

DEMOGRAPHIC AGING: A POPULATION CRISIS?

Demographic aging and its projected societal effects is receiving a great deal of media attention.[10] For example, a story in the *Globe and Mail*

Figure 2.4
Change in Overall Sex Ratio in Canada, 1881–2001

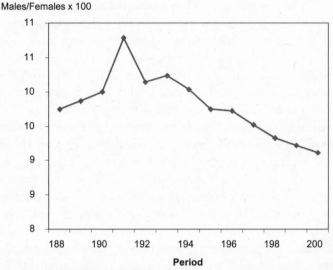

Sources: Wayne Mc Vey Jr and Warren E. Kalbach. 1995. *Canadian Population*, 57. Toronto: Nelson; Statistics Canada. 2002. *Age and Sex for the Population of Canada*. *2001 Census*. Ottawa (July 16). Catalogue no. 95F0300XCB01004.

(Stackhouse 1994) points to the worldwide aging trend and the pressures this is likely to impose on the public pension systems of industrialized countries, and also some developing economies. For the American case, Gendel (2002) warns that as the large baby boom cohorts approach retirement years, there will be great pressure on the social security system of the United States. Compounding this situation is the fact that many workers now tend to retire on the average a few years before reaching age 65. Gendel (2002 2) opines that "we cannot afford to keep putting off coping with this issue."

More recently, *The Economist* (2004) reported on the case of Japan, one of the world's leading economies. Japan's population is aging quickly, it is noted, and this poses serious implications for the country's economy and for the society at large. The combination of a shrinking population and an increasingly elderly one will have a growing impact on everything from demand for goods and services, to public finances, to the structure of the workforce. In the near future, it is stated, Japan's universities will have more available university spaces than applicants. As for its labour force, it is anticipated that it will shrink from 87 million in 1995 to 70 million in 2030. The post-retirement population aged 65 and older is expected to soar from less than one-fifth of the total population in 2003, to one-third over the next several decades.

Faced with these kinds of prospects, Japan and other industrialized countries are looking for ways to avert what appears to be a looming social
security crisis. Bongaarts (2004) has concluded that although societies are
not identical in their projected old age burden, they will all see, between
2000 and 2050, a substantial rise in old age dependency ratios, with Japan
and Italy representing the most severe cases, and the United States the least.
Bongaarts shows that as the pensioner to worker ratio increases, the average
value of public pension benefit declines, while at the same time, the average expenditure in relation to earnings per person rises. These anticipated
developments are not favourable for the average pensioner or for his society.

The severity of the public pension crisis will depend on the extent to
which governments may be able to generate interest in their populations to
retire later rather than early and to their efficacy in creating work for those
above the age of 65. Later retirement should ease the burden on the public
pension system, as will the continued work activity of the elderly. It is likely,
however, that a probable solution should also entail the unpalatable option
of governments reducing the value of public pension benefits per retiree.
Bongaarts (2004,21) adds that even though Organization for Economic
Cooperation and Development (OECD) countries have been trying to reform
their public pension systems to avert impending difficulties, it seems highly
likely that "today's workers will have to save more, work longer, retire later,
receive less generous benefits, and perhaps pay more taxes."

For countries such as Canada and the United States that have experienced
large baby booms in the two decades following the end of World War II,
pressure on the public pension system is projected to intensify between 2011
and 2036, when the front and tail ends of the baby boom generations enter
retirement age. Recent generations of elderly tend to be relatively healthier
than preceding ones; thus, assuming a retirement age of 65, and life expectancy at this age being in the range of 25 years, the cumulative amount of
public pension payments is bound to increase substantially.

To the public pensions scenario is the added possibility of growing
health-care costs because, on the aggregate, with population aging, there
will likely be increased prevalence of chronic disabilities, especially among
the oldest-old (i.e., 85 and older) segment of the senior population (Manton
1982; Manton, Guo, and Lamb 2006; Olshansky and Ault 1986; Stone
and Fletcher 1994; Suzman, Willis, and Manton 1992; Kinsella and Velkoff
2001, 45).

Not all views on this question are pessimistic. For instance, a headline in
the *Globe and Mail* (Little 1999) reads: "The coming glut of seniors won't
be so taxing." The article affirms that the old age dependency ratio for

Canada is indeed expected to keep on increasing over the current century, but adds that the presumed future costs associated with the provision of health care to the growing senior population are likely to be counteracted by the declining youth dependency ratios. Another report in the *Globe and Mail* (Laghi 2002) presents the view that the baby boom generation is no big threat to Canada's publicly funded health care system, and that the effects of aging population on health costs can be easily managed by government if it takes action now as opposed to later. While it is acknowledged that there will be pressures on the system as a result of the population bulge and that cost could rise by 30 percent by the year 2030, it is argued that major surgery on the system is unjustified because the baby boom aging effect would represent a one-time pressure on expenditures and not a continuing matter over the long term.

Of course, many of these issues surrounding population aging and its anticipated effects are open for debate. For instance, the costs of health care for an aging population may far exceed the savings incurred from a reduced youth dependency ratio. Indeed, based on his detailed analysis of population projections for Canada and Quebec province, Henripin (1994, 86) concluded that "our society will have to face increasing costs in health care and pensions that will not be offset by decreases in education and child allowance costs associated with lower fertility."

Another perspective on the demographics of aging is premised on the idea that population aging *per se* is not the main factor in many of the presumed future "crises" envisioned by some analysts and the media. The "anti-apocalyptic demography" perspective (Gee and Gutman 2001) considers demographic aging as being inextricably connected to the socio-economic situation in which it occurs and cannot be understood apart from the broader societal context. For example, the aging paradigm has been explicitly used by government to justify changes in the levels of immigration and to justify cutbacks to education

The society creates images and ideas of aging, then scientists and policy makers work towards ameliorating the "problems" of an aging society within the paradigms established by these images. The "aging paradigm" as a basis for public policy, it is argued, may be taking a reality of its own – a self-fulfilling prophecy – a prophecy that comes true not because it was true at first, but because people acted as if it were true, thus ultimately making it true. Thus according to the anti-apocalyptic demography perspective, invoking population aging as the cause of shifting markets, the aged welfare burden, and increased health care costs is to miss the mark as to the real causes of these problems. Politicians tend to erroneously attribute the problem of depletion of the pension fund to population aging instead of problems with the system itself and possibly its mismanagement. Finally, overreliance on the "demographics of aging" paradigm encourages erroneous conceptualizations of the health care burden as lying in the demographic realm rather than in the domain of health care management and policy.

A synthesis of these contrasting paradigms – the "demographic crisis" and the "anti-apocalyptic," would call for the incorporation of elements of both schools of thought in the assessment and implementation of policies associated with the aging situation. The demographic crisis approach to aging hinges on the idea that population projections have a reality of their own. The critical voice of the "anti-apocalyptic" perspective suggests that the demographic weight of seniors on society, while real, is blown out of proportion by governments and certain sectors of academe and the media. A middle ground approach is possible: We can anticipate significant demographic pressures emanating from the aging of the population, but the severity of impact of this reality on the society will depend on structural conditions, such as the degree of economic growth of the nation and its ability to absorb increasing costs. If the rate of economic growth exceeds the rate of costs incurred by population aging, the latter may not pose as severe a crisis as many envision.

CONCLUSION

In its early days, in its formative stages as a country, the population of Canada was youthful, with a median age of about 20 years in the late 1800s. As the twentieth century unfolded, Canada became increasingly industrialized and urbanized, and fertility rates embarked on a secular trend of decline, interrupted temporarily by the two-decade rise in birth rates during the post-War baby boom from 1946 to 1966. After this point, the birth rate resumed its long term declining trend, reaching current low levels. Decades of subreplacement fertility has led to an increasingly older population, the median age fast approaching 40 years.

The greying of the population poses some challenges for the country. By midway in the 21st century, Canada will see a shrinking of its working-age population while the population of old age dependents rises and youth dependency ratios decline. In this context, the "old-old" component of the population (ages 85 and older) is expected to increase significantly as survival probabilities in the seniors population are bound to improve further. Health care costs may increase significantly. Moreover, a projected shortage of workers also implies the necessity to boost immigration levels to help supplement a shrinking labour force population. Finally, as is the case with all demographically mature societies, there is bound to be some pressure on the public pension system.

Notwithstanding these concerns, as a prosperous advanced society, Canada should more than adequately meet the challenges of an increasingly aging population. As aptly argued by Day (1992: xvii), although demographic phenomena once they unfold take on a momentum of their own, our collective well-being is likely to be threatened more by non-demographic factors than the greying of the population:

> The social consequences of … older age structures and declining numbers of people … will depend … not so much on demographic dimensions as on a variety of essentially nondemographic factors: on, for example, the types of social policies in force, the distribution of wealth and income; the availability of health services, housing, and public transportation; and on such conditions of the physical and social environment as air quality, noise, personal safety, and opportunities for both social interaction and enjoyment of privacy."

The main societal challenge will be to maintain and promote for all age groups and future generations universal principles of equity, freedom, and access to socioeconomic opportunities. Demographic aging may turn out to be a problem to the extent that society fails to operate on these basic principles.

NOTES

1 The arithmetic average age is not very useful because it is highly sensitive to extreme values in the age distribution.
2 As for migration, its role in affecting change in the age composition of national populations would, in most cases, be relatively minor (Preston, Heuveline, and Guillot 2001).
3 One may also plot the absolute age-sex specific counts to form the population age pyramid.
4 The terminal age group in the age-sex pyramid is not restricted to 85+; it can be an older age category, such as 90+ or 100+. However, the initial age category is customarily set to be 0–4.
5 Statistics Canada (Cat.96F0030XIE2001002 16 July 2002: 15) gives the start and end dates of the baby boom as being 1946–1965. In 2001, the baby boomers were therefore aged 36–55. The baby bust cohort – the cohort immediately following the

baby boom – is listed as occurring between 1966 and 1979. Following this cohort is that of the "children of the boomers" (1980–1995); and finally, children of the baby bust cohorts (from 1996 on).

6 A measure of aging commonly used in the demographic literature is the "aging index," expressed as the number of persons 60 years old or over per hundred persons under age 15 (United Nations Department of Economic and Social Affairs Population Division 2002, 41).

7 In the demographic literature this measure is also referred to as the "masculinity ratio."

8 In some countries (e.g., India) this measure is transposed, with females being the numerator and males the denominator (Clarke 2003).

9 Across populations the sex ratio at birth is usually in the range of about 105 baby boys to 100 baby girls. This parameter is frequently applied in formal demographic analysis.

10 In his 1978 monograph, *What Will a ZPG Society Look Like?* Lincoln Day listed 26 countries that as of about 1976 had reached, or were close to attaining, zero population growth rates and therefore an older age structure. Out of these 26 countries only Singapore was a developing country. Today, the list of countries falling into demographic maturity has grown considerably. Out of 54 countries examined by Frejka and Ross (2001: 222) in 1997, two had a net reproduction rate (NRR) of between 1.00 and 1.19 (NRR of exactly 1.00 means the population is just replacing itself, while a value above 1.00 indicates above-replacement reproductivity; and less than 1.00 means below-replacement). Twenty countries had NRRs between 0.80 and 0.99; 23 ranged between 0.60 and 0.79; and 7 had NRRs below 0.60. Twenty-five of the 54 countries are Western societies, 22 Eastern European, and 6 Asian (including Japan and China).

REFERENCES

Bongaarts, John. 2004. "Population Aging and the Rising Cost of Public Pensions." *Population and Development Review* 30 (1): 1–24

Clarke, John I. 2003. "Sex Ratio." In *Encyclopedia of Population*, eds. Paul Demeny and Geoffrey McNicoll, 875–8. New York: Macmillan Reference USA

Coale, Ansley J. 1957. "How the Age Distribution of a Human Population is Determined." Cold Spring Harbor Symposia on Quantitative Biology 22: 83–9

– 1964. "How a Population Ages or Grows Younger." Chapter 3 in *Population: The Vital Revolution*, ed. Ronald Freedman. Garden City, NY: Anchor Books, Doubleday and Co

– 1972. *The Growth and Structure of Human Populations: A Mathematical Investigation*. Princeton: Princeton University Press

Day, Lincoln H. 1978. "What Will a ZPG Society Look Like?" *Population Bulletin* 33 (3). Washington: Population Reference Bureau

– 1992. *The Future of Low-Birthrate Populations*. London: Rutledge

Denton, Frank, and Byron G. Spencer. 1975. *Population and the Economy*. Lexington, MA: Saxon House/Lexington Books

– 1998. Economic Costs of Population Aging. IESOP Research paper no. 32. Program for Research on the Independence and Economic Security of the Older Population. McMaster University, Faculty of Social Sciences. Hamilton, Ontario

– 2000. "How Old is Old? Revising the Definition Based on Life Table Criteria." In *Independence and Economic Security in Old Age*, eds. Frank T. Denton, Deborah Fretz, and Byron G. Spencer, 15–26. Vancouver: University of British Columbia Press

– and Christine H. Feaver. 2000. "The Future Population of Canada and its Age Distribution." In *Independence and Economic Security in Old Age*, eds. Frank T. Denton, Deborah Fretz, and Byron G. Spencer, 27–56. Vancouver: University of British Columbia Press

The Economist. 2004. "Employment: Return of the Wrinklies." (17 January): 48

– 2004. "Japan: A Shrinking Giant." (10 January): 38

Frejka, Thomas, and John Ross. 2001. "Paths to Subreplacement Fertility: The Empirical Evidence." In *Global Fertility Transition. Population and Development Review*, eds. Rodolfo A. Bulatao and John B. Casterline, 213–54. Supplement to vol. 27. New York: The Population Council

Gee, Ellen M., and Gloria Gutman, eds. *The Overselling of Population Aging: Apocalyptic Demography, Intergenerational Challenges, and Social Policy*. Don Mills, Ontario: Oxford University Press

Gendel, Murray. 2002. "Boomers' Retirement Wave Likely to Begin in Just 6 Years." *Population Today* (April 30, no. 3): 4–5

George, M.V. et al. 2001. "Population Projections for Canada, Provinces and Territories, 2000–2026." Ottawa: Ministry of Industry. Cat. no. 91–520

Greeley, Andrew, and Michael Hout. 1999. "Americans' Increasing Belief in Life After Death: Religious Competition and Acculturation." *American Sociological Review* 64 (6): 813–35

Grindstaff, Carl F. 1981. *Population and Society: A Sociological Perspective*. West Hanover, MA: The Christopher Publishing House

Guttentag, Marcia, and Paul F. Secord. 1983. *Too Many Women? The Sex Ratio Question*. Beverly Hills: Sage

Henripin, Jacques. 1994. "The Financial Consequences of Population Aging." *Canadian Public Policy* 20 (1): 78–94

Hirschi, T., and M. Gottfredson. 1983. "Age and the Explanation of Crime." *American Journal of Sociology* 89: 552–84

Hout, Michael, Andrew Greeley, and Melissa J. Wilde. 2001. "Demographic Imperative in Religious Change." *American Journal of Sociology* 107 (2): 468–500

Kannisto, Vaino, Jens Lauritsen, A. Roger Thatcher, and James W. Vaupel. 1994. "Reductions in Mortality at Advanced Ages: Several Decades of Evidence from 27 Countries." *Population and Development Review* 20 (4): 793–810

Kinsella, Kevin, and Victoria A. Vlekoff. 2001. An Aging World: 2001. US Census Bureau, series P95/01–1. Washington, DC: US Government Printing Office

Laghi, Brian. 2002. "Baby Boomers No Big Threat, Romanow Told." *The Globe and Mail* (11 October): A7

Little, Bruce. 1999. "Boomer Gloom's Voice of Reason." *The Globe and Mail* (19 July): A2

Manton, Kenneth G. 1982. "Changing Concepts of Mortality and Morbidity in the Elderly Population." *Milbank Memorial Fund Quarterly/Health and Society* 60 (2): 183–244

– Xi Liang Gu, and Vicky L. Lamb. 2006. "Long-Term Trends in the Life Expectancy and Active Life Expectancy in the United States." *Population and Development Review* 32 (1): 81–105

McVey, Wayne W. Jr, and Warren E. Kalbach. 1995. *Canadian Population*. Toronto: Nelson Canada

Olshansky, S. Jay, and Brian A. Ault. 1986. "The Fourth Stage of the Epidemiological Transition: The Age of Delayed Degenerative Diseases." *Milbank Quarterly* 64: 355–91

Perls, Thomas T., and Ruth C. Fretts. 2002. "Why Women Live Longer than Men." In *Population and Society: Essential Readings*, ed. Frank Trovato, 101–6. Don Mills, Ontario: Oxford University Press

Preston, Samuel H., Patrick Heuveline, and Michel Guillot. 2001. *Demography: Measuring and Modeling Population Processes*. Oxford: Blackwell Publishers

Pryor, Edward T., and Douglas A. Norris. 1988. "Religion and the Family Life Cycle." *Canadian Studies in Population* 15 (2): 159–80

Stackhouse, John. 1994. "Worldwide Aging Crisis Feared." *The Globe and Mail* (4 October): A1, A10

Statistics Canada. 2002. *Profile of the Canadian Population by Age and Sex: Canada Ages*. Cat. no. 96F0030XIE2001002 (16 July 2002)

Stone, Leroy O., and Susan Fletcher. 1994. "The Seniors Boom: Dramatic Increases in Longevity and Prospects for Better Health." In *Perspectives on Canada's Population: An Introduction to Concepts and Issues*, eds. Frank Trovato and Carl F. Grindstaff, 96–111. Toronto: Oxford University Press

Suzman, Richard M., David P. Willis, and Kenneth G. Manton, eds. *The Oldest Old*. New York: Oxford University Press

Teitelbaum, Michael S. 1972. "Factors Associated with the Sex Ratio in Human
    Populations." In *The Structure of Human Populations*, eds. G.A. Harrison and
    A.J. Boyce, 90–109. Oxford: Clarendon Press
United Nations Department of Economic and Social Affairs, Population Division.
    2002. "World Population Ageing 1950–2050." New York: United Nations. ST/
    ESA/SER.A/207
– 2004. "World Population Prospects: The 2002 Revision." New York: United
    Nations
United Nations Secretariat, Department of Economic and Social Affairs, Population
    Division. 2003. "World Population Prospects: The 2002 Revision." Vols. I & II.
    New York: United Nations. ST/ESA/SER.A/223

3

Households and Housing in Canada

FERNANDO RAJULTON

INTRODUCTION

Households are basic socio-demographic units as much as families are. In practice, we use the two terms, households and families, interchangeably since in most contexts family types determine household types. Yet, the distinction between the two is important while computing statistical measures because most of these measures depend on the base used in the calculations (that is, whether households or families). The measures presented in this chapter are based on households, unless stated otherwise.

Households and families are dynamic not only in their composition, but also in their definition. The two were assumed to be identical in their definitions, therefore in their composition, until 1950s. Since then their definitions have changed considerably, especially during the late 1990s.[1] Some caution is therefore necessary when interpreting various measures over time. To be on the safeguard, time series measures presented in this chapter will not go further than the 1960s.

Households and families are also dynamic in another sense in that they evolve over the life courses of individuals. Census data cannot adequately capture the life course impact on the evolution of households and families. Yet, we can get some insight into the pattern of evolution by linking the information from various censuses, especially through age, period, and cohort components.

There has been a tremendous growth in the number of households all over the world during the second half of the 20th century. Much of this growth was due to the rate of population increase. In developed societies like Canada, other demographic processes such as union formations and dissolutions, population aging, and proliferation of individual lifestyles have also given a spurt to the growth of households. A study of households, therefore, cannot be done in a vacuum; it has to be done in the context of socio-demographic changes over time.

Homes, sweet homes, are places for building personal relationships with spouses and children as well as with neighbours and communities. Well-maintained, suitable, and affordable houses contribute not only to the general physical and mental well-being of their occupants, but also to building and strengthening of neighbourhoods and communities. Housing ultimately reflects the quality of life of a community or neighbourhood or even of a nation at large.[2] Thus, housing and associated issues such as housing conditions and affordability are also important topics in a study of households. These issues, however, depend much on the socioeconomic conditions prevailing in a society. The healthy social life of a nation is therefore inextricably linked to its healthy economic life.[3]

A study of households and housing conditions at the national level, as in this study, because of space limitations, ignores the large variation that can exist at regional, provincial, community, and individual levels. Where possible, this chapter tries to explore variations in the pattern of households and housing conditions. To tap into all these variations would call for a volume of its own because of the in-built diversity in the Canadian population due to its immigrant and Aboriginal subpopulations. Fortunately, census data on these subgroups are readily available, and interested readers are encouraged to explore these variations on their own.

With these points in mind, this chapter explores the prevailing status of households and housing conditions in Canada by looking at the data collected by the 2001 Census. And, wherever possible, the chapter will also highlight the changes over time by looking at similar measures from previous censuses; this may give some insight into possible future patterns. Since major changes in families and households started only after the 1950s, the earliest census considered in this chapter would be that of 1961.

NUMBER AND TYPES OF HOUSEHOLDS IN CANADA

As mentioned earlier, there has been a tremendous growth in the number of households all over the world during the second half of the last century. Canada is no exception. Census data show the total number of Canadian households in 2001 is 2.5 times larger than what it was in 1961 (with 11.6 million households in 2001 compared with 4.5 million in 1961). What is unique to Canada and other developed societies is the onset of second demographic transition[4] (van de Kaa 1987, 1994; Lesthaeghe 1995) during the last quarter of the 20th century and its consequences such as population aging (McDaniel 1986; Stone and Frenken 1988; Gee and Gutman 2000), proliferation of lifestyles and different forms of family support (Riley and

Riley 1992; Rajulton and Ravanera 2006). These socio-demographic changes had marked effects on the household and housing patterns during the last four decades.

Since the 1960s, the percentage change in the number of households from census to census increased much faster than the Canadian population. The latter witnessed a steady decline in its percentage change from 10 percent in 1960s to 4 percent at the turn of the century, except for a unique spike during the period of 1986–91. In contrast, the percentage change in Canadian households increased from 14 percent in the sixties to 19 percent in the seventies before starting to decline to reach 7 percent at the turn of the century, again except for the unusual period of 1986–91.[5] The dramatic increase in the number of households in the seventies was because of "boomers"[6] starting to form households around that period. The rate of household growth in the 1970s was well above that of any other period in Canadian history. The second spike in the years 1986–91 was mainly due to the sudden and huge increase in the number of immigrants into the country. During the last five year period 1996–2001, the percentage change in households continued to drop from eight to seven percent. But the percentage change in population kept the same level as in the immediately previous five year period. Coupled with ever-declining fertility since the mid-sixties, an obvious and important outcome was a steady decline in average household size, which has not shown any reverse trend since the sixties (see Table 3.2, Panel B).

Table 3.1 presents the data on household type and size obtained by Census 2001. Twenty nine and a half million Canadians were living in 11.6 million households, with an average of 2.6 persons per household (see the last row of table 3.1). Broken down by household type and the number of persons, the table yields interesting points. As the column titled "% of total households" reveals, 70 percent of households were family households, consisting mainly of one-family type (69 percent of all households or 98 percent of family households). *Of these one-family households*, married couples with or without children made up 71 percent, while common-law couples with or without children and lone parents shared almost equally the remaining 29 percent of households (14 percent and 15 percent respectively). Although only 13 percent of Canadians were living in non-family households, these households made up 30 percent of all households, and a vast majority of them (87 percent) were one-person households.

Concerning the number of persons, it is clear from table 3.1 that 58 percent of households had only one or two persons, and only 10 percent had five or more persons. Although multiple-family households comprised only 2 percent of all family households, they housed the highest average number of

Table 3.1:
Household Type by Household Size, with Average Number of Persons per Household, Census 2001

Household Type	Total Number of households	% of Total Households	Row percentages of Number of Persons						Total # Persons	Average # Persons
			1	2	3	4	5	6+		
Family households	8155565	0.705	–	0.419	0.223	0.225	0.091	0.043	25586660	3.1
One-family households	7951965	0.688	–	0.430	0.229	0.224	0.086	0.031	24430370	3.1
Married couples with children	3338630	0.289	–	0.000	0.330	0.432	0.174	0.063	13329525	4.0
Married couples without children	2300585	0.199	–	0.967	0.029	0.003	0.001	–	4690520	2.0
Common-law couples with children	518995	0.045	–	–	0.452	0.380	0.121	0.047	1961765	3.8
Common-law couples without children	609595	0.053	–	0.943	0.049	0.006	0.001	–	1259975	2.1
Lone parents	1184165	0.102	–	0.521	0.324	0.112	0.031	0.012	3188585	2.7
Multiple-family households	203595	0.018	–	–	–	0.237	0.265	0.498	1156290	5.7
Non-family households	3407415	0.295	0.874	0.105	0.017	0.004	–	–	3935640	1.2
One person only	2976875	0.257	1.000	–	–	–	–	–	2976875	1.0
Two or more persons	430535	0.037	–	0.828	0.132	0.029	0.008	0.003	958765	2.2
Total - Household type	11562975		2976880	3772430	1875215	1843795	741520	353135	29522305	2.6

Source: Census of Canada 2001.

Table 3.2
Changes in Household Type and Household Size from 1961 to 2001, Canada

A) Household Type

	Total # Households	Row percentages of Type of Household				
		One-family	Multiple-family	Non-family	Lone parent[a]	Common-law[a]
1961	4554736	83.0	3.7	13.3	9.2	
1971	6041302	79.6	2.0	18.3	10.0	
1981	8281530	74.1	1.1	24.8	11.6	6.4
1991	10108270	71.1	1.2	27.8	13.4	5.6
2001	11562975	68.8	1.8	29.5	14.9	9.8

B) Household size

	Total # households	Row percentages of size of household						
		1	2	3	4	5	6+	Average # persons
1961	4554736	9.3	22.2	17.8	18.4	13.3	19.0	3.9
1966	5180473	11.4	23.1	17.0	17.6	12.9	18.0	3.7
1971	6034505	13.4	25.3	17.3	17.6	11.9	14.5	3.5
1976	7166095	16.8	27.8	17.5	18.2	10.5	9.2	3.1
1981	8281530	20.3	29.0	17.5	18.6	9.1	5.5	2.9
1986	8991675	21.5	30.0	17.8	18.7	8.1	3.9	2.8
1991	10108270	22.9	31.4	17.4	17.7	7.3	3.3	2.7
1996	10820050	24.2	31.6	16.9	17.0	7.1	3.2	2.6
2001	11562975	25.7	32.6	16.2	15.9	6.4	3.1	2.6

a: The base for Lone Parent and Common-law households is one-family households.
Source: Data for 1961 to 1991 from Peron et al. (1999), tables 1.9 and 2.15. Data for 2001 are from Census 2001.

persons (5.7, in the last column) among the various households. Households of married and common-law couples with children had an average of about four persons per household, while those of lone-parents had an average of 2.7 persons per household.

Combined with data from previous censuses, we can see the trend over time of the household types and average number of persons per household. Table 3.2 highlights the changes in broad categories of household type over the last forty years in Panel A. One-family households show a steady decline from 83 percent in 1961 to 69 percent in 2001. So, too, multiple-family households that are now only half of what they were in 1961. In contrast, non-family households have steadily grown from 13 percent in 1961 to 30 percent in 2001. Non-family households consist of persons living alone or living with relatives and non-relatives. The proportion of non-family persons is negligible among children, rather large among young adults who are usually at an important life course stage of forming their own families and households, smaller again among adults who are busy raising their children, and progressively higher among older adults and the elderly when the family unit starts contracting and dissolving. Low fertility, longer life, and population aging have all played significant roles in the increase of non-family households. One-person households in particular show the fastest growth and have more than tripled between 1971 and 2001.

Lone-parent and common-law households also show a steady increase. *With the one-family households as the base*, the lone-parent households have increased from 9 percent to 15 percent and the common-law households (for which data are available only from 1981) increased from 6 to 10 percent. The increase in common-law households is due to the growing "popularity" and legalization of such unions. The households comprising couples with children also grew during this period (not shown in the table, see table 2.15 of Peron 1999) but more slowly than lone-parent, common-law and couples-without-children households. Socio-demographic factors such as increased marital dissolutions and pluralistic lifestyles are responsible for the observed pattern of changes over time among these family households.

No wonder, then, as a consequence of all these changes, the average number of persons in Canadian households has declined steadily since 1961 (see the lower Panel B of Table 3.2). Between 1961 and 2001, one-person households nearly tripled, two-person households increased by 50 percent, three-person households have remained steady around 17 percent, and four-or-more-person households steadily declined, with six-plus-person households almost disappearing.

HOUSEHOLDS BY TENURE

The fact that the number of households has increased while the average number of persons in households has decreased with some prominent changes in household types leads us to inquire about the type of dwellings these households are occupying. There are two important aspects of dwellings; one is structural and the other is economic. The major categories of the structural aspect are usually seen as: single detached houses, apartment buildings with five or more storeys, movable homes, and others such as single attached houses, apartment buildings with less than five storeys and duplexes. The economic aspect focuses on the ownership or tenure of houses, therefore on the financial viability of households. What are the most common types of households that fall into one category or other, either structural or economic? Table 3.3 gives a summary picture of household type by ownership or tenure[7], and table 3.4 classifies household type further by structural aspect, both as obtained from Census 2001.

Although there are no legal or institutional impediments to home ownership in Canada, there can be various socio-economic impediments to ownership. In the case of women, for example, ownership may be closely related to their family (or marital) status than in the case of men. According to the 2001 Census data, 78–80 percent of women in two-spouse households owned their homes, depending on whether they were living with children or not. But only 48–58 percent of women in common-law households, 46–54 percent of women in lone-parent households, and 39–45 percent of women in non-family households owned their homes. The corresponding percentages for men are: 80–84 percent for two-spouse households, 57–67 percent for common-law households, 63–64 percent for lone-parent households, and 35–43 percent for non-family households. As mentioned earlier, such variations deserve a study of their own, and only some of them are highlighted in this paper.

As table 3.3 reveals, overall, two-thirds of Canadian households fall under the category "Owned" (with or without mortgage). Classified by household type, it is understandable that 75 percent of one-family households and 79 percent of multiple family households own their dwellings, while only 43 percent of non-family households do so. This large difference between family and non-family households is obviously because of the presence of children and parents' feelings of obligation to provide space and other amenities to their children. This is especially so among the married couples with children, who are the most likely to own their homes; 84 percent of them own their homes. Married couples without children are also almost as likely (83 percent) to own their homes as those with children. But the absence of children arrives later in the life course, when children have left homes, with an increasing possibility of returning home sometime or other for various reasons (for this interesting phenomenon known as "boomerang," see Goldscheider 2000; Mitchell 2006). Common-law couples with or without children are 20 to 30 percent less likely than married couples to own their homes. Reasons for this may be many, and one needs to combine life course information with qualitative interviews to get at plausible reasons. However, it is possible the uncertainty of long-term relationships among cohabiting couples is acting as a barrier to such large investments as housing.

Table 3.3 also shows that among the family households, lone parents are the least likely to own their homes. Actually, they are almost equally split among owners and renters (51 percent versus 49 percent respectively). Problems of financial viability faced by most lone parents, either as unmarried

Table 3.3
Tenure by Household Type – Census 2001

| | Total Number of Households | Row percentages of Types of Tenure | | |
		Owned	Rented	Band housing
Family households	8155560	0.754	0.242	0.005
One-family households	7951965	0.753	0.243	0.004
Married couples with children	3338630	0.843	0.154	0.003
Married couples without children	2300585	0.829	0.170	0.001
Common-law couples with children	518995	0.644	0.343	0.014
Common-law couples without children	609595	0.544	0.453	0.002
Lone parents	1184160	0.505	0.487	0.008
Multiple-family households	203600	0.787	0.189	0.025
Non-family households	3407415	0.430	0.568	0.002
One person only	2976880	0.439	0.559	0.002
Two or more persons	430540	0.366	0.632	0.003
Total – Household type	11562975	7610390	3907170	45415
% of total		0.658	0.338	0.004

or previously married, are certain factors that can explain this rather low proportion of home ownership among lone parents.

Household ownership classified further by type of dwelling shows an interesting pattern too, as shown in table 3.4. Fifty-seven percent of all households in Canada live in single detached houses. The main household type occupying single detached houses consists of married couples with children (77 percent), 86 percent of whom own. In contrast, non-family households are the least likely to be occupying single detached houses (only 34 percent), out of whom only 65 percent own them. It is also interesting to see that while only about 46–47 percent of lone parents and common-law couples without children are able to occupy single detached houses, 72–73 percent of them are actually able to own.

Belying common opinion, only 9 percent of all households live in apartment buildings with five or more storeys. Non-family households are the dominant type to occupy these apartments (17 percent), out of whom only 7 percent own them. Thirty-two percent of all households live in other types of dwellings, such as single attached houses, duplexes, and apartment buildings with less than five storeys. The highest percentages living in these other types of dwellings include non-family households (47 percent), lone-parent households (45 percent), and common-law couples without children (43 percent). Roughly 25 percent of these three types of households own these dwellings.

Table 3.4
Household Type by Dwelling Type and by Tenure – Census 2001

Household Type	Total Tenure					Owned				
	Total Structural Type of dwelling	Single-detached house	Structural Type of Dwelling Apartment, building that has five or more storeys	Movable dwelling	Other dwelling	Total Structural Type of dwelling	Single-detached house	Structural Type of Dwelling Apartment, building that has five or more storeys	Movable dwelling	Other dwelling
Total	11,562,975	57.4	9.1	1.4	32.2	7,610,385	78.5	2.8	1.7	17.0
Family households	8,155,560	67.2	5.6	1.3	25.8	6,145,835	81.8	1.8	1.5	15.0
One-family households	7,951,960	67.1	5.7	1.3	25.9	5,985,695	81.9	1.8	1.5	14.9
Married couples with children	3,338,625	76.6	4.0	0.9	18.5	2,814,020	85.5	0.9	1.0	12.6
Married couples without children	2,300,585	70.5	7.1	1.5	20.9	1,907,860	81.4	3.0	1.7	14.0
Common-law couples with children	518,995	63.1	2.2	2.2	32.5	334,000	80.5	0.4	2.5	16.6
Common-law couples without children	609,595	47.1	8.2	1.9	42.8	331,840	72.7	3.1	2.8	21.4
Lone parents	1,184,165	46.1	7.9	1.4	44.6	597,970	72.2	2.3	2.0	23.5
Multiple-family households	203,600	70.0	4.9	0.6	24.6	160,140	77.9	1.6	0.5	19.9
Non-family households	3,407,415	33.8	17.3	1.5	47.4	1,464,555	64.8	7.0	2.8	25.4
One person only	2,976,880	33.6	17.9	1.5	46.9	1,307,170	64.4	7.3	2.9	25.4
Two or more persons	430,535	35.3	13.2	1.3	50.2	157,380	67.6	4.4	2.4	25.6

The above picture presents clearly the economic viability of households or of household maintainers, either in the type of dwellings they are able to live in or in the type of tenure. We shall therefore examine the picture of ownership and affordability in the next two sections.[8]

HOME OWNERSHIP BY INCOME

No doubt home ownership is mainly determined by income, either personal income of household maintainer or total household income. The relationship between ownership and household income is presented in table 3.5 with census 2001 data. The summary statistics given at the bottom of table 3.5 clearly show that, on the average, homeowners need at least twice the income of renters whether one considers mean or median household income. Actually, the average number of persons in a homeowner household is larger than that in a renter household (2.9 versus 2.1) and even larger (3.2) when ownership with mortgage is considered. The same pattern holds with the average number of income recipients in a household.

Table 3.5 presents two types of percentages. Row percentages give the percentage of owners and renters within each income group, hence telling us about the "impact" of income on ownership. Column percentages are calculated *within* owners and renters category, thereby telling us how owners or renters in 2001 are distributed by income (*among owners or renters themselves*).

Looking at the row percentages, it is obvious that as income increases, ownership steadily increases and renting steadily decreases. The column percentages *among owners* (with or without mortgage) show that ownership increases steadily with income until it reaches an abrupt peak at an income in the range of 50 to 60 thousand dollars. Such an abrupt peak in home ownership around 60 thousand dollars is no surprise given that mortgages are not generally available from financial institutions for households with lower income. What is more surprising, however, is the start of decline in ownership from this point on, such that at an income nearing 100 thousand dollars the decline reaches a level that is comparable to the one just before the peak. For income in the range of 100 to 125 thousand dollars, there is a 2 percent increase, only to decrease further at much higher income. It may sound strange that the distribution of owners by income starts declining at higher income. What it tells us is that large proportions of homeowners in 2001 are from the 50–to 70–thousand dollar income bracket. But at higher incomes, which are usually associated with higher ages at least until retirement, the profile of ownership by age and life course stages takes precedence over the profile by income. In contrast to homeowners, the column percentages *among renters* reach a peak

Table 3.5
Tenure by Household Income and Ownership with Mortgage – Census 2001

Household Income	Total Number	Owned Number	Owned Row %	Owned Col %	Rented Number	Rented Row %	Rented Col %	Owned with Mortgage* Number	Owned with Mortgage* Row %	Owned with Mortgage* Col %
Under $5,000	390125	109565	28.1	1.6	280555	71.9	7.2	55195	50.4	1.6
$ 5,000 - $ 9,999	382130	93375	24.4	1.4	288750	75.6	7.4	43975	47.1	1.2
$ 10,000 - $ 14,999	779860	267155	34.3	4.0	512705	65.7	13.2	68555	25.7	1.9
$ 15,000 - $ 19,999	737605	301375	40.9	4.5	436230	59.1	11.2	85380	28.3	2.4
$ 20,000 - $ 24,999	684265	339595	49.6	5.1	344665	50.4	8.9	102345	30.1	2.9
$ 25,000 - $ 29,999	649895	343135	52.8	5.1	306760	47.2	7.9	123105	35.9	3.5
$ 30,000 - $ 34,999	621805	343730	55.3	5.1	278070	44.7	7.2	147530	42.9	4.2
$ 35,000 - $ 39,999	604815	357750	59.2	5.4	247060	40.8	6.4	173775	48.6	4.9
$ 40,000 - $ 44,999	574515	361010	62.8	5.4	213505	37.2	5.5	190875	52.9	5.4
$ 45,000 - $ 49,999	553195	371795	67.2	5.6	181400	32.8	4.7	208620	56.1	5.9
$ 50,000 - $ 59,999	1021945	743380	72.7	11.1	278560	27.3	7.2	447690	60.2	12.6
$ 60,000 - $ 69,999	856170	673880	78.7	10.1	182290	21.3	4.7	426655	63.3	12.0
$ 70,000 - $ 79,999	684550	568595	83.1	8.5	115955	16.9	3.0	368375	64.8	10.4
$ 80,000 - $ 89,999	532370	458145	86.1	6.9	74225	13.9	1.9	298560	65.2	8.4
$ 90,000 - $ 99,999	386575	341385	88.3	5.1	45190	11.7	1.2	220075	64.5	6.2
$100,000 - $124,999	570300	514275	90.2	7.7	56020	9.8	1.4	321715	62.6	9.1
$125,000 - $149,999	246950	226480	91.7	3.4	20470	8.3	0.5	134790	59.5	3.8
$150,000 and over	283635	261495	92.2	3.9	22135	7.8	0.6	132755	50.8	3.7
Total	10560685	6676125		100.0	3884565		100.0	3549985		100.0
Average household income $	52969	64466			33211			69234		
Median household income $	43841	56038			26310			62983		
Standard error of average household income $	32	45			31			49		
Average number of persons	2.6	2.9			2.1			3.2		
Average number of income recipients	1.9	2.1			1.6			2.2		

Note: * - These percentages are computed with owners as the base.

at incomes in the range of 10 to 20 thousand dollars and thereafter steadily decline for higher incomes. Thus, the renters' profile is influenced by income as well as by age and life course stage.

Table 3.5 gives also the row and column percentages of owners with mortgage by income. Fifty-three percent of homeowners in 2001 were owners with mortgages (that is, 3,549,985 out of 6,676,125). The row percentages are calculated by using the number of owners at each income group as the base, and therefore their complement will reflect ownership without mortgage. The column percentages calculated by using the number of owners with mortgage as the base give the distribution of owners with mortgage in the year 2001. These column percentages *among owners with mortgage* show the expected pattern, similar to the one for all owners, of steady increase until the peak around 50–59 thousand dollars and decline thereafter at higher incomes.

The row percentages of owners with mortgages reveal an interesting non-linear pattern. Rather high proportions of owners with mortgages (nearly 50 percent) are found at the lowest two income categories. Possible home buyers at these income levels are: i) the young with low income but from high-income families; ii) the old whose income might have dropped but who have saved enough in their lives. Those from less affluent families would need more time to amass the capital needed to buy homes. This is confirmed by the steady trend shown in the mid-portion of the distribution. At incomes of 15 thousand dollars or higher, the percentages show a steady increase until around 90 thousand dollars, after which they decline again to the starting point of 50 percent at incomes 150 thousand or higher.

The whole picture of home ownership with mortgage in the census year 2001 needs to be seen in terms of the economic fluctuations during the last decade.[9] There was a rise in housing demand in the late 1990s, triggered by the most obvious economic factors of job creation, income growth, and low mortgage rates. After a few lean years in the early nineties, employment grew steadily until 2001. The unemployment rate in Canada in the early 1990s was as high as 11 percent. But it fell to 6.9 percent in 2000 (and remained below eight percent through 2003). Economic consequences of job creation and income growth were inevitable. Housing demand increased in the late 1990s, which led to tightening of supply conditions. For example, rental vacancy rates hit a low point of 3.2 in 1999 (and a much lower point of 2.2 in 2000) and new houses available for rent or buying became rare. Rising demand and tightening supply conditions resulted in greater housing prices and rents from 1996 to 2001 than in the first half of the 1990s. Because of the interplay between these market conditions, the mortgage rates were steadily falling from 13.4 percent in 1990 to 6.1 percent in 2001 (only to hit a historic low of 4.8 percent in

2003)[10]. Given this situation, Canadians were more willing to buy houses under mortgage than to pay high rents. The nonlinear pattern revealed by the row percentages in table 3.5 clearly shows that buying a home with mortgage was (and still is) a strategy of everybody, irrespective of income threshold.

AFFORDABLE HOUSING BY HOUSEHOLD TYPE

Affordable housing is measured by housing costs that are less than 30 percent of total before-tax household income. For renters, housing costs include rent, payments for electricity, fuel, water, and other municipal services. For owners, costs include mortgage payments (principal and interest), property taxes, any condominium fees, payments for electricity, fuel, water, and other municipal services.

Using a cut-off value of 30 percent of before-tax household income does not necessarily imply that households spending 30 percent or more of incomes on shelter costs have an affordability problem. Households with high incomes or households that choose to spend more on housing than on other goods are clear exceptions. The reference years by which censuses in Canada get information on income and shelter costs also create a minor problem. The reference period for shelter costs is usually the census year (here, 2001), while that for household income is the year before the census. Despite these drawbacks, such a measure of affordability serves as a useful benchmark for assessing trends in housing affordability.

Besides affordability, two more indicators, adequacy and suitability, are also considered for studying housing conditions. Adequate housing is one that needs no major repairs, such as defective plumbing and electrical wiring or structural repairs. Suitable housing is one with enough bedrooms for the size and makeup of a household, according to National Occupancy Standard (NOS) requirements. Overall, the term "acceptable housing" is used for housing that meets all the three conditions of affordability, adequacy, and suitability (for details, see CMHC 2003).

Inadequate and unsuitable housing (that is, housing in need of major repairs and crowding) are both rare in Canada. Going through 2001 and earlier censuses, we find that in general about 93 percent of Canadian households report adequate and suitable housing conditions. Non-affordability however is much more common, with the affordability percentage hanging around 78 to 80 percent. This pulls down the acceptable housing index to around 68 percent over various censuses, with moderate fluctuations arising from the prevailing economic conditions. We shall therefore focus our attention on affordability in this chapter.[11]

Table 3.6 breaks down affordability by tenure type further by three broad categories of household type for the year 2001. Three fourths of Canadian households meet the affordability criterion (see the Total column in table 3.6). Eighty-four percent of owners spend less than 30 percent of their incomes on housing, while only sixty percent of renters do so. However, variations within the owners and renters groups exist, as seen when we cross-classify the table by household type. While 87 to 88 percent of owners in one-family and multiple-family households meet the affordability criterion, only 72 percent of owners living in non-family households meet the criterion. Similarly, paying the rent is more affordable to those living in multiple-family households (80 percent) than in one-family (68 percent) and in non-family households (52 percent). Since non-family households are comprised mostly of one-person households (with old and unattached individuals), we can say that 50 percent of these household maintainers have to cope with the problem of affordability.

Limited space does not allow us to examine many other possible explanations for this social problem. We shall, however, look at the differentials in affordability by province since Canadian provinces are often seen as "have" and "have-not" provinces in terms of economic opportunities they enjoy. Table 3.7 gives the percentage of households that spend less than 30 percent of their before-tax income for housing in each province for the year 2001. As seen in table 3.7, the largest housing affordability is found in Nunavut and the Northwest Territories, even reaching 90 percent in the former. The lowest affordability is found in British Columbia (71 percent), where housing prices have skyrocketed during the last decade, followed by Ontario (75 percent), Nova Scotia (77 percent), and Alberta (78 percent). Thus, it looks like the economic performance of a province is *not* a guarantee for housing affordability. Rather, the overall economic performance can camouflage serious social problems underneath, with large percentages of immigrants and new settlers living in rented apartments that may also fall below the expected standards of adequacy and suitability. A breakdown of affordability by tenure type confirms this. Rather low affordability in the so-called "have" provinces arises mainly from rented households. In general, owned households in each province have much higher affordability than rented households. The highest affordability among owners is found in Manitoba (89 percent), while the lowest is again in British Columbia (79 percent). Rented households, on the other hand, have much lower affordability, hanging around from 55 to 65 percent, except in the case of Nunavut and the Northwest Territories. The variation by provinces among renters is much larger than among owners.

Table 3.6
Affordability by Tenure and Major Categories of Household Type – Census 2001

	Household Type							
	Total		One-family		Multiple-family		Non-family	
	Number	%	Number	%	Number	%	Number	%
a) All Households								
Affordability								
Spending less than 30% of household income on housing costs	8559255	75.9	6345440	82.1	168665	86.8	2045150	60.9
Spending 30% or more of household income on housing costs	2720070	24.1	1381105	17.9	25660	13.2	1313305	39.1
Total	11279330		7726545		194325		3358460	
b) Owned Households								
Affordability								
Spending less than 30% of household income on housing costs	6222750	84.0	5043890	86.7	138630	88.5	1040225	72.4
Spending 30% or more of household income on housing costs	1188470	16.0	773335	13.3	18060	11.5	397070	27.6
Total	7411215		5817225		156695		1437300	
c) Rented Households								
Affordability								
Spending less than 30% of household income on housing costs	2336510	60.4	1301550	68.2	30030	79.8	1004925	52.3
Spending 30% or more of household income on housing costs	1531605	39.6	607775	31.8	7595	20.2	916235	47.7
Total	3868115		1909325		37630		1921160	

Table 3.7
Housing Affordability by Provinces and by Tenure Type, Census 2001

	All households		Owned households		Rented households	
	# households	% Spending < 30%	# households	% Spending < 30%	# households	% Spending < 30%
Newfoundland and Labrador	188440	80.5	147340	87.3	41100	55.8
Prince Edward Island	49410	80.1	35940	88.0	13470	59.0
Nova Scotia	355095	77.1	252020	86.4	103075	54.5
New Brunswick	279515	80.5	208935	87.1	70575	60.9
Quebec	2944465	76.7	1702740	85.9	1241730	64.1
Ontario	4152635	74.7	2813785	82.7	1338850	57.8
Manitoba	403185	80.6	276530	88.7	126655	62.9
Saskatchewan	334460	80.4	235130	88.5	99330	61.4
Alberta	1050985	78.4	735395	84.5	315585	64.0
British Columbia	1491055	71.4	987980	79.3	503075	55.9
Yukon Territory	10590	79.0	7075	85.4	3515	66.1
Northwest Territories	12325	83.7	6615	86.4	5710	80.5
Nunavut	7175	89.3	1735	85.9	5440	90.4
Total – Canada	11279330	75.9	7411215	84.0	3868115	60.4

CONCLUSIONS

With the data available from the Census 2001 in Canada, this study has highlighted the importance of studying households and housing conditions over time. The snapshot picture obtained by a census at a particular time point hides underneath the evolution of various processes – social, economic, and political – that impact on the growth and type of households and the housing conditions in which these households live.

Housing in Canada has changed dramatically during the last four decades in terms of structure or composition, hence in the number of persons in households. Reasons for all these changes are many, especially demographic and socio-economic. International migration has played its own role during the last decade, whereby the mosaic of the Canadian population has changed dramatically. Despite this immigration flow, the Canadian population is certainly aging. Seniors like to live independently, on their own. Thus, one-person households have shown the fastest growth between 1971 and 2001, followed by lone-parent and couples-without-children households. We can expect this trend to continue well into the near future.

While the number of households is constantly on the increase, the number of persons in them is constantly shrinking. Yet, data from the housing market show that homes are getting larger. The pattern of owner and renter households is also constantly changing over time because of their dependence on the economy. Roughly, two-thirds of Canadian households are homeowners, and home ownership rates have shown only minor increase in recent years. Home ownership among those under 50 (especially among the busters and the echoers) has not shown much improvement when compared to the 1960s. It is difficult to foresee what the future holds in store for Canadian households because people are increasingly finding themselves in non-standard work situations, such as part-time work or short-term and contractual work. Housing requires households to make long-term financial commitments. Prolonged or repeated bouts of unemployment or short-term and contractual work certainly do not support such commitments. Persons and households with weak labour force ties are more likely to rent and are much more likely to be in core-housing need, and ultimately will be excluded from community and social participation and activities.

For lack of space, this study has not touched on many differentiating factors at subnational levels, including specific segments of the Canadian population, such as immigrants and Aboriginals. Such studies are warranted for any policy on households and housing, no matter at what level. Challenges in providing affordable housing to all citizens of the country are galore, and one is struck with the conspicuous silence on the part of governments, either federal or provincial, on this primary social provision, especially in many of Canada's major urban centres.

NOTES

1 For detailed descriptions of changes in the definitions of family and household, see Statistics Canada's documentation for various censuses. For a short description, see Peron (1999).

2 Realizing the importance of housing in people's lives, the United Nations held a second conference on Human Settlements, *Habitat II*, in Istanbul, Turkey, in June 1996 to discuss issues of shelter and human settlements in a rapidly urbanizing world. Canada is a signatory to this Habitat Agenda. And, in 2001, in response to the UN's invitation to submit a report on the agenda on behalf of the government, Canadian Mortgage and Housing Corporation (CMHC) prepared a country report titled "Implementing the Outcomes of the Second United Nations Conference on Human Settlements (Habitat II): Canada's Response." It is a document worth reading along with this chapter (see Govt. of Canada 2001).

3 The former, however, does not necessarily follow the latter, nor does the latter invariably lead to the former. This fact gives rise to serious social concerns, for example, homelessness in urban centres and shanty towns in the midst of skyscrapers. This is a topic that is beyond the scope of this chapter.

4 The second demographic transition refers to a set of socio-demographic changes such as decline in fertility to below replacement level, a rise in mean age at marriage of both men and women, and a rise in the rate of divorce and extramarital births. More importantly, it also refers to attitudinal changes such as self-fulfillment in partnerships and in childbearing, and pluralism in lifestyles.

5 During this period 1986–91, there was an unusual increase in the number of births (the number of births steadily increasing from year to year from about 372 thousand births in 1986 to 403 thousand in 1991), as well as in the number of immigrants allowed into the country (from about 25 thousand in 1986 to a whopping 200 thousand in 1991).

6 The "baby boomers" are those who were born during the period from the end of World War II until mid 1960s, that is, roughly from 1945 to 1965. These birth cohorts were quite large compared with the previous and subsequent ones. The birth cohorts from 1965 to 1980, in contrast, were smaller in number and are called "baby busters." The birth cohorts after this period, typically from 1980 to 1995, are called the "echo" generations. The boomer, bust, and echo generations (Foot with Stoffman 1996) have their own similarities and differences, especially in in-

come, education, and economic opportunities that affect housing demand, housing choice, and affordability. The boomers had good educational and financial opportunities, and they were pioneers in introducing many changes in the social fabric. Thanks to improved educational opportunities, the busters make up a highly educated group. But their high education levels have not been matched by improved employment or income opportunities because of economic downturns they have experienced. They are also often faced with precarious and insecure job positions. Because of the lack of opportunities, they are highly mobile, willing to relocate to areas offering greater economic opportunities. The echoers are still too young and are going through secondary-or post-secondary education. They are faced with the problem of rising tuition costs and debts.

7 Band-housing included in table 3.3 refers to households maintained on an Indian reserve or settlement. These households are usually excluded from calculations of shelter costs and ownership because their housing costs are paid through band housing arrangements and the census does not collect their shelter costs.

8 A demographic profile of home ownership by age and by birth cohorts is also useful, since these variables clearly define the likelihood of ownership by life course stages. Due to space limitations, such a profile is not presented in this study. Interested readers can contact the author for this profile.

9 For a complete description of the economic forces and statistics, see Engeland et al. 2004.

10 By the time this chapter is published, we will have seen another historic low of 2.5 percent in 2009 because of the global financial crisis that started in 2008 and its consequences on the housing market.

11 The original version of this chapter included a section on affordable and acceptable housing conditions for the years 1991 to 2001. Again, for reasons of space limitations, the section had to be removed. Interested readers can contact the author for details.

REFERENCES

Arestis, Philip, and Elias Karakitsos. 2003. "How Long Can the U.S. Consumers Carry the Economy on Their Shoulders?" Working Paper #380. The Levy Economics Institute of Bard College, Annandale-on-Hudson, NY. www.levy.org/pubs/wp/380.pdf

CMHC (Canada Mortgage and Housing Corporation). 2002. "Housing the Boom, Bust and Echo Generations. Research Highlights." Socio-economic Series 02–077

– 2003. 2001 Census. Housing Series, Issue 1: "Housing Affordability Improves. Research Highlights." Socio-Economic Series 03–017

Engeland, John, Roger Lewis, Steven Ehrlich, and Janet Che. 2004. *Evolving Housing Conditions in Canada's Census Metropolitan Areas, 1991–2001.* Trends and Conditions in Census Metropolitan Areas Series. Ottawa: Statistics Canada. Cat. no. 89–613–MWE2004005

Foot, David K., and Daniel Stoffman. 1996 (republished in 2000) *Boom, Bust & Echo.* Toronto: Macfarlane Walter & Ross

Gee, Ellen M. and Gloria M. Gutman. 2000. *The Overselling of Population Aging: Apocalyptic Demography, Intergenerational Challenges, and Social Policy.* Don Mills, Ont.: Oxford University Press

Goldscheider, Frances. 2000. "Why Study Young Adult Living Arrangements? A View of the Second Demographic Transition." Paper presented at the workshop, Leaving Home: A European Focus, at the Max Planck Institute for Demographic Research, Rostock, Germany. 6–8 September 2000. Available at www.demogr. mpg.de/Papers/workshops/000906_paper05.pdf

Government of Canada. 2001. *Implementing the Outcomes of the Second United Nations Conference on Human Settlements (Habitat II): Canada's Response.*

Haan, Michael, 2005. *The Decline of the Immigrant Ownership Advantage: Life-Cycle, Declining Fortunes and Changing Housing Careers in Montreal, Toronto and Vancouver, 1981 to 2001.* Analytical Studies Research Paper Series. Ottawa: Statistics Canada. Cat. no. 238

Lesthaeghe, Ron, 1995. "The Second Demographic Transition in Western Countries: An Interpretation." In *Gender and Family Change in Industrialized Countries,* eds. K.O. Mason and A. Jensen, 17–62. New York: Oxford University Press

McDaniel, Susan. 1986. *Canada's Aging Population.* Toronto: Butterworth

Mitchell, Barbara A. 2006. *The Boomerang Age: Transitions to Adulthood in Families.* New Brunswick, NJ: Aldine Transaction

Mongeau, Jael, and Evelyne Lapierre-Adamcyk. 1999. "Variations in the Housing Conditions of Canadian Families." Chapter 7 in *Canadian Families at the Approach of the Year 2000,* eds. Yves Peron et al. Ottawa: Statistics Canada. Cat. no. 96–321–MPE No.4

Peron, Yves. 1999. "Households and Families." Chapter 1 in *Canadian Families at the Approach of the Year 2000,* eds. Peron et al. Ottawa: Statistics Canada. Cat. no. 96–321–MPE No.4

Rajulton, Fernando, and Zenaida R. Ravanera. 2006. "Degrees of Family Solidarity: An Exploration with the Canadian General Social Survey on Family and Community Support, 1996." In *Canada's Changing Families: Implications for Individuals and Society,* eds. Kevin McQuillan and Zenaida R. Ravanera. Toronto: Toronto University Press

Riley, Matilda W., and John W. Riley Jr. 1992. "Generational relations: a future perspective." Chapter 12 in *Aging and Generational Relations, Life Course and Cross-cultural Perspectives*, ed. T. Hareven. NY: Aldine de Gruyter

Stone, Leroy, and Hubert Frenken. 1988. *Canada's Seniors*. Ottawa: Statistics Canada. Cat. no. 98–121.

Van de Kaa, Dirk J. 1987. "Europe's Second Demographic Transition." *Population Bulletin* 42 (1). Washington: The Population Reference Bureau.

– 1994. "The Second Demographic Transition Revisited: Theories and Expectations." In *Population and Family in the Low Countries 1993*, eds. G.C.N. Beets et al., 81–126. Lisse, Netherlands: Swets and Zeitlinger. (Updated and abbreviated version of PDOD *Werkstukken* no. 109 [1988])

PART TWO

Social Stratification

4

The Educational Attainment of Canadians

KEVIN McQUILLAN AND ERIN GIBBS VAN BRUNSCHOT

The coming of post-industrial society, as Daniel Bell (1973) presciently observed over thirty years ago, placed knowledge workers at the centre of the modern economy. The steady growth of technology and intense competition from societies in the developing world, with lower costs of production, have led to significant declines in employment, first in primary industries, and, more recently, in manufacturing. Manual skill and strength count for less while the ability to work with information is now a prerequisite for employment in the modern economy. And, as Peter Drucker (1994, 2) has observed, "the knowledge worker gains access to work, job and social position through formal education." Some critics argue that the importance of the formal education system lies as much in its ability to bestow credentials on its students as in its success in transmitting knowledge and expertise (e.g. Collins 1979); nevertheless, it is widely accepted by scholars, governments, and the general public that education is the essential pathway to rewarding employment. The result is that education has become an almost unquestioned good in advanced societies. Governments invest huge sums in supporting educational institutions and use both the law and public education campaigns to convince young people to stay in school. Parents, especially those who are knowledge workers themselves, are willing to spend their own resources to increase the chances that their children will succeed at school. Not surprisingly, then, in Canada as in other advanced industrial nations, each successive generation is acquiring more formal education.

EDUCATION IN THE 2001 CENSUS OF CANADA

The census is an essential source for tracking changes in the educational attainment of Canadians. Through many censuses, Statistics Canada has gathered information on the educational experiences of Canadians. The long form of the 2001 census, which was distributed to 20 percent of Canadian households, included six questions related to education that were asked of respondents 15 years of age and over (Statistics Canada 2004a). The questions touched on school attendance; years of schooling; certificates, diplomas, and degrees received; and major field of study. Despite some changes in the wording of questions, most allow for historical comparison with the results of earlier censuses. The analysis in this paper was conducted using the Public Use Microdata File (PUMF) for individuals, which consists of a 2.7 percent sample of the total population recorded in the census (Statistics Canada 2005). It is important to note that in preparing the file, Statistics Canada suppresses some variables and collapses response categories for others in order to protect the confidentiality of individual respondents. It is therefore not possible to conduct as fine-grained an analysis with the PUMF as is true with the complete census file, which Statistics Canada relies on for the analysis presented in its publications (Statistics Canada 2003). Nevertheless, the ability to work with the unaggregated data more than offsets the problems created by the suppression of some of the original information.

RISING LEVELS OF EDUCATIONAL ATTAINMENT IN CANADA

The expansion of formal schooling has been a constant theme in Canadian history. In the nineteenth century, the struggle was to make schooling mandatory for all Canadian children. Through the first half of the twentieth century, completion of secondary school became a central goal of educational policy and a high school diploma was seen as essential for employment in an industrializing society. The nineteen sixties saw enormous growth in the size of Canada's post-secondary institutions, and growing numbers of young Canadians aspired to earn a university degree, which for long had been a credential held by only a privileged minority. Guppy and Davies (1998), in their monograph based on the 1991 census, traced the changes in the educational achievements of Canadians, with special attention to the phenomenal growth in the decades after World War II. Data from the first post-War census, conducted in 1951, showed that more than half the population aged 15 and over had less than nine years of completed schooling, while less than 2 percent of Canadians held a university degree (Guppy and Davies 1998, 19). In the decades that followed, the proportion of young Canadians graduating from high school rose dramatically, and, by 1991, the proportion of those aged 20–29 who had completed high school reached almost

Table 4.1
Highest Level of Education Attained for Persons 25 Years of Age and Over, Canada, 1991
and 2001, in percentages

Highest level of education	1991	2001
< Grade 9	16.1	11.3
Grades 9–13	20.9	17.8
High School graduate	14.1	13.8
Trades certificate or diploma	4.5	4.0
College without certificate or diploma	6.0	5.8
College with trades certificate or diploma	7.0	7.4
College with college certificate or diploma	10.1	13.1
University without certificate, diploma or degree	3.2	3.1
University with non-university certificate or diploma	5.4	6.4
University with bachelor's degree or higher	12.8	17.5

Source: 1991 Statistics Canada 1993: 24–5.
    2001 Public Use Microdata File (Individual), author's calculations.
Note: Percentages do not add to 100% due to rounding.

80 percent (Guppy and Davies 1998, 23). This growing pool of high-school graduates fueled a major increase in enrollment in post-secondary institutions, and, by 1991, 11.4 percent of Canadians aged 15 and over had earned a university degree (Guppy and Davies 1998, 19).

Table 4.1 presents a detailed tabulation of the distribution of Canadians according to the highest level of education they attended for the years 1991 and 2001.[1] Given that the completion of post-secondary education almost always requires school attendance through the late teens and early twenties, the data presented refer to the population 25 years of age and over. The results show a continuation of the trends noted by Guppy and Davies. The proportion of Canadians with low education (less than nine years of schooling) declined from 16.1 percent in 1991 to just 11.3 percent in 2001. Perhaps most striking, for the first time, a majority of Canadians (25+ years of age) had received at least some training and education beyond secondary school; 53.3 percent had attended, though not necessarily graduated from, a college or university; and almost one in five (17.5 percent) held a university degree.

Data for the whole adult population obscures the rising educational achievements among younger Canadians. Table 4.2 presents information on educational levels by age. We have collapsed the twelve categories used in the previous table to just four broad categories of achievement. Given the history of educational expansion in Canada, it is not surprising that there are larger differences in the educational experiences of older and younger Canadians. For those 65 years of age and older, more than half had not completed high school. This proportion declines steadily among the younger

Table 4.2
Highest Level of Education Attained by Age Group, Canada, 2001

	Age Category					
Highest level of education	25–34	35–44	55–64	55–64	65+	Total 25+
Less than high school	15.2	19.7	23.3	37.8	57.5	29.1
High school graduate	11.8	15.4	16.2	13.6	11.1	13.8
Post-secondary without degree	47.8	45.6	41.5	34.6	24.1	39.7
University with bachelor's degree or higher	25.2	19.3	19.0	14.0	7.2	17.5

Source: Public Use Microdata File (Individual), author's calculations.
Note: Percentages do not add to 100% due to rounding.

cohorts, reaching 23.3 percent for the early baby boomers who were in the age group 45–54 at the time of the 2001 census, and falling to a low of just 15.2 percent for those aged 25–34, the first of the "baby-bust" cohorts. Expanding university enrollment is clear among this cohort as well. One in four earned a university degree, while almost half attended a college or trades program beyond high school. The wide access to schooling and the variety of programs available beyond the secondary-school level are good news for the country and allow Canada to compare favourably with other highly developed societies in terms of academic achievement. Still, it is troubling to note that in an era when post-secondary education is becoming the norm, a sizeable group of young people do not complete high school. And, as we shall see later in the chapter, problems with school completion are more common in certain segments of the population.

Table 4.3 and figure 4.1 complete this preliminary look at education in Canada by presenting data by province/territory. Historically, there have been wide differences in educational attainment by region. In 1991, for example, the percentage of persons 25 and over with a university degree ranged from 7.8 in Newfoundland to 14.6 in Ontario. The 2001 figures show that, while achievement levels have increased in all provinces, significant differences remain. Ontario, British Columbia, and Alberta, the three traditional donor provinces to the Canadian equalization system, lead the way with only about one-quarter of their populations recording less than a completed high school education. Newfoundland and Labrador continues to trail the other provinces in educational attainment, though very significant progress has been made. Almost half of the province's residents who were 25 and over had received some post-secondary education and 11 percent had earned a university degree.

Another simple way to look at the different educational profiles of the provinces and territories is to calculate the ratio of those in the lowest category

Table 4.3
Highest Level of Education Attained by Province/Territory, Canada, 2001

| | Highest level of education | | | |
Province/Territory	Less than high school	High school graduate	Post-secondary without degree	University with bachelor's degree or higher
Newfoundland and Labrador	41.9	8.9	38.3	11.0
Prince Edward Island	35.6	11.5	39.3	13.7
Nova Scotia	32.9	9.2	42.4	15.5
New Brunswick	35.8	14.5	37.3	12.4
Quebec	31.3	17.5	35.5	15.7
Ontario	26.9	14.0	39.3	19.8
Manitoba	35.5	11.0	39.0	14.5
Saskatchewan	36.3	10.3	40.7	12.7
Alberta	27.2	10.8	44.6	17.3
British Columbia	25.1	11.9	44.6	18.4
Territories	26.2	7.3	49.5	16.9

Source: Public Use Microdata File (Individual), author's calculations.
Note: Percentages do not add to 100% due to rounding.

Figure 4.1
Ratio of Low Education to High Education Individuals, by Province/Territory

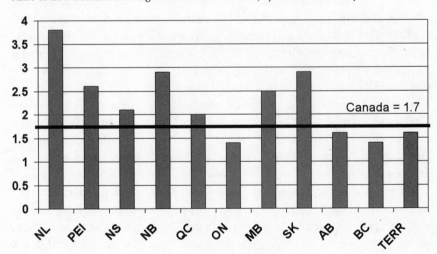

Source: Statistics Canada, 2001 Public Use Microdata File (Individual).

(less than completed high school) to those in the highest category (a university degree or higher). For Canada as a whole, the ratio is 1.7, meaning that for every 100 university graduates in the country there are 170 people with less than a high school diploma. As the bars in figure 4.1 demonstrate, the ratios differ quite substantially across the provinces. In Ontario and British Columbia, there are only 140 persons with less than a completed high school education for every 100 university graduates. Alberta and the territories[2] also have ratios below the national average, while the ratios for the other seven provinces are above the national average. Interestingly, Quebec, which for a long period had a low level of educational attainment, is now only slightly above average and in fourth place among the provinces.

GENDER AND EDUCATIONAL ACHIEVEMENT

Perhaps no topic has received as intense scrutiny from analysts of education as has gender differences in educational experience and attainment. Restricted opportunity for women was seen as both a cause and a consequence of women's subordinate position in society. For long, formal barriers to women's participation in some parts of the education system existed. As these barriers began to come down, sociologists of education pointed to a number of less obvious but equally restrictive practices in families, the schools, and the larger society, pratices that discouraged women from proceeding as far in school or from entering certain courses of study. Not surprisingly, then, as opportunities in post-secondary education expanded, women were slower in taking advantage of them and, when they did, women were often heavily concentrated in a limited range of programs. More recently, however, the situation has changed dramatically. Many of the differences in educational achievement between women and men have either disappeared or been reversed. Indeed, there is now concern that young males are at a growing disadvantage in the school system, and that this may pose serious problems for society in the future (Head 1999; Statistics Canada 2004b).

We begin our analysis of this issue by looking at census data on educational attainment by gender and age. Again, the focus is on the highest level of schooling attended by respondents. To simplify the presentation, we use just four major categories of achievement. The figures in table 4.4 suggest that the later baby boomers, those aged 35–44 in 2001, form a "hinge" generation in terms of educational attainment. Among previous cohorts, the educational achievements of males clearly exceeded those of females. For the oldest groups, those 55 and older at the time of the census, significantly more men earned university degrees while a higher proportion

Table 4.4
Highest Level of Education Attained by Age and Gender, Canada, 2001

| Age/Gender | Highest level of education | | | |
	Less than high school	High school graduate	Post-secondary without degree	University with bachelor's degree
18–24				
Male	25.2	20.5	48.4	5.8
Female	18.5	16.8	54.8	9.9
25–34				
Male	17.2	12.7	47.2	22.9
Female	13.2	11.0	48.4	27.3
35–44				
Male	21.7	13.7	45.3	19.3
Female	17.8	16.9	46.0	19.3
45–54				
Male	23.4	13.9	42.0	20.7
Female	23.2	18.4	41.0	17.4
55–64				
Male	36.0	11.3	35.4	17.2
Female	39.6	15.8	33.7	10.8
65+				
Male	54.3	9.0	26.2	10.5
Female	60.0	12.8	22.5	4.7

Source: Public Use Microdata File (Individual), author's calculations.
Note: Percentages do not add to 100% due to rounding.

of women failed to complete high school. Among the early baby boomers, the achievements of men and women grew remarkably similar. The proportion not completing high school was almost identical by gender, though a slightly higher percentage of males received a university degree. For the later baby boomers, there is almost no difference with respect to participation in post-secondary education, while, for the first time, a gap is apparent between women and men in the proportion who graduate from high school. This difference is also apparent in the youngest cohort, those aged 25–34. Although the proportion completing high school rose for both males and females, there is a four percentage point difference between young men and women. And, for the first time, a significant difference is observed by gender in the proportion completing university: 27.3 percent of women in this cohort had achieved at least a bachelor's degree against only 22.9 percent of men. Although not shown in the table, more detailed data suggest that even the traditional advantage enjoyed by men in advanced degrees is eroding. Almost identical percentages of men and women 25–34 had earned master's degrees, and only a small advantage remained for men in the doctoral category.

Figure 4.2
Percent of men and Women with University Degree by Age

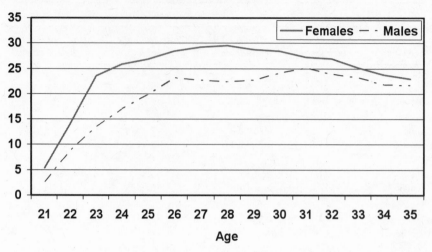

What lies ahead with respect to gender differences in educational attainment? As young men become increasingly aware that the erosion of the primary and manufacturing industries reduces the demand for low-skill labour, will they increase their rate of participation in higher education, or will the gap in rates we have seen among young adults continue to grow in the next generation? It would be mistaken to draw strong conclusions from data on younger adults, many of whom are still in school. Nevertheless, the figures for 18–24 olds in table 4.4 and the data on university completion rates for those 21–35 (figure 4.2) raise concern about the situation of young men in Canada. There is almost a seven point difference between young women and men in the proportion completing high school and, while almost one in ten women aged 18–24 has earned a university degree, only 5.8 percent of males have done so. The data by single year of age presented in figure 4.2 suggest a widening gap between young men and women in post-secondary education. For example, while 23.6 percent of 23–year-old women have earned a university degree, only 13.5 percent of men have done so. To be sure, the difference may reflect, in part, a tendency for young men to proceed more slowly through the school system or to take time off before completing their education. Still, the problems many young men are encountering in the school system are likely to be an important focus of educational research in the years ahead.

Women are steadily increasing their rate of participation in higher education, but some critics point to their under-representation in certain fields of study, especially in sciences and engineering. This is a particular source of

Table 4.5
Major Field of Study for Certificate, Diploma, and Degree Holders by Level of Education and
Gender, Canada, 2001

| Major Field of Study | College Diploma and Certificate Recipients | | |
	Male	Female	Total
Education	2.1	9.3	5.7
Arts and Social Sciences	11.7	19.1	15.5
Business	14.3	37.2	25.9
Science and Engineering	68.7	12.8	40.4
Health	2.9	21.5	12.3
Other Fields	0.2	0.2	0.2
	University Degree Recipients		
Education	11.3	24.6	17.9
Arts and Social Sciences	28.4	36.4	32.3
Business	18.9	13.0	16.0
Science and Engineering	35.0	14.0	24.5
Health	6.3	11.8	9.0
Other	0.2	0.2	0.2

Source: Public Use Microdata File (Individual), author's calculations.
Note: Only persons aged 25–64 are included in the analysis. Percentages do not add to 100% due to rounding.

concern as study in these areas may lead to more lucrative employment in
the future. To look at this issue, we present in table 4.5 data on major field
of study for men and women who have earned a certificate, degree, or diploma at the post-secondary level. Because programs that might be grouped
under the same heading differ significantly at the college and university
level, the data are presented separately for those who have earned a university degree and those who have not. Finally, to see whether significant changes are occurring among younger people, the data are shown for those who
have finished their schooling fairly recently (ages 25–34) and those who
likely finished some time ago (ages 35–64). The results point to substantial
differences by gender even among more recent graduates. Among college
and trade school graduates, gender differences are especially evident with
men heavily concentrated in the science, engineering, and trades category
whereas women follow more diverse courses of study. Among university
graduates, gender differences are less stark, though still evident. Although
not as markedly as at the college level, men significantly outnumber women
in the science and engineering fields. By contrast, women predominate in the
education and health fields.

Interestingly, comparing more recent graduates with those from earlier
years reveals only small changes over time. The proportion of women in the

sciences and business at the university level has increased modestly, while the percentage of women in both the education and health fields has declined, suggesting that traditional female occupations such as teaching school and nursing, while still attractive to women, no longer dominate career choice. Especially interesting is the growing number of female university graduates in the business area. Among those over 35 years of age, there were more than twice as many female degree holders in education as in business. Among the more recent graduates, there are only 30 percent more graduates in education than in business. It should also be remembered that the absolute number of women earning degrees in the most recent cohorts is significantly greater than the number of men. Thus, while almost 20 percent of recent male graduates are in the area of business versus only 15 percent among women, the numbers of men and women earning degrees in business are now almost the same.

ETHNICITY, IMMIGRATION, AND EDUCATIONAL ATTAINMENT

The expansion of schooling that has occurred in advanced industrial societies like Canada has been closely tied to the ideal of equal opportunity. Functionalists and human capital theorists argued that as knowledge and skill became the basis for employment, education would replace family background as the key to occupational success. If true, this would allow people from all social backgrounds to translate academic success into occupational status. For such a system to work, of course, the school system must offer real opportunity to all. In the past, social class background, ethnicity, and gender were obstacles to success in the school system and, ultimately, to attainment of higher occupational status and wealth. Porter's (1965) classic analysis of inequality in Canada drew attention to the significance of such factors and created a tradition of empirical research in Canadian sociology on issues of inequality and social mobility. More recent studies have demonstrated that social class continues to play an important role in explaining inequality in schooling and occupational status (Davies 2004; Krahn 2004).

The census is an excellent resource for assessing the influence of some characteristics on educational achievement but not others. It is not possible, for example, to examine the influence of such parental characteristics as occupational status or income on the educational attainment of their children using census data.[3] On the other hand, census data are quite useful in illuminating differences in educational attainment by gender and ethnicity. As we saw in the previous section, over the last generation very substantial

Figure 4.3
Percent of Persons 25–64 with University Degree or Higher, by Visible Minority Membership and Immigration Status

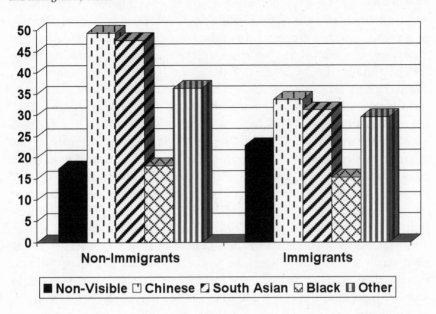

differences in schooling that once existed between men and women have disappeared. In this section, we turn to an analysis of the role of the intertwined factors of ethnicity and place of birth on educational achievement.

Canada has a long history of immigration and, today, is more open to the arrival of newcomers than any industrialized nation. The 2001 census shows that 18.4 percent of the population was born outside Canada, and many younger Canadians are the children of parents who have arrived in the country in recent decades. These demographic patterns raise interesting questions for the study of educational attainment. On the one hand, Canadian immigration policy gives preference to applicants with high levels of education, and the emphasis on educational credentials has increased in recent years. This would lead us to expect that a substantial proportion of those born outside the country would be well educated. Moreover, as parental education is strongly linked to the school success of children, we might also anticipate that the children of recent immigrants will go far in school as well. On the other hand, we know that ethnicity has been an obstacle to success in Canadian society in the past. Moreover, the fact that many recent immigrants belong to visible minority groups may serve as an additional hurdle that stands in the way of educational attainment.

This is a complex problem to study, and we can present only a limited analysis in this chapter. Figure 4.3 contains data on the percentage of persons of working age (25–64) who have attained at least a bachelor's degree according to their place of birth (Canada or elsewhere) and their membership in a visible minority group. The categorization is necessarily broad, as the PUMF provides limited data on ethnicity, but the results are striking, nevertheless.[4] Immigrants, regardless of the group to which they belong, have relatively high levels of education. The only exception is immigrants who identify themselves as black, among whom only 15.3 percent reported holding a university degree. This figure is marginally lower than that for non-visible minority persons born in Canada, among whom 17.4 percent had a university degree (Milan and Tran 2004). The attainment of immigrants from China and South Asia is especially striking, with almost one-third of these new residents reporting having earned a university degree. But even more remarkable is the achievement of members of these groups who were born in Canada. Almost half of Chinese and South Asian men and women who indicate they were born in Canada have obtained a university education, which is nearly three times the proportion among Canadians who are not members of a visible minority community. Although it is beyond the scope of this paper, it is important to remember that the higher educational achievements of those who are members of a visible minority community, many of whom are recent immigrants, do not always translate into occupational success and an income commensurate with their educational credentials (Galarneau and Morisette 2004; Picot and Sweetman 2005).

The analysis above used a simple distinction between immigrants and non-immigrants. Before we leave this topic, we look at a somewhat finer distinction regarding immigration. In table 4.6, data on education are presented for persons aged 25–64 according to whether they were born outside Canada, one or both of their parents were born outside Canada, or both they and their parents were born in Canada. Again, we find evidence of the high achievement of new arrivals in the country: 26.7 percent of first-generation Canadians have at least a university degree and almost two-thirds have at least some post-secondary education. At the same time, more than one in five did not complete high school. Second-generation Canadians show the highest levels of achievement (Boyd 2002; Farley and Alba 2002). Whether one or both parents were born outside Canada, the proportion with post-secondary education is higher and the proportion failing to complete high school is lower than among immigrants or among those Canadians whose parents were born in the country. It is worth noting that the lower level of achievement among longer-term Canadian residents reflects, in part, the

Table 4.6
Highest Level of Education Attained by Place of Birth of Respondent and Respondent's Parents, Canada, 2001

Place of birth of respondent and parents	Less than high school	High school graduate	Post-secondary without degree	University with bachelor's degree
Respondent born outside Canada (1st generation)	22.1	12.0	39.2	26.7
One parent born outside Canada (2nd generation)	13.9	12.4	47.3	26.4
Both parents born outside Canada (2nd generation)	19.0	13.1	46.0	22.0
Both parents born in Canada (3rd generation)	24.3	15.7	43.8	16.2

Source: Public Use Microdata File (Individual), author's calculations.
Note: Only persons aged 25–64 are included in the analysis. Percentages may not add to 100% due to rounding.

regional distribution of the population. Those who have come to Canada more recently tend to reside in the provinces and regions of the country where education levels are higher.

CONCLUSION

The last decade of the twentieth century saw a continuation of the expansion of formal schooling, with over half of the population 25 years of age and over reporting at least some education beyond the high school level. More education is widely accepted as a good thing by governments, industry, families, and young people themselves. While students and their families have come to bear a larger share of the cost in recent years, research suggests that an investment in higher education still brings a good return (Finnie 2000). Whether this will continue to be the case in the future remains an open question (Johnson and Kuhn 2004; Morissette et al. 2004). While possessing a college diploma or university degree may become the essential credential for most occupations, the growing proportion of those in recent cohorts who hold these credentials may limit the financial returns they bring.[5]

The data from the recent census document the great success of two groups in particular – women and recent immigrants and their children. The last twenty years have seen an amazing transformation in the participation rates of women. Of course, women had long played an important role in the education system through their involvement in teaching. And, as Guppy and Davies noted (1998), prior to the period when attendance at high school became universal, women had higher enrollment rates than men. Yet, women's participation at the post-secondary level was restricted and, even among the early baby boom generation, men were significantly more likely to obtain a university degree. When women did enroll at university, they were concentrated in a relatively narrow range of disciplines. As the analysis here has shown, most of this has now changed. Women's rate of participation in college and university now exceeds that of men and the gap appears to be growing. With few exceptions, women are now well represented in most programs in universities. Professional schools, such as medicine and law, which were long male preserves, now have nearly equal numbers of women and men students. Many factors have contributed to this, among them the changing nature of work in the modern labour force, the perception that two incomes are needed to support a family, and a growing realization among parents that their daughters as well as their sons needed and deserved the opportunity to develop their talents. Changes in policy and curriculum, as well as in the attitudes and practices of teachers and school administrators, also contributed to this dramatic increase in women's involvement in education.

Just as striking are the data on the achievements of immigrants and their children. The increasing preference given to applications for immigration from those who possess advanced education no doubt played an important role in creating this situation. Yet, it is also true that, despite the difficulty that many recent immigrants have experienced in the labour market, they have been remarkably successful in encouraging their children to persevere in the school system. Not all groups show the same level of success in the education system. The proportion of black respondents reporting a university education was about the same as for the non-visible minority population, suggesting important diversity in the experience of minority populations. Davies and Guppy (1998), using more detailed data on ethnicity from the 1991 census that are not available in the 2001 PUMF, emphasized the differing attainments of various ethnic groups. Nevertheless, the data are, on the whole, encouraging. The challenge for Canadian society is to see the impressive educational performance of minority group members translate into greater success in the labour market.

An emerging issue that will require careful study in the years ahead are the problems being experienced by many young men. The proportion of young people who do not complete high school – almost one in six for those aged 25–34 – is troubling in itself. The problem is even more acute among boys. As the types of jobs that often provided a decent living to young men with limited formal education continue to shrink in the Canadian economy, more attention will need to be paid to the lagging level of achievement among a significant minority of young males.

NOTES

1 The variable used here refers to the highest level of education a respondent attended. This usually implies that the individual completed lower levels of education, but it is not always the case. Many older Canadians, for example, may have obtained trades certificates without having completed high school. For full details, see Statistics Canada 2004a.
2 The PUMF groups residents of the three territories (Yukon, Northwest Territories, and Nunavut) into one category.
3 Knighton and Mirza (2002) provide a valuable analysis of this issue using data from the Survey of Labour and Income Dynamics.
4 Corbeil (2003) provides an interesting breakdown by language that complements the analysis presented here.
5 Interestingly, in their analysis of data for the period 1981–2000, Morisette et al. (2004) find that, in contrast to the situation in the United States, there has been no increase in Canada in income inequality between the university educated and those with only high school.

REFERENCES

Bell, Daniel. 1973. *The Coming of Post-Industrial Society: A Venture in Social Forecasting*. New York: Basic

Boyd, Monica. 2002. "Educational Attainments of Immigrant Offspring: Success or Segmented Assimilation?" *International Migration Review* 36: 1037–60

Collins, Randall. 1979. *The Credential Society: An Historical Sociology of Education and Stratification*. New York: Academic Press

Corbeil, Jean-Pierre. 2003. "30 Years of Education: Canada's Language Groups." *Canadian Social Trends* 71: 8–12

Davies, Scott. 2004. "Stubborn Disparities: Explaining Class Inequalities in Schooling." In *Social Inequality in Canada*, eds. James Curtis, Edward Grabb, and Neil Guppy, 173–86. 4th edition. Toronto: Pearson

Drucker, Peter. 1994. *Knowledge Work and Knowledge Society: The Social Transformations of This Century*. The 1994 Edwin L. Godkin Lecture, Harvard University www.iop. harvard.edu/Multimedia-Center/All-Videos/Knowledge-Work-And-Knowledge-Society-The-Social-Transformations-Of-This-Century2 (accessed 21 March 2010)

Farley, Reynolds, and Richard Alba. 2002. "The New Second-Generation in the United States." *International Migration Review* 36: 669–701

Finnie, Ross. 2000. "Holding Their Own: Employment and Earnings of Postsecondary Graduates." *Education Quarterly Review* 7: 21–37

Frenette, Marc. 2004. "Access to College and University: Does Distance to School Matter?" *Canadian Public Policy* 30: 427–43

Galarneau, Diane, and René Morisette. 2004. "Immigrants: Settling for Less?" *Perspectives on Labour and Income* 16: 7–18

Guppy, Neil, and Scott Davies. 1998. *Education in Canada: Recent Trends and Future Challenges*. Ottawa: Statistics Canada, Minister of Industry; Scarborough, Ont.: Nelson Canada

Head, John. 1999. *Understanding the Boys: Issues of Behaviour and Achievement*. London and New York: Falmer Press

Johnson, Susan, and Peter Kuhn. 2004. "Increasing Male Earnings Inequality in Canada and the United States, 1981–1997: The Role of Hours Changes Versus Wages Changes." *Canadian Public Policy* 30: 155–75

Knighton, Tamara, and Sheba Mirza. 2002. "Post-secondary Participation: The Effects of Parents' Education and Household Income." *Education Quarterly Review* 8: 25–32

Krahn, Harvey. 2004. "Choose Your Parents Carefully: Social Class, Post-secondary Education, and Occupational Outcomes." In *Social Inequality in Canada*, eds. James Curtis, Edward Grabb, and Neil Guppy, 187–203. 4th edition. Toronto: Pearson

Milan, Anne, and Kelly Tran. 2004. "Blacks in Canada: A Long History." *Canadian Social Trends* 72: 2–7

Morissette, René, Yuri Ostrovsky, and Garnett Picot. 2004. *Relative Wage Patterns Among the Highly Educated in a Knowledge-based Economy*. Ottawa: Statistics Canada Analytical Studies Branch Research Paper Series. 11F0019MIE no. 232

Picot, Garnett, and Arthur Sweetman. 2005. *The Deteriorating Economic Welfare of Immigrants and Possible Causes: Update 2005*. Ottawa: Statistics Canada, Business and Labour Market Analysis Division. Analytical Studies Research Paper Series no. 262

Porter, John. 1965. *The Vertical Mosaic: An Analysis of Social Class and Power in Canada*. Toronto: University of Toronto Press

Statistics Canada. 2003. *Education in Canada: Raising the Standard*. 2001 Census Analysis Series. Ottawa: Minister of Industry

Statistics Canada. 2004a. *2001 Census User Guide: Schooling and Major Field of Study*. www12.statcan.ca/english/census01/Products/Reference/tech_rep/school.cfm (Accessed April 2010).

Statistics Canada. 2004b. "The Gap in Achievement Between Boys and Girls." *Education Matters*. www.statcan.gc.ca/bsolc/english/bsolc?catno=81-004-X&CHROPG (Accessed April 2010).

Statistics Canada. 2005. *Inidviduals File*. 2001 Census. Public use microdata files. www.statcan.gc.ca/bsolc/olc-cel/olc-cel?lang=eng&catno (Accessed April 2010).

5

Low Income Status by Population Groups, 1961–2001

RODERIC BEAUJOT, JIANYE LIU, AND DON KERR

INTRODUCTION

In the 1961 census monograph series, Podoluk (1968) included a chapter on "Low income and poverty" as part of *Incomes of Canadians*. The concept of low income was initially developed by Podoluk, and it has become the most common concept used in the discussion of poverty in Canada. This chapter makes comparisons between the 1961 and 2001 census, in terms of the population groups that are most affected by low income.

The 1961 census was the information base on which much of Canada's welfare state was developed in the 1960s. Canada was rather different forty years ago. Families were mostly of the breadwinner type, fertility was high, and the elderly comprised a significant pocket of poverty. In *The Work World*, The Royal Commission on Bilingualism and Biculturalism (1969) reported that persons of French ethnic origin had the lowest average income among the major ethnic groups, second only to the recently arriving persons of Italian origin.

The situation is rather different at the beginning of the 21st century. When early results were released from the 2001 census, there was much public interest in understanding how the country was changing. Attention focused on the changing growth and distribution of the population, aging, and the changing composition resulting from the greater importance of immigration. Completed results show that in effect, Canada faces powerful demographic changes, including population aging, unequal distribution of population, increased diversity and changes in family structure. These questions can be linked to the second demographic transition, which brings low fertility and aging, more diverse families, and a greater contribution of immigration to population change. These demographic and family changes point to certain groups who are at risk, including persons in less stable families, persons who are not living in family households, and recent immigrants.

To compare the groups most subject to low income in 1961 and 2001, we consider population groups as defined by age and sex, then family structure, to then compare across groups defined by ethnicity, language, and place of birth.

MEASURING LOW INCOME AND POVERTY

Low income measures the levels of income that are significantly below the standard, relative to a given society at a given time (see Canadian Council on Social Development 2002). When comparisons are made across countries, low-income is typically measured as below half of median income, adjusting for household size (Hagenaars and De Vos 1988). For comparisons within Canada, the most commonly used measure is the low income status as defined by Statistics Canada. This measure was first developed in relation to the 1961 census. Based on the 1959 Family Expenditure Survey, the average family was found to be spending 50 percent of their income on the necessities of food, shelter, and clothing (Cotton et al. 1999). It was arbitrarily decided that those who spent 70 percent or more of their income on these necessities would be classified as having low income status. Using the same 20 percent difference from the average, the low income line involved spending more than 58.5 percent of income on necessities in 1981 and 54.7 percent in 2001. Besides changing the base of the low income lines, annual adjustments are made for inflation. Statistics Canada (2004, 165) has emphasized that these Low Income Cut-Offs (LICOs) are not measures of poverty, but they reflect a consistent methodology to identify those who are substantially worse off than average.

Table 5.1 shows the low income lines for the 1961, 1981, and 2001 censuses, expressed in the year 2000 dollars. Low income is based on the concept of economic families and unattached individuals. As of the 1971 census, the calculation of low income is based on size of family and size of the place of residence. Thus, adjusting for the consumer price index and expressed in 2000 dollars, it can be seen that a family of four would have low-income status with an income below $21,473 in 1961, compared to an income range of $23,174 to $31,505 in 1981, and a range of $23,892 to $34,572 in 2001 (depending on the size of the place of residence). Most of the data for 2001 are taken from the household file, which includes economic families and persons who are not attached to economic families.

Income-based indicators of economic well-being have many well known limitations (see Cotton et al. 1999; Wolfson and Evans 1989). For example,

Table 5.1
Low Income Cut-offs, before Taxes, Canada, 1960, 1980, 2000 (in 2000 dollars)

Number of persons	1960	1980					2000				
		Rural	LT30K	30-99K	100-499K	MT500K	Rural	LT30K	30-99K	100-499K	MT500K
1	9,203	11,456	12,758	13,800	14,712	15,491	12,696	14,561	15,648	15,757	18,371
2	15,338	14,972	16,793	18,097	19,397	20,439	15,870	18,201	19,561	19,697	22,964
3	18,405	20,049	22,522	24,214	25,908	27,340	19,738	22,635	24,326	24,497	28,560
4	21,473	23,174	26,036	27,989	29,941	31,505	23,892	27,401	29,448	29,653	34,572
5	24,541	26,948	30,201	32,417	34,758	36,712	26,708	30,629	32,917	33,148	38,646
6		29,421	32,937	35,410	37,884	40,095	29,524	33,857	36,387	36,642	42,719
7		32,417	36,322	39,056	41,789	44,133	32,340	37,085	39,857	40,137	46,793

K = 1000's; LT = less than; MT = more than.
Sources: Podoluk (1968, 185); Statistics Canada (1984b xxv); Statistics Canada (2004, 165).

while income is measured after transfers, they exclude various types of in-kind public assistance, the sharing of resources and services across households and generations, the impact of exchanges in the informal economy, and various types of employment benefits such as extended medical insurance and drug plans. This is particularly problematic in documenting economic well-being, since these resources and entitlements can vary considerably across individuals and households, and over time. Nonetheless, given the consistent methodology, this measure allows for the identification of low-income families and individuals and to follow their changing composition.

LOW INCOME STATUS, 1980-2004

Before turning to the census data, it is useful to present the time series generated by Statistics Canada, based on the Survey of Consumer Finances and the Survey of Labour and Income Dynamics. The information in Table 5.2 uses the 1992 base, adjusting for inflation. In order to be consistent with the census data, the low income measure is calculated after transfers but before tax. The overall trends show higher rates in the recessions of 1982–84 and 1992–96, but declines to historically low levels by 2004. In the early 1990s, the difficulties in the economy were compounded by budgetary constraints, as governments that had hitherto run large fiscal deficits reduced the direct transfers to families (Picot et al. 1998). There are persistent gender differences, with higher proportions with low income for women at ages 18 and over, especially at ages 65 and over. In 1980, there are markedly higher levels at ages 65 and over compared to ages 0–17, but the pattern has been much more downward for ages 65 and over, so that by 1990 the male elderly have lower rates than that those of children, and by 2004 the female elderly have

Table 5.2

Percent with Low Income (before Tax), by Age and Sex, Canada, 1980–2004

Year	Total		Children < 18		Persons 65+		18–64 years	
	Male	Female	Male	Female	Male	Female	Male	Female
1980	13.9	18.1	15.8	16.6	26.4	40.0	11.4	15.2
1982	15.4	19.1	18.7	19.8	20.4	36.6	13.3	15.9
1984	16.8	20.6	20.9	20.8	22.3	35.8	14.5	17.9
1986	14.6	18.1	17.5	17.5	19.5	32.3	12.8	15.9
1988	12.9	17.2	15.4	16.0	16.6	32.6	11.3	14.8
1990	14.1	18.2	17.8	18.8	14.0	27.5	12.7	16.2
1992	16.5	20.0	19.7	20.0	13.2	27.7	15.8	18.4
1994	16.6	20.6	20.0	21.2	10.9	26.3	16.1	19.2
1996	19.1	22.1	24.0	23.1	13.0	26.3	18.2	20.8
1998	17.1	20.0	21.2	20.0	12.6	24.8	16.3	19.0
2000	14.6	18.1	17.7	18.4	10.3	21.5	14.2	17.3
2002	15.0	17.4	18.7	17.3	10.5	20.1	14.4	16.9
2004	14.4	16.6	17.7	17.6	9.3	17.8	14.1	16.1

Source: Statistics Canada. 2005. *Income Trends in Canada 1980–2004*, table 202–0802.

Table 5.3

Incidence of Low Income (before tax) for Family-Unit Types, Canada, 1980–2004

Family-unit types	1980	1985	1990	1995	2000	2004
Economic families, two persons or more	13.2	14.2	12.8	15.4	12.3	11.5
Non-elderly families	12.4	14.1	13.7	16.7	13.0	12.4
Married couples, 1 earner	11.9	13.8	12.8	16.6	12.4	11.8
Married couples, 2 earners	1.6	3.2	4.0	5.1	3.7	3.7
Two-parent families & children	9.9	11.7	10.2	13.8	11.0	10.0
Two-parent families & children, 1 earner	16.9	21.0	23.8	28.1	29.5	26.5
Two-parent families & children, 2 earner	6.1	7.7	6.8	7.9	6.1	6.6
Lone-parent families	53.3	57.2	55.9	55.7	41.7	42.6
Male lone-parent families	25.9	27.4	27.3	33.2	16.3	22.2
Female lone-parent families	57.6	61.1	60.6	59.2	46.8	47.1
Elderly families	19.1	15.5	7.9	8.2	7.5	6.7
Unattached individuals	44.3	44.3	41.0	43.6	41.3	37.6

Source: Statistics Canada. 2005. *Income Trends in Canada 1980–2004*, table 202–0804.

reached the rates for children. This downward trend for the elderly is much less affected by the recessions of the early 1980s and early 1990s.

Table 5.3 shows the low income rates by various family statuses over this period 1980–2004. The overall trend is downward for both economic families and unattached individuals. The major exception to this downward trend is for two parent families with children and one earner, where 16.9 percent have low income in 1980 compared to 26.5 percent in 2004.

For these two parent families with children, the gap has widened between the one earner and the-two earner categories. The gap between two parent families with children and lone-parent families has declined, but remains large. In 1980, the male lone-parent families had a rate of low income that was 16.0 percentage points above that of two-parent families with children, and by 2004 this gap was 12.2 percentage points. For female lone-parent families, the gap, compared to two-parent families, has declined from 47.7 to 37.1 percentage points. In each of the one-earner and two-earner categories, there are higher rates of low income when children are present. The most significant decline is for elderly families, who had a low income rate of 19.1 percent in 1980 compared to 6.7 percent in 2004. In 2004, the highest rates occur for female lone-parent families, followed by unattached individuals, one earner, two-parent families with children, and male lone-parent families. In contrast, the lowest rates, below 10 percent, occur for married couples with two earners and for elderly families.

LOW INCOME STATUS, BY DEMOGRAPHIC GROUPS, 1961 AND 2001

The 1961 census monograph on income includes a chapter on low income (Podoluk 1968), but the income monographs or profiles for subsequent censuses have not included sections on low income (Rashid 1977; Statistics Canada 1984a; Rashid 1994). The regular census tables include low income (e.g. Statistics Canada 1977; 1984b). For the purpose of this chapter, tables have been derived from the 2001 census that would be comparable to those published from the 1961 census. Partly because the economic circumstances of the farm population were rather different, the 1961 monograph includes only the non-farm population. Given the separate low-income line for the rural population, the 2001 data include the farm population.

In 1961, 25.3 percent of families and 43.5 percent of unattached individuals were classified as having low income. In 2001, these figures are 13.0 percent for families and 35.8 percent for unattached (table 5.4). While both types of units have made progress, the gap between economic families and unattached is higher in 2001 than in 1961. The provincial differences have declined markedly, both for families and unattached individuals (table 5.4). In 1961, the Atlantic provinces, and to a lesser extent Saskatchewan, had incidences of low income that were significantly above the average. As another example, while Ontario remains advantaged compared to Quebec, the difference in the incidence of low income for economic families was 9.3 percentage points in 1961 compared to 2.9 percentage points in 2001.

Table 5.4
Percentage of Families and Unattached Individuals with Low-Income Status, Canada and
Provinces, 1961 and 2001

Province	1961		2001	
	Families	Unattached	Families	Unattached
Newfoundland	55.7	64.9	16.1	45.8
P.E.I.	49.2	64.6	8.6	37.2
Nova Scotia	40.3	57.5	13.6	37.5
New Brunswick	43.5	56.7	13.2	37.1
Quebec	27.9	43.7	14.7	42.2
Ontario	18.6	39.3	11.8	31.5
Manitoba	26.1	45.3	14.3	38.1
Saskatchewan	34.8	50.2	12.9	34.4
Alberta	22.9	40.2	10.8	30.0
British Columbia	21.3	44.9	14.1	35.0
TOTAL	25.3	43.5	13.0	35.8

Sources: Podoluk (1968, 196, 202); Census of Canada, 2001, Public Use Microdata File (Household File).

The comparisons by demographic characteristics of families is difficult because in 1961 all two-spouse families are classified by the characteristics of the male head of family. Thus the families with a male head include the two-spouse families plus the lone-parent families with a male head. The 7.8 percent of economic families with female head in 1961 are all lone-parent families. In 2001, there is no longer a concept of "head" of family or household. The concept of "main household maintainer," which is used in 2001, is a rather different concept from that of household head, and thus two-spouse families are tabulated according to the characteristics of both male and female spouses. Of all economic families, 83.1 percent are two-spouse, 2.2 percent are male lone-parent families, 9.9 percent are female lone-parent families, and 4.9 percent are other economic families. In 1961, the incidence of low income is 23.8 percent for male heads and 42.6 percent for female heads (Table 5.5). In 2001, the figures are 9.3 percent for two-spouse families, 18.6 percent for male lone-parent families and 38.7 percent for female lone-parent families. The only direct comparison that can be made is for female lone-parents, who were 17.3 percentage points above the average for all families in 1961 compared to 25.7 percentage points in 2001. This is partly due to the changing demographics of lone-parent s, who were more likely to be widows in 1961 but separated or divorced with young children in 2001.

The reduced gender differences are more readily visible in the unattached population. In 1961, the percent low income was 35.0 for males and 51.2 for females, while in 2001 these figures are 31.0 for males and 39.8 for females (table 5.5). For families in 1961, the highest instances by age and sex occur

Table 5.5
Percentage of Families and Unattached Individuals with Low Income, by Age and Sex, Canada, 1961 and 2001

Age and sex	1961		2001		
	Families	Unattached	2 Spouse	1 Parent	Unattached
Male under 25	27.3	30.0	27.9	69.2	53.4
25–34	22.8	17.2	11.6	30.4	25.6
35–44	20.5	21.5	9.9	21.8	25.0
45–54	17.5	27.6	7.7	15.6	30.8
55–64	20.9	39.1	9.5	19.1	38.2
65+	46.4	66.1	6.4	12.4	30.8
TOTAL	23.8	35.0	9.3	18.6	31.0
Female under 25	65.5	47.3	24.2	88.9	67.1
25–34	68.7	27.6	11.7	64.1	26.8
35–44	59.0	30.6	9.5	43.5	28.3
45–54	40.7	38.0	7.0	25.1	34.0
55–64	32.1	51.1	9.8	22.3	42.8
65+	33.3	72.2	5.3	15.7	43.2
TOTAL	42.6	51.2	9.3	38.7	39.8

Notes: 1. In 2001, two-spouse families are shown twice, by characteristics of male and female spouse.
Sources: Podoluk (1968, 197, 203); Census of Canada, 2001, Public Use Microdata File (Household File).

for male heads of families aged 65 and over, along with female heads under 45 years. In families with male heads in 1961, those under 25 years have the second highest incidence, after the 65 and over. For the unattached in 1961, for both genders, the highest incidence is at ages 65 and over, with second highest at ages 55–64 and third highest at ages under 25 years. In 2001, for both two-spouse families and lone-parent families, the highest incidence occurs at ages under 25, the second highest at ages 25–34, and the lowest incidence at ages 65 and over. Among the individuals who are not attached to economic families, those aged 65 and over had the highest incidences of low income in 1961, but in 2001 it is those under 25 years. For unattached women in 2001, the incidence increases over age groups 25–34 to 65+, while for men it is the age group 55–64 that stands out with the second highest incidence, after those under 25 years of age. The most significant observation in table 5.5 is that the under-25 age group has replaced the 65 and over as the group with the highest incidence of low income.

LOW INCOME STATUS BY FAMILY CHARACTERISTICS, 1961 AND 2001

Besides the family structures as defined by two-spouse, lone-parent and unattached individuals, it is useful to consider the number of children, sources

Table 5.6
Percentage of Families with Low Income, by Number of Children <16, Income Earners, and
Family Type, 1961 and 2001

	1961			2001			
	Total	Male Headed	Female Headed	Total	Two Parent	Male lP	Female lP
Number of children							
no children	23.9	23.1	29.4	9.1	7.6	13.5	20.0
1 child	20.5	17.8	54.1	18.4	10.8	24.1	48.0
2 child	23.0	21.2	62.3	16.3	10.8	25.6	55.3
3 & more	33.1	31.5	74.9	23.4	16.7	29.0	73.8
TOTAL	25.3	23.8	42.6	13.0	9.3	18.6	38.7
Number of income earners							
0 earner	81.2	79.6	87.4	31.3	21.2	64.1	81.3
1 earner	28.3	27.2	43.7	21.4	16.9	16.1	34.5
2 earner	12.7	12.2	20.0	6.1	5.4	6.6	14.0
3& more	7.3	7.0	11.2	3.3	2.9	3.9	10.0
TOTAL	25.3	23.8	42.6	13.0	9.3	18.6	38.7

Sources: Podoluk (1968, 198–9); Census of Canada, 2001, Public Use Microdata File (Household File).

of income, and other characteristics of families. Table 5.6 uses children under 16. Across the categories of "one" to "three or more" children, in 1961, the incidence of low income increases markedly by number of children. The difference between one and two children is minimal in 2001, except in the case of female lone-parent families. In 1961, the male heads with no children under 16 had higher incidence than those with one or two children. In 2001, the two-spouse families with no children have the lowest incidence of low income. Mostly, we can observe that in two-spouse families, having children presents a larger disadvantage in 2001, with the main difference occurring between "two" and "three or more" children.

The number of income earners makes a large difference in the incidence of low income (table 5.6). In 1961, over 80 percent of families with no earners had low income, and this applies to 31 percent of families with no earners in 2001. Female heads with one earner had an incidence of 43.7 percent in 1961 but 34.5 percent in 2001. In comparison, the 2001 rate for male lone-parents with one earner was 16.1 percent, and for two-spouse families it was 16.9 percent. The comparison of one earner male and female lone-parents clearly show the influence of lower female wages and average hours of work. The two-spouse economic families with no earners are much less disadvantaged in 2001 than in 1961, which probably reflects the better situation of persons over 65 who are not in the labour market.

Table 5.7
Percentage of Families and Unattached Individuals with Low Income, by Major Source of
Income, Canada, 1961 and 2001

	1961		2001	
Major Source of Income	Families	Unattached	Families	Unattached
Wages and salaries	18.3	23.3	6.2	18.5
Self-employment	24.9	29.9	13.3	32.0
Transfer payments	90.3	92.6	42.9	65.1
Investment income	35.2	42.6	13.4	20.3
Other income	44.9	40.2	6.1	12.8
No income	100.0	100.0	100.0	100.0
TOTAL	25.3	43.5	13.0	35.8

Sources: Podoluk (1968, 199–200, 203); Census of Canada, 2001, Public Use Microdata File (Household File).

In 1961, the incidence of low income is clearly lowest when wages and salaries are the major source of income, and this incidence is highest when transfer payments are the major source of income (Table 5.7). By 2001, persons with wages and salaries remain relatively advantaged, but there is also relatively low incidence for those who have investment income or other income as their major source of income. In 1961, the incidence of low income was over 90 percent for families and unattached individuals who had transfer payments as their major source of income, and by 2001 the incidence is reduced to 42.9 percent for economic families and 65.1 percent for persons who are not part of economic families. It is probably mostly among elderly families that transfer payments as the major source of income are reducing the levels of low income.

In *Incomes of Canadians*, Podoluk (1968, 202) included an interesting table on the income composition of low-income families. Table 5.8 includes these results along with comparable data from 2001, based on census families. Only low-income families are included in the table, which comprise 25.3 percent of all families in the 1961 non-farm population and 12.9 percent of all census families in 2001. In 1961, 70.3 percent of the income of low-income families came from employment, while this figure is only 39.3 percent in 2001. Family allowances or child tax benefits amounted to 6.6 percent of the income of low-income families in 1961 and 17.3 percent in 2001. Old age pensions and other transfers made up 17.3 percent of this income in 1961, compared to 36.3 percent in 2001. The last column for each year shows the percent of all family income from a given source that goes to low-income families in particular. It is noteworthy that the 25.3 percent

Table 5.8
Income Compositions of Low-Income Families, Canada, 1961 and 2001

| Income Component | 1961 | | | | 2001 | | | | |
	Male Heads	Female Heads	Total	%	2-Spouse	Lone Parent Male	Female	Total	%
Employment	72.5	49.7	70.3	7.5	44.9	33.6	30.1	39.3	2.4
Fam. Allowance	6.5	7.3	6.6	29.3	11.9	23.4	26.0	17.3	92.3
Old age pension	8.4	11.9	8.7	44.3	14.2	11.8	8.0	12.0	25.7
Other transfers	7.3	20.9	8.6	38.0	21.1	28.1	29.7	24.3	48.1
Investment	2.8	5.7	3.1	6.7	5.1	1.5	1.4	3.7	1.6
Other income	2.4	4.6	2.6	15.3	2.9	1.6	4.8	3.5	20.1
TOTAL	100.0	100.0	100.0	9.4	100	100.0	100.0	100.0	4.7

Notes: 1. In 2001, "Old age pension" includes Old Age Security, Guaranteed Income Supplement, and
Canada/Quebec Pension Plan, but not pension plans from employers; "Investment" includes pension
plans from employers and other private pension plans; "Fam. Allowance" includes child tax credits.
    2. Percentage is the % of total family income from a source going to low-income families.
Sources: Podoluk, 1968, Census of Canada 2001, Public Use Microdata File, census families.

of families who were low-income received 7.5 percent of all employment
income in 1961, and the 12.9 percent of families who were low-income
received 2.4 percent of employment income in 2001. The concentration of
family allowances and child tax benefits has increased, with low-income
families receiving 29.3 percent of these allowances in 1961 compared to
92.3 percent in 2001. The same applies to other transfers, with 38.0 percent
of these going to low-income families in 1961 and 48.1 percent in 2001.
The opposite occurs for old age pension, which includes Old Age Security,
Guaranteed Income Supplement, and Canada/Quebec Pension Plan; the
low-income families received 44.3 percent of this transfer income in 1961
compared to 25.7 percent in 2001. While the categories are not exactly comparable, there has clearly been reduced targeting with old-age benefits and
greater targeting for family benefits and other transfers.

ETHNIC ORIGIN, LANGUAGE, AND IMMIGRATION STATUS

Among the major ethnic groups reported in 1961 (by single origin), which
excluded persons of Aboriginal ethnicity, the French had second lowest average income after persons of Italian origin. This was reported by the Royal
Commission on Bilingualism and Biculturalism (1969), which also reported
figures by category of knowledge of official languages. Table 5.9 includes
these results along with the comparable data from 2001, based only on

Table 5.9
Index of Average Total Income of the Male Labour Force, by Ethnic Origin and Knowledge of
Official Languages, Canada and Quebec, 1961 and 2001

		1961		2001	
Ethnic Origin	Knowledge of Official Languages	Canada	Quebec	Canada	Quebec
British	Overall average	109.9	140.0	108.4	107.6
	English only	107.8	143.1	108.0	104.6
	French only	57.4	65.8	76.8	88.0
	Both	142.4	140.3	115.5	113.5
French	Overall average	87.7	91.8	96.5	106.3
	English only	91.0	136.6	96.6	106.1
	French only	70.2	73.5	80.1	90.7
	Both	98.6	107.0	103.3	116.4
All origins	Overall average	100.0	100.1	100.0	100.0
	English only	102.9	130.2	103.0	91.0
	French only	70.0	73.3	77.4	87.5
	Both	107.5	112.9	101.2	109.9

Notes: 1. With French and British, ethnicity includes only single origin.
　　　　2. The index uses the overall average for all origins as a base.
Sources: Royal Commission on Bilingualism and Biculturalism (1969);
Census of Canada, 2001, Public Use Microdata File (Household File).

the male non-agricultural labour force (that is, the subsample as used by this Royal Commission). The average incomes of those with French ethnic origin in Canada represented 87.7 percent of the average for all origins in 1961, compared to 96.5 percent of this overall average in 2001. Even if they knew both official languages, the average for French of ethnic origin in 1961 was 98.6 percent of the overall average, while those of British origins who knew both languages had 142.4 percent of the average income. In 2001, the French who know both languages had 103.3 percent of the average income, while the British who knew both languages had 115.5 percent of average income.

　　The change in Quebec is even more striking. In 1961, the British had an index of 140.0 while the French were at 91.8 percent of the overall provincial average. By 2001, the British were at 107.6 and the French at 106.3. In 1961, knowledge of both languages (for all origins) presented an average of 112.9, compared to 130.2 for English only and 73.3 for French only. The highest group in 2001 were the French in Quebec who knew both languages, at 116.4, while the British who knew both languages had 113.5. The knowledge of both languages represented an average advantage of 109.9, while knowing only English or only French in Quebec represented a disadvantage.

In 2001 the highest group in Canada as a whole were the British who knew both languages, while in Quebec the French who know both languages displaced the British. While the disadvantage of knowing only French has declined, it remains significant both for the whole of Canada and for Quebec. In Quebec, knowing only English has become a disadvantage.

The data on immigration status by place of birth uses the 1981 census, since there are no comparable data from the 1961 census. Table 5.10 excludes persons who arrived in the year preceding the census, for whom the income measure could include income before arriving to Canada. The categories of birthplace are somewhat different in 1981 and 2001, as noted in the footnote to the table. The first observation is that for all foreign-born families there was a lower incidence of low-income compared to the Canadian-born in 1981, but a much higher incidence in 2001. In 1981, the total incidence of low-income is higher than that of the Canadian-born for persons born in Caribbean, Latin America, Southeast Asia, East Asia, and Western Asia. In 2001, incidence above the Canadian-born occurs for persons born in Latin America (this includes the Caribbean in 2001), along with Eastern Europe, Africa, South Asia, Southeast Asia, East Asia, Western Asia, and Oceania.

At both dates, there is a systematic pattern of higher incidence of low-income for those who have arrived more recently. In 1981, this applied to those who had arrived 10 to 20 years before the census from Caribbean, Latin America, Southern Europe, and Western Asia. This higher incidence of low income than that of the Canadian-born also occurred for persons who arrived 5 to 10 years before the census from Eastern Europe and Oceania, and for those who arrived in the 5 years preceding the census from United States, Other Western Europe, Central Europe, Africa, South Asia, Southeast Asia, and East Asia. In 2001, the incidence above that of the Canadian-born occurred for those who had arrived more than 20 years before the census from Central/South America and Western Asia. For 10 to 20 years before the census, we add Southern Europe, Africa, South Asia, Southeast Asia, East Asia, and Oceania. The United States, other Western Europe, Central Europe, and Eastern Europe are added at 5 to 10 years before the census. Thus in the last 5 years before the census, it is only those from the United Kingdom who have a lower incidence than the Canadian born, while in 1981 this also applied to persons from Northern Europe. The situation has changed markedly from the time of the 1971 census, where Richmond and Kalbach (1980) found that most age and sex groups of immigrants of the 1946–60 period had already exceeded the Canadian-born average income(see also Beaujot 2003).

Table 5.10

Percentage of Foreign-born and Canadian-born Families with Low Income, by Period of Immigration, Canada, 1981 and 2001

	1981					2001				
	Total	<1960	1960–69	1970–74	1975–79	Total	<1980	1980–89	1990–94	1995–99
Canadian-born	13.1	N.A.	N.A.	N.A.	N.A.	11.9	N.A.	N.A.	N.A.	N.A.
Foreign-born	11.6	9.4	11.6	15.5	19.0	19.8	8.5	16.3	24.4	32.7
United States	11.5	10.0	13.3	13.3	14.8	10.8	6.4	8.3	15.5	17.6
Caribbean	24.2	9.3	16.1	30.2	31.5					
Latin America	19.9	12.9	14.5	21.2	23.9	22.8	12.6	21.5	26.6	30.4
United Kingdom	7.5	7.5	7.1	8.0	7.9	5.8	4.8	5.7	9.2	11.5
Other West Europe	9.4	8.8	10.3	11.5	14.8	10.5	6.3	10.0	14.5	18.6
Central Europe	10.2	9.9	10.5	12.1	16.2	12.0	8.9	11.3	13.1	20.8
Southern Europe	13.3	10.9	14.6	16.7	17.9	11.9	11.3	14.4	13.5	18.3
Eastern Europe	10.7	9.9	13.2	14.4	22.3	21.1	8.0	10.9·	14.2	29.5
Northern Europe	10.3	10.1	11.4	10.2	8.9					
Africa	12.2	7.9	9.3	12.6	17.1	30.0	9.5	18.3	32.4	41.7
South Asia	10.2	7.1	6.1	11.4	14.4	25.6	8.3	17.1	23.8	30.3
Southeast Asia	15.1	4.6	4.7	6.9	25.3	29.7	9.9	19.9	31.1	47.4
East Asia	14.5	13.4	9.4	13.2	22.3	23.8	9.0	15.1	23.7	30.7
Western Asia	21.2	11.6	15.9	25.4	28.7	38.4	15.7	25.3	37.5	46.9
Oceania & other	11.7	6.2	9.5	16.8	14.7	14.4	8.7	14.5	20.9	18.5

Notes: In 2001, "Latin America" includes Caribbean, "Other Western Europe" includes Northern Europe, and "Other Europe" has been placed in "Central Europe."

Sources: Beaujot et al. (1988, 82); Census of Canada, 2001, Public Use Microdata File (Individual File).

These results by birthplace and immigrant cohort need to be interpreted in the context of specific historical circumstances that lead to migration of specific people. There are typically both push and pull factors at stake. The push factors are probably more important for persons coming from Latin America and the Caribbean, Asia, and Africa, while the pull factors may play a larger relative role for persons from the United States, Western, Northern, and Southern Europe. That is, these differences in selectivity by push and pull factors may explain part of the differences across birthplace groups. It could also be hypothesized that the overall numbers of immigrants are relevant to their relative situations in Canada. Massey (1995) has proposed that the immigrants of the post-war period profited from the long hiatus of low immigration in the period 1915–45. These immigrants, especially those who arrived before 1960, would have had less competition since there were fewer immigrants who preceded them. Picot and Sweetman (2005) have more recently observed that the worsening situations of some immigrant groups tends to be occurring most notably from places of origin that are sending more immigrants. In contrast, the average situation of immigrants is improving among immigrants from parts of the world that are decreasing in their relative share of total immigration, including Southeast Asia, United States, Latin America, and the Caribbean.

SUMMARY AND DISCUSSION

Levels of income and their distribution can be analyzed in relation to individuals, the economy, and policy. Picot et al. (1998) highlight three distinctive types of events as potential explanations of variations in inequality: (i) demographic events that influence the types of families and living arrangements in which Canadians share and pool income; (ii) economic events that influence the availability of jobs and the wages available in the labour market; and (iii) political events that influence the types of transfer payments that Canadians receive from government. Individuals are therefore relevant to levels of income in terms of abilities, resources, and the supply of labour. The economy is relevant in terms of the demand for labour, levels of employment, and opportunity structures. Policy seeks to address issues at various levels, including macro-economic growth, unequal opportunities, and caring for the disadvantaged.

In reflecting on the patterns of income inequality at the time of the 1961 census, Podoluk (1968) observed that low-income was no longer associated with all segments of the population, but that it applied to specific population groups. If there was one characteristic that was dominant in 1961, this was the non-working population. Thus low-income was more prevalent if no member of the family worked during the year, and for economic families whose head was over 65 years of age. The sex of the family head was also related to work since women had much lower labour force participation. Other economic characteristics involved residence in rural areas or in the Atlantic region. Family characteristics were also important, especially the disadvantage of female lone-parent families, but also of not being attached to an economic family. Summarizing the situation at the time of the Royal Commission on the Economic Union and Development Prospects for Canada, Vaillancourt (1985) pointed especially to the elderly and families headed by women as two groups more subject to low-income. In *The New Face of Poverty*, the Economic Council of Canada (1992) pointed to persons with disabilities, lone-parent families, and older workers. The risk of poverty was found to especially increase with divorce and with a reduction in the number of job earners in the family.

While many differentials have declined since the 1961 census, the family characteristics remain significant. While labour force participation remains important, that is not the case for the elderly population who have come to have low incidence of low-income, at least for those living in economic families. Both for persons living in economic families and for the unattached, the biggest change is by age, with the elderly no longer being a significant pocket of low-income, and young families now being more disadvantaged. The family characteristics that continue to be important include lone parenthood, especially among women, not being attached to an economic family, having three or more children, being under 25 years of age, and having only one member in the labour force. "One earner" two-parent families with children now have a relatively high incidence of low-income, but not as high as among female lone-parent families and unattached individuals.

In terms of social characteristics, the 1961 census identified persons of French origin as having significant disadvantages, while the 2001 census points to recent immigrants to Canada. Even for the total foreign-born population, the 1981 census found lower incidence of low-income in comparison to the Canadian-born, but the foreign-born incidence is much higher in the 2001 census. Based on the Survey of Labour and Income Dynamics, Hatfield (2004) identified five groups that are subject to persistent low-income: lone-parent s, unattached persons aged 45–64, recent immigrants, persons with work-limiting disabilities, and Aboriginal populations. While persons with work disabilities cannot be identified in the 2001 census, the low-income of these other groups can be documented. The incidence of low-income is high in all these groups, with 39.4 percent low-income for the total Aboriginal population, 37.4 percent for unattached 45–64, 35.3 percent for recent immigrants, and 35.1 percent for lone-parent families. Persons belonging to one or the other of these four categories comprise 22.5 percent of Canada's population but 45.5 percent of persons with low-income.

The macro-economic context is clearly relevant to these patterns. In particular, the economic growth, especially in the 1960s and to the mid-1970s, has reduced the overall incidence of low-income, both for economic families and for persons not attached to economic families. The economic difficulties of the early parts of the decades of the 1980s and 1990s have made for reversals or slow change, but the early part of the 21st century has brought record lows in levels of unemployment (Statistics Canada 2005). Given the importance that Podoluk (1968) had attached to work status, it is significant to observe that the employment rate, defined as the percentage employed in the population aged 15 and over, was at a low level in 1961, at 50.2 percent(Beaujot 2000, 136). By 2005, those employed represented 62.6 per 100 population aged 15 and over. While the percentage of persons working part time has also increased, this higher employment rate is clearly very significant in the overall incidence of low-income, and it especially affects groups that previously had lower levels of employment, including women in particular. By now, two-parent families with children are disadvantaged if they have only one earner.

Besides individual characteristics and the macro-economic context, policy questions are also relevant. Given the patterns of the early 1960s, it is quite understandable that the Royal Commission on Bilingualism and Biculturalism (1969) had a whole volume on *The Work World*. The policies of the federal government to promote the two national languages, and those of the Quebec government to increase the opportunities of persons speaking French, have clearly had their impacts. Given the disadvantaged situation of the elderly in the 1960s, it is also understandable that the evolving welfare state paid particular attention to this population. Relatively speaking, much less attention has been paid to children and young adults (Cheal 1999). The stronger welfare state is clearly visible in these data: there are very large reductions in the incidence of low-income for families with no earners and for families where transfer payments are the major source of income. Transfers to the elderly have become less focused on the economically disadvantaged, but other family transfers have become more targeted to those with low-income. Transfers have come to occupy a larger role in the income of disadvantaged families, but these have hardly kept up with other family changes, especially the higher likelihood of lone parenthood (Rashid 1999). The limited support to children and youth can also be seen in the high incidence of low-income at ages under 25, and even in one earner two-parent families with children.

There are significant differences across societies in the extent to which policy structures involve transfers from the working to the older population (Bongaarts 2004; Légaré 2001). Comparing poverty rates in eight rich countries, Smeeding (2003) finds that Canadian poverty rates are second highest, after the United States, for families with children, but second lowest, after the Netherlands, for the elderly. Among these eight countries, the social expenditure on the non-elderly as a percent of GDP is also second lowest in Canada. Further comparisons indicate that Canada is the country that has made the greatest progress in terms of reducing poverty in the elderly population, especially in elderly families (Picot and Myles 2005; Myles 2000). It may be concluded that Canada's welfare state has come to benefit the elderly, more so than young families. Several analyses have concluded that young adults face difficult economic outcomes (Morissette 1998; Picot 1998).

While the challenge of the 1960s involved the elderly and increasing the proportion of the population who were employed, the challenge of the early part of the 21st century involves youth and young families. Increasing the welfare of the young poses the complexity that this needs to be done without undermining the incentive to work, and the context of the large budgetary commitments toward the elderly, who comprise an increasing component of the population. There are persistent challenges for the Aboriginal population and lone-parent families, two population groups that are also growing in relative size. There is the further challenge of integrating new Canadians, especially in the context that immigration has become an increasing component of demographic change. Both young adults and recent immigrants are having difficulty in the phase of labour force entry, in spite of high average levels of education and training. These challenges may include conflicts of interest in relation to groups who have more seniority in the labour market.

REFERENCES

Beaujot, Roderic. 2000. *Earning and Caring in Canadian Families*. Toronto: Broadview Press
– 2003. "Effect of Immigration on Demographic Structure." In *Canadian Immigration Policy for the 21st Century*, eds. C.M. Beach, A.G. Green, and J.G. Reitz, 49–91. Montreal: McGill-Queen's University Press
– K.G. Basavarajappa, and R. Verma. 1988. *Income of Immigrants in Canada: A Census Data Analysis*. Ottawa: Statistics Canada. Cat. no. 91–527

Bongaarts, John. 2004. "Population Aging and the Rising Costs of Public Pensions." *Population and Development Review* 30 (1): 1–23

Canadian Council on Social Development. 2002. *The Canadian Fact Book on Poverty.* Ottawa: CCSD

Cheal, David. 1999. *New Poverty: Families in Postmodern Society.* Westport: Praeger

Cotton, C., M. Webber, and Y. Saint-Pierre. 1999. *Should the Low Income Cutoffs be Updated?* Ottawa: Statistics Canada. Cat. no. 75F0002MIE-99009

Economic Council of Canada. 1992. *The New Face of Poverty: Income Security Needs of Canadian Families.* Ottawa: Economic Council of Canada

Hagenaars, Aldi, and Klaas De Vos. 1988. "The Definition and Measurement of Poverty." *Journal of Human Resources* 23 (2): 211–21

Hatfield, Michael. 2004. "Vulnerability to Persistent Low Income." *Horizons* 7 (2): 19–26

Légaré, Jacques. 2001. "Ageing and Social Security Program Reforms: Canada in International Perspective." *ISUMA: Canadian Journal of Policy Research* 2 (2): 110–18

Massey, D.S. 1995. "The New Immigration and Ethnicity in the United States." *Population and Development Review* 21 (3): 631–52

Morissette, René. 1998. "The Declining Labor Market Status of Young Men." In *Labor Markets, Social Institutions, and the Future of Canada's Children,* ed. M. Corak. Ottawa: Statistics Canada. Cat. no. 89–553

Myles, John. 2000. "The Maturation of Canada's Retirement Income System: Income Levels, Income Inequality and Low Income among Older Persons." *Canadian Journal on Aging* 19 (3): 287–316

Picot, Garnett. 1998. "What Is Happening to Earnings Inequality and Youth Wages in the 1990s." *Canadian Economic Observer* 11 (9): 3.1–3.18

– Myles, John, and Wendy Pyper. 1998. "Markets, Families and Social Transfers: Trends in Low-Income Among the Young and Old, 1973–1995." In *Labour Markets, Social Institutions, and the Future of Canada's Children,* ed. Miles Corak, 11–30. Ottawa: Statistics Canada. Cat. no. 890553-XPB

– and Arthur Sweetman. 2005. "The Deteriorating Economic Welfare of Immigrants and Possible Causes: Update 2005." Ottawa: Statistics Canada, Analytical Studies Research Paper no. 262

– and John Myles. 2005. "Income Inequality and Low Income in Canada: An International Perspective." Analytical Studies Research Paper Series 11F0019 MIE2005240. Ottawa: Statistics Canada

Podoluk, Jenny. 1968. *Incomes of Canadians.* Ottawa: Dominion Bureau of Statistics

Rashid, A. 1977. *Sources and Distribution of Canadian Income.* Ottawa: Statistics Canada. Cat. no. 99–721

– 1994. *Family Income in Canada.* Ottawa: Statistics Canada. Cat. no. 96–318

– 1999. "Family Incomes: 25 Years of Stability and Change." *Perspectives on Labour and Income* 11 (1): 9–15

Richmond, Anthony, and Warren Kalbach. 1980. *Factors in the Adjustment of Immigrants and Their Descendants*. Ottawa: Statistics Canada. Cat. no. 99–761

Royal Commission on Bilingualism and Biculturalism. 1969. *Report of the Royal Commission on Bilingualism and Biculturalism*. Book III: *The Work World*. Ottawa: Queen's Printer

Smeeding, Timothy. 2003. "Government Programs and Social Outcomes: The United States in Comparative Perspective." Paper prepared for the Smolensky Conference on Poverty, the Distribution of Income and Public Policy. University of California Berkeley, 12–13 December 2003

Statistics Canada. 1977. *Families: Statistics on Low Income*. 1971 Census of Canada. Ottawa. Cat. no. 93–773

– 1984a. *Changes in Income in Canada: 1970–1980*. Ottawa. Cat. no. 99–941

– 1984b. *Economic Families in Private Households: Income and Selected Characteristics*. 1981 Census of Canada. Ottawa. Cat. no. 92–937

– 2004. *2001 Census Dictionary*. Ottawa. Cat. no. 92-378-XIE

– 2005. *Income Trends in Canada*. Ottawa. Cat. no. 75-202-XIE

Vaillancourt, Francois. 1985. *Income Distribution and Economic Security in Canada*. Toronto: University of Toronto Press

Wolfson, M., and J. Evans. 1989. *Statistics Canada's Low Income Cutoffs: Methodological Concerns and Possibilities*. Ottawa: Statistics Canada, Analytical Studies Branch

6

Labour Force

BILL MARR

INTRODUCTION AND CONTEXT

This chapter examines the Canadian and provincial/ territorial labour force from the perspective of the 2001 Canadian Census with appropriate use of the 1991 Canadian Census when it is useful to show changes over that ten year time period. Since a Canadian census is taken only every five years, the emphasis will be on structural changes to the Canadian labour force rather than on cyclical changes. It would be inappropriate to use census data for the latter changes because they can occur at intervals of less than ten years or even five years and they tend to exhibit no trend; a good example is the unemployment rate for the nation or for provinces or territories. Therefore, this chapter explores the levels and changes in structural factors of the Canadian labour force; some examples of those factors, which will be examined in this chapter, are the size of the labour force and its provincial/territorial distribution, the occupational and industrial structures, full-time versus part-time work, the labour force participation rate, and class or worker designations.

THE LABOUR FORCE

In this chapter, the general dimensions of Canada's labour force in 2001 and over the decade 1991 to 2001 will be described. In the first place, the size of that labour force, its growth rate, and its distribution by one spatial dimension (namely province and territory) and two demographic dimensions (sex and age group) are three useful ways to appreciate the changes over that time period. Except where specifically noted, all data come from the Census section of Statistics Canada's web site, and relate to the population aged 15 and older.

Table 6.1

Title	Labour Force Canada 2001			Participation Rate (%) Canada 2001			Labour Force Growth Rates (%) Canada 1991–2001		
	Total – Sex	Male	Female	Total – Sex	Male	Female	Total – Sex	Male	Female
Age Groups									
15-24 years	2,581,445	1,333,020	1,248,425	64.389	65.523	63.221	0.673	-0.611	2.081
25-34 years	3,393,625	1,777,780	1,615,840	84.948	90.391	79.670	-18.674	-21.276	-15.606
35-44 years	4,388,140	2,293,575	2,094,560	86.015	91.133	81.031	15.830	12.358	19.887
45-54 years	3,649,575	1,929,640	1,719,940	82.583	88.332	76.963	50.847	42.108	62.025
55-64 years	1,537,930	900,725	637,205	53.623	63.846	43.727	22.624	15.815	33.740
65 years and over	321,355	217,265	104,090	8.264	13.067	4.676	16.486	19.732	10.247
15+ years	15,872,070	8,542,015	7,420,055	65.367	71.774	59.333	9.652	6.210	13.855

In 2001, Canada's labour force was 15,872,070 from a population age 15+ of 24,281,560; this results in a labour force participation rate (i.e., the labour force as a percentage of the population age 15+) of 65.4 percent (see table 6.1). In comparison, in 1991 Canada's labour force was about 14.7 million from a population age 15+ of about 21.6 million; the participation rate was 67.0 percent. So while Canada's population grew about 12.4 percent over that decade, the labour force grew by just 9.7 percent. As described in the previous paragraph, the growth rate of the labour force is the product of the growth rates of the population age 15+ and the labour force participation rate; the fact that the labour force grew more slowly than the growth rate of the population age 15+ attests to the fact that the participation rate declined between the 1991 Census and the 2001 Census.

While most comparisons for the Census in 2001 will be with the Census in 1991, it is sometimes useful to also include the data from the Census in 1981. This is one of those times. Over the decade 1981 to 1991, Canada's labour force grew about 20.1 percent, which is much more robust than the period from 1991 to 2001. At least from the viewpoint of this labour force, the 1980s had a labour force dynamic that was not present from 1991 to 2001.

In 2001, about 53.3 percent of the labour force was male and the other 46.7 percent was female. This contrasts with about 55 percent being males and 45 percent being females in 1991. Clearly the growth rate of the female labour force was greater than the growth rate of the male labour force over the decade, namely 13.9 percent versus 6.2 percent. It is interesting to note that both growth rates are much lower than those from 1981 to 1991; over that decade, the male labour force grew 11.2 percent and the female labour force grew 33.0 percent. So the growth rate of the labour force is declining over time, and this is reflected in a decline in its growth rate for both males and females.

In 2001, the labour force participation rates for males and females were 71.8 percent and 59.3 percent respectively. This compares with 75.5 percent and 58.9 percent in 1991. Therefore, the male participation rate fell over the decade while the female participation rate remained steady or increased slightly. As with the relative growth rates, the feminization of the Canadian labour force continues.

When attention turns to the labour force by age groups in table 6.1, the obvious thing to note is the –18.7 percent growth rate in the 25 to 34 age group. In other words, the number in the labour force in that age group decreased by 18.7 percent between the 1991 Census and the 2001 Census. This represents a population growth rate in that age group of –17.9 percent and a small decrease in the labour force participation rate in that age group, both of which act to decrease the growth rate of the labour force. Both males and females showed a decreased labour force growth rate between 1991 and 2001 of –21.3 percent and –15.6 percent respectively in that age group. The only difference was that the female participation rate increased over that decade, which offset some of the negative population growth.

The other age groups all showed positive growth rates between 1991 and 2001 in keeping with the overall increase in the labour force that was noted above. In particular, the labour force in the 45 to 54 age group grew by 50.9 percent, which attests to the well-documented aging of the Canadian labour force, as that group will be aged 55 to 64 in 2011. Both the male and female labour forces showed very high growth rates in this age group.

Labour force participation rates increase from the 15 to 24 age group to the 35 to 44 age group, and decrease thereafter. This pattern is found in the total figure as well as for both males and females. When those rates in 2001 are compared to 1991, there is no easy pattern. For the younger age groups, the participation rate decreased over that decade while it increased for older age groups; but, for the oldest age group, those older than 64 years, the participation rate was lower in 2001 than in 1991. This finding is a bit surprising given the notion that people are working longer. Labour force participation rates generally rise across age groups for females, except for the youngest and the oldest two age groups. The overall pattern for female rates to increase is especially noticeable in the age groups 45 to 54 and 54 to 64, where the increases are about 4–5 percent between 1991 and 2001. In contrast, the male labour force participation rates decreased in every age group.

Table 6.2
Labour Force 15 Years and Over by Province and Sex, 2001

	Sex			Growth Rates: 1991 to 2001		
	Total	Male	Female	Total	Male	Female
Newfoundland	241,495	128,640	112,855	-9.6	-13.9	-4.2
Nova Scotia	451,380	238,440	212,940	0.9	-4.4	7.5
New Brunswick	371,805	197,610	174,195	4.5	-0.5	10.9
Prince Edward Is.	73,635	38,395	35,240	7.8	3.9	12.4
Quebec	3,742,485	2,012,340	1,730,145	5.8	2.0	10.5
Ontario	6,086,815	3,214,995	2,871,825	10.4	7.6	13.8
Manitoba	585,420	311,355	274,070	3.1	0.1	6.8
Saskatchewan	512,240	273,900	238,335	1.2	-2.5	5.8
Alberta	1,696,760	920,145	776,615	19.6	17.4	22.2
British Columbia	2,059,945	1,089,740	970,210	17.8	13.2	23.4
Yukon Territory	17,950	9,210	8,735	5.5	-0.6	12.9
Northwest Territories	20,785	11,115	9,670	3.5	-0.9	9.3
Nunavut	11,355	6,130	5,225	39.2	30.3	51.2

Table 6.2 presents the labour force and its growth rates by province or territory in 2001 by sex. Recall that Canada's total labour force grew by 9.7 percent from 1991 to 2001. The provincial and territorial distributions of Canada's labour force show no surprises in table 6.2; they are well known and are unlikely to change very much over the course of just ten years. However, it is important and useful to notice the amount of variation in the provincial and territorial growth rates of their labour forces around the country's growth of 9.7 percent. There was a decrease of 9.6 percent in Newfoundland and Labrador's total labour force at the one extreme, while Nunavut's labour force increased by 39.2 percent. On the high end of the spectrum, the labour forces in Alberta and British Columbia increased by 19.6 percent and 17.8 percent respectively. They were clearly the high growth areas of the decade. As well as Newfoundland and Labrador, other lower growth areas were Nova Scotia and Saskatchewan.

The feminization of the Canadian labour force, noted previously, is evident at the provincial and territorial levels too. In every geographical area in table 6.2, the growth rate of the female labour force exceeded the growth rate of the male labour force. Even in Newfoundland and Labrador, where the total labour force decreased over the decade, the negative growth rate of the female labour force was smaller than the negative growth rate of the male labour force. In Quebec and Ontario, the growth rates of the female labour force were more than double the growth rate of the male labour force. In Nova Scotia, New Brunswick, Saskatchewan, and the Yukon

Territory, the total male labour force decreased between 1991 and 2001. The only comparatively large increases in the male labour force were in Alberta and British Columbia.

The statistics for each province and territory that are equivalent to table 6.1 are available on request, but they are not shown here in order to save space. Clearly Alberta and British Columbia were the labour force growth areas between the 1991 Census and the 2001 Census. If the identity at the start of this section is used to describe that growth in terms of the growth rate of the population age 15+ and the growth rate of the labour force participation rate, it is interesting to note for both Alberta and British Columbia that all of the growth in the labour force was due to population growth; Alberta's population age 15+ grew by 21.3 percent over the decade, while the overall participation rate actually decreased by about 1 percent. In British Columbia, the population age 15+ grew 22.2 percent and the participation rate declined by about 2 percent. At the other end of the spectrum, in Newfoundland and Labrador, between 1991 and 2001, the population decreased by 3.7 percent and the labour force participation rate declined by about 3.5 percent.

Ontario has not been mentioned so far because the growth rate of its labour force was neither at one extreme nor the other. Its overall labour force grew by 10.4 percent between 1991 and 2001, and of course had the largest labour force of any province or territory in 2001. Its male and female labour forces grew by 7.6 percent and 13.8 percent respectively over that same time period. Among the provinces, Ontario had the third highest labour force growth rates overall and by sex. As with Alberta and British Columbia, the growth rate of the total labour force was due entirely to the growth of the population age 15+, which was 14.3 percent; the participation rate declined by about 2.3 percent. Therefore, population growth as the cause of labour force growth, while participation rates decline slightly in the relatively fast growth provinces, presents a dominant pattern. However, the statistics from all provinces indicate that the overall participation rate decreases in all of them over this decade. Differentiating by sex, the labour force participation rate for females increased or did not change in every province except Newfoundland and Labrador, and it decreased for males in every province.

Therefore, while the growth rate of the overall and the male labour force between 1991 and 2001 was dominated by the growth rate (or lack of growth) of the population age 15+, both the growth rate of the female population age 15+ and the increase of the labour force participation rate of females caused the female labour force to grow (with the exception of

Newfoundland and Labrador, and the female participation rate hardly changing at all in the key provinces of Ontario and British Columbia).

WEEKS WORKED AND FULL-TIME VERSUS PART-TIME

Besides the levels and growth rates of the labour force, it is also important to examine the distribution of labour between full-time and part-time work, and the distribution of those two work options over the spectrum of the number of weeks worked. For example, someone may work full-time but for only 10 weeks while someone else may work mainly part-time but for 40 weeks. The total contribution of the second person in terms of hours worked in the year could well be greater than for the person who worked full-time. It is also interesting to see if the distribution between full-time and part-time work has changed over the time period 1991 to 2001.

Table 6.3 contains the percentage distributions between full-time and part-time work for Canada by sex and age group. The question in the Census asks if the person worked mainly full-time or part-time in the reference year. In 2001, about 78 percent of all people in the labour force worked mainly full-time; as might be hypothesized, that percentage was much greater for males than for females: 85.4 percent versus 69.4 percent. Especially for males, the percentage working mainly full-time has decreased since 1991; turning this around, for all people in the labour force, the percentage working mainly part-time has increased by about 2 percent.

Staying with Canada-wide data for now, table 6.3 presents the distribution between full-time and part-time work by age group. For all people in the labour force from the 2001 Census, the percentage working mainly full-time looks like an inverted "U" across the age groups: 47.6 percent for people aged 15 to 24 (i.e., the majority of those workers work mainly part-time), increasing to 86.4 percent for people aged 45 to 54, and decreasing to 53.9 percent for people age 65+. It is interesting to note that the majority of people aged 65+ who are in the labour force work mainly full-time. This pattern is also evident for both sexes. For the prime working age groups, namely age 25 to 54, not many changes are evident between the 1991 and 2001 censuses. The differences occur at the ends of the age spectrum. For people in the age group 15 to 24 who were in the labour force, the percentage working mainly full-time decreased very dramatically for all workers and for both sexes; there is clearly a trend towards part-time work in that age group. For people in the age groups 55 to 64 and 65+, the same change is seen; fewer of those people are working mainly full-time in the 2001 Census than in the 1991 Census. For the youngest workers, this may reflect

Table 6.3
Worked Mostly Full-Time or Part-Time

		Percentage Distribution			
		2001 (%)		1991(%)	
		Full-Time	Part-Time	Full-Time	Part-Time
Canada	All Workers	77.9	22.1	80.0	20.0
	Males	85.4	14.6	87.9	12.1
	Females	69.4	30.6	70.4	29.6
Age 15 to 24	All Workers	47.6	52.4	56.3	43.7
	Males	53.1	46.9	60.4	39.6
	Females	41.7	58.3	51.9	48.1
Age 25 to 34	All Workers	85.2	14.8	86.5	13.5
	Males	92.2	7.8	94.2	5.8
	Females	77.7	22.3	77.7	22.3
Age 35 to 44	All Workers	86.0	14.0	86.4	13.6
	Males	95.1	4.9	96.2	3.8
	Females	76.1	23.9	75.1	24.9
Age 45 to 54	All Workers	86.4	13.6	86.7	13.3
	Males	94.5	5.5	95.9	4.1
	Females	77.5	22.5	75.4	24.6
Age 55 to 64	All Workers	78.3	21.7	82.2	17.8
	Males	86.7	13.3	91.0	9.0
	Females	66.8	33.2	68.4	31.6
Age 65+	All Workers	53.9	46.1	62.5	37.5
	Males	59.4	40.6	68.1	31.9
	Females	43.1	56.9	52.0	48.0

the fact that they are staying in school longer, and for the oldest workers, this may reflect a desire to retire at a younger age, at least from full-time work, and perhaps greater wealth, allowing people to move to part-time work at a younger age.

Turning to the provincial statistics, which are available on request, there are some differences in the percentage of people working mainly full-time in the 2001 Census across those provinces and territories. For example, 83.4 percent of people in the labour force in the Northwest Territories worked mainly full-time, but only 74.1 percent in British Columbia's labour force were in the same category. However, their relative positions were the same in the 1991 Census, which indicates that a structural factor is at work here. As noted above for the Canadian labour force, all provinces and territories showed an increase in the percentage working mainly part-time between the two censuses. The largest increases were in Newfoundland and Labrador, British Columbia, the Yukon Territory, and Nunavut.

Table 6.4
Weeks Worked

Canada 2001

Worked in the reference year	Total – Sex (%)	Male (%)	Female (%)	Worked Mostly Full-Time in the Reference Year	Total – Sex (%)	Male (%)	Female (%)	Worked Mostly Part-Time in the Reference Year	Total – Sex (%)	Male (%)	Female (%)
1–13 weeks	7.32	6.57	8.17	1–13 weeks	4.06	3.73	4.51%	1–13 weeks	18.81	23.20	16.46
14–26 weeks	9.83	8.99	10.78	14–26 weeks	7.14	6.75	7.66	14–26 weeks	19.31	22.07	17.84
27–39 weeks	7.26	6.98	7.57	27–39 weeks	6.04	6.09	5.96	27–39 weeks	11.55	12.16	11.22
40–48 weeks	13.79	13.46	14.16	40–48 weeks	13.59	13.61	13.57	40–48 weeks	14.50	12.62	15.50
49–52 weeks	61.79	63.99	59.32	49–52 weeks	69.18	69.82	68.30	49–52 weeks	35.82	29.94	38.98

The other dimension to the weeks-worked data is the distribution by weeks worked for all people in the labour force divided into people who worked mainly full-time or part-time. Statistics for all of Canada are presented in table 6.4. For all workers, the distribution is of course weighted towards working 40 or more weeks; for all people in the Canadian labour force from the 2001 Census, about 75 percent worked 40 or more weeks in the reference year. This percentage is actually slightly higher than from the 1991 Census; people are working more weeks. In the 2001 Census, for all workers, females are more likely to be in the lower weeks worked categories (i.e., under 39 weeks). As expected, for people who worked mainly full-time, the percentage working 40 or more weeks is even higher, at about 83 percent. But among people who worked mainly part-time, the majority in the 2001 Census still worked 40 or more weeks, although the distribution across the weeks worked categories is much flatter than for people who worked mainly full-time. Note that for people who worked mainly part-time, the percentage working more weeks has increased between 1991 and 2001. Once again, people are working more weeks. If males and females are compared in the 2001 Census, differences in their distributions are more marked for people who worked mainly part-time. In fact, the distributions are very similar for people who worked mainly full-time. For people who worked mainly part-time, females are more likely to have worked more weeks in the reference year.

Data are available from the 2001 Census at the provincial and territorial levels that are equivalent to the national data in table 6.4. In the interest of space, those sub-national data are not presented here, but they are available on request. A few highlights will be noted. For Newfoundland and Labrador, 47 percent of all workers worked 49 to 52 weeks in the reference year; the corresponding statistics for males and females were 45 percent and 49 percent. These percentages are quite a bit lower than those in table 6.4 for all workers in Canada. In fact in that province, 22 percent of all workers and 24 percent and 19 percent respectively of males and females worked only 14 to 26 weeks, which is much higher than the national statistics in table 6.4. Prince Edward Island showed a very similar pattern in the 2001 Census, while Nova Scotia and New Brunswick were much more like the Canada-wide pattern, although all workers in those two provinces did work fewer weeks than the average across Canada. For all workers in Quebec, the distribution across weeks worked was almost identical to those in table 6.4, while in Ontario, 65 percent of all workers worked 49 to 52 weeks in the reference year, which is above the national average; the corresponding data for males and females in Ontario were 67 percent and 61 percent. Looking at the Prairies, Manitoba and Saskatchewan were like Ontario with above average percentages in the 49 to 52 weeks-worked category, while Alberta, like Quebec, was at the national average. British Columbia had slightly lower percentages of all workers, working 49 to 52 weeks as compared with the national average, while the territories and Nunavut were more like Newfoundland and Labrador. Just to emphasize the two ends of the spectrum, all workers in Ontario in the 2001 census worked an average of about 44 weeks in the reference year; in contrast, all workers in Newfoundland and Labrador and Nunavut worked about 36 weeks on average.

Even for workers who worked mainly full-time in the 2001 Census, only 52 percent worked 49 to 52 weeks in Newfoundland and Labrador as compared to 69 percent nation-wide. The relative patterns across provinces and territories for all workers described in the previous paragraph carry over to people who worked mainly full-time. For people who worked mainly part-time in the reference year, as with the full-time workers, the distribution over the weeks-worked categories is more likely to be skewed towards the 1 to 13 and the 14 to 26 weeks categories in the provinces and territories, where people worked fewer weeks on average; examples are Newfoundland and Labrador, Prince Edward Island, and the Yukon Territory. In Ontario, everyone worked more weeks on average, even people who worked mainly part-time: 34 weeks as compared with 28 weeks in Newfoundland and Labrador. In fact from the 2001 Census, except for Newfoundland and Labrador, there was little difference among the provinces in the average number of weeks worked for people who mainly worked part-time. However, the territories were different: 30 weeks in the Yukon Territory, 28 weeks in the Northwest Territories, 25 weeks in Nunavut.

As a final aspect of weeks worked, the 1991 and 2001 Censuses present statistics on the average number of weeks worked for all people who worked in the reference year. The point was made previously that Canadians are working more, and this can be seen also in that average number of weeks worked. For all people who worked, there was a one-week increase in the average number of weeks worked over that decade: from 41.9 weeks to 43 weeks. Males increased their weeks worked by exactly one week, while females actually increased average weeks worked by more than one week, from 40.8 weeks to 42.2 weeks. This same increase was seen for people who worked both mainly full-time and mainly part-time. The increase was very pervasive. When the average number of weeks worked is examined across age groups, that average showed no change at all for people aged 65+; they worked on average 38 to 39 weeks in 1991 and 2001. Also, the average number of weeks worked for males between the ages of 35 and 64 did not increase by very much; they showed only a small rise over the decade. This is expected since those groups have always been active in Canada's labour force.

In sum, Canadians are working more in the paid labour force on average and the feminization of that labour force, a trend noted before, is evident in weeks worked as well as in the labour force participation rate and the growth rate of the female labour force.

THREE STRUCTURAL DIMENSIONS: INDUSTRY, OCCUPATION, AND CLASS OF WORKER

In 2001 there were three industries with greater than 10 percent of the total labour force, namely manufacturing (14.2 percent), retail trade (12 percent), and health and social services (10.2 percent). As one comparison, in the 1991 Census only manufacturing and the retail trade had more than 10 percent of the total labour force distribution; health and social services was in third place with about 9 percent of the total labour force. Over the decade, the former two industries about held their own while the latter increased in an important way.

For males, the two highest percentages in the 2001 Census were manufacturing, at 18.6 percent, and the retail trade, at 10.8 percent. The construction trades followed them at 9.8 percent and business services at 8.8 percent. Only 3.5 percent of the male labour force was in health and social services. On the other hand, for females, 17.8 percent of the labour force was in health and social services, 13.4 percent was in the retail trade, 9.8 percent in educational services, and 9.1 percent was in manufacturing. For males and for females, the pattern of the distribution in the 1991 Census was about the same as in 2001, although the percentage of males in business services grew about 3 percent over the decade. As has been noted previously, it would be unusual if the industrial structure of Canada changed dramatically over a decade.

When the provinces and territories are compared to the national distribution, some differences show up. For example, as is well known, Ontario and Quebec had a higher percentage in manufacturing while government services were more important in the Yukon Territory, the Northwest Territories, and Nunavut, and agriculture had higher percentages in Saskatchewan, Prince Edward Island, and Alberta. As would be expected given the nature of the industry, the percentages in the retail trade; construction; real estate and insurance; educational services; and accommodation, food, and beverage services were much tighter across the provinces and territories. Business services were more important in Ontario, Alberta, and British Columbia, while mining, quarrying, and oil well industries were more important to

Newfoundland and Labrador, Saskatchewan, Alberta, the Yukon Territory, the Northwest Territories, and Nunavut.

Turning now to the occupational distributions, occupations that dominate the Canadian distributions in the 2001 Census were sales and services, business, finance and administration, trades and transport, and management. In the 1991 Census, the same four occupations had the highest percentages also. For males in the 2001 Census, the only differences were that occupations unique to processing, manufacturing, and utilities had about 10 percent and natural and applied sciences had 9.5 percent of the occupational distribution, which put those occupations in fourth and fifth places behind trades and transport (24.5 percent), sales and services (19 percent), and management (12.6 percent). The distribution for females in 2001 was actually more skewed than for males. For females, 30.9 percent were in sales and services; 27.8 percent were in business, finance, and administration; and 9.2 percent were in social science, education, and government. For both males and females, the relative position in the occupations distribution in 1991 was the same as in 2001. The only small difference was that females in health occupations (8.8 percent) were just ahead of females in social science, education, and government in the 1991 Census.

Turning to the provinces and territories, perhaps it is not surprising that outside of occupations unique to primary industry, the percentages across the provinces and territories are quite alike. After all, there are, for example, management occupations in almost all industries. So no matter a province or territory's industrial structure, the percentage of the labour force in management occupations can be the same. That, for the most part, seems to be the situation from the 2001 Census. Saskatchewan is the obvious outlier, but even for that province the difference with respect to the other provinces and territories appears to be with mainly one occupation. That province had a much higher percentage of its labour force in occupations unique to primary industry and then slightly lower percentages of its labour force in a number of other occupations. British Columbia also had a relatively high percentage of its labour force in occupations unique to primary industry.

Considering Canada's industrial and occupational structures from the 2001 Census, one might note with interest the industries and occupations that showed the highest growth between 1991 and 2001. For all members of the labour force for all of Canada, people in the business service industry grew by 61.8 percent over that decade, while the corresponding growths for males and females were 65.6 percent and 57.2 percent. That sector demonstrated major growth. Wholesale trade industries grew by 33.3 percent (males by 30 percent and females by 40.9 percent), and health and social services increased by 24 percent (males by only 14 percent but females by 26.5 percent). Closely grouped were other service industries (19.1 percent); real estate operator and insurance agent industries (17.4 percent); and accommodation, food, and beverage service industries (16 percent). People who classified themselves as being in manufacturing industries grew by 6 percent (males by 5.5 and females by 7.3 percent). The total number of people in government service industries; finance and insurance industries; construction industries; mining, quarrying, and oil well industries; logging and forestry industries; and agriculture and related service industries all declined between 1991 and 2001; with the exception of males in finance and insurance industries, the total number of both males and females decreased in all of those industries. It is interesting to note that the number of males in retail trade industries and in educational service industries also declined, while the number of females in the latter industry increased by 18.3 percent.

The only two occupations that saw a decrease in the total number of people in them were trades, transport, and equipment operators (0.3 percent), and occupations unique to primary industry (9.1 percent). The occupations that had the largest growth in numbers were natural and applied sciences at 41.9 percent; occupations in art, culture, recreation and sport at 29.2 percent; and management occupations at 17.2 percent. The total number of females in management occupations grew by 40.5 percent, and, as well, they saw a 26 percent increase in the total number of females in occupations in social science, education, government service, and religion (males in that industry grew by only 3.4 percent). Growth in the "traditional" industries of processing, manufacturing and utilities, and sales and service occupations increased by 11.4 percent and 10 percent respectively. Finally, the total number in health occupations increased by 13.8 percent over the decade.

The growth rates of the total labour force in various industries in Quebec and Ontario were very close to those for Canada as a whole; business service industries, wholesale trade industries, and health and social service industries led the way. But in Quebec, people in real estate and insurance increased by 21.8 percent, which exceeded health and social service industries. In Ontario, the labour force in transportation and storage industries grew by 21.9 percent, about the same as in health and social service industries. Recall from table 6.2 that Alberta had the highest growth rate of the labour force of all provinces and territories between 1991 and 2001. Partly as a result of that, many industries in Alberta showed large increases over that decade: business service industries (84.5 percent), wholesale trade industries (42.8 percent), construction industries (34.6 percent, which actually declined for Canada), manufacturing industries (30.6 percent), accommodation, food and beverage service industries (29.3 percent), transportation and storage industries (26.7 percent), and health and social service industries (25 percent). British Columbia, with the second highest growth rate of the total labour force among all provinces and territories over the decade, was more like Canada, Ontario, and Quebec in terms of the industries that grew the most; but it is interesting to note that the labour force in B.C. in health and social service industries increased by 41.7 percent and the labour force in educational service industries grew by 31.9 percent, which are well above the national growth rates for those two industries.

While Newfoundland and Labrador saw the same high growth rates in business service industries and health and social service industries, the labour force in manufacturing industries decreased by 32.9 percent and in government service industries by 40.9 percent. Declines in those two industries also characterized Nova Scotia and New Brunswick over the decade. Prince Edward Island actually had a 10 percent increase in the labour force in manufacturing industries.

In the 1990s there was a spate of newspaper articles and research publications that stressed the growth of self-employment in Canada. From reading this literature, one would think that the Canadian labour force was turning into store owners, restaurant owners, doctors, lawyers, and independent consultants. What does the Census say about that growth from 1991 to 2001? In fact, we are a nation of employees; most of us work for somebody else: according to the 2001 Census, 86 percent people who were in the labour force were employees; they worked for somebody else. Now the number of people in the labour force who were self-employed did grow over that decade: from about 1.4 million in 1991 to just over 1.8 million in 2001. This represents an increase from 9.7 percent of the labour force in 1991 to 11.7 percent in 2001, a small change. The picture was about the same for men and women separately. For males, the percentage that was self-employed increased from 12.7 percent to 14.6 percent, and for females it increased from 6 percent to 8.5 percent. Most Canadians find work working for somebody else.

In 2001, the self-employed made up various percentages of each province or territory's labour force, and the pattern seems to generally fit the industrial structure as it shifts from some primary production to a preponderance of secondary industry. The areas with more primary production (for example, agriculture or logging) tended to have a higher percentage of the labour force in self-employment. Some examples include Prince Edward Island at 12.4 percent, Saskatchewan at 18.2 percent, British Columbia at 14.2 percent, Alberta at 14.1 percent, and the Yukon at 13 percent. The rest of Atlantic Canada, the Northwest Territories, and Nunavut were in the 5 percent to 9 percent range.

As has been noted before, Quebec and Ontario were at about the national average of 11 percent. For the most part, provinces and territories showed an increase in the percentage of the labour force that was self-employed between 1991 and 2001 of from 1 percent to 2 percent, with the exception of Saskatchewan and Nunavut, where the percentage did not change.

CONCLUSIONS

So, what were some of the important changes in Canada's labour force and its structures between the 1991 Census and the 2001 Census?

1 In total, and for both males and females, the labour force growth rate was substantially lower in the 1990s than in the 1980s.
2 The feminization of the Canadian labour force continued between 1991 and 2001.
3 The age structure of the labour force shifted towards the older age groups for those in the labour force.
4 There was a slight shift towards more people working part-time, which was especially evident in the age groups 15 to 24, 55 to 64, and 65+.
5 People were working longer, at least in terms of weeks worked.
6 The industries with the highest growth rates over that decade were business services, the wholesale trades, and health and social services, while negative growth rates were evident in government services, construction, and primary industries. Alberta had very high growth rates in several industries.
7 While there was a slight increase in the percentage of people in the labour force who were self-employed, Canadians remain overwhelmingly a nation of employees.

ACKNOWLEDGMENT

The author would like to thank Rong Yan for valuable assistance with the data collection for this project.

REFERENCES

Statistics Canada. 2001 Census of Canada www.12.statcan.gc.ca/english/census01/home/Index.cfm

Statistics Canada. 2003. *The Changing Profile of Canada's Labour Force.* 2001 Census. Analysis series. Cat. no. 96F0030XIE2001009

7

Occupation and Industry

RICHARD A. WANNER

INTRODUCTION

The division of labour in any society can be characterized by observing both what is produced and the tasks that individual workers engage in to produce it. These two aspects of the division of labour are measured in the Census of Canada by means of questions that ascertain a respondent's industry of employment (what does he or she produce, or what is the nature of the business carried out by the respondent's employer?) and occupation (what kind of work does the person do?). Industry structure represents a horizontal dimension of the division of labour, since there is no implication that industries are unequal in some sense. They simply produce different products or services. On the other hand, the occupational structure is frequently seen as the vertical dimension of the division of labour, since occupations not only differ in the nature of the work involved; they may also be ranked in terms of the skills and formal education required and the earnings typically associated with them. In addition, occupational distributions tend to vary by such ascribed traits as gender, race, or ethnicity. Thus the occupational structure is a key element in a society's class or stratification system. While this chapter will pay some attention to Canada's industry structure and changes in it over time, a majority of our attention will focus on the occupational structure. I will particularly examine gender differences and differences by ethnicity and immigrant status in occupational attainment.

MEASURING INDUSTRY AND OCCUPATION

One of the challenges in studying changes over time in Canada's industry and occupational structures is related to the changing measures used by

Statistics Canada. Industry codes have remained relatively constant over time, with the 1980 Standard Industrial Classification (SIC) being used to classify industry in all censuses since 1986. In the 2001 census, a new classification, the 1997 North American Industry Classification System (NAICS) was introduced alongside the older SIC to improve industry comparability among the three North American Free Trade Agreement partners, Canada, the U.S., and Mexico.

Statistics Canada has changed markedly its occupational classification nearly every decade, with a significant change introduced to the Standard Occupational Classification (SOC) for the 1991 census, making it non-comparable to the 1980 SOC or the 1971 Occupational Classification Manual. For 2001, the 1991 SOC was revised and relabeled the National Occupational Classification for Statistics (NOC-S) (Statistics Canada 2001). Another version of the NOC-S, confusingly known as the NOC, was developed for the Federal Department now known as Human Resources and Skills Development Canada (Social Development Canada 2001). The NOC is particularly useful, because it groups occupations on the basis of skill and training required and level of responsibility. It is this classification that I use extensively in this chapter.

Given the centrality of occupation to understanding a society's stratification system, sociologists and demographers have devised numerous methods for scaling occupations along such dimensions as prestige or status or classifying them into more meaningful social classes. Perhaps the best-known Canadian scale of occupational status is the Blishen scale (Blishen 1967). It ranks occupations on the basis of the average educational level and earnings of their incumbents for the Canadian labour force, using methods similar to those developed by Duncan in the U.S. Blishen's initial socioeconomic index used data from the 1961 Census of Canada and was updated for the 1971 and 1981 censuses. It has not been updated since, though it is still widely used.

Like the Blishen scale, the categories of the NOC show a distinct gradient by average education and earnings, as shown in table 7.1.[1] These categories are somewhat abstract,since they were constructed on the basis of both the type of work involved (e.g., occupations in social science) and the skill level required of the work (e.g., occupations that usually require a university education). For example, the "skilled sales and service" category includes specific occupations like police officers and firefighters or insurance and real estate salespersons; "elemental sales and service" includes occupations like security guards, cleaners, or cashiers; "skilled crafts and trades" includes practitioners of the construction trades and auto mechanics. For both men and women, professionals and senior managers have the highest mean years

Table 7.1
Average Years of Schooling and Earnings by Occupation and Sex for Full-Time, Full-Year
Workers Age 25 and Over, Canada 2001

Occupation	Women		Men		Women's Earnings as a Percent of Men's
	Mean Years of Schooling	Median Earnings	Mean Years of Schooling	Median Earnings	
Senior managers	15.0	54000	14.9	72000	75.0
Middle, other managers	13.9	37700	13.9	50000	75.4
Professionals	15.7	45723	16.2	56000	81.6
Semi-professionals	13.7	32000	13.7	43000	74.4
Supervisors	12.9	30000	12.9	37800	79.4
Supervisors in crafts/trades	12.0	17000	11.8	35235	48.2
Admin, senior clerical	13.2	31500	14.0	45000	70.0
Skilled sales/service	12.6	24632	13.0	42000	58.6
Skilled crafts/trades	11.6	24000	12.1	40587	59.1
Clerical personnel	13.0	30000	12.9	35000	85.7
Intermediate sales/service	12.6	23000	13.0	37000	62.2
Semi-skilled manual	11.2	22712	11.5	35000	64.9
Elemental sales/service	11.5	19000	11.8	26690	71.2
Manual labour	10.9	22875	11.4	35000	65.4
TOTAL	13.4	31000	13.2	41500	74.7

of schooling and median earnings, while the lowest educational levels and earnings are found among semi-skilled manual workers, elemental sales and service workers, and manual labourers. Although mean years of schooling differ very little between men and women at all levels of the occupational structure, in 2001 women still earned less on average than men. Overall, women's earnings were about 75 percent of men's, but in skilled sales and service and skilled crafts and trades the ratio was considerably lower. In the professional and clerical ranks, women's earnings exceeded 80 percent of men's on average.

LONG-TERM TRENDS

From the perspective of social change, both the occupational and industry structures are central to understanding how technological change influences the social structure. The decline of the agricultural sector in the early twentieth century was accompanied by an increase in both the goods-producing sector, including manufacturing and construction, and the service sector, including business services, consumer services, and government. More recently, the goods-producing sector has also declined, and the service sector has become so dominant that we now refer to the new social formation as

Figure 7.1
Long-Term Trends in Major Industry Sectors, Canada 1881–2001

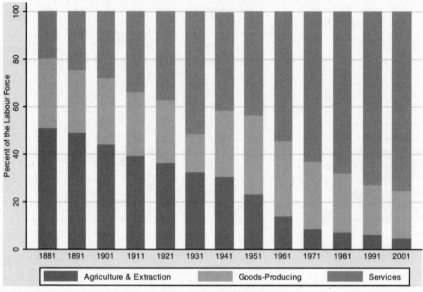

Source: Smucker (1980, 78) and Census Public Use Microdata Files 1981, 1991, and 2001.

"postindustrial" society (Bell 1973). This transformation, according to Bell, is accompanied by changes in the occupational distribution characterized by major growth in professional and technical employment. However, in the intervening decades since Bell made his observations, it has become clear that the service jobs created in a postindustrial economy are as likely to pay low wages and require few skills as they are to pay high wages and require a university education, particularly in the burgeoning personal and retail service industries (Clement and Myles 1994).

Industry Structure

Figure 7.1 shows the extensive change in Canada's industry structure since the late 1800s, based on decennial censuses since that time. In 1881 roughly half of Canada's labour force was engaged in agriculture and extraction, and such primary industries remained a significant component of economic activity until the mid-twentieth century. With the decline in agriculture and extraction, both goods-producing and service industries expanded. By the mid-twentieth century, the goods-production sector reached its maximum, approximately a third of the labour force, and has declined since, falling below 20 percent by 2001. This is a result of a number of factors, including enhanced efficiency through technological advances in transportation, communication, and the productive process; the centralization and concentration of business enterprises; falling profitability in manufacturing compared to services; and the export of many manufacturing jobs to low-wage countries (Bluestone and Harrison 1982). While the US experienced a similar pattern, several more developed countries reached as much as two-fifths (France and Italy) or even one-half (England and Germany) of their labour force in goods producing industries before the proportion declined (Singelmann 1978). The decline in manufacturing has been so significant in some countries that the term 'deindustrialization' (Bluestone and Harrison 1982) has come into common use to describe it. The most obvious feature of figure 7.1 is the enormous increase in the proportion of the labour force employed in service industries. By 2001, these industries comprised fully three-quarters of employment in Canada, though the rate of increase seems to be declining in recent decades.

To produce this long-term time series on industry composition, I was forced to simplify industry structure considerably, particularly the service sector. Table 7.2 shows a more detailed picture of Canada's industry structure based on the 2001 census. The primary sector includes the categories labeled 'agriculture and other primary,' while the goods-producing sector includes manufacturing and construction. Taken together, these sectors employ a bit less than 25 percent of Canada's labour force. All the remaining industries listed in table 7.2 make up the service sector. One of the ways in which work in Canada is gendered is in terms of differences in industry between men and women. While over 35 percent of men were employed in primary and goods-producing industries in 2001, just 13.4 percent of women were found in these industries. However, women are overrepresented in service industries, particularly in retail trade, education, health and social services, and hospitality services. As we shall see below, these differences in the industry distributions of men and women are closely related to differences in their occupational distributions. Has the promise of the prophets of a postindustrial society to deliver increasing numbers of "good jobs" that require greater amounts of training, pay well, and offer more meaningful work been realized with the rise of the service sector? As we shall see below, well-paying professional and managerial jobs, many in the service sector, have been increasing. Yet at the same time, the lower tier of the service sector, including jobs in retail trade, hospitality services, and other services, remains a significant segment of the labour force, particularly in the case of women (Krahn and Lowe 2002). As the figures in table 7.2 show, these three

Table 7.2
Industry by Sex for Workers Age 15 and Over, Canada 2001

Industry	Women	Men	Total
Agriculture	2.3	3.6	3.0
Other primary	0.7	3.3	2.1
Manufacturing	9.0	18.4	14.0
Construction	1.4	9.8	5.8
Transport and storage	1.8	6.2	4.1
Communication and utilities	2.2	3.4	2.8
Wholesale trade	3.5	6.6	5.1
Retail trade	13.6	11.0	12.2
Finance, insurance, and real estate	6.8	4.0	5.3
Business services	7.8	8.6	8.2
Federal government	2.2	2.3	2.3
Other government	3.3	3.3	3.3
Education	9.8	4.5	7.0
Health and social services	17.5	3.5	10.1
Hospitality services	9.2	5.3	7.2
Other services	8.8	6.3	7.5
TOTAL	100%	100%	100%
Number	7,918,122	8,818,587	16,736,709

lower-tier industries accounted for 31.6 percent of employed women and 22.6 percent of employed men, though the industry structure we have observed is by no means uniform across Canada with a considerable amount of specialization within census metropolitan areas.

The steady growth in the service sector over the twentieth century is by no means limited to Canada. All the more developed countries have experienced it to some degree. (OECD 2000) Among OECD countries, Canada and the United States have the highest percentages of their labour forces employed in this sector, but are closely followed by European countries such as Sweden, Belgium, and the Netherlands. The next group, including Italy, Spain, Germany, and South Korea, either retain a substantial proportion of the labour force in goods-producing industries, or still have a relatively large agricultural sector, such as Spain, Portugal, and Greece. Less developed, low-income countries in general tend to have a large proportion of their labour forces engaged in agriculture, yielding a fairly strong correlation between the proportion of the labour force in service industries and gross national income.

Occupational Structure

Figure 7.2 shows trends in Canada's occupational structure from 1891 to 2001 using a limited set of occupational categories. Trends are shown separately for

Figure 7.2
Long-Term Trends in Canada's Occupational Structure, 1891–2001

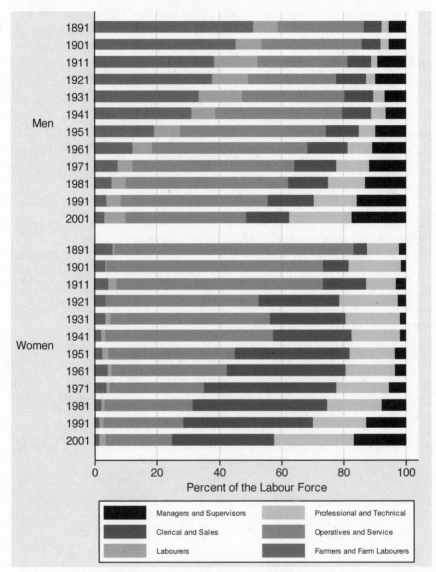

Sources: Leacy (1983, Series D86–106) and Statistics Canada (1981; 1993; 2001).

men and women to emphasize both historical differences between them and the different patterns of change they have experienced over time. Mirroring the trend in figure 7.1 of a declining primary sector, the proportion of men engaged in farming declined dramatically since 1891, from over half the male labour force to less than three and one-half percent. As farming declined among men, growing numbers of them were employed in operative and service occupations up to 1961, reflecting mainly the growth in manufacturing employment. Since 1951, an increasing proportion of men is found in both managerial and professional and technical employment, consistent with Bell's (1973) forecast for postindustrial societies. At the same time, unskilled manual occupations declined after reaching a peak of nearly 14 percent of the male labour force in the 1930s, though some 6 percent of men were still found in such occupations by 2001.

The story for women is considerably different. While a substantial proportion of women early in the twentieth century were engaged in farming as unpaid family workers, they do not show up in census figures on the paid labour force as farmers, hence the very small fraction of women in farming occupations throughout the century. Before the 1950s, a higher proportion of women were found in the amorphous operative and service category. Early in the century this meant mainly domestic service employment, while during and after World War II many women were employed as factory operatives. Since the 1950s, this form of employment for women has declined, while first clerical employment, then managerial and professional and technical occupations expanded. In the latter half of the century, clerical employment among women first grew rapidly, then began to decline: by 1981, over 43 percent of women in the labour force were in clerical employment, declining to about 33 percent by 2001. Since the 1960s, there has been substantial growth in the proportion of women employed as managers or in the professional and technical category. A substantial amount of sex segregation remains in Canada's occupational structure, but it is clear that women are increasingly found in higher-status, higher-wage occupations. In the next section, I explore gender differences in occupation in more detail.

While the evolution of Canada's occupational structure portrayed in figure 7.2 appears to be gradual, this understates the radical and fairly rapid change that was taking place, particularly during the 1970s. As I have already noted, during this period many relatively high-paying jobs requiring little education in goods-producing industries were being replaced by either high-paying jobs in the professional or managerial ranks, requiring a substantial amount of education, or by low-paying jobs in the service sector, requiring little education. Not only was this transition in Canada's economy painful for employees in so-called "sunset" industries in Canada's industrial heartland in southern Ontario and parts of Quebec (High 2003), it also has become evident that, in part at least, this transformation led to a greater degree of income inequality in Canada (Richardson 1997), as it has in many other postindustrial societies.

GENDER AND OCCUPATION

While these long-term changes have been taking place in Canada's industry and occupational structures, another equally momentous change has been taking place in the composition of the labour force: the surge in employment among women, coupled with a decline in the male labour force participation rate, particularly at older ages. The result is that between 1951 and 2001, women more than doubled their share of the labour force from 22 percent to nearly 47 percent (Leacy 1983; Statistics Canada 2001). Although, as we shall see, there has been some reduction in recent decades in the extent of sex segregation in the occupational structure, occupations in Canada remain extensively sex segregated, with women remaining clustered in a relatively small number of female-stereotyped occupations, particularly in the clerical field.

Table 7.3 provides not only a comparison of the overall occupational distributions of men and women in 2001 (in the Total column), but also separate distributions for persons with different levels of education. To be sure that these respondents have had an opportunity to attain their highest level of education, only those age 25 or over are included in the table. As we would expect from the differences between women and men in industry distributions, their occupational distributions are substantially different. Given their over-representation in service industries and under-representation in goods-production, considerably smaller percentages of women are found in the skilled crafts and trades and other manual categories, as well as in supervisory positions in crafts and trades. At the same time, women remain highly overrepresented in clerical occupations, with nearly 26 percent of employed women working in clerical or administrative and senior clerical positions, compared to just 6.1 percent of employed men. Fewer women than men are also in managerial occupations, although a higher percentage of women are found in professional and semi-professional positions. At the other end of the occupational hierarchy, few women work as manual labourers, but over 8 percent of women are found in low-paying elemental sales and service occupations, compared to 5 percent of men.

The separate occupational distributions for each level of educational attainment shown in table 7.3 underscore the strong association between

Table 7.3

Occupation by Highest Level of Education and Sex, Canadian Employed Population Age 25 and Over, 2001

Occupation	Women						Men					
	Less than HS Diploma	High School Diploma	Some Post-sec	Bachelor's Degree	Advanced Degree	Total	Less than HS Diploma	High School Diploma	Some Post-sec	Bachelor's Degree	Advanced Degree	Total
Senior managers	0.4	0.6	0.7	1.3	2.2	0.8	0.9	1.4	1.9	4.0	5.4	2.1
Middle, other managers	6.2	7.7	7.7	9.9	11.2	8.0	7.7	10.9	12.7	16.8	16.4	12.1
Professionals	2.0	4.4	15.5	50.2	64.0	19.7	1.5	3.3	10.1	46.1	58.7	15.5
Semi-professionals	3.6	5.1	11.9	8.8	6.4	8.4	2.3	4.2	10.8	7.4	5.1	6.9
Supervisors	1.8	2.2	1.6	1.0	0.5	1.6	0.9	1.4	1.1	0.8	0.4	1.0
Supervisors in crafts/trades	3.0	1.8	1.3	0.8	0.5	1.5	9.1	6.7	5.3	1.9	1.0	5.6
Admin, senior clerical	7.3	14.6	13.3	6.8	4.3	10.9	0.8	1.5	1.9	2.7	1.9	1.7
Skilled sales/service	5.3	4.9	4.4	1.9	1.0	4.0	3.4	4.4	5.5	3.4	1.5	4.3
Skilled crafts/trades	2.4	1.4	0.9	0.3	0.2	1.1	16.7	19.7	19.7	2.0	1.3	15.3
Clerical personnel	11.6	20.6	17.5	8.5	4.4	14.9	4.1	5.6	4.8	3.7	2.1	4.4
Intermediate sales/service	17.7	15.9	15.2	7.0	3.4	13.7	4.9	6.8	6.8	5.0	2.5	5.8
Semi-skilled manual	13.5	7.1	3.3	1.2	0.7	5.2	30.4	22.0	12.0	3.5	2.0	15.9
Elemental sales/service	19.8	11.2	5.7	2.0	1.1	8.2	8.2	6.5	4.4	1.9	1.3	5.0
Manual labour	5.4	2.6	1.1	0.4	0.3	1.9	9.2	5.6	3.0	0.8	0.5	4.3
TOTAL	100%	100%	100%	100%	100%	100%	100%	100%	100%	100%	100%	100%

education and occupation. At one extreme, over 77 percent of men and over 80 percent of women holding advanced degrees (M.A., Ph.D., or professional degrees) are found in professional or managerial occupations. At the other extreme, over 56 percent of women and nearly 52 percent of men lacking a high school diploma are found in the four low-wage occupational groups. While some men and women without a bachelor's degree are found in the managerial and professional ranks, particularly as "middle and other managers," few members of the labour force without at least a bachelor's degree are found there.

Beyond this common overall pattern, the distribution of men and women across occupational categories differs considerably, depending upon their level of education. Among men with less than a high-school diploma, over 65 percent are found in just four occupational categories: manual labour, semi-skilled manual, skilled crafts and trades, and supervisors in crafts and trades. You will note that the occupations in all these categories involve manual work, or what is often called blue-collar work. In contrast, a majority (56 percent) of women with less than a high-school diploma are found in so-called white-collar jobs in the administrative and senior clerical, clerical, intermediate sales and service, and elemental sales and service, categories in which many of the jobs are low paying (see median earnings in table 7.1).

It is apparent from table 7.3 that as level of education increases, the similarity between the occupational distributions of women and men also increases. This is shown in summary form in figure 7.3, which reports values for an index of dissimilarity between the male and female occupational distributions, both by level of education and for two census years, 1991 and 2001.[2] It is clear from this figure that the occupational distributions of men and women with less education differ more than the occupational distributions of those holding a bachelor's or advanced degree. In fact, in 2001 just 12 percent of women holding an advanced degree would have to change occupations to eliminate sex segregation among advanced degree holders, compared to nearly four times as many women (45 percent) with a high-school diploma who would have to change to eliminate segregation among high school diploma holders. In the decade between the 1991 and 2001 censuses, there has been an overall decline in occupational sex segregation of nearly 9 percent, and declines have taken place at all educational levels, with the possible exception of those with less than a high-school diploma. This represents a continuation of the decline in sex segregation that began in the 1960s (Fox and Fox 1987).

Despite the decline that has continued between the 1991 and 2001 censuses, figure 7.3 indicates that occupational sex segregation remains

Figure 7.3
Index of Occupational Sex Segregation by Level of Education, Canada 1991–2001

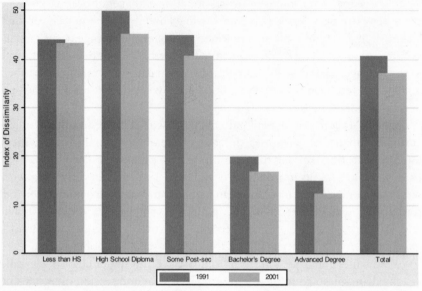

Note: Index based on the 14 category classification of the NOC using data from 1991 and 2001 Census
Public Use Microdata Files.

substantial, with 37 percent of women in the labour force being required
to change occupations to eliminate sex segregation. This estimate is likely
conservative, since it is based on an occupational classification with relatively few categories and does not reflect differences within categories. The
continued high level of occupational sex segregation is puzzling given the
general rise in egalitarian values during the past five decades, along with the
striking increase in female labour force participation and the elimination of
the gender gap in educational attainment. Canada is by no means unique
since, with some variation, high levels of occupational sex segregation continue to characterize all postindustrial societies (Charles and Grusky 2004).

IMMIGRATION, VISIBLE MINORITIES,
AND OCCUPATION

With over 18 percent of its population born elsewhere, Canada remains one
of the world's chief immigrant-receiving countries. In recent decades immigrants increasingly arrive from regions such as Asia, Latin America and the
Caribbean, and Africa instead of Europe or the United States, producing a

growing visible minority population. An important issue, which many scholars have addressed, is the extent to which immigrants and members of visible minority groups are afforded labour market opportunities commensurate with their education and job experience. A key dimension of labour market opportunity is the extent to which these groups have access to higher status occupations, compared to the Canadian-born or those with European or North American ancestry.

Table 7.4 shows distributions of the NOC occupational categories by visible minority status for all Canadian workers over age 15, including those who are not members of a visible minority group for purposes of comparison. It is clear from a comparison of the occupational distributions represented there that the catchall category 'visible minority' masks some important differences.[3] Compared to census respondents who do not belong to a visible minority group, blacks seem particularly disadvantaged in terms of occupational attainment. Among both women and men, they are underrepresented in the professional and managerial ranks, but overrepresented in lower-paying occupational groups, such as intermediate and elemental sales and service and semi-skilled manual.

In contrast to the situation of blacks, Canadians of Chinese origin are actually overrepresented among professionals and managers, particularly in the case of men. Nearly twice the percentage of Chinese-origin men, 25.7 percent, is employed in professional occupations than for men who are not members of visible minority groups. At the same time, considerably fewer Chinese men are engaged in manual occupations of all kinds, particularly skilled crafts and trades. Chinese women, while somewhat more likely to be professionals than nonvisible minority women, are also more likely to be engaged in low-paying semi-skilled manual and manual-labouring occupations. Occupational patterns among male Canadians of South Asian origin are roughly bimodal, with overrepresentation, compared to workers who are not members of a visible minority, apparent in better jobs in the professions and worse jobs in semi-skilled manual and elemental sales and service categories. In contrast, South Asian women are underrepresented in management and the professions, but considerably overrepresented in clerical, semi-skilled manual, and manual-labouring occupations.

All these comparisons of visible minority groups with Canadian workers who are not members of a visible minority are quite crude, since they fail to take into account either differences in human capital – mainly education, experience, and language ability – among these groups or differences in immigrant/non-immigrant status. In fact some Canadian research has indicated that it is mainly immigrant members of visible minorities not educated

Table 7.4
Occupation by Visible Minority Status and Sex for Workers Age 15 and Over, Canada 2001

	Women				
Occupation	Black	South Asian	Chinese	Other Visible Minorities	Not a Visible Minority
Senior managers	0.2	0.5	0.5	0.4	0.7
Middle, other managers	4.0	5.5	7.7	6.4	7.1
Professionals	14.3	14.2	20.1	13.3	17.3
Semi-professionals	7.7	6.6	7.0	7.9	8.7
Supervisors	1.6	1.4	1.2	1.3	1.6
Supervisors in crafts/trades	0.6	0.7	0.4	0.7	1.4
Admin, senior clerical	6.9	6.5	7.9	6.1	10.0
Skilled sales/service	2.8	3.0	4.2	4.0	4.0
Skilled crafts/trades	1.2	1.1	1.5	1.4	1.0
Clerical personnel	17.9	17.3	14.3	13.7	14.4
Intermediate sales/service	18.3	12.7	13.7	19.9	16.4
Semi-skilled manual	6.7	11.0	9.7	8.1	4.5
Elemental sales/service	14.4	13.1	9.1	14.1	11.1
Manual labour	3.7	6.4	2.8	2.8	1.8
TOTAL	100%	100%	100%	100%	100%
Number	173,127	215,658	255,578	363,005	6,910,022

	Men				
Occupation	Black	South Asian	Chinese	Other Visible Minorities	Not a Visible Minority
Senior managers	0.8	1.2	1.5	1.1	1.9
Middle, other managers	6.4	9.7	12.7	9.9	10.4
Professionals	12.7	16.8	25.7	14.9	13.0
Semi-professionals	6.9	6.0	8.7	7.8	6.9
Supervisors	1.2	1.1	0.8	1.3	1.0
Supervisors in crafts/trades	2.1	1.9	1.0	1.9	5.3
Admin, senior clerical	1.6	1.4	1.7	1.0	1.6
Skilled sales/service	4.5	3.8	8.9	4.9	4.2
Skilled crafts/trades	10.8	7.6	5.9	10.4	15.0
Clerical personnel	9.0	7.6	6.3	6.4	4.7
Intermediate sales/service	7.7	6.4	7.8	7.7	6.7
Semi-skilled manual	19.3	21.0	9.2	16.7	15.9
Elemental sales/service	11.9	10.5	6.8	11.7	7.8
Manual labour	5.2	5.1	3.2	4.3	5.7
TOTAL	100%	100%	100%	100%	100%
Number	164,902	275,964	268,281	381,413	7,727,741

Figure 7.4
Occupation by Place of Birth and Sex, Canada 2001

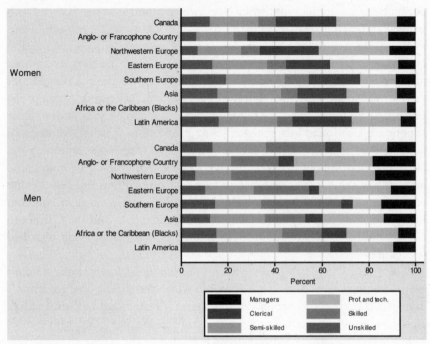

Source: Tabulation from the 2001 Census Public Use Microdata File.

in Canada who have lower levels of occupational and earnings attainments, controlling for human capital factors, than the native born (e.g. Wanner and Ambrose 2003).

Although it does not control for human capital, data in figure 7.4 indicate differences between the occupational structure of native-born Canadians and immigrants from several regions of the world in 2001. To facilitate presentation, I have collapsed the NOC categories into just six groups.[4] Once again, results are shown separately for men and women. By far the most advantaged group is not the Canadian-born, but immigrants from anglo- or francophone countries, mainly the US and UK Over half of the men and 44 percent of the women born in these countries are in professional, technical, and managerial occupations, compared to approximately a third of native-born men and women. Why should immigrants from these countries do so well? Little research has paid specific attention to their situation, but it is likely a combination of their language ability, recognition of their credentials, and the fact that most immigrants from anglo- and francophone countries come to Canada as economic immigrants, often with arranged employment or as a result of a corporate transfer. Other groups that also exceed the Canadian-born in attainment of professional and managerial occupations are immigrants from Northwestern and Eastern Europe, both women and men, likely for similar reasons.

As was the case with visible minority groups in general, immigrants originating in less developed countries do not follow a single pattern. Asian-born men are more likely to be found in professional and managerial occupations than are Canadian-born men, but men born in Latin America or Africa or the Caribbean are less likely to be found in such occupations. Men born in these regions are also found in somewhat larger proportions in unskilled positions than are the Canadian-born. Non-European-origin women are uniformly less likely than native-born women to have attained professional or managerial occupations, though their representation in such occupations still exceeds that of Southern European-born women. Along with women born in Southern Europe, women originating in Latin America and Africa and the Caribbean are more likely than native-born women to be found in low-paying, unskilled occupations.

A recurrent issue both in research on the economic integration of immigrants and in policy circles is the extent to which the educational credentials immigrants earn in their countries of origin are recognized in the Canadian labour market. It is likely that the concentration of some immigrant groups in low-paying occupational categories is related to the failure of employers to give full value to their credentials, particularly if they were obtained in a less developed country. Table 7.5 addresses this issue by reporting both the occupations immigrants arriving in Canada between 1996 and 2001 indicated that they intended to practice in Canada, as recorded on their landing documents, and the occupations that were reported for this group of immigrants in the 2001 census.

It is clear that, for both women and men, the disparities in these distributions are considerable. Particularly striking is the observation that 59 percent of the men and nearly 44 percent of the women recently arrived in Canada intended to work in a professional occupation. By 2001, just 23.6 percent of the men and 17.5 percent off the women were actually observed in such occupations. Was their intention realistic? According to the 2001 census, over 52 percent of these men and nearly 38 percent of these women held at least one university degree, normally the requirement for professional employment, so only a fraction of them had unrealistic aspirations. When we recognize that half or more of Canadian-born workers with at least one degree are found in the professional ranks (see table 7.3), it becomes obvious that many of these immigrants are not working in occupations for which

Table 7.5
Intended and Observed Occupations of Immigrants Arriving in Canada 1996–2001 by Sex

Occupation	Intended Occupation Upon Landing[a]		Occupation Observed in Census[b]	
	Women	Men	Women	Men
Senior managers	0.1	0.3	0.4	0.8
Middle, other managers	2.3	3.3	5.3	8.6
Professionals	43.8	59.0	17.5	23.6
Semi-professionals	8.4	10.2	7.8	7.8
Admin, senior clerical	16.4	2.9	5.5	1.3
Skilled sales/service	4.8	5.2	4.0	4.7
Skilled crafts/trades	3.4	9.2	2.3	9.4
Clerical personnel	4.4	1.4	12.2	6.0
Intermediate sales/service	11.2	2.9	15.6	6.4
Semi-skilled manual	1.0	2.1	10.1	16.5
Elemental sales/service	1.1	0.6	14.6	10.1
Manual labour	3.2	3.1	4.8	4.9
TOTAL	100%	100%	100%	100%

a Tabulated from Citizenship and Immigration Canada's Landed Immigrant Data System.
b Tabulated from the 2001 Census of Canada Public Use Microdata File.

they were trained. Where are they found? By 2001, both women and men are overrepresented in the lowest paying occupational groups – semi-skilled manual, elemental sales and service, and manual labour.

DISCUSSION

As I indicated at the outset, the occupational structure in many respects forms the basis for a society's stratification system. Not only does it serve to transfer educational attainment and training into locations in the labour force, but also it attaches, in the form of earnings, rewards to specific jobs that form the occupational structure. Although not dealt with here, sociologists, and to a considerably lesser extent economists, have studied the mechanisms whereby status is transmitted across the generations in the form of occupational mobility processes. One of the main conclusions of such research is that there is considerable inheritance of occupational status, if not specific occupations, that remains in all advanced industrial societies, despite the decline in such inheritance that has taken place in the course of the twentieth century (Wanner 2005). Nevertheless the occupational structure is evolving over time, as we saw above, producing new opportunities and eliminating old ones, resulting in a certain amount of so-called structural mobility as some occupational categories shrink and others expand.

We have surveyed the long-term trends in Canada's industry and occupational structures, but it is dangerous to extrapolate those trends to a future filled with uncertainty. However, over the past few decades it has become clear that the rise of the service economy has been a mixed blessing, bringing with it both "good jobs" and "bad jobs," polarizing the occupational structure. Accompanying this trend has been increased income inequality, driven in part by lower earnings among young entrants to the labour market and recent immigrants. At the same time, employers have opted for more flexibility in their work forces, creating increasing numbers of part-time and temporary jobs, often outsourcing their employment requirements (Krahn and Lowe 2002).

With Canada's population aging and current government policy calling for yet more immigrants to make up for a flagging rate of natural increase, we must address the problem of utilizing fully the skills that immigrants bring to this country. It does not benefit Canada's economy to have trained engineers cleaning buildings. It is clear that the real problem lies in employers' failure to recognize credentials not earned in Canada, since immigrants who came to this country at an early age and are educated in Canada receive about the same return in the form of earnings to their credentials as do the Canadian born (Wanner 1998). While skills assessment programs are already in place in many provinces, governments must do more to convince employers of the value of immigrants' skills and eliminate artificial barriers to their ability to practice regulated occupations.

Aside from some comparisons to the industry structures of other countries, we have been looking at Canada's occupational structure in isolation instead of in the environment of economic globalization in which it functions. Just as in the past few decades manufacturing jobs have been "exported" to low-wage countries by multinational corporations intent on increasing profits, service jobs are beginning to be exported. These are not just low-wage telemarketing jobs being done by English-speaking telemarketers in Bangalore, India. Technological advances, particularly the growth of the Internet, have made it possible for companies to export virtually any business function, including accounting, computer programming, and even some medical and legal services (Babcock 2004). It is not clear what the implications of such "offshoring" of high-quality jobs will be for Canada specifically or the advanced industrial countries generally, since proponents argue that by enhancing productivity and profitability, offshoring will in the long run create even more jobs in the more developed countries. Regardless of the outcome, it is clear that, to succeed in the globally connected service economy that now exists, Canadians in increasing numbers must obtain advanced education and training to qualify for the better-quality jobs and avoid the low-paying jobs that are being created in our postindustrial economy.

NOTES

1 Unless otherwise noted, data reported in tables and figures are based on tabulations by the author using the 2001 Census of Canada Public Use Microdata File (Statistics Canada 2005).

2 The index of dissimilarity is computed as:

$$D = \sum\nolimits_{j=1}^{J} |\, F_j \,/\, F - M_j \,/\, M \,| \times 100 \times \frac{1}{2}$$

where J is the total number of occupations or occupational groups, F_j and M_j are the number of women or men in the jth occupation, and F and M represent the total number of women and men. The index has a straightforward interpretation: it represents the percentage of women (or men) who would have to change occupations to eliminate sex segregation in the labour force.

3 The term 'visible minority' is of Canadian origin, first appearing in the 1984 *Royal Commission Report on Equity in Employment* to identify one of the groups designated for special treatment by employers in government-regulated businesses under the *Employment Equity Act* of 1986. See Li (2003).

4 The categories have been collapsed as follows: managers (including senior, middle, and other managers); professional and technical (including professionals and semi-professionals); clerical (including administrative, senior clerical, clerical, and related supervisors); skilled (including skilled crafts and trades and sales and service); semi-skilled (including intermediate sales and service and semi-skilled manual); and unskilled (including manual labour and elemental sales and service).

REFERENCES

Babcock, Pamela. 2004. "America's Newest Export: White-Collar Jobs." HR *Magazine* 49: 50–7

Bell, Daniel. 1973. *The Coming of Post-Industrial Society: A Venture in Social Forecasting.* New York: Basic Books

Blishen, Bernard R. 1967. "A Socio-Economic Index for Occupations in Canada." *Canadian Review of Sociology and Anthropology* 4: 41–53

Bluestone, Barry, and Bennett Harrison. 1982. *The Deindustrialization of America.* New York: Basic Books

Charles, Maria, and David B. Grusky. 2004. *Occupational Ghettos: The Worldwide Segregation of Women and Men.* Stanford, CA: Stanford University Press

Clement, Wallace, and John Myles. 1994. *Relations of Ruling: Class and Gender in Postindustrial Societies.* Montreal: McGill-Queen's University Press

Fox, Bonnie J., and John Fox. 1987. "Occupational Gender Segregation of the Canadian Labour Force, 1931–1981." *Canadian Review of Sociology and Anthropology* 24: 374–97

High, Steven C. 2003. *Industrial Sunset: The Making of North America's Rust Belt, 1969–1984*. Toronto: University of Toronto Press

Krahn, Harvey J., and Graham S. Lowe. 2002. *Work, Industry, and Canadian Society*. Toronto: Thomson Nelson

Leacy, F.H., ed. 1983. *Historical Statistics of Canada*. Ottawa: Statistics Canada

Li, Peter S. 2003. *Destination Canada: Immigration Debates and Issues*. Toronto: Oxford University Press

OECD. 2000. "Employment in the Service Economy: A Reassessment." In OECD *Employment Outlook*, 79–128. Paris: Organization for Economic Cooperation and Development

Richardson, David H. 1997. "Changes in the Distribution of Wages in Canada, 1981–1992." *Canadian Journal of Economics* 30: 622–43

Singelmann, Joachim. 1978. "The Sectoral Transformation of the Labor Force in Seven Industrialized Countries, 1920–1970." *American Journal of Sociology* 83: 1224–34

Smucker, Joseph. 1980. *Industrialization in Canada*. Scarborough, Ont.: Prentice-Hall of Canada

Social Development Canada. 2001. "National Occupational Classification." www.sdc.gc.ca/en/hip/hrp/noc/noc_index.shtml (Accessed April 2010)

Statistics Canada. 1983. *Population: Labour Force Occupation Trends*. 1981 Census of Canada. Vol. 1. National Series. Ottawa, Ministry of Supply and Services. Cat. no. 92–920

– 1993. *The Nation: Employment Income by Occupation*. 1991 Census of Canada. Ottawa. Cat. no. 93–332

– 2001. 2001 Census of Canada. www12.statcan.ca/english/census01 (Accessed April 2010)

– 2005. 2001 Census. Public Use Microdata File: Individuals File User Documentation. Cat. no. 95M0016XCB

Wanner, Richard A. 1998. "Prejudice, Profit, or Productivity: Explaining Returns to Human Capital among Male Immigrants to Canada." *Canadian Ethnic Studies* 30: 24–55

– 2005. "Twentieth-Century Trends in Occupational Attainment in Canada." *Canadian Journal of Sociology* 30: 441–67

– 2009. "Social Mobility in Canada: Concepts, Patterns, and Trends." In *Social Inequality in Canada: Patterns, Problems, Policies*, eds. E. Grabb and N. Guppy, 116–32. 5th edition. Toronto: Pearson Prentice-Hall

Wanner, Richard A. and Michelle Ambrose. 2003. "Trends in the Occupational and Earnings Attainments of Women Immigrants to Canada, 1971–1996." *Canadian Studies in Population* 30: 355–88

PART THREE

Population Distribution and Migration

8

Spatial Distribution of Racial and Ethnic Groups in Canada

ERIC FONG AND ELIC CHAN

INTRODUCTION

Canada is a country of immigrants. People from many different countries have arrived in different periods. They settled in different parts of the country in response to the social and economic contexts at the time of their arrival. Gradually, settlement patterns associated with distinctive ethnic and linguistic groups in different regions emerged, sometimes referred to "multicultural regionalism" (Driedger 1996).

One of the most discussed and documented patterns of multicultural regionalism is the majority French population in Quebec. Their settlement pattern dates back to a few centuries ago when Samuel de Champlain settled in Montreal in 1608 (Quellet 1980). Since then, the French have maintained numeric dominance in the province.

In the east, the dominant ethnic group in the provinces of Newfoundland, Nova Scotia, and Prince Edward Island is British. Although these provinces took different paths to join Canadian confederation, they all share a strong British influence. Newfoundland was a British colony and joined confederation in 1949 (Neary 1988). Prince Edward Island, called Island of Saint John at the time, became a British colony in 1769 and joined the Dominion of Canada in 1873 (Bumsted 1987). New Brunswick was first settled by the French, who came to be known as Acadians. It became a British colony in 1784 and joined the original Confederation in 1867. The colonial period under the British has considerably influenced the ethnic representations in these provinces up to the present time. Their population still maintains a high British representation (Kalbach 1987).

There is also a considerable number of blacks clustered in Nova Scotia (Winks 1997). The considerable presence of blacks dates back to the American Revolution. British Empire loyalists fled the American colony with their possessions, including their slaves, and other blacks responded to the British offer of freedom and land.

Ontario developed differently. The southern part, previously called Upper Canada, also had an early concentration of British. Since the 1900s, Ontario, especially the city of Toronto, has attracted settlements of immigrants from different countries, largely because the region has been the engine of the Canadian economy and immigrants have been attracted to jobs available there (Lemon 1985). Immigrant groups arriving from a variety of countries in different periods contributed to Toronto becoming multi-ethnic. These immigrants include a large proportion of southern Europeans who arrived before and after the Second World War and a large number of non-Europeans who have come since the 1970s (Troper 2003).

Western Canada has been the home of early immigrants from Asian and European countries. A large number of Asians, first Chinese and later Japanese, arrived in British Columbia at the beginning of the last century (Lai 1988). Their immigration virtually stopped due to the Chinese Exclusion Act in 1923 and later the revised Japanese Gentlemen's Agreement in 1928. The Chinese moved eastward and gradually settled in other western provinces (Baureiss and Driedger 1982). With the development of the Prairies and the expansion of the country's economy at the beginning of the twentieth century, large numbers of northern and western Europeans were directly recruited to emigrate there. Later, many eastern and southern European immigrants settled there before and after the two world wars (Lemon 1985).

Since the change in immigration policies in the 1970s, Canada has experienced a new wave of immigration, bringing a large number of immigrants from non-European countries. With a growing visible-minority in the country, the dynamics of the settlement patterns of groups may be different from previous centuries. In this chapter, we identify the settlement patterns of major racial and ethnic groups in Canada at the beginning of the millennium. Our discussion includes settlement patterns in provinces and cities. To provide a more comprehensive understanding of these patterns, we also explore the neighbourhoods where these groups reside. In particular, we compare neighborhood qualities and racial and ethnic compositions. Taken together, the information not only helps us to understand the geographic distribution of groups, but also informs us of their neighborhood characteristics.

RACIAL AND ETHNIC DISTRIBUTION
IN CANADIAN PROVINCES

To understand the settlement patterns of major racial and ethnic groups in the Canadian provinces, we discuss the patterns of European groups, then visible-minority groups. European groups are discussed first because they arrived in large numbers in earlier periods. For space considerations, we discuss the settlement patterns of most major European groups reported in the national census, but not including the smaller groups. Nevertheless, the discussion still provides a general picture of geographic distribution of groups in Canada. In our report, we only include single ethnic responses. To avoid potential complication of interpretation, we do not include the people who gave multiple ethnic responses to avoid potential complication of interpretation.[1]

In table 8.1, we report the distribution among European ethnic groups in each province. Reflecting the historical settlement patterns in previous centuries, the two charter groups, English and French, still maintain different settlement patterns. Only two provinces, Ontario and British Columbia, account for more than two-thirds of the English population in Canada. About half of them are disproportionately concentrated in Ontario. However, the overwhelming majority of French, about 63 percent, resides in Quebec, while only 18 percent are in Ontario.

Other old European immigrant groups, such as Irish, German, and Dutch, are also heavily settled in Ontario and British Columbia. However, a considerable proportion of Germans are in the western provinces, such as Alberta. In the prairie provinces, German has the highest representation of all older European immigrant groups, such as Irish and Scottish, at 44 percent.

The new European immigrant groups, such as Polish, Italian, Portuguese, and Greek, are not as widely dispersed as the old European immigrant groups. Instead, they are heavily concentrated in Ontario, where more than half of their members reside. This pattern may reflect their ethnic clustering partly due to their recent arrival in previous decades. It is noteworthy to point out that the settlement patterns of Ukrainians are uniquely different from other new European immigrant groups. A large proportion of them reside in the west. Altogether, about 69 percent of Ukrainians are in the four provinces west of Ontario.

In short, the results show a common pattern among most European groups clustered in Ontario, with the exception of the French, Germans, and Ukrainians. These patterns may reflect the dominant population size of Ontario among all other provinces, and also the historical settlement of these groups.

Table 8.1
Distribution Among Major European Groups by Province, 2001

Province	English (%)	French (%)	Scottish (%)	Irish (%)	German (%)	Dutch (%)	Ukrainian (%)	Polish (%)	Italian (%)	Portuguese (%)	Greek (%)	Jewish (%)
British Columbia	18.4	3.5	15.9	10.3	17.5	18.6	12.5	9.1	6.4	6.5	5.8	5.3
Prairies	15.9	7.6	17.4	13.7	44.3	23.2	56.4	20.0	4.5	6.3	4.6	7.9
Ontario	47.3	17.8	46.4	47.0	32.1	53.5	27.6	62.2	66.3	72.3	56.4	57.8
Quebec	3.0	63.4	4.1	10.8	2.9	1.5	2.8	7.7	22.3	14.5	31.9	28.2
Maritimes Provinces	15.1	7.7	16.0	17.9	3.0	3.1	0.5	1.0	0.5	0.4	1.2	0.8
The Territories	0.2	0.1	0.2	0.2	0.2	0.1	0.2	0.1	0.0	0.0	0.0	0.0
TOTAL N	1,479,530	1,060,750	712,790	565,155	1,018,165	389,685	510,195	312,555	758,745	268,785	150,455	201,230

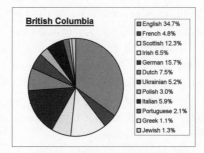

British Columbia

| English 34.7% |
| French 4.8% |
| Scottish 12.3% |
| Irish 6.5% |
| German 15.7% |
| Dutch 7.5% |
| Ukrainian 5.2% |
| Polish 3.0% |
| Italian 5.9% |
| Portuguese 2.1% |
| Greek 1.1% |
| Jewish 1.3% |

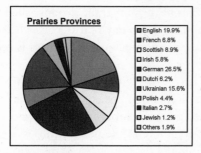

Prairies Provinces

| English 19.9% |
| French 6.8% |
| Scottish 8.9% |
| Irish 5.8% |
| German 26.5% |
| Dutch 6.2% |
| Ukrainian 15.6% |
| Polish 4.4% |
| Italian 2.7% |
| Jewish 1.2% |
| Others 1.9% |

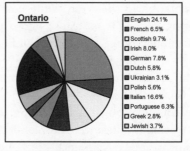

Ontario

| English 24.1% |
| French 6.5% |
| Scottish 9.7% |
| Irish 8.0% |
| German 7.8% |
| Dutch 5.8% |
| Ukrainian 3.1% |
| Polish 5.6% |
| Italian 16.6% |
| Portuguese 6.3% |
| Greek 2.8% |
| Jewish 3.7% |

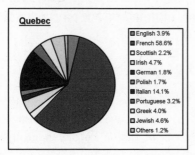

Quebec

| English 3.9% |
| French 58.6% |
| Scottish 2.2% |
| Irish 4.7% |
| German 1.8% |
| Polish 1.7% |
| Italian 14.1% |
| Portuguese 3.2% |
| Greek 4.0% |
| Jewish 4.6% |
| Others 1.2% |

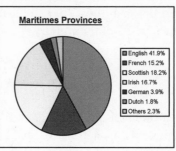

Maritimes Provinces

| English 41.9% |
| French 15.2% |
| Scottish 18.2% |
| Irish 16.7% |
| German 3.9% |
| Dutch 1.8% |
| Others 2.3% |

Graph 8.1
Distribution Among Major European Groups in Provinces and Regions, 2001

To further explore group settlement patterns, we turn our discussion to group representation in each province, reported in graph 8.1. This information provides another means to understanding group settlement in Canada. We realize that group sizes in each province are strongly affected by their overall population size in Canada. Therefore, instead of comparing group sizes within provinces, our discussion will focus on the variations of group representation in provinces.

As expected, the large size of the English population reflects their considerable representation in all provinces, especially in the Maritimes. Forty-two percent of the population of the Maritime provinces is English. Together with the Scots and Irish, they represent more than 77 percent of the total population there. Despite their high concentration in Ontario, as suggested in the previous table, the English represent a moderate percentage of that province. The results reflect the multi-ethnic component of Ontario, where many diverse groups have also settled. French, the other Charter group, has larger representation not only in Quebec (59 percent) but also in the Maritimes (15 percent). Their representation largely reflects the early French settlement in Canada.

Old European immigrant groups, especially German, show higher representation in the west, while new European immigrant groups, such as Portuguese and Greek, show higher representation in Ontario. Nevertheless, the population of new European immigrant groups in all provinces is relatively small in general.

In sum, the results show a continuation of regional ethnic distribution in Canada (Driedger 1996). Although Canadian society has experienced the continuation of urbanization, fast growing suburbanization, and the increasing significance of a high-tech economy in the past centuries, these major societal developments have not altered the settlement patterns of major European groups. They still maintain disproportionate representation in different parts of the country.

DISTRIBUTION OF EUROPEAN GROUPS
IN MAJOR CITIES

Given the high level of urbanization in Canada, we focus our discussion in this section on the settlement patterns of major European groups in Canadian cities. We report distribution among European groups in the major Canadian cities in table 8.2.

The results in table 8.2 echo findings described in earlier tables. As expected, most English are in Toronto and Vancouver, two major cities in Ontario and British Columbia, while the French are mainly in Montreal and Quebec City, both cities in Quebec. The distribution of old European immigrant groups such as Scottish, Irish, German, and Dutch, are more dispersed. Among the included cities, Toronto and Vancouver have 15 percent or more of each of these groups (except Irish has close to 10 percent in Vancouver). In addition, Montreal and Ottawa have more than 10 percent Irish; Calgary and Edmonton, German; and Edmonton, London, and Hamilton, Dutch. New European immigrant groups, such as the Italians, Portuguese, and Greeks, are mainly clustered in Toronto and Montreal. Over 50 percent of the new European immigrant groups are settled in these two cities.

Table 8.2

Distribution Among Major European Groups by Major Canadian Cities, 2001

Major Canadian Cities	English (%)	French (%)	Scottish (%)	Irish (%)	German (%)	Dutch (%)	Ukrainian (%)	Polish (%)	Italian (%)	Portuguese (%)	Greek (%)	Jewish (%)
WESTERN CANADA												
Vancouver	16.77	2.86	15.37	9.64	19.59	18.10	12.62	8.58	5.10	4.61	5.11	4.75
Victoria	5.45	0.56	4.02	2.06	3.01	3.57	1.78	0.92	0.34	0.76	0.34	0.36
Calgary	7.49	1.98	8.84	6.59	15.01	9.80	10.47	5.46	1.90	0.99	1.43	2.11
Edmonton	5.88	2.84	6.74	5.48	18.05	11.92	31.08	7.57	1.57	2.35	1.06	1.35
ONTARIO												
Toronto	31.46	4.85	30.95	30.63	22.55	23.43	28.31	48.87	53.18	62.79	48.97	55.68
Hamilton	7.89	1.28	8.80	5.53	4.93	12.95	5.14	8.35	6.86	5.34	2.35	1.11
London	5.57	0.76	5.33	4.10	3.66	11.02	1.67	4.88	1.26	3.99	2.00	0.48
Ottawa	5.89	11.11	6.86	10.43	4.57	5.10	2.78	4.44	2.91	3.24	2.32	3.22
QUÉBEC												
Montréal	4.34	55.72	5.28	11.39	5.81	2.50	5.59	10.06	26.48	15.32	35.26	30.40
Québec City	0.16	16.27	0.63	1.87	0.51	0.12	0.06	0.26	0.17	0.39	0.20	0.03
ATLANTIC PROVINCES												
Halifax	4.04	1.62	6.52	4.71	2.15	1.42	0.47	0.58	0.19	0.18	0.94	0.50
St John's	5.06	0.14	0.67	7.56	0.15	0.09	0.02	0.05	0.02	0.04	0.03	0.01
TOTAL N	673,345	526,165	272,755	239,730	226,990	116,680	143,765	170,450	581,675	205,895	126,520	171,330

Table 8.3
Distribution Among Major European Groups in Major Canadian cities, 2001

Major Canadian Cities	English (%)	French (%)	Scottish (%)	Irish (%)	German (%)	Dutch (%)	Ukrainian (%)	Polish (%)	Italian (%)	Portuguese (%)	Greek (%)	Jewish
WESTERN CANADA												
Vancouver	32.72	4.36	12.15	6.70	12.88	6.12	5.26	4.24	8.60	2.75	1.87	2.36
Victoria	48.72	3.94	14.57	6.56	9.08	5.54	3.40	2.08	2.64	2.08	0.56	0.83
Calgary	26.66	5.51	12.74	8.36	18.01	6.04	7.96	4.92	5.85	1.08	0.96	1.91
Edmonton	18.32	6.91	8.51	6.08	18.96	6.43	20.68	5.97	4.23	2.24	0.62	1.07
ONTARIO												
Toronto	17.75	2.14	7.07	6.15	4.29	2.29	3.41	6.98	25.91	10.83	5.19	7.99
Hamilton	26.46	3.35	11.95	6.60	5.58	7.52	3.68	7.09	19.86	5.48	1.48	0.94
London	32.17	3.43	12.46	8.43	7.12	11.02	2.06	7.13	6.27	7.04	2.17	0.70
Ottawa	19.65	28.97	9.27	12.40	5.14	2.95	1.98	3.75	8.40	3.31	1.45	2.74
QUÉBEC												
Montréal	4.25	42.64	2.10	3.97	1.92	0.42	1.17	2.49	22.40	4.59	6.49	7.57
Québec City	1.11	88.39	1.78	4.63	1.20	0.14	0.09	0.45	1.05	0.84	0.26	0.05
ATLANTIC PROVINCES												
Halifax	35.57	11.11	23.23	14.76	6.39	2.16	0.88	1.29	1.45	0.48	1.56	1.12
St John's	61.27	1.36	3.26	32.59	0.63	0.18	0.06	0.14	0.25	0.14	0.06	0.04
TOTAL N	461,405	497,505	190,865	190,420	134,155	73,025	97,650	144,520	536,975	195,865	117,985	164,800

Table 8.3 continues to examine distribution among European groups in major Canadian cities, and compares the composition of European groups in each of these cities. The representations of these groups in major cities generally reflect their provincial distribution, such as the English having considerable representation in cities in British Columbia and Ontario, or the French in Quebec. However, their presence is substantially varied among cities within each province. Results show that a higher percentage of English is reported in Victoria than in Vancouver, and a higher percentage of French in Quebec City than in Montreal. In addition, there is a much higher percentage of Ukrainians in Edmonton than in Calgary, and Italians have a higher percentage in Toronto and Hamilton than in other Ontario cities.

With the results from the previous two tables, it is clear that multicultural regionalism still persists, and that European groups are clustered in some provinces and cities. We now turn to discuss the visible-minority settlement patterns in Canada. Most visible-minority groups arrived in Canada in recent decades. By taking their patterns into account, we are able to provide a more comprehensive picture of the settlement patterns of groups in Canada.

DISTRIBUTION OF VISIBLE MINORITIES IN CANADIAN PROVINCES

One of the major changes in Canadian society at the end of the last century was an extremely large increase in the number of visible minorities. At the beginning of the twentieth century, their presence was negligible. The 1901 census recorded about 17,000 blacks, 17,000 Chinese, 4,700 Japanese, the three major visible-minority groups at that time (Fong 1993; Adachi 1976). In 2001, about six million visible minorities were counted in the census.

The significant growth of visible minorities in Canada began in the late 1970s. The implementation in 1967 of the point system, which emphasizes the human capital of immigrants instead of ethnic origin, led to a growing number of applicants from non-European countries.

To examine the settlement patterns of the visible-minority population in Canada, we first report the provincial distribution among the five largest visible-minority groups in table 8.4. Results clearly suggest an uneven provincial distribution of these groups. Ontario and British Columbia stand out as having the largest visible-minority population. Ontario alone contains half of Canada's visible-minority population (over 1.7 million). At the same time, other provinces in the Maritimes and the territories in the north have only about 1 percent of Canada's total visible-minorities. The results strongly point out that the growing representation of visible minorities is concentrated in a few provinces.

Table 8.4
Distribution Among Major Visible Minority Groups by Province, 2001

Province	Chinese (%)	South Asian (%)	Black (%)	Filipino (%)	Latin American (%)
British Columbia	35.5	22.9	3.8	20.8	11.0
Prairies	11.6	9.4	7.3	21.9	11.8
Ontario	46.8	60.5	62.1	50.8	49.3
Quebec	5.5	6.5	23.0	6.0	27.4
Maritime Provinces	0.6	0.6	3.7	0.4	0.5
The Territories	0.0	0.0	0.0	0.0	0.0
TOTAL N	1,028,880	916,650	710,230	375,295	242,400

Although visible-minority groups tend to be concentrated in a few provinces, their representation there varies. The Chinese are heavily concentrated in British Columbia and Ontario, about 82 percent. Although other visible-minority groups are also concentrated in these two provinces, a considerably higher percentage settles in Ontario than in British Columbia.

There is also a high proportion of Chinese in the Prairies. This pattern may reflect Chinese historical settlement patterns in the west, which began as early as the late 1880s. Traveling across the Pacific, they mostly clustered in British Columbia and later migrated eastward to Alberta and Saskatchewan.

Among the visible-minority groups in the Maritime provinces, there is a larger percentage of blacks. About 4 percent of blacks as compared to only about 0.5 percent of other visible-minority groups are settled in these provinces. There is also a high proportion of blacks in Quebec, reflecting recent French-speaking immigrants from African countries.

In graph 8.2, we present distribution among visible-minority groups in each province/region in Canada. The results show that the Chinese have a high representation among all visible-minority groups in the western provinces (British Columbia and the Prairie provinces). Over one-third of the visible-minority population in the Prairie provinces is Chinese. Filipinos, on the other hand, have a higher concentration in the Prairies than in other provinces. Blacks are heavily represented in the Maritime provinces and Quebec. In short, the data show that patterns of multicultural regionalism have emerged among visible-minority groups.

We follow the earlier discussion and explore the settlement patterns of visible minorities in major cities. Table 8.5 shows distribution among five visible-minority groups in the major Canadian cities. Most striking is the high concentration of visible minorities in the three largest cities: Toronto,

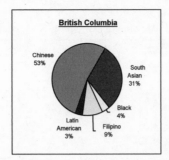

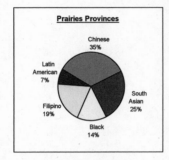

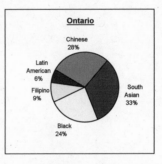

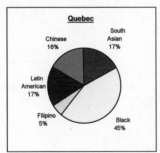

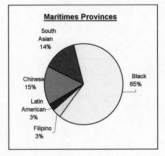

Graph 8.2
Distribution Among Major Visible Minority Groups in Provinces and Regions, 2001

Montreal, and Vancouver. They comprise over 80 percent of the total visible-minority population in major Canadian cities. The six cities that have the most visible-minority population are Toronto, Vancouver, Montreal, Ottawa, Calgary, and Edmonton. Together, they hold more than 90 percent of the visible-minority population in major Canadian cities. In particular, Toronto is the most popular city for all visible-minority groups. All groups have at least 40 percent of their population residing in Toronto. The data seem to suggest a general immigrant settlement pattern that recently arrived immigrants are attracted to places where ethnic communities are located

Table 8.5

Distribution Among Major Visible Minority Groups by Major Canadian Cities, 2001

Major Canadian Cities	Chinese (%)	South Asian (%)	Black (%)	Filipino (%)	Latin American (%)
WESTERN CANADA					
Vancouver	35.87	20.22	3.21	22.51	10.14
Victoria	1.18	0.71	0.38	0.71	0.63
Calgary	5.43	4.53	2.38	6.46	4.66
Edmonton	4.32	3.58	2.46	5.59	4.07
ONTARIO					
Toronto	42.87	58.30	54.11	52.76	41.12
Hamilton	0.94	1.76	2.24	1.95	2.68
London	0.49	0.61	1.33	0.64	2.42
Ottawa	3.02	2.74	6.65	2.06	4.15
QUÉBEC					
Montréal	5.45	7.13	24.27	7.06	28.80
Québec City	0.13	0.04	0.63	0.02	1.09
ATLANTIC PROVINCES					
Halifax	0.26	0.29	2.28	0.19	0.22
St John's	0.05	0.09	0.06	0.05	0.03
TOTAL N	955,390	812,710	573,855	253,385	184,610

Table 8.6

Distribution Among Major Visible Minority Groups in Major Canadian Cities, 2001

Major Canadian Cities	Chinese (%)	South Asian (%)	Black (%)	Filipino (%)	Latin American (%)
WESTERN CANADA					
Vancouver	57.0	27.3	3.1	9.5	3.1
Victoria	50.7	26.1	9.8	8.2	5.2
Calgary	40.7	28.9	10.7	12.9	6.8
Edmonton	38.9	27.4	13.3	13.4	7.1
ONTARIO					
Toronto	29.2	33.8	22.1	9.5	5.4
Hamilton	19.5	31.0	27.9	10.8	10.8
London	20.0	21.1	32.7	7.0	19.2
Ottawa	28.2	21.8	37.4	5.1	7.5
QUÉBEC					
Montréal	16.3	18.1	43.5	5.6	16.6
Québec City	17.4	4.7	49.7	0.8	27.4
ATLANTIC PROVINCES					
Halifax	13.0	12.5	69.8	2.5	2.2
St John's	29.1	41.6	19.6	6.4	3.4
TOTAL N	955,390	812,710	573,855	253,385	184,610

and job opportunities are available. Subsequently, visible minorities concentrate in large urban areas, and the growing multi-ethnic component largely occurs there.

Table 8.6 reports the distribution among visible-minority groups in each city. The patterns largely reflect their clustering in different provinces. However, there are considerable variations in the cities within provinces. As reported in table 8.6, the Chinese are heavily represented in cities in the west. They are the largest visible-minority group in Vancouver, Victoria, Calgary, and Edmonton. However, their representation in these cities varies from 39 percent to 57 percent. The larger settlement of South Asians is found in Ontario, but mainly in cities with a large industrial base, such as Toronto and Hamilton. Given the large settlement of blacks in the maritime provinces and Quebec, their representations in cities there is substantial in comparison with other visible-minority groups. In addition, they have large representation in major cities in Quebec, such as Montreal and Quebec City.

Overall, tables 8.5 and 8.6 show that visible-minority groups are clustered in a few provinces and highly concentrated in a few major cities in these provinces. The settlement patterns of these visible-minority groups imply that Canada is only multi-ethnic in a few major large cities in a few provinces. At the same time, despite the recent arrival of these new immigrants, their present settlement patterns show an uneven distribution of visible-minority groups in different parts of the country.

NEIGHBOURHOOD QUALITIES
AMONG RACIAL AND ETHNIC GROUPS

The settlement patterns of racial and ethnic groups in Canada inform us of the regional distribution of groups. However, we do not know about the neighborhood characteristics where they reside in these provinces and cities. In the following sections, we explore the patterns of neighbourhood characteristics among racial and ethnic groups. We focus on two aspects of neighborhood characteristics: neighbourhood qualities and group composition in neighbourhoods.

A comparison of neighbourhood qualities among groups has significant implications. Since neighbourhood qualities are associated with the life chances of those residing there, group disparity in neighbourhood qualities suggests unequal life chances (Massey and Denton 1998; Wilson 1987). In addition, neighbourhood qualities among groups inform their residential integration, especially for visible-minority groups who arrived in recent decades.

We report the neighbourhood qualities of European and visible-minority groups in table 8.7.[2] The analysis only included neighbourhoods of the four largest cities, Toronto, Montreal, Vancouver, and Calgary, because visible minorities are highly concentrated in these cities.[3] Eight characteristics that reflect the social, demographic, and economic dimensions of neighbourhoods are discussed. Together, they portray a comprehensive picture of the neighbourhoods where these groups reside.

The results show a clear pattern that English and old European immigrant groups, followed by recent European immigrant groups, are living in neighbourhoods with better qualities. Visible-minority groups are residing in the least desirable neighbourhoods. Specifically, English and old European immigrant groups are living in neighbourhoods with a lower proportion of residents not knowing either official language, a lower unemployment rate, a lower percentage of low-income households, higher housing values, and lower housing density.

The neighbourhood qualities of French are uniquely different from other European groups. On the one hand, their neighbourhoods have a lower proportion of residents not knowing either official language and a lower immigrant population than other old European immigrant groups. On the other hand, their neighbourhoods have lower household income and housing values than those of visible-minority groups. These patterns may in fact reflect the general neighbourhood pattern in Quebec, as the majority of French concentrate there.

Of all groups, Vietnamese are the most disadvantaged. They live in neighbourhoods with the lowest proportions of university-educated residents, the highest unemployment rates, the highest proportion of low-income households, the lowest average household income, the lowest housing values, and the lowest rental values. Despite being in Canada for more than 20 years, when the majority of them arrived as refugees, most of them have not been able to move into neighbourhoods with better qualities.

NEIGHBOURHOOD RACIAL AND ETHNIC COMPOSITION AMONG GROUPS

The second aspect of the racial and ethnic settlement patterns in our study is the group composition in neighbourhoods. The comparison provides information on the level of sharing neighbourhoods among groups. Such information helps us to understand the possibilities for group interaction in an informal environment, which is considered to be crucial in fostering intergroup understanding (Forbes 1997).

Table 8.7

Neighbourhood Qualities of Major Racial and Ethnic Groups in Toronto, Montreal, Vancouver, and Calgary, 2001

Major European Groups	English	French	Scottish	Irish	German	Dutch	Italian	Portuguese	Greek	Jewish
Proportion of pop. w/ no knowledge of official language	0.024	0.013	0.023	0.022	0.024	0.021	0.040	0.059	0.046	0.028
Proportion of Immigrant Population (after 1991)	0.314	0.301	0.313	0.306	0.319	0.293	0.278	0.314	0.337	0.341
Population 15 years and over – Unemployment rate	5.829	6.943	5.797	5.946	5.896	5.557	6.295	6.526	7.669	6.361
Proportion of population with a University degree	0.331	0.271	0.330	0.320	0.320	0.307	0.262	0.266	0.320	0.481
Population in private households – Incidence of low income %	15.28	20.40	15.24	16.07	15.72	13.90	17.55	19.65	21.51	17.57
Household income – Average household income $	$ 77,530	$ 58,982	$ 77,145	$ 74,907	$ 74,890	$ 76,984	$ 70,089	$ 63,408	$ 65,997	$ 90,622
Average value of dwelling $	$ 263,899	$ 156,923	$ 257,650	$ 242,986	$ 250,208	$ 256,953	$ 242,364	$ 223,353	$ 227,278	$ 331,966
Household Density (persons/household)	2.735	2.443	2.713	2.682	2.741	2.787	2.911	2.857	2.762	2.695

Major Visible Minority Groups	Chinese	East Indian	Filipino	Jamaican	Vietnamese	Blacks
Proportion of pop. w/ no knowledge of official language	0.071	0.054	0.048	0.045	0.060	0.041
Proportion of Immigrant Population (after 1991)	0.438	0.415	0.430	0.405	0.398	0.394
Population 15 years and over – Unemployment rate	7.408	7.211	7.492	7.265	8.573	8.155
Proportion of population with a University degree	0.361	0.284	0.316	0.266	0.263	0.265
Population in private households – Incidence of low income %	22.32	19.91	22.71	22.19	26.74	25.31
Household income – Average household income $	$ 69,144	$ 68,031	$ 62,652	$ 63,933	$ 55,663	$ 58,580
Average value of dwelling $	$ 275,948	$ 233,776	$ 233,304	$ 217,529	$ 211,197	$ 201,295
Household Density (persons/household)	2.948	3.212	2.865	3.098	2.820	2.848

In tables 8.8 and 8.9, we report the racial and ethnic composition of groups in the four largest Canadian cities. The table shows five major patterns. First, all groups are residing in multi-ethnic neighbourhoods. All neighbourhoods have a considerable proportion of diverse racial and ethnic groups. This pattern reflects the growing multi-ethnic composition in these major cities. No group experiences extreme segregation. The results may reflect the increase in various racial and ethnic groups due to recent immigration. Second, despite the multi-ethnic composition of neighbourhoods, results indicate that, among all major European groups, English and old European immigrant groups are more likely to share their neighbourhoods with their own groups. Their neighbourhoods have a higher percentage of English, German, Scottish, and Dutch. These results suggest that visible-minority groups may have less opportunity to share neighbourhoods with the charter groups and old European immigrant groups. Third, new European immigrant groups are residing in ethnic-clustered neighbourhoods. They are more likely to share their neighbourhoods with their own group. For example, Italians are residing in neighbourhoods that are 41 percent Italian, Portuguese in neighbourhoods that are 20 percent Portuguese. Fourth, similar to new European immigrant groups, though visible-minority groups are not necessarily residing in neighbourhoods with a high concentration of their own group, they are more likely to share neighbourhoods with other visible-minority groups. Their neighbourhoods are about 50 percent visible minorities. The results of high clustering of new European immigrant groups and visible-minority groups may reflect that their recent arrival draws their members together. Finally, Chinese, Italians, and Jews are highly concentrated. Although their arrival periods are varied, their own groups comprise 47 percent, 41 percent, and 36 percent respectively of their neighbourhood population. The concentration implies existing ethnic neighbourhoods and support for ethnic activities. In turn, concentration serves as a centrifugal force that further attracts members to the neighbourhoods and sustains the presence of ethnic neighbourhoods.

CONCLUSION

At the beginning of a new century, multicultural regionalism in Canada has not disappeared. Various European groups still are unevenly represented in different regions, provinces, and cities. Compounding the complexity of the situation, the newly arrived European groups and visible-minority groups in the last few decades also show a considerably uneven distribution in provinces and cities. The uneven distribution of visible-minority groups

Table 8.8

Group Composition in Neighbourhoods by Major European Groups in Toronto, Montreal, Vancouver, and Calgary, 2001

Group Composition in Neighbourhoods	English (%)	French (%)	Scottish (%)	Irish (%)	German (%)	Dutch (%)	Ukrainian (%)	Polish (%)	Italian (%)	Portuguese (%)	Greek (%)	Jewish (%)
English	15.4	5.8	14.7	13.5	14.3	15.9	11.7	9.2	4.4	5.4	4.9	4.2
French	2.9	31.4	3.3	5.3	3.4	2.8	3.0	2.9	3.3	2.9	3.5	2.6
Italian	8.3	12.4	8.4	9.4	8.0	8.1	10.0	11.2	41.2	15.2	9.3	7.1
German	4.9	2.3	4.9	4.3	6.5	6.0	4.6	3.0	1.5	1.6	1.6	1.3
Scottish	5.9	2.7	6.5	5.6	5.7	6.3	4.8	3.7	1.8	2.2	2.1	1.6
Irish	4.4	3.5	4.5	5.1	4.1	4.6	3.7	3.2	1.6	1.9	1.8	1.3
Ukrainian	2.4	1.3	2.5	2.4	2.8	2.6	4.9	3.2	1.1	1.5	0.9	1.1
Dutch	2.4	0.9	2.4	2.1	2.6	4.7	1.9	1.3	0.7	0.8	0.5	0.5
Polish	3.3	2.1	3.3	3.5	3.2	3.0	5.5	7.8	2.1	3.2	1.8	1.8
Portuguese	3.1	3.4	3.2	3.4	2.6	3.2	4.2	5.2	4.7	19.7	2.9	1.3
Jewish	2.3	2.9	2.2	2.3	2.0	1.8	3.0	2.9	2.1	1.3	3.8	35.5
Greek	2.0	2.9	2.1	2.3	1.9	1.4	1.9	2.0	2.0	2.0	11.3	2.8
Chinese	16.5	7.6	16.0	14.4	17.8	14.9	15.7	11.7	8.8	11.3	14.4	11.4
East Indian	9.6	4.0	9.7	9.0	10.2	10.6	8.8	10.7	7.8	9.4	8.2	3.8
Filipino	4.3	2.2	4.3	4.2	4.4	3.7	4.8	5.5	2.5	3.8	3.6	4.4
Jamaican	2.5	1.0	2.5	2.6	1.8	2.1	2.0	3.3	2.6	3.6	2.0	1.2
Vietnamese	1.3	1.9	1.2	1.2	1.6	1.3	1.6	2.0	1.6	2.4	1.3	0.9
Black	8.5	11.9	8.4	9.5	7.0	6.8	8.0	11.1	10.2	11.8	8.7	5.3

Table 8.9

Group Composition in Neighbourhoods by Major Visible Minority Groups in Toronto, Montreal, Vancouver, and Calgary, 2001

Group Composition in Neighbourhoods	Chinese (%)	East Indian (%)	Filipino (%)	Jamaican (%)	Vietnamese (%)	Blacks (%)
English	5.6	5.5	6.2	5.4	4.8	5.3
French	1.3	1.2	1.6	1.1	3.6	3.7
Italian	5.6	8.4	6.8	10.5	11.4	12.0
German	2.1	2.0	2.2	1.4	2.0	1.5
Scottish	2.2	2.3	2.5	2.1	1.9	2.1
Irish	1.6	1.7	2.0	1.8	1.5	1.9
Ukrainian	1.1	1.1	1.4	0.9	1.2	1.0
Dutch	0.8	0.9	0.8	0.7	0.7	0.6
Polish	1.4	2.2	2.8	2.5	2.6	2.5
Portuguese	2.2	3.2	3.2	4.5	5.3	4.3
Jewish	2.1	1.2	3.6	1.5	1.8	1.8
Greek	2.0	1.9	2.1	1.8	1.9	2.2
Chinese	47.3	16.6	21.5	11.7	21.1	11.5
East Indian	9.8	27.6	14.1	16.6	11.6	13.5
Filipino	5.0	5.6	11.2	5.4	6.3	5.2
Jamaican	1.8	4.4	3.6	8.5	3.2	6.3
Vietnamese	1.9	1.8	2.5	1.9	6.4	2.1
Black	6.2	12.4	12.0	21.7	12.5	22.3

in provinces and cities suggests that the growing multi-ethnic nature of Canada only occurs in a few major cities. Thus, there is strong evidence of a continuation and growing divergence of racial and ethnic composition among provinces and cities at the beginning of the new millennium.

Not only are groups unevenly distributed among cities, they are also unevenly distributed within cities and living in neighbourhoods with uneven qualities. We have found evidence that English and other old European immigrant groups are living in neighbourhoods with better qualities, followed by new European immigrant groups. Visible minority groups usually are living in neighbourhoods with the least desirable characteristics. We have also found that English and older European immigrant groups are more likely to share neighbourhoods among themselves, while new European immigrant groups and visible-minority groups tend to cluster.

This chapter has focused on the geographic settlement patterns and neighbourhood characteristics of racial and ethnic groups in Canada. Both are essential for understanding the changing context of racial and ethnic relations in Canada. Since the geographic settlement patterns of groups continue to be distinctive among cities and within cities, the issues that confront these groups vary according to the regions, provinces, cities, and neighbourhoods where they are concentrated. Porter (1965) proposed the concept of the vertical mosaic to describe the social- and political-resource distribution among groups in Canada almost half a century ago. He did not envision that at the beginning of a new century, the "horizontal mosaic," in which groups are distributed unevenly, would be another important dimension to understand in Canadian society.

NOTES

1 Respondents were asked to self identify up to four ethnic backgrounds. The single ethnic response comprises those respondents who reported only one ethnic background. Multiple ethnic responses are those reporting more than one ethnic background.
2 We used census tracts as proxy for neighbourhoods. Census tracts are defined by Statistics Canada as the geostatistical areas with an average of 4000 persons with similar social background. The boundaries of census tracts are usually along major roads, landmarks, or geographic landscape.
3 The results are the average of neighbourhood characteristics weighted by the number of group members in the neighbourhoods.

REFERENCES

Adachi, Ken. 1976. *The Enemy That Never Was: History of Japanese Canadians.* Toronto: McClelland & Stewart

Andrew, Sheila M. 1996. *Development of Elites in Acadian New Brunswick, 1861–1881.* Montreal: McGill-Queen's University Press

Baureiss, Gunter, and Leo Driedger. 1982. "Winnipeg's Chinatown: Demographic, Ecological and Organizational Change, 1900–1980." *Urban History Review* 10: 11–24

Bumsted, J.M. 1987. *Land, Settlement, and Politics on Eighteenth-Century Prince Edward Island.* Montreal: McGill-Queen's University Press

Driedger, Leo. 1996. *Multi-Ethnic Canada: Identities and Inequalities.* Toronto: Oxford University Press

Fong, Eric. 1993. *Racial Residential Segregation in American and Canadian Cities.* Unpublished Dissertation. University of Toronto

Forbes, H. Donald. 1997. *Ethnic Conflict: Commerce, Culture, and the Contract Hypothesis.* New Haven, CT: Yale University Press

Kalbach, Warren E. 1987. "Growth and Distribution of Canada's Ethnic Populations, 1871–1981." In *Ethnic Canada: Identities and Inequalities,* ed. Leo Driedger, 82–110. Toronto: Copp Clark Pitman Ltd

Lai, Chuen-yan David. 1988. *Chinatowns: Towns within Cities in Canada.* Vancouver: University of British Columbia Press

Lemon, James. 1985. *Toronto Since 1918: An Illustrated History.* Toronto: James Lorimer & Company

Massey, Douglas, and Nancy Denton. 1998. *American Apartheid: Segregation and the Making of the Underclass.* Boston: Harvard University Press

Neary, Peter M. 1988. *Newfoundland in the North Atlantic World, 1929–1949.* Montreal: McGill-Queen's University Press

Ouellet, Fernand. 1980. *Economic and Social History of Quebec, 1760–1850.* Ottawa: Carleton University Press

Porter, John. 1965. *The Vertical Mosaic: An Analysis of Social Class and Power in Canada.* Toronto: University of Toronto Press

Troper, Harold. 2003. "Becoming an Immigrant City: A History of Immigration into Toronto Since the Second World War." In *The World in a City*, eds. Paul Anisef and Michael Lanphier, 19–65. Toronto: University of Toronto Press

Wilson, William J. 1987. *The Truly Disadvantaged: The Inner City, the Underclass, and Public Policy.* Chicago: University of Chicago Press

Winks, Robin W. 1997. *The Blacks in Canada.* Montreal: McGill-Queen's University Press

9

Urbanization and the Growth
of the Canadian City

K. BRUCE NEWBOLD

INTRODUCTION

According to the 2001 Census, nearly 80 percent of Canada's population lived in an urban area, with Canada's urban hierarchy dominated by Toronto, Montréal, and Vancouver. With populations of 4.7, 3.4, and 2.0 million, respectively, these three metropolitan areas accounted for 35 percent of Canada's population in 2001. Canada's evolving urban settlement system is, however, much more than these three centres. Over the 1996 to 2001 interval, Canada's urban population grew faster (6.5 percent) than its overall population growth (4.0 percent), Ottawa-Gatineau joined the list of one-million cities, and Canada's population became increasingly concentrated in its largest urbanized regions, creating new "megapolitan" areas such as Southern Ontario's Golden Horseshoe or the West Coast's Vancouver-Victoria megapolitan region.

The growth of Canada's urban system represents a remarkable transformation in the character, structure, and distribution of its population. As Canada transitioned into the twentieth century, its population totaled just 5.4 million. With less than 40 percent of its population living in urban areas, its society was predominately rural and agricultural. Even by mid-century, Canada's population had grown to just 7.9 million, and less than 60 percent of Canadians lived in metropolitan areas. As Canada entered the twenty-first century, its population exceeded 30 million, and it was one of the most urbanized countries in the world. The vast majority of Canadians now live in urban places, with Canada's remnant rural population largely located in the peripheral areas around urban areas. In fact, only 2.4 percent of Canada's population was defined as "rural farm" in 2001, down from 3.0 percent in 1996 (Statistics Canada 2005a).

Although the outcome of a process that spanned a century, Canada's urban growth was initiated with industrialization that created labour demand within the cities, and the concomitant mechanization of agriculture that freed individuals from agricultural occupations. The growth of urban areas based on industrialization attracted migrants not just from rural areas, but also prompted immigration, with most immigrants drawn to urban locations following 1851 (Marr and Paterson 1980), a pattern that continues to this day. Not surprisingly, the most rapid rates of urban growth occurred in Ontario, Quebec, and British Columbia, the three provinces with the largest industrial and service sectors. The growth of Canada's urban areas reflects the availability of employment opportunities and the growth of the financial and services sectors, amenities, the dominance of urban-centered immigration, and the decline of the proportion of the population actively engaged in agriculture and/or resource extraction.

The following chapter explores the growth of Canada's urban population, with the discussion reflecting trends noted in the 2001 Census. Specifically, the chapter will first document the growth of Canada's metropolitan areas as well as the increasing importance of a handful of major metropolitan or "megapolitan" regions, before exploring the two drivers of city growth – internal migration and immigration, with references back to reasons why Canadians choose to live in cities. The chapter closes with a discussion of future prospects and associated implications.

DEFINING URBAN AREAS IN CANADA

What constitutes a place being urban? There is, in fact, considerable variation in the definition of an urban place across countries. Statistics Canada defines urban places as those having a minimum population of 1,000 and a population density of at least 400 people per square kilometre. Statistics Canada also recognizes Census Areas (CAs), or areas where the population count of the urban core is at least 10,000. At the time of the 2001 Census, Statistics Canada identified 27 Census Metropolitan Areas (CMAs), defined as urban areas consisting of one or more adjacent municipalities situated around a major urban core. To form a census metropolitan area, the urban core must have a population of at least 100,000, with adjacent municipalities having a high degree of integration with the central urban area, as measured by commuting flows derived from census place of work data. For example, the Toronto CMA includes the City of Toronto, as well as cities or towns including Mississauga, Vaughn, Oakville, Newmarket, and Aurora.

Table 9.1
Growth of the Canadian Urban System: Number of Urban Places and Levels of Concentration, 1921–2001

	1921	1941	1961	1981	1991	2001
Number of urban places by population size						
Number of CMAs (100,000+)	6	7	16	23	24	27
Number of CAs (10,000 – 99,999)	37	556	77	129	123	112
TOTAL	43	63	93	152	147	139
Levels of metropolitan concentration						
Number of CMAs with 1 million or greater	–	1	2	3	3	4
% urban	49.5	54.3	60.7	75.7	77.0	79.9
Urban growth rate (%)	3.3	1.2	3.9	3.1	1.4	1.4
% population in CMAs	35.4	40.2	48.3	55.3	61.1	64.5
% population in 3 largest CMAs	18.8	22.2	25.0	29.1	31.6	35.0
TOTAL urban population (000s)	4,352	6,252	11,068	18,436	22,008	23,908
TOTAL population (000s) in 3 largest CMAs	1,651	2,551	4,725	7,095	8,622	9,422

THE GROWTH OF CANADA'S URBAN AREAS

Table 9.1 documents the growth of Canada's urban areas since the 1920s (see also Ley and Bourne 1993; Simmons and McCann 2000). Although slowing in the past two decades, Canada's urbanization represents an extraordinary transformation. In 1901, only 37.5 percent of Canada's population was defined as urban. By 1921, approximately one-half of it lived in urban areas, a proportion that barely changed over the span of the Depression and World War II, when fewer jobs meant that domestic migrants were not attracted to urban areas, and restrictionist immigration policies and poor economic prospects limited the number of new immigrants. Even by 1951, and despite the industrial demands placed upon the Canadian economy during World War II, only 56.7 percent of Canada's population resided in an urban area. By 1981, however, over three-quarters of its population resided in urban centres, with a corresponding decline in the rural population. With the 2001 Census, 80 percent of Canada's population was urban.

Corresponding to Canada's increasingly urban population, the types of cities that Canadians live in have also changed. Prior to 1941, Canada could not boast a single city with a population greater than one million, when Montréal finally surpassed that milestone. At the same time, only 40 percent of Canada's population lived in one of the seven CMAs. By 2001, however, this proportion had grown to nearly 65 percent, and the number of CMAs grew to twenty-seven (table 9.1). While the population size of Canada's urban areas are relatively small by world (and even North American) standards, the growth of Canada's largest CMAs in the post-War period is impressive, with the number of urban settlements quickly growing. For example, the number of urban places grew three-fold to 139 between 1921 and 2001. In addition, urban places with populations between 100,000 and 1 million nearly doubled from 16 in 1961 to 27 in 2001, led by the growth of cities around Toronto such as Oshawa, as well as western cities such as Calgary and Edmonton.

A ranking of Canadian CMAs by population size in 2001 shows considerable variation in population size, share, and growth rates (table 9.2). With greater than 15 percent of the nation's population in 2001, Toronto's population exceeded 4.6 million, making it the nation's (and one of North America's) largest urban areas, a position that it has held since the 1970s when it eclipsed Montréal as Canada's largest urban centre (Anderson and Papageorgiou 1992). Montréal, Vancouver, and Ottawa-Gatineau rounded out the list of metropolitan areas with populations exceeding one million. Yet, even amongst these four metropolitan areas, there is considerable diversity. For example, Montréal's population grew at only 3.0 percent between 1996 and 2001, less than half the national average of 6.5 percent. Although Toronto experienced a healthy growth rate of 9.8 percent between 1996 and 2001, it was closely followed by Vancouver (8.5 percent). Both lagged Calgary, which posted the largest growth rate of all Canadian CMAs (15.8 percent). Edmonton also experienced above average growth (8.7 percent), with the growth of both Edmonton and Calgary fueled by the expansion of Alberta's resource sector and accompanying jobs. Other CMAs in the growth shadow of Toronto, including Oshawa, Kitchener-Waterloo, and Hamilton also experienced growth rates equivalent to, or greater than, the national average (6.5 percent), driven by a combination of immigration and movement out of the Toronto CMA and into its neighbouring areas.

At the other end of the spectrum, Abbotsford, BC, was a newly minted CMA in the 2001 Census, and Thunder Bay, with a 2001 population of 121,986, was the 27th ranked CMA. Typically, these smaller CMAs represent those located in more peripheral areas or reliant upon the resource extraction and processing sector. For the first time, seven CMAs, including Thunder Bay, experienced declines in their total population and proportional shares between 1996 and 2001, with the Greater Sudbury CMA having the largest decline (6 percent). Other CMAs with population declines included Regina, St John's, Chicoutimi-Jonquière, Trois-Rivières, and Saint John.

Table 9.2
Growth of Canada's CMAS, 1996–2001

CMA	1996			2001			% Change 1996–01
	N	%	Rank	N	%	Rank	
Toronto	4,263,759	14.78	1	4,682,897	15.61	1	9.8
Montréal	3,326,447	11.53	2	3,426,350	11.42	2	3.0
Vancouver	1,831,665	6.35	3	1,986,965	6.62	3	8.5
Ottawa-Gatineau	998,718	3.46	4	1,063,664	3.54	4	6.5
Calgary	821,628	2.85	5	951,395	3.17	5	15.8
Edmonton	862,597	2.99	6	937,845	3.13	6	8.7
Québec City	671,889	2.33	7	682,757	2.28	7	1.6
Winnipeg	667,093	2.31	8	671,274	2.24	8	0.6
Hamilton	624,360	2.16	9	662,401	2.21	9	6.1
London	416,546	1.44	10	432,451	1.44	10	3.8
Kitchener	382,940	1.33	11	414,284	1.38	11	8.2
St Catharines-Niagara	372,406	1.29	12	377,009	1.26	12	1.2
Windsor	286,811	0.99	15	307,877	1.24	13	4.7
Halifax	342,966	1.19	13	359,183	1.20	14	2.5
Victoria	304,287	1.05	14	311,902	1.04	15	7.3
Oshawa	268,773	0.93	16	296,298	0.99	16	10.2
Saskatoon	219,056	0.76	17	225,927	0.75	17	3.1
Regina	193,652	0.67	18	192,800	0.64	18	-0.4
St John's	174,051	0.60	19	172,918	0.59	19	-0.7
Sudbury	165,618	0.57	20	155,601	0.52	20	-6.0
Chicoutimi-Jonquière	160,454	0.56	21	154,938	0.52	21	-3.4
Sherbrooke	149,569	0.52	22	153,811	0.51	22	2.8
Abbotsford	136,480	0.47	26	147,370	0.49	23	8.0
Kingston	144,528	0.50	23	146,838	0.49	24	1.6
Trois-Rivières	139,956	0.49	24	137,507	0.46	25	-1.7
Saint John	125,705	0.44	28	122,678	0.41	26	-2.4
Thunder Bay	126,643	0.44	27	121,986	0.41	27	-3.7
TOTAL CMA	18,178,597	63.0		19,359,926	64.5		6.5
Canada	28,846,761			30,007,094			

THE PREFERENCE FOR LARGE URBAN AREAS:
METROPOLITAN CANADA

The evidence garnered from the 2001 Census suggests that Canadians have become more metropolitan, seemingly reflecting a range of values, including an increasing preference to live in larger cities, cultural and social amenities, a diversified population, and economic potential. In essence, Canada's demographic composition is now one of a growing metropolitan core and declining rural area, along with a set of smaller, declining urban centres. Between

1996 and 2001, for example, Canada's urban population growth was led by urban areas with populations exceeding 100,000 (6.2 percent), exceeding the growth rate of urban areas in general (5.2 percent) and Census Areas, which grew at a much more modest rate of 1.5 percent. At the same time, the population of other areas declined by 0.4 percent. Moreover, there has been an increasing concentration of the country's population in the largest urban centres. In 1941, just 22.2 percent lived in the three largest metropolitan area CMAs, comprised of Toronto, Montréal, and Vancouver. By 2001, 35 percent, or 9.4 million, Canadians resided in one of these three areas.

Beyond the statistically defined metropolitan areas, Canada's population is increasingly concentrated in a handful of (unofficial) "megapolitan" areas. These large-scale metropolitan areas often include CAs adjacent to CMAs and/or clusters of CMAs and CAs, such as Southern Ontario's Golden Horseshoe, which includes the Oshawa CMA in the east, the Barrie-Orilla CAs to its north, and the Hamilton and St Catharines-Niagara CMAs in the west. Growing at a rate of 9.2 percent in 1996–2001, a total of 7.5 million people live in this extended urban region. Other megapolitan areas include Montréal and its adjacent urban region, including Saint-Hyacinthe, Sorel, Joliette, and Lachute; the Vancouver-Victoria region, including British Columbia's lower mainland; the Calgary-Edmonton corridor; and Ottawa-Gatineau. In total, these five megapolitan regions saw the continued concentration and growth of population within their borders, and grew at a combined rate of 7.6 percent while accounting for 51 percent of the nation's population in 2001. Individually, Montréal grew at a rate of 3.0 percent, while Vancouver-Victoria and Ottawa-Gatineau grew by 7.3 and 6.5 percent, respectively. The Calgary-Edmonton megapolitan area grew at the rapid rate of 12.3 percent between 1996 and 2001. Some of the strongest CMA growth rates between 1996 and 2001 were located in these five large, urbanized regions (table 9.2), including places such as Oshawa, Calgary, Edmonton, and Kitchener. Exceptions included Windsor and Halifax, both of which posted robust growth over the 1996–2001 period (7.3 and 4.7 percent, respectively).

The preference for residing in larger urban areas is also reflected in the number of defined urban places, which peaked at 152 in 1981 (Ley and Bourne 1993). Subsequently, the number declined to 147 in 1991, and 139 in 2001, reflecting the retirement of CAs by Statistics Canada as their population dropped below the 10,000 threshold. This decline in the number of urban areas was lead by smaller urban areas with populations less than 100,000. For example, urban areas with a population between 30,000 and 100,000 declined from 57 in 1991 to 49 in 2001, and the number of urban areas with populations between 10,000 and 30,000 declined from 74 in 1981 to 56 in 2001.

REASONS FOR URBAN GROWTH

Despite the overall growth of Canada's urban areas, the growth (decline) of individual urban areas varies widely and reflects a variety of issues, including changing economic conditions and the attractiveness of individual urban areas to internal migrants and immigrants. In the past, natural population growth associated with higher fertility levels enabled cities to grow. However, with below-replacement fertility levels and near constant mortality schedules across the country, differential urban-growth patterns typically reflect differences in migration into and out of urban areas, as well as immigration. Indeed, Canadians are highly mobile (Newbold 1997), frequently responding to employment opportunities and amenities in the origins and destinations, while immigration is selective on the largest metropolitan areas.

The growth of medium- and large-sized cities over the last two or three decades has been largely driven by internal migration, immigration, and consolidation of the urban settlement pattern. Calgary and Edmonton's growth over the 1996 to 2001 Census interval was, for example, due to domestic in-migration, and to a lesser extent immigration associated with economic growth. Although not an immigrant magnet, Halifax grew largely due to its continued evolution as a regional centre servicing the Atlantic provinces. Amongst the largest metropolitan areas, population growth was largely associated with immigration. Canada now accepts in excess of 200,000 immigrants per year, with the vast majority electing to settle in urban areas, and in particular Toronto, Vancouver, and Montréal.

INTERNAL MIGRATION

Internal migration has generally shifted the population westward over time, as new frontiers and opportunities appeared. In the post-World War II era, population movements have reflected departures from the Atlantic and Prairie provinces, and movement into Ontario, British Columbia, and Alberta in search of employment or amenities, while movement into and out of Québec tends to be structured by language effects (Newbold and Liaw 1994). These shifts in the Canadian population continued in the final years of the twentieth century, and are reflected in table 9.3, which illustrates the impact of net inter-provincial (between provinces) and intra-provincial (within provinces) migration on CMA populations between 1996 and 2001. Between 1996 and 2001, internal migration flows had differential effects on Canadian metropolitan areas. First, the largest CMAs, including Toronto,

Table 9.3

Net Population Changes Attributable to Internal Migration between CMAS, 1996–2001

	In-Migration			Out-Migration			
	Intra	Inter	TOTAL	Intra	Inter	TOTAL	Net
Toronto	127,275	86,500	213,775	198,215	60,060	258,275	-44,500
Montréal	137,555	32,525	170,080	106,285	76,395	182,680	-12,600
Vancouver	54,095	66,785	120,880	71,650	69,760	141,410	-20,530
Ottawa-Gatineau	64,820	45,090	109,910	53,425	30,050	83,475	26,435
Calgary	43,150	96,255	139,405	36,895	45,525	82,420	56,985
Edmonton	46,190	61,510	107,700	41,415	37,115	78,560	29,170
Québec City	50,325	4,465	54,790	57,995	10,140	68,135	-13,345
Winnipeg	22,205	26,555	48,760	16,935	39,800	56,735	-7,975
Hamilton	56,815	10,345	67,160	42,725	7,805	50,530	16,630
London	38,415	6,925	45,340	37,575	7,940	45,515	-175
Kitchener	37,675	9,240	46,915	33,305	5,955	39,260	7,655
St Catharines-Niagara	22,065	4,900	26,965	19,880	3,990	23,870	3,095
Windsor	19,310	5,175	24,485	15,475	2,905	18,380	6,105
Halifax	16,515	31,565	48,080	11,390	29,005	40,395	7,685
Victoria	23,830	17,795	41,625	22,385	16,975	39,360	2,265
Oshawa	41,855	5,045	46,900	26,080	3,380	29,460	17,440
Saskatoon	17,810	11,820	29,630	12,630	18,765	31,395	-1,765
Regina	12,435	8,015	20,450	9,915	16,395	26,310	-5,860
St John's	9,775	5,955	15,730	4,575	16,690	21,265	-5,535
Sudbury	10,820	1,965	12,785	16,880	3,225	20,105	-7,320
Chicoutimi-Jonquière	9,360	935	10,295	14,805	1,180	15,985	-5,690
Sherbrooke	17,745	1,105	18,850	18,315	2,270	20,585	-1,735
Abbotsford	19,060	4,450	23,510	15,675	5,450	21,125	2,385
Kingston	16,365	7,045	23,410	17,315	5,785	23,100	310
Trois-Rivières	12,440	425	12,865	14,370	635	15,005	-2,140
Saint John	3,860	5,420	9,280	4,585	6,955	11,540	-2,260
Thunder Bay	6,245	2,430	8,675	7,865	5,700	13,565	-4,890
TOTAL CMA	938,010	560,240	1,498,250	928,560	529,850	1,458,410	39,840

Montréal, and Vancouver lost population through internal migration over 1996–2001. As Canada's largest CMA, Toronto might be expected to experience population gain through internal migration, yet it had a net population loss due to internal domestic migration of -44,500 individuals, composed of a net in-migration of 26,440 individuals from outside the province and a net loss to other locations in Ontario (-70,940), a trend that has been recorded since the mid-1980s (Hou and Bourne 2004). More than likely, a large proportion of this loss was to neighbouring CMAs such as Hamilton, Oshawa, and Kitchener, all of which experienced net gains due to intra-provincial migration (14,090, 15,775, and 4,370, respectively). Toronto's population growth is attributed solely to immigration, which injected nearly 375,000 people into the CMA over the 1996–2001 period. Montréal also had a net loss of population (-12,600) between 1996 and 2001, reflecting a loss of -43,870 through inter-provincial migration and a gain of 31,270 from within the province. Like Toronto, its growth over the Census interval was due to immigration. Continuing a trend that started in the early 1990s, Vancouver lost population to other locations within the province as well as to locations outside the province, potentially reflecting a downturn in the BC economy in the late 1990s.

Second, many of the mid-sized CMAs such as Ottawa-Gatineau, Calgary, Edmonton, and Oshawa experienced a net population increase through internal migration. Amongst those CMAs that had net in-migration, Calgary and Edmonton were the two largest gainers, attracting a total (inter-provincial and intra-provincial) of 56,985 and 29,170 internal migrants, respectively. No doubt, these internal migrants were attracted by employment potentials in these two metropolitan areas, and the province in general. In addition, Ottawa-Gatineau had a net inflow of domestic migrants, as well as Windsor, Halifax, Victoria, St Catharines-Niagara, and Kingston.

Third, many of the smaller CMAs, including Sudbury, Thunder Bay, Kingston, Saint John, Chicoutimi, and Sherbrooke, lost population through internal migration, a problem exacerbated by their inability to attract foreign arrivals. The exception was Abbotsford, BC, which had a modest net gain attributable to inter-provincial migration.

IMMIGRATION

Accounting for over one-half of Canada's population growth between 1996 and 2001 (Schellenberg 2004), immigration has had a substantial effect on the growth of Canadian cities, with table 9.4 further exploring the impact of immigration on metropolitan populations. Despite attempts through federal policy to distribute immigrants throughout Canada, the immigrant population is predominately an urban one, with approximately 88 percent residing in a metropolitan area in 2001. Moreover, 94 percent of immigrants arriving between 1996 and 2001 settled in Canada's urban areas. More precisely, immigrants are concentrated in the three immigrant gateway cities of Toronto, Montréal, and Vancouver. Proportionately, 37.3 percent (2,032,960) of Canada's total immigrant population resided in Toronto in 2001, while Vancouver and Montréal were each home to 12.7 and 11.8 percent (738,550 and 621,890), respectively. In total, these three CMAs accounted for 62 percent of the total immigrant population in 2001.

Table 9.4
Growth of CMAs by Immigration, 1996–2001

	2001			1996–01		
				1996–01	1996–01	% 1996–01
	N	% Total	% CMA	Growth	Arrivals	Arrivals
Toronto	2,032,960	37.3	43.7	14.7	415,505	43.1
Montréal	621,890	11.4	18.4	6.0	114,175	11.9
Vancouver	738,550	13.6	37.5	16.5	169,620	17.6
Ottawa-Gatineau	185,005	3.4	17.6	14.3	38,170	4.0
Calgary	197,410	3.6	20.9	15.5	36,390	3.8
Edmonton	165,235	3.0	17.8	4.3	21,005	2.2
Québec City	19,685	0.4	2.9	13.2	5,285	0.5
Winnipeg	109,390	2.0	16.5	-2.1	13,415	1.4
Hamilton	154,660	2.8	23.6	6.2	18,685	1.9
London	80,410	1.5	18.8	5.8	10,065	1.0
Kitchener	90,570	1.7	22.1	9.4	14,180	1.5
St Catharines-Niagara	66,045	1.2	17.8	-1.9	5,490	0.6
Windsor	67,880	1.2	22.3	19.1	14,690	1.5
Halifax	24,390	0.4	6.9	3.2	4,435	0.5
Victoria	57,590	1.1	18.8	-0.4	4,750	0.5
Oshawa	46,150	0.8	15.7	4.6	2,950	0.3
Saskatoon	16,865	0.3	7.6	2.5	3,150	0.3
Regina	14,015	0.3	7.4	-8.0	1,780	0.2
St John's	4,885	0.1	2.9	-3.6	825	0.1
Sudbury	10,775	0.2	7.0	-10.4	505	0.1
Chicoutimi-Jonquière	1,335	0.0	0.9	15.1	305	0.0
Sherbrooke	6,850	0.1	4.6	10.0	2,085	0.2
Abbotsford	31,660	0.6	21.8	16.0	5,105	0.5
Kingston	17,675	0.3	12.4	-0.9	1,905	0.2
Trois-Rivières	2,065	0.0	1.5	-7.2	460	0.0
Saint John	4,615	0.1	3.8	-6.2	520	0.1
Thunder Bay	13,320	0.2	11.1	-12.8	615	0.1
TOTAL CMA	4,781,880		87.8	11.4	906,065	94.1
TOTAL Canada	5,448,480			9.6	963,325	

By far, Toronto was the most important immigrant destination, attracting a near majority (415,505 or 43.1 percent) of arrivals between 1996 and 2001. Vancouver was a distant second, attracting nearly 170,000 (17.6 percent) of arrivals over the same interval, while Montréal attracted 114,175 immigrants (11.9 percent). Together, these three immigrant magnets attracted 73 percent of all new arrivals. In comparison, only 58 percent of immigrants arriving between 1971 and 1981 settled in the same three CMAs (Schellenberg 2004). As mentioned, the large number of new immigrant arrivals to these areas offset net population losses due to either inter-provincial or intra-provincial migration. In other words, without immigration to offset their loses due to internal migration, the populations of Toronto and Montréal would have declined over the Census period, situations not dissimilar to population change within some of the largest metropolitan cities in the United States, including New York City.

Outside of these three immigrant gateways, the number of new immigrants settling in any one CMA was significantly less, with immigration consequently playing a smaller role in the population growth of these centers. Still, several CMAs had a none-trivial inflow of new immigrant arrivals. For example, Ottawa-Gatineau, Calgary, and Edmonton each attracted substantial numbers of immigrants (38,170 [4.0 percent], 36,390 [3.8 percent], and 21,005 [2.2 percent], respectively). Finally, some of the smallest CMAs, including Sudbury, Thunder Bay, Saint John, and Chicoutimi-Jonquière, were only able to attract a few hundred immigrants each.

The net result has been the concentration of immigrants within a handful of metropolitan areas. Nearly 44 percent of Toronto's population is, for example, foreign-born. In addition, and echoing the relative attractiveness of the top three CMAs amongst new arrivals, nearly 38 percent of Vancouver's population is foreign-born. Despite Montréal's position as the third (numerically) largest immigrant centre, just 18.4 percent of its population was foreign-born. In fact, the proportional share of immigrants relative to the total CMA was greater in several cases, including Calgary, where 20.9 percent its total population is foreign-born. Other CMAs with a large immigrant component include Hamilton (23.6 percent), London (18.8 percent), Windsor (22.3 percent), Kitchener (22.1 percent), Victoria (18.8 percent), and Abbotsford (21.8 percent). Conversely, immigrants in many of the smaller CMAs represent less than 10 percent of their total population. In the case of Trois-Rivières, just 1.5 percent of its population is foreign-born.

CONCLUSIONS

Like all other developed countries, Canada's population was transformed during the twentieth century from a predominately rural, agricultural society to an urban, metropolitan one. Urban growth has been uneven and has essentially resulted in two types of regions, typified on the one hand by slow growth or declining areas, and the concentration of population and economic activities in a handful of large, integrated metropolitan centres on the other. These large "megapolitan" centres include Toronto, Montréal, Ottawa-Gatineau, Vancouver-Victoria, and Calgary-Edmonton, which have grown at the expense of smaller urban areas. Moreover, growth in these places will continue, exemplified by the Calgary CMA, which joined the one-million club before the 2006 Census. Other regional centres, such as Halifax, Saskatoon, or Winnipeg have also grown, but more so through domestic in-migration and with relatively slow growth of their population.

One interesting aspect of metropolitan growth trends that is not immediately apparent is the "donut" effect (Statistics Canada 2005b). With the important exceptions of Ottawa-Gatineau, and Abbotsford, the population of the core municipalities grew slower than the areas around them, forming the donut. In particular, Saskatoon and Regina were two centres where the core population grew more slowly than the surrounding municipalities. In the case of Saskatoon, the core increased at a rate of 1.6 percent between 1996 and 2001, while the surrounding urban area grew at a rate of 14.6 percent, while the core and surrounding areas of Regina grew at -1.2 percent and 10 percent, respectively.

Although the processes of urbanization and metropolitan growth will likely continue in the coming years, albeit at a potentially reduced pace, future changes to Canada's urban structure will likely reflect two non-exclusive trends relating to the growth (decline) of individual CMAs. First, although Canadians demonstrate a preference for urban areas, the reasons for growth will differ across the individual CMAs. More generally, economic potential and on-going structural shifts in the Canadian economy as it moves from one reliant upon the resource sector to a service- and information-based economy will create winners and losers amongst Canada's CMAs. Concurrently, high-order services including finance, media, medical, and educational services are increasingly concentrated in larger urban areas (Coffey and Shearmur 1996). As seen with the 2001 Census, CMAs located in peripheral areas and/or reliant upon resource extraction will likely continue to decline, unless they can reposition themselves.

Second, internal migration and immigration will continue to promote population concentration in large metropolitan areas. Large- and mid-sized CMAs will most likely grow from a mix of internal migration and immigration, while smaller CMAs and CAs will lose population through out-migration. More generally, changing economic conditions will drive changes to internal migration. However, the potential for internal migration will decrease with population aging, although the attraction of high amenity retirement areas such as Victoria will benefit such areas.

Immigration will instead drive future metropolitan population growth, especially for Toronto, Montréal, and Vancouver. Moreover, it is unlikely that this new immigrant population will disperse over time. As Ley and Hiebert (2001) argue, immigration is Canada's population policy, and as a result it is urban policy. While the federal government has attempted to steer new arrivals to destinations other than the top three metropolitan areas through various incentives and programs, they have met with only limited success. In short, immigration flows will continue to focus upon the same handful of metropolitan centres, resulting in a growing population diversity of these centres, with Statistics Canada concluding that over 50 percent of Toronto's population will be a visible minority by 2017 (Statistics Canada 2005c). However, the literature also suggests that there is a link between immigrant and domestic out-migration from these centres, with the less-educated native-born moving out of the immigrant gateways (Champion 1994; Frey 1996; Hou and Bourne 2004; Ley 2003).

The growth of Canada's largest urban areas, which is basically occurring at the expense of other, smaller urban areas or rural areas, implies different and distinct social, economic, and policy challenges, some of which are explored elsewhere in this book. The contrasts between growing urban areas and slow growth or declining urban areas will create dissimilar urban environments with different economic and social policies. As large metropolitan areas dominate the landscape, new "fault lines" – or the divide between growing and declining places – may be created (Bourne and Simmons 2003).

In addition, cities are increasingly defined as key components to Canada's future economic success, representing and increasingly demanding greater political representation, flexibility, and monetary assistance from both the provincial and federal governments (Bourne and Simmons 2003; Donald 2001). In Ontario and Quebec, for example, the Windsor-Quebec City corridor represents more than one-third of Canada's population, creating a high degree of demographic, economic, and political concentration. Yet, there are no elected bodies or effective planning agencies that oversee growth in these megapolitan areas, and there is relatively little history of direct and consistent political interest in urban areas (Bourne and Simmons 2003). Additionally, the growth of urban areas implies other issues that must be addressed, including service provision, aging populations, transportation, segregation, and the integration of newcomers, as well as negative effects such as congestion, housing costs, and pollution. To this end, the federal and provincial governments have started to pay greater attention to the fiscal needs of cities, although this cannot be seen as being at the expense of rural and/or smaller urban areas.

REFERENCES

Anderson, William A., and Yorgos Y. Papageorgiou. 1992. "Metropolitan and Non-metropolitan Population Trends in Canada, 1966–1982." *The Canadian Geographer* 36 (2): 124–43

Bourne, Larry S., and Jim Simmons. 2003. "New Fault Lines? Recent Trends in the Canadian Urban System and Their Implications for Planning and Public Policy." *Canadian Journal of Urban Research* 12 (1), Supplement: 22–47

Champion, Anthony G. 1994. "International Migration and Demographic Change in the Developed World." *Urban Studies* 31 (4/5): 653–77

Coffey, William, and Richard Shearmur. 1996. *Employment Growth and Change in the Canadian Urban System.* Ottawa: Canadian Policy Research Network

Donald, Betsy. 2001. "Economic Competitiveness and Quality of Life: Compatible Concepts?" *Canadian Journal of Urban Research* 10 (2): 259–74

Frey, William. 1996. "Immigration, Domestic Migration and Demographic Balkanization in America: New evidence for the 1990s." *Population and Development Review* 22 (4): 741–63

Hou, Feng, and Larry S. Bourne. 2004. *Population Movement into and out of Canada's Immigrant Gateway Cities: A Comparative Analysis of Toronto, Montréal and Vancouver.* Ottawa: Statistics Canada. Research Paper Series 229

Ley, David. 2003. "Offsetting Immigration and Domestic Migration in Gateway Cities: Canadian and Australian Reflections on an 'American Dilemma.'" Vancouver Centre of Excellence Research on Immigration and Integration in the Metropolis. Working Paper Series: 03–01

Ley, David, and Larry S. Bourne. 1993. "The Social Context and Diversity of Urban Canada." In *The Changing Social Geography of Canadian Cities*, eds. L.S. Bourne and D. Ley, 3–32. Montreal: McGill-Queen's University Press

– and Daniel Hiebert. 2001. "Immigration Policy as Population Policy." *The Canadian Geographer* 45 (1):120–6

Marr, William L., and Donald G. Paterson. 1980. *Canada: An Economic History.* Toronto: Gage

Newbold, K. Bruce. 1997. "Primary, Return and Onward Migration in the U.S. and Canada: Is There a Difference?" *Papers in Regional Science* 76 (2): 175–98

– and Kao-Liee Liaw. 1994. "Return and Onward Interprovincial Migration through Economic Boom and Bust in Canada: From 1976–81 to 1981–86." *Geographical Analysis* 26 (3): 228–45

Schellenberg, Grant. 2004. *Immigrants in Canada's Census Metropolitan Areas.* Ottawa: Statistics Canada. Cat. no. 89–613–MIE

Simmons, Jim, and Larry McCann. 2000. "Growth and Transition in the Canadian Urban System." In *Canadian Cities in Transition*, eds. Pierre Filion and Trudi Bunting, 97–120. Toronto: Oxford University Press

Statistics Canada. 2005a. *Farm population and total population by rural and urban population, by province* (2001 and 2006 Census of Agriculture and Census of Population) www.statcan.ca/english/Pgdb/agrc42k.htm (Accessed March 2010).

- 2005b. *A Profile of the Canadian Population: Where We Live.* 2001 Census Analysis Series. Ottawa. Cat. no. 96F0030XIE2001001
- 2005c. "Canada's Visible Minority Population in 2017." *The Daily* (March 22). Online publication

10

Internal Migration

BARRY EDMONSTON

INTRODUCTION

The residents of Canada are a very mobile population. During a single year, more than 2 million, or about 13 percent, of the nation's population move from one house to another, about 4 percent move within their province of residence, and 1–in–100 move from one province to another. Relatively few Canadians spend their entire lives in their communities of birth, and many move from one province to another more than once. The purpose of this chapter is to show that internal migration is not the movement of only a few residents or an aimless wandering, but that it is a common occurrence and has definite patterns related to economic and social changes.

Populations can change in only three ways: births, deaths, or the movement of people into and out of the population. Migration is thus one of the three fundamental subjects for the study of population change. A community or nation can gain population by births or in-migration. It can lose population by deaths or by out-migration. As a component of population change, migration occupies a central place in demographic analysis.

Demographers customarily divide the study of migration into two categories – international migration and internal migration. This division into two categories is convenient because international migrants face special rules for entrance into national populations and receive interest because immigrants often have different linguistic and cultural origins than people in their countries of settlement. International migration is discussed in another chapter in this volume (see Chapter 11). Previous reports on internal migration in Canada, based on census analysis, include ones based on 1961 census data (George, 1970; Stone 1969), 1971 census data (Stone 1977), and 1991 census data (Ram, Shin, and Pouliot 1994).

Importance of Migration

Internal migration is a necessary part of population changes associated with employment mobility. Within Canada, some communities have expanding employment opportunities, while other communities are areas with stable or declining economic opportunities. As a result, some younger persons are born and raised in communities that offer little promise for satisfactory employment as adults. By moving to new areas with better employment prospects, internal migration provides both a mechanism for personal employment improvements as well as a process that maintains a better connection between available workers and job opportunities. If internal migration were to cease, it would result very shortly in communities with plentiful jobs and no workers, and communities with increasing unemployment. Migration is a vital demographic process in a dynamic economy.

The process of internal migration has important consequences for the communities of departure and arrival. Along with its effects on employment, migrants influence the housing markets, schools, public services, and retail establishments in both communities.

Measurement of Internal Migration

Demographers usually consider two types of internal migration. One type is local movement, or the changing of residence within a community. The second type is migration, or the changing of the community of residence. In the first type, a person moves locally and usually does not disrupt his regular daily social and economic ties. In the second type, a person changes his community of residence and generally interrupts his social and economic ties with the original community.

Both of these types of internal migration are important and deserve separate study. Local movement can alter the spatial distribution of population within communities and can affect residential housing markets. Migration between communities affects both the origin and destination communities. When a large number of people leave a single community or settle in a new community, this can alter quickly the community's population characteristics. For these reasons, there tends to be greater interest in internal migration involving changes in the community of residence.

The mobility status of a population is measured in censuses and special surveys. By comparing current place of residence with prior residence (usually one or five years ago), it is possible to determine the proportion of the population who are local movers or migrants. This chapter discusses these various measures of internal migration in the following sections.

Type of Migrants

Although migrants often move for economic reasons, not all mobility is related to employment. There are many reasons for moving, either within communities or between communities. For within-community movement, families often move because of the desire to change their housing, to be closer to work, to be in an area with the desired school for their children, to be closer to suitable transportation, and for other reasons that make a new place more desirable.

For between-community movement, economic reasons are often a primary reason for moving because job opportunities are an important motivation to leave a community with high unemployment and move to a community with greater opportunities for employment. People move for other reasons as well. A large number of young adults move to a new place for job training and college. Other young adults want to see what life is like in a new place and head to larger towns or new areas, even if job opportunities may be limited in the destination community. Retirees select places to settle based on available suitable housing, climate, and desirable amenities. Stated generally, people may move from one place to another for many reasons and will give preference to some comparisons more than others, based on their own situations and interests.

Types of Mobility

Mobility status refers to the relationship between a person's current residence and his residence at some previous time. Using census data reported by Statistics Canada, we define the following hierarchy for types of mobility status:

1 *Non-movers*: persons who are in the same dwelling as the one they were in at the previous date.
2 *Movers*: persons who are in a different dwelling from the one they were in at the previous date.
  2.1 *Non-migrants*: persons who are in a different dwelling but in the same census community at the previous date.
  2.2 *Migrants*: persons who are residing in a different census community than at the previous date.

2.2.1 *Internal migrants*: migrants who were living in Canada at a previous date, including *intraprovincial migrants* (who were living in the same province at the previous date) and *interprovincial migrants* (who were living in a different province at the previous date).

2.2.2 *External migrants*: migrants who were living outside Canada at the previous date.

Lifetime Migration

A common mobility measure is a comparison of current residence with the place of residence at birth. Place-of-birth mobility is ascertained from a census question asking, "Where were you born?" and comparing responses with the person's current residence. Tabulations for interprovincial lifetime migration are possible only for persons who were born in Canada, of course. The major limitation of a place-of-birth reference is that the time at which the migration took place is not known. Movement could have occurred at any time between birth and the current date.

Figure 10.1 presents information for 1901–2001 on the percent of persons born in Canada who live in a different province than their province of birth. In 1901, the overwhelming number of Canadians, about 94 percent, lived in their province of birth. Mobility within Canada increased in the first decades of the twentieth century. Throughout the 1911 to 1941 period, about 10 percent of Canadians lived in a province different than their province of birth. During the 1940s and afterwards, the pace of interprovincial migration increased, with steady gains after 1941 in the percent of Canadians who lived in a province different than their province of birth. By 1981, the percent increased to almost 16 percent, and remained about 15 percent in 1991 and 2001. If anything, it appears that the major peak in the interprovincial migration of Canadians was prior to 1981.

Variations in Mobility Status

There have been modest changes in the mobility status of Canada's residents during the previous four decades, as reported in the 1961 to 2001 censuses. During 1961 to 2001, the percentage of non-movers increased from 55 percent in 1961 to 58 percent in 2001 – the highest level of the past forty years.

About one-in-four Canadian residents move within their community over a five-year period. These residents change their place of residence but remain in the same municipality. The percentage of non-migrant movers has

Figure 10.1
Percent of Canada-born Persons Living in a Different Province than Their Province of Birth,
1901 to 2001

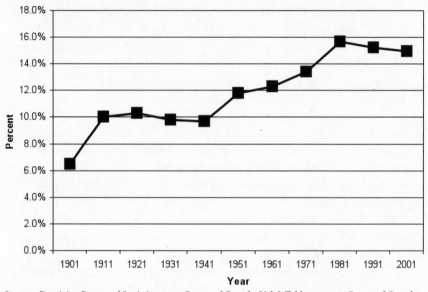

Sources: Dominion Bureau of Statistics, 1931 Census of Canada, Vol. I, Table 75; 1941 Census of Canada,
Vol. III, Table 19; 1951 Census of Canada, Vol. X, Table 20; 1961 Census of Canada, Vol. I, Part II, Table
49; Statistics Canada, 1971, 1981, 1991, and 2001 census microdata samples (data tabulated by author).

declined during the past forty years, decreasing from 25 percent in 1961 to
22 percent in 2001.

The rate of intraprovincial migrants increased from 13 percent in 1961 to
16 percent in 1991 before decreasing to 13 percent in 2001.

Interprovincial and external migrants constitute the smallest percentage
of Canadian residents. Interprovincial migration rates increased from 3 percent in 1961 to about 6 percent in 1971 and 1981 before decreasing to
3 percent in 1991 and 2001. The percentage of Canadian residents who
are external migrants (primarily foreign-born persons moving to Canada)
decreased from 3 percent in 1961 to about 2 percent in 1971 and 1981, and
then increased to 4 percent in 1991 and 2001.

PROVINCIAL VARIATIONS

There are considerable variations in mobility status for provinces, as well as
in the relative proportion of persons moving in and of provinces.

Table 10.1
Percent Distribution of Population, Five Years of Age and Older, by Mobility Status, for Provinces, 1996–2001

	Non-Mover	Non-Migrant Mover	Migrant			
			Total Migrant	Intra-provincial	Inter-provincial	External
CANADA	58.1	22.4	19.5	12.7	3.3	3.5
PROVINCE						
Newfoundland	73.4	14.2	12.4	8.4	3.4	0.6
Prince Edward Island	67.5	17.7	14.8	7.5	6.3	1.0
Nova Scotia	63.8	22.2	14.0	6.5	6.4	1.1
New Brunswick	67.3	18.3	14.5	9.1	4.8	0.6
Quebec	61.1	20.1	18.8	15.9	0.9	2.0
Ontario	57.2	23.2	19.5	12.4	2.3	4.8
Manitoba	61.3	24.6	14.1	8.0	4.2	1.9
Saskatchewan	62.0	20.7	17.2	11.4	4.8	1.0
Alberta	50.8	26.4	22.7	11.1	8.8	2.8
British Columbia	53.6	23.2	23.1	13.6	4.1	5.4
Yukon, Northwest Territories, and Nunavut	45.7	31.7	22.6	7.6	13.8	1.2

Variations in Mobility Status

Table 10.1 displays the percent distribution for Canadian residents, by mobility status, for the national and provincial populations in 2001. Based on the percentage of residents who are non-movers during the 1996 to 2001 period, Newfoundland and Labrador had the highest figure: almost three-fourths of residents remained in the same house over the five-year period. Prince Edward Island, Nova Scotia, New Brunswick, Quebec, Manitoba, and Saskatchewan also had higher proportions of non-movers than the national average. Ontario had a rate of non-movers that was similar to the national average. Two provinces, Alberta and British Columbia, as well as the combined populations of Yukon Territory, Northwest Territories, and Nunavut had considerable lower rates of non-movers than the national average.

The causes of the higher rates of non-movers vary by provinces. In general, provinces with higher rates of non-movers have lower rates of non-migrant movers and lower rates for the three types of migrants. The following patterns prevail for provinces with higher rates of non-movers:

• Except for Quebec, all have *higher* rates of interprovincial migration. These provinces present two faces of mobility. On the one hand, they have a large proportion of residents who do not change their dwelling, yet on the other hand have higher rates of interprovincial migration than the national average.

- Quebec has higher rates of intraprovincial migration and lower rates of interprovincial migration. The province of Quebec represents a population in which most migration occurs within the province and not with other provinces.
- All these provinces have lower rates of external migrants. They represent more-settled populations with higher rates of non-movers and are less likely to attract immigrants.

Ontario's residents resemble fairly closely the national average for mobility status, with the one caveat that Ontario has a higher level of external migrants than the national average.

Alberta and British Columbia have lower rates of non-movers. The causes differ. Alberta's population has substantially higher rates on non-migrant movers and interprovincial migration than the national average. This reflects the attractiveness of Alberta for migrants from other provinces, and because they are younger and more recent arrivals they have greater mobility within Alberta after their arrival. British Columbia's population has Canada's highest relative rate of external migration, which increases the province's overall migration rates. British Columbia has slightly higher rates of interprovincial migration than the national average.

Interprovincial Migration

Over a five-year period, about 1 million Canadian residents move from one province to another. Interprovincial migration involves both the movement into as well as out of provinces (see table 10.2). We calculate the net interprovincial migration by subtracting out-migrants from in-migrants. During the 1996 to 2001 period, three provinces (Nova Scotia, Ontario, and Alberta) experienced a net in-migration of interprovincial migrants. The other provinces and territories witnessed net out-migration of interprovincial migrants.

The patterns of interprovincial migration for the 1996 to 2001 period are similar to previous periods for some provinces. There has been net in-migration to Ontario for many previous decades. There has been net out-migration from the Atlantic provinces and Quebec, Manitoba, and Saskatchewan since the 1950s. The level of net migration for Alberta and British Columbia, however, has fluctuated during the prior five decades. Both provinces have

Table 10.2
Number of Interprovincial Migrants Into, Out of, and Net Migrants and Migration Rates
(per 1,000 Resident Mid-period Population) for the Population Five Years of Age and Older,
for Provinces, 1996–2001

Province	Into		Out of		Net Migrants	
	Number	Rate	Number	Rate	Number	Rate
Newfoundland	16,422	30.8	49,912	-93.8	-33,490	-62.9
Prince Edward Island	7,876	58.4	8,025	-59.5	-149	-1.1
Nova Scotia	54,802	60.3	53,314	-58.7	1,488	1.6
New Brunswick	32,422	44.2	40,858	-55.7	-8,436	-11.5
Quebec	61,907	8.6	119,239	-16.6	-57,332	-8.0
Ontario	241,607	21.8	192,599	-17.4	49,008	4.4
Manitoba	43,784	39.2	59,224	-53.0	-15,440	-13.8
Saskatchewan	43,437	44.1	67,393	-68.4	-23,956	-24.3
Alberta	243,428	85.8	122,201	-43.1	121,227	42.7
British Columbia	151,706	39.8	177,830	-46.6	-26,124	-6.8
Yukon, Northwest Territories, and Nunavut	11,754	125.1	18,368	-195.5	-6,614	-70.4

experienced periods of boom and bust, with variations in the level and direction of net migration.

Several provinces and territories had unusually low rates of in-migration (Quebec) or relatively high rates of in-migration (Prince Edward Island, Nova Scotia, Alberta, and the combined areas of Yukon, Northwest Territories, and Nunavut).

Out-migration rates vary for provinces. Newfoundland and Labrador, as well as the combined areas of Yukon, Northwest Territories, and Nunavut had very high rates of out-migration. Quebec and Ontario experienced out-migration rates of less than 20 per 1,000 residents during the five-year period prior to 2001.

Some provinces, such as Newfoundland and Labrador, witnessed high in-migration and even higher out-migration – producing substantial net out-migration. There was net in-migration into Ontario (about 4 per 1,000 residents) and Alberta (about 40 per 1,000) during the five-year period from 1996 to 2001. All other provinces experienced net out-migration during 1996 to 2001, with higher levels of out-migration for New Brunswick, Manitoba, and Saskatchewan.

METROPOLITAN VARIATIONS

Compared to the national average, Canada's metropolitan areas have slightly lower rates of non-movers, higher rates of non-migrant movers, and higher rates of migration (see table 10.3). Metropolitan areas have considerably higher rates of external migration but have rates of intraprovincial and interprovincial migration that are not greatly different from the national average.

Table 10.3 reports variations in the types of mobility status for the larger Census Metropolitan Areas (CMAs) of Canada for the 1996 to 2001 period. In statistical analysis not reported here, cluster analysis reveals five groups of CMAs that have similar mobility rates within each group. These groups and their mobility rates are as follows:

- Group #1: 6 CMAs have higher levels of external migration as well as levels of other mobility rates that are closely similar to the overall averages for all CMAs, including Toronto, Kitchener, London, Windsor, Vancouver, and Victoria. These CMAs are Canada's major gateway areas of immigrants.
- Group #2: 5 CMAs are characterized as having lower rates of external and intraprovincial migration and higher rates of interprovincial migration, including Halifax, Ottawa-Hull, Winnipeg, Regina and Saskatoon, and Edmonton.
- Group #3: 3 CMAs are noteworthy for having lower rates of external, interprovincial, and intraprovincial migration and, as a result, considerably higher rates of non-movers, including Hamilton, St. Catharines-Niagara, and Sudbury and Thunder Bay.
- Group #4: 4 CMAs have lower rates of external and interprovincial migration and higher rates of intraprovincial migration, including Quebec, Montreal, Sherbrooke and Trois-Rivieres, and Oshawa.
- Group #5: 1 CMA, Calgary, had a unique pattern of higher rates of external and interprovincial migration and lower rates of intraprovincial migration. Overall, Calgary had especially higher rates of migration and non-migrant movers, yielding unusually lower rates of non-movers.

SELECTIVITY OF MIGRATION

When people move, some groups are more likely to move than others. The study of groups that are more likely to move is referred to as the selectivity of migration. Demographers usually examine migration selectivity for a limited set of demographic characteristics, including age and sex, social and economic characteristics (such as educational attainment and occupation), and nativity. This section discusses the selectivity of migration for several important demographic characteristics.

Table 10.3
Percent Distribution of Population, Five Years of Age and Older, by Mobility Status, for Census
Metropolitan Areas, 1996–2001

	Non-Mover	Non-Migrant Mover	Migrant			
			Total Migrant	Intra-provincial	Inter-provincial	External
CANADA	58.1	22.4	19.5	12.7	3.3	3.5
CENSUS METROPOLITAN AREA (CMA)						
All CMA's	55.0	24.8	20.2	11.9	3.2	5.1
Halifax	54.3	29.1	16.6	4.8	9.8	1.9
Quebec	61.0	19.8	19.2	17.6	0.6	0.9
Montreal	56.7	22.4	20.9	16.3	1.0	3.6
Sherbrooke and Trois-Rivieres	58.3	21.0	20.7	19.2	0.4	1.2
Ottawa-Hull	54.2	26.3	19.5	9.1	6.1	4.2
Oshawa	55.9	20.4	23.7	20.8	1.8	1.1
Toronto	54.6	24.1	21.3	10.7	2.0	8.6
Hamilton	58.6	24.6	16.8	11.8	1.6	3.5
St.Catherines-Niagara	62.9	21.6	15.5	12.5	1.4	1.6
Kitchener	53.8	26.1	20.1	13.8	2.7	3.6
London	54.9	27.5	17.6	12.7	1.9	3.0
Windsor	56.6	26.4	17.0	11.0	1.4	4.6
Sudbury and Thunder Bay	63.3	27.3	9.4	6.9	1.9	0.6
Winnipeg	58.2	30.0	11.8	5.1	4.5	2.2
Regina and Saskatoon	55.4	27.6	17.0	10.1	5.3	1.7
Calgary	45.4	32.8	21.8	6.5	10.6	4.7
Edmonton	51.5	28.0	20.5	10.5	7.5	2.6
Vancouver	52.0	23.2	24.8	12.1	3.5	9.1
Victoria	54.0	25.5	20.5	11.7	6.1	2.7

Age and Sex

During the 1996 to 2001 period, men and women appear to be equally mobile (see table 10.4). These is little evidence, for various measures of mobility
status, that either men or women were more mobile than the other. Overall,
58 percent of men and women were non-movers during the five-year period
from 1996 to 2001. More than one-fifth of men and women were non-
migrant movers, and almost one-fifth were migrants. Most migrants moved
within their province, as indicated by the intraprovincial migration rates –
about two-thirds of migrants were intraprovincial migrants. Slightly more
than 3 percent of men and women were interprovincial migrants during
1996 to 2001. More than 3 percent of men and women residing in Canada
in 2001 were external migrants who were living outside Canada in 1996.

Table 10.4
Mobility Rates by Type of Mobility, by Sex and Age, for Population Five Years of Age
and Older, 1996–2001

			Migrant			
	Non-Mover	Non-Migrant Mover	Total Migrant	Intra-provincial	Inter-provincial	External
MALES						
All Ages	58.1	22.4	19.5	12.6	3.3	3.5
5-17	56.9	24.0	19.1	12.0	3.1	4.0
18-34	39.3	30.5	30.2	19.2	5.5	5.5
35-54	59.1	22.9	18.0	11.6	3.1	3.4
55-64	75.2	13.1	11.7	8.5	1.8	1.3
65+	81.8	9.6	8.6	6.5	1.1	0.9
FEMALES						
All Ages	58.1	22.5	19.4	12.8	3.2	3.4
5-17	56.5	23.8	19.7	12.5	3.3	3.9
18-34	34.8	32.4	32.8	21.2	5.5	6.0
35-54	60.9	22.1	17.0	11.1	2.8	3.1
55-64	74.9	13.4	11.7	8.6	1.7	1.3
65+	80.2	11.5	8.3	6.2	1.3	0.9

Table 10.5
Net Interprovincial Migration Rates (per 1,000 mid-period residents), by Age, for Population
Five Years of Age and Older, for Provinces, 1996–2001

	Age Groups					
Province	All Ages	5–17	18–34	35–54	55–64	65+
Newfoundland	-69.4	-57.6	-188.5	-35.3	-8.5	-0.5
Prince Edward Island	-1.2	9.6	-33.4	6.0	14.5	8.9
Nova Scotia	1.8	4.3	-22.3	8.9	16.1	9.3
New Brunswick	-12.3	-8.4	-41.7	-7.1	7.0	4.7
Quebec	-8.5	-10.1	-12.0	-7.8	-4.6	-5.3
Ontario	4.6	5.0	9.1	4.3	-1.1	1.0
Manitoba	-15.0	-4.5	-26.7	-16.6	-15.5	-6.6
Saskatchewan	-26.5	-12.9	-62.6	-22.0	-6.2	-12.8
Alberta	44.0	35.9	85.3	34.5	13.8	11.4
British Columbia	-7.1	-11.8	-14.2	-8.0	6.8	2.9
Yukon, Northwest Territories, and Nunavut	-101.0	-154.2	-25.2	-111.1	-170.5	-76.8

Persons in their late teens, their twenties, and their early thirties are more mobile than the general population. As shown in table 10.5, younger adult persons have both higher migration as well as local mobility than the overall average. The high degree of mobility prevailing among the younger adult population is a fundamental aspect of population dynamics.

The mobility of children and youth, aged 17 years and younger, reflects the movement, both local and migratory, of their parents. The higher mobility rates above 17 years, in the younger adult years, reflects the completion of secondary education, and the going to college, seeking work, enlistment in military service, or movement based on personal preferences. Mobility among younger adults is also affected by choices about marriages or partnerships, which typically involve change of residence for one or both persons.

There are differences in the age pattern of interprovincial migration for Canada's provinces and territories (see table 10.5). In several areas with net out-migration, there is net out-migration for all age groups (Newfoundland and Labrador, Quebec, Manitoba, Saskatchewan, and the combined areas of Yukon, Northwest Territories, and Nunavut); even in these areas, however, there is substantial variation in the level of net out-migration by age.

In the Atlantic provinces of Prince Edward Island, Nova Scotia, and New Brunswick, the highest rate of net out-migration is for younger adults, aged 18 to 34 years. Although these three provinces experienced overall net out-migration, all three had net in-migration of older adults, 55 to 64 years and 65 years of age and older, evidencing the combination of in-migration of retired persons and the possible return of older persons who were originally born in the Atlantic region. Prince Edward Island and Nova Scotia also witnessed a net in-migration of children and youth, aged 5 to 17 years: this suggests that there is in-migration of younger adults with children that counterbalanced an out-migration of younger adults without children.

Alberta had a net in-migration of all age groups, with especially high rates of net in-migration of younger adults and adults with children.

Although British Columbia had an overall net out-migration during 1996 to 2001, it was primarily due to the out-migration of younger adults and adults with children. British Columbia retained its appeal to older adults, especially those around the age of retirement, and had net in-migration of persons aged 55 to 64 years and 65 years and older.

Education

There is considerable variation between age groups in the level of educational attainment. Because older people tend to have less education than younger generations, the population at older ages typically has a lower average number of years of completed schooling than the younger adult age group. Because mobility varies sharply with age, a comparison of mobility status by education needs to recognize that relationship is influenced by differences in age composition.

Table 10.6
Mobility Rates (per 1,000 Mid-period Residents) by Type of Mobility, by Educational Attainment,
Household Income, and Occupation, for Population Five Years of Age and Older, 1996–2001

			Migrant			
	Non-Mover	Non-Migrant Mover	Total Migrant	Intra-provincial	Inter-provincial	External
EDUCATIONAL ATTAINMENT						
All Persons	58.7	22.0	19.3	12.7	3.2	3.4
Less than High School	66.2	20.2	13.6	9.4	2.1	2.1
High School	61.9	21.9	16.2	12.2	2.5	2.5
Some College or University	55.7	23.6	20.7	14.8	3.5	2.4
University Degree or more	50.2	22.3	27.5	15.1	4.9	7.5
OCCUPATION						
All Persons	54.4	24.4	21.2	14.2	3.7	3.2
Managers	55.4	23.9	20.7	14.7	4.3	5.1
Professionals	51.2	23.2	25.6	15.6	4.9	2.5
Technicians, Supervisors, and Senior Clerical	57.0	22.8	20.2	14.4	3.4	2.0
Skilled Workers	55.8	24.8	19.4	14.1	3.3	2.9
Clerical and Intermediate Sales Workers	52.7	25.8	21.5	14.5	4.1	3.5
Manual, Sales, and Service Workers	55.4	25.3	19.3	12.8	3.0	3.2

Although the most mobile segment of the population appears to be those with above-average educational attainment (see the top panel of table 10.6), this is due primarily to the higher levels of migration for college and university-educated persons. The patterns for local mobility, as indicated for non-migrant movers, are highest for persons with some college or university, and are slightly lower for those at the upper end and lowest for those at the lower end of educational attainment. For migration and especially for interprovincial migration, the highest rates are for those with a university degree or more, and are much lower for those with less than a high-school education.

Occupation

Mobility patterns vary greatly for occupational groups (see the second panel of table 10.6). One of the most mobile segments of the population includes managers and professionals. The above-average mobility of clerical and intermediate sales workers is due to both higher levels of local mobility as well as migration. The least mobile occupational group (with respect to local mobility and migration) is technicians, supervisors, and skilled clerical workers. Managers, and manual, sales, and service workers also tend to have below-average mobility.

Occupational groups also vary with respect to the kind of mobility. Professionals have higher rates of intraprovincial and external migration. Clerical and intermediate sales workers, and manual, sales, and service workers have higher rates of local residential mobility. The high total mobility of the professional group results from high rates of migration. Managers have unusually high rates of external migration, reflecting the large in-flow of immigrants into the managerial occupational group. Clerical and intermediate service workers also have high rates of interprovincial migration. Manual, sales, and service workers are noteworthy for having relative low rates of intraprovincial migration.

These inter-occupational differences reflect, in part, differences in the age composition of members of particular occupational groups. The pattern also probably results from job opportunities for particular occupations and migration required by employees of different companies.

Nativity

Immigration and internal migration overlap in two areas. One aspect is that immigrants often settle in areas with better economic opportunities, the same areas that attract internal migrants. The second aspect is that, after settling in Canada, immigrants also move, either as local movers or as migrants.

If types of mobility are compared for the Canada-born and foreign-born population (see the first two panels of table 10.7), it is apparent that the Canada-born population has slightly higher rates of non-movers. Both groups have similar rates of non-migrant movers. The lower rates of non-movers for the foreign-born are due to higher rates of migration, which are in turn based entirely on the higher rates of external migration.

We can take external migrants into account for the analysis by examining only foreign-born residents who lived in Canada in 1996 (see third panel of table 10.7). If we compare the Canada-born (top panel) with the foreign-born who resided in Canada in 1996 (bottom panel), we limit attention to the population who may have moved internally within Canada during the 1996 to 2001 period. In this case, the comparison reveals that the foreign-born population had higher rates of non-migrant movers (25.8 percent compared to 22.6 percent) and lower rates of migration (12.6 percent compared to 17.8 percent). Once arriving in Canada, the foreign-born are more likely to move within their community and somewhat less likely to migrate within or between their province of settlement.

Table 10.7
Mobility Rates (per 1,000 Mid-period Residents) by Type of Mobility, by Nativity and Age,
for Population Five Years of Age and Older, 1996–2001

			Migrant			
	Non-Mover	Non-Migrant Mover	Total Migrant	Intra-provincial	Inter-provincial	External
CANADA-BORN						
All Ages	59.6	22.6	17.8	13.8	3.5	0.4
5-17	59.4	24.2	16.4	12.7	3.2	0.5
18-34	39.2	31.9	28.9	22.2	6.0	0.6
35-54	62.5	21.8	15.7	12.2	3.0	0.4
55-64	76.1	12.7	11.2	9.2	1.8	0.3
65+	82.1	10.1	7.8	6.5	1.2	0.1
FOREIGN-BORN						
All Ages	52.0	21.8	26.2	8.3	2.3	15.6
5-17	26.1	21.4	52.5	7.3	2.5	42.8
18-34	26.9	29.4	43.7	11.0	3.4	29.3
35-54	51.4	24.8	23.8	8.5	2.4	12.8
55-64	72.4	14.7	12.9	7.1	1.6	4.2
65+	77.9	12.0	10.1	6.1	1.2	2.8
FOREIGN-BORN, RESIDENT IN CANADA IN 1996						
All Ages	61.6	25.8	12.6	9.9	2.7	–[1]
5-17	45.6	37.5	16.9	12.6	4.3	–[1]
18-34	38.0	41.6	20.4	15.6	4.8	–[1]
35-54	58.9	28.5	12.6	9.8	2.8	–[1]
55-64	75.6	15.4	9.0	7.4	1.7	–[1]
65+	80.1	12.4	7.5	6.2	1.3	–[1]

[1] No external sources of migration because all individuals were in Canada in 1996.

These mobility patterns for the foreign-born have two implications. Once foreign-born persons have decided to emigrate to Canada, they still need to decide upon where they will settle in Canada. Second, it is clear that immigrants continue to move around Canada even as they adjust to a new life.

CONCLUSION

Internal migration is one of the fundamental processes of population change. It is one of the critical mechanisms that change communities, altering population size and characteristics for both the community of origin and the community of destination. If internal migration were to cease, populations would accumulate in areas with weak job opportunities, and unfilled jobs would increase in areas with greater economic growth. If migration were suddenly to become random, there would be an increasing mismatch between jobs and workers, between students and colleges, and social and economic institutions would not operate efficiently. Internal migration is a common non-random occurrence, integral to the population adjustments related to social and economic processes. Internal migration operates as a central mechanism for adjusting populations to social and economic changes.

Internal migration is unquestionably one of the most impressive features of the Canadian population. Mobility at the local and provincial level is such a routine occurrence that it is easy to overlook the ways in which it changes communities across the nation. Mobility involves the comparative desirability of different areas with local areas and provinces as well as in different provinces as seen by potential migrants. The migration process involves judgments about the current place of residence, judgments that are usually fairly well-informed because most persons are familiar with social and economic conditions in their place of residence. The decision to move also involves an appraisal of opportunities in potential new places of settlement. Not infrequently, the appraisal may be inadequate or misleading because potential migrants have no information or information is limited to hearsay. Indeed, some potential migrants may decide not to move or decide to move to the "wrong" place because of lack of factual information about potential places of destination. Stated differently, the effect of knowledge about places of destination can affect the decision to migrate as well as the choice of final settlement. While decisions to migrate have some factual basis, migration does not depend upon perfect and complete information about possible places of settlement.

Internal migration has major effects on population change for communities and provinces in Canada. The movement of a person from one community to another changes the population at both the origin and destination. The movement of people not only subtracts and adds a resident for the communities of origin and destination; the communities are changed by the characteristics of the internal migrant. Migration is a process of cultural change and social integration. The person who migrates from one community to another provides a link between the two communities, at least temporarily. If the new arrival is "different" than members of the new community of settlement, he or she may form the onset of arrivals who will become a new social group, either adjusting to the new community over time or changing the community itself.

This chapter emphasizes that migration is one of the fundamental demographic processes shaping Canadian communities. The internal migration of residents is a common occurrence and is a population response to social and economic changes.

With lower rates of natural increase, internal migration has become a more important component of population change at the provincial, metropolitan, and local levels. Unlike fertility and mortality, however, the determinants of internal migration change quickly and move up or down – producing sudden positive or negative migration flows. As a result, internal migration patterns evidenced in the 1996–2001 period are intricately related to the social and economic structure of this period. Although many features common to internal migration in the 1996–2001 period are likely to persist, future changes in Canadian society and the economy will alter previous patterns.

REFERENCES

George, M.V. 1970. *Internal Migration in Canada: Demographic Analysis.* 1961 Census Monograph, Dominion Bureau of Statistics. Ottawa: The Queen's Printer

Ram, Bali, Edward Y. Shin, and Michel Pouliot. 1994. *Canadians on the Move.* Focus on Canada Series. Ottawa: Statistics Canada; Prentice Hall Canada

Stone, Leroy O. 1969. *Migration in Canada: Regional Aspects.* 1961 Census Monograph, Dominion Bureau of Statistics. Ottawa: The Queen's Printer

– 1977. "Migration in Canada." 1971 Census Canada. Profiles Series. *Bulletin* 5: 1–5. Ottawa: Statistics Canada

11

Immigrants in Canada: Trends and Issues

MONICA BOYD

INTRODUCTION

International migration, here defined as the movement of people across international borders for purposes of permanent settlement, has long contributed to Canada's population growth, economic and political development, and demographic and social diversity. Following the ancient settlement of Canada by the Aboriginal peoples, British and French migrants began to arrive in the 1600s. Although migration from France virtually ceased after British victory in the Seven Years War (1756–1763), British migration continued. During the 1700 and 1800s, migrants also came from the United States, Ireland, Northern Europe, and by the second half of the 19th century, many were from Eastern Europe (Kelley and Trebilcock 1998; Knowles 2007).

A century later, international migration is still a defining characteristic of Canada. Indeed, as shown in chart 11.1, the numbers entering Canada throughout the 1900s often were higher than those observed earlier. Precipitous declines shown in the chart reflect the difficulties of travel associated with World Wars I and II and the lack of economic opportunities in Canada during the 1930s Depression years. The flow of migrants increased again after World War II, and by the start of the 21st century, more than 200,000 people were entering Canada yearly for permanent residence.

However, for students of immigration, the second half of the 20th century is noteworthy for more than just the numbers of people migrating to Canada. Seismic shifts occurred within the immigrant population with respect to source country, racial and ethnic composition, language first learned, and destination in Canada. Further, although historically migration was encouraged for purposes of settlement and the supply of labour for Canada's agrarian and manufacturing economy, by the end of the century

Chart 11.1
Canada's International Migration Flows, 1860–2005

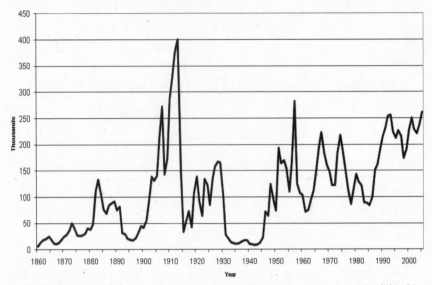

Source: Canada, Citizenship and Immigration 2002. Facts and Figures 2002. www.cic.gc.ca/english/pub/
facts2002/immigration/immigration_1.html and Canada, Citizenship and Immigration 2005. Facts and
Figures 2005. www.cic.gc.ca/english/pub/facts2005/overview/01.html.

those patterns had shifted and the type of labour altered (Boyd and Vickers
2000). Paradoxically, although immigrants were better educated than those of
earlier decades, by the 1990s these better-educated new arrivals were doing less
well in the labour force than earlier migrants. Because today's new immigrants
are overwhelmingly from areas other than Europe, their altered fortunes raise
the possibility that the "vertical mosaic" advanced by Porter (1965), as based
on ethnic origins, is now based on race. Moreover, the economic difficulties of
new migrants, however caused, prompt the question of whether their children
will do as well as immigrant offspring of the 1950s and 1960s.

This chapter uses 2001 Canadian census data from the Public Use
Microdata File on Individuals (PUMF) to demonstrate the temporal alterations in immigrants. Throughout the chapter, we use terminology employed
by Statistics Canada: immigrant population refers to permanent residents of
Canada; "non-immigrant" population refers to Canadian citizens by birth
(also called the Canadian-born). Reflecting changes in source countries, we
pay particular attention to visible minorities, a designation referring to persons of colour. We conclude with a brief look at the Canadian-born children
of immigrants.

IMMIGRATION AND CANADA'S CENSUS

International migration has always been an important contributor to Canada's population growth. With the decline in the birthrate beginning in the 1970s, net migration became the most important factor fueling population growth, currently accounting for approximately two-thirds of Canada's annual increase (Statistics Canada 2008). Immigration also now contributes to Canada's increasing labour force and could account for all of Canada's net labour force growth by 2011 (Zietsman 2007,7) because international migration is most likely to occur in the adult years, when labour force participation is most likely (Statistics Canada 2008: chart 4.3).

ENTRY COHORTS AND THEIR DIFFERENCES

The terms "immigrant" and "permanent resident" artificially create an allusion of homogeneity. In fact, the Canadian immigrant population is an amalgamation of groups that have entered Canada at different times. Because of alterations in immigration policy that determine the criteria of admission, earlier groups may differ from later ones with respect to origins, ethnicity and race, and socioeconomic characteristics. With time, less-recent-entry cohorts have entered mature stages of their life and employment cycles; such progressions mean they are likely to differ from more recently arrived cohorts with respect to economic consumption, such as home ownership and labour market income.

When we compare the non-immigrant (or Canadian-born) population and the immigrant population in table 11.1 (columns 1 and 2), we see that in comparison with the Canadian-born population, the immigrant population is older, far more likely to be legally married, and less likely never to have been married. Although differences in family type are not large, the immigrant population has higher percentages with children over the age of 15, and the average size of immigrant economic families is larger, consistent with a higher percentage living in multiple families. Compared to the non-immigrant or Canadian-born population, the immigrant population has slightly higher percentages of renters living in households with incomes below Statistics Canada Low Income Cutoffs. This term, often shortened to LICOs, represents a series of income thresholds based on family expenditure data, below which families must devote a larger share of income to the necessities of food, shelter, and clothing than the average family (Paquet 2002).

As noted previously, the total immigrant population is a composite of groups arriving in Canada at different times. According to the 2001 census,

Table 11.1
Select Demographic, Family, and Household Characteristics for the Non-Immigrant and Immigrant Populations, by Period of Arrival, Canada 2001

	Non-Immigrant[a] (1)	Immigrant Population[b]					
		Total (2)	<1961 (3)	1961–1970 (4)	1971–1980 (5)	1981–1990 (6)	1991–2001 (7)
Numbers, in '000s	24004	5434	898	741	926	1036	1833
Percentage		100	17	14	17	19	34
Average Age	35	46	67	56	49	41	33
Age Groups	100	100	100	100	100	100	100
0–14	22	6	–	–	2	2	16
15–24	14	9	–	–	2	15	16
25–64	52	67	39	76	85	73	63
65 and Older	11	19	61	24	13	9	5
Marital Status	100	100	100	100	100	100	100
Single, Never Married	45	22	4	7	13	28	39
Legally Married	36	60	66	71	66	57	52
Common-Law	9	4	3	4	5	4	2
Other[a]	10	14	27	17	15	11	7
Family Type	100	100	100	100	100	100	100
Married or Common-Law	72	71	68	74	71	69	70
Single Parent Family	11	9	6	7	9	11	9
Multiple Family	3	9	2	5	7	11	13
Non-Family, 1 Person	10	9	21	12	9	6	4
Non-Family, 2 Persons	3	3	2	2	3	3	3

Presence of Children							
No Child Present	54	43	64	43	34	39	41
One or More < Age 6	14	16	1	7	13	19	26
One or More, Ages 6–14	16	17	6	14	20	23	18
One or More, Ages 15 Plus	16	25	30	36	34	19	15
Average Size of Economic[d] Family	3.2	3.4	2.3	2.9	3.3	3.8	3.9
Average Size of Census[e] Family	3.1	3.0	2.1	2.6	3.0	3.3	3.4
Accommodation	100	100	100	100	100	100	100
Renter	28	32	16	16	23	32	51
Owner – Condominium	4	8	8	7	8	9	9
Owner – Other Types	69	60	76	76	70	59	40
Density (rooms per person)	2.6	2.3	3.4	2.9	2.4	2.0	1.7
% in Households with 2000 Income $50,000 or More	58	54	46	62	67	61	45
% Living in Households Below the Low Income Cutoffs[f]	15	22	14	12	14	20	35

(Presence of Children row: 100, 100, 100, 100, 100, 100, 100)

(a) The non-immigrant population refers to those who are Canadian citizens by birth.

(b) The immigrant population refers to those who are landed immigrants; these individuals have been granted the right to live in Canada permanently by immigration authorities.

(c) Includes legally separated, divorced, and widowed who are not in common-law unions.

(d) An economic family consists of two or more household members who are related to each other by blood, marriage, common-law, or adoption.

(e) A census family is composed of a married couple or two persons living common-law, with or without children, or of a lone parent living with at least one child in the same dwelling.

over one-third of Canada's immigrant population has arrived since the early 1990s. This figure attests to the increasing numbers of persons admitted to Canada late in the 20th century. But earlier waves of migrants are also present; data from the 2001 census show that almost two-thirds of Canada's immigrant population arrived before 1991. Because the prevalent pattern is to migrate in adulthood, as shown in table 11.1, the average age of those arriving before 1961 is 67 years, compared to declining average ages for groups arriving thereafter. Many individuals in the pre-1961 cohort can be said to have aged "in place" after immigrating as adults, or to a lesser extent, as children. In contrast, the most recent entry cohort – the 1990s – are now working-age adults, and the children accompanying them add to the more youthful age structure. Four decades from now, this cohort will represent a footprint of previous migration; the children now aged 0–14 will be 40–54, and those in their 40s will be 80 and older.

Chronological age is highly associated with stages in the life cycle. It therefore comes as no surprise to find that compared to recent arrivals, immigrants arriving before 1961 are most likely not to be married, to be living alone in non-family settings, and to have either no children present or only children aged 15 and older. At the same time, they are more likely than those arriving in the 1980s and beyond to own their own homes. And compared to groups arriving in the 1980s and 1990s, those arriving before 1961 and during the 1960s and 1970s have lower percentages living in households with incomes below the low income cutoffs.

Canada's newest immigrants are unlike the entry cohorts preceding them and unlike the non-immigrant population. Recent arrivals are the most likely to be part of multiple families residing together; over half are renting (compared to slightly over one-quarter of the non-immigrant population), and over one-third live in households with incomes below the low income cutoffs. By definition, recent arrivals have not been in Canada very long, and these findings may simply reflect the initial adjustment stages that come with international migration. However, when considered in combination with other indicators discussed later in this chapter, they fuel concern that immigrants arriving in today's Canada may not be doing as well as those of previous decades.

ALTERED GEOGRAPHIES AND CULTURAL CHARACTERISTICS

Recent arrivals differ from the Canadian-born and earlier cohorts in other ways. For example, they are more likely to live in Canada's large cities. To be sure, immigrants have always located where work can be found. Early in the 20th century, this meant settling in agrarian areas or industrial cities (Boyd and Vickers 2000). Today's immigrants are more likely to focus on big cities (Schellenberg 2004), especially those arriving in the past ten years. Nearly three-quarters (73 percent) of those who entered Canada between 1991 and 2001 reside in Montreal, Toronto, or Vancouver. Toronto is the major residential and work area for permanent residents, with over 40 percent of recent arrivals (table 11.2).

As well, immigrant cohorts differ with respect to places of origin. Starting in the 1960s, altered immigration regulations and legislation enshrined in the 1976 Immigration Act removed national origins as a criterion of admissibility. In *defacto* and *dejure* operation since Confederation and reaffirmed in Canada's 1953 Immigration Act, the national-origin criterion restricted entry to persons from the UK and European countries. The new admissibility criteria adopted in the 1960s are based on family reunification, economic contribution, and humanitarian concerns. Provided prospective immigrants or a family's principal applicant meet one of these criteria, persons from around the world can be granted legal entrance to Canada as permanent residents.

The effects of these changes were evident by the end of the 1970s and remained visible throughout the 1980s and 1990s. Table 11.2 shows the increasing percentages of immigrants born outside the US or Europe by the decade of their legal admission into Canada. Of those immigrants enumerated in the 2001 census, 94 percent arriving before 1961 were born in the US, the UK, or elsewhere in Europe; only 22 percent arriving in the 1990s came from these areas, with the balance from other areas of the world. Of those arriving between 1991 and 2001, half were from Southern Asian and East and Southeastern Asian countries.

Country and region of origin are closely associated with membership in visible minority populations, and recent immigrants are more likely to be visible minorities than earlier immigrants. The term "visible minority" was first used by the Canadian federal government in the early 1980s to denote groups other than the Aboriginal peoples who are distinctive by virtue of race, colour, or "visibility." The phrase was integral to the development of federal employment equity legislation and program requirements of the mid-1980s. In the 2001 PUMF, information is provided for Chinese, South Asian, and Black populations – the largest visible minority groups in Canada. The non-visible minority category includes those who identify as members of Canada's Aboriginal peoples, although most of the non-visible minority population is "white."

Table 11.2
Select Geographical and Socio-Cultural Characteristics of the Non-Immigrant and Immigrant Populations, by Period of Arrival, Canada 2001

| | Non-Immigrant[a] | Immigrant Population[b] | | | | | |
	(1)	Total (2)	<1961 (3)	1961–1970 (4)	1971–1980 (5)	1981–1990 (6)	1991–2001 (7)
CMA Place of Residence	100	100	100	100	100	100	100
Montreal	11	11	9	12	11	12	12
Ottawa-Hull	4	3	3	3	3	4	4
Toronto	11	37	25	34	37	40	43
Calgary	3	4	3	3	4	4	4
Edmonton	3	3	3	2	4	4	2
Vancouver	5	14	8	10	13	14	18
Other select CMAs[c]	19	14	21	18	14	12	10
All Other Areas	44	13	27	18	13	10	7
Birthplace		100	100	100	100	100	100
USA, UK &Other Europe	(nr)	46	94	76	42	29	22
West Central Asia & Middle East	(nr)	5	1	2	3	7	9
South Asia	(nr)	9	0	4	9	10	16
East & SE Asia	(nr)	22	2	7	22	30	34
Central & S. America & Caribbean	(nr)	11	1	8	17	17	11
Oceania, Africa and Other	(nr)	6	1	4	7	7	8
Visible Minority Status	100	100	100	100	100	100	100
Not a Visible Minority	95	51	97	81	48	35	26
Chinese	1	14	2	5	13	17	22
South Asian	1	12	0	4	13	13	18
Black	1	6	0	5	9	8	8
Other Visible Minority	2	17	1	5	17	27	26

Religion	100	100	100	100	100	100	100
Catholic	46	33	41	44	34	33	24
Protestant	31	20	39	27	21	15	11
Other religions(d)	6	30	9	15	28	35	44
No religious affiliation	16	17	11	14	16	18	21
Mother Tongue	100	100	100	100	100	100	100
Eng, Fr, or Aboriginal	94	30	37	43	41	27	19
Other	6	70	63	57	59	73	81
Home Language(e)	100	100	100	100	100	100	100
Eng, Fr, or Aboriginal only	95	41	64	58	51	34	22
Other	5	59	36	42	49	66	78
Official Language Knowledge(f)	100	100	100	100	100	100	100
English and/or French	100	94	98	96	95	93	91
No English or French	0	6	2	4	5	7	9

(a) The non-immigrant population refers to those who are Canadian citizens by birth.

(b) The immigrant population refers to those who are landed immigrants; these individuals have been granted the right to live in Canada permanently by immigration authorities.

(c) Consists of Halifax, Québec, Sherbrooke, Trois-Rivières, Oshawa, Hamilton, St Catharines – Niagara, Kitchener, London, Windsor, Sudbury, Thunder Bay, Winnipeg, Regina, Saskatoon, and Victoria.

(d) Includes Christian Orthodox, Muslim, Jewish, Buddhist, Hindu, Sikh, Baha'i, Jains, Shinto, Taoist, Zoroastrian, Zoroastrian, and smaller Eastern religions, and religions as Pagan, Scientology, and Rastafarian.

(e) Refers to language regularly used at home. The "Other" category includes persons who speak at least one language other than English, French, and/or Aboriginal languages regularly in the home.

(f) Respondents were asked if they could speak English and/or French well enough to carry on a conversation.

According to the 2001 Census, of those arriving before 1961 only three percent are visible minorities, slightly lower than today's Canadian-born population (table 11.2). However, with increased admission of immigrants from Asia, Africa, the Caribbean, and Latin and South America, the near absence of visible minorities in the immigrant population is reversed: of those entering Canada in 1991–2001 and enumerated in the 2001 Census, nearly three-quarters (74 percent) are members of visible minority groups, with Chinese and South Asian groups predominating.

Altered source countries are associated with religious and linguistic diversity as well. Slightly under one-third of all immigrants have a religion that is neither Catholic nor Protestant, compared to only six percent of the Canadian-born; the percentage declaring non-Catholic, non-Protestant religions increases with recent arrival. Of those arriving 1991–2001, over four out of ten declare themselves non-Catholic, non-Protestant. Immigrants also are more likely than the Canadian-born to declare no religious affiliation, and again percentages are highest for those entering Canada in the 1990s (table 11.2).

There are similar trends for indicators of language use. Table 11.2 shows that new arrivals are the most likely to have mother tongue languages (the first language learned and still understood) that are not English or French; over three-quarters of those arriving in the 1990s speak a language other than English or French at home. This is problematic because lack of language proficiency in host-country language(s) can create barriers to learning for school-age children and may reduce economic opportunities for immigrants (Boyd 1999; Chiswick and Miller 2003).

DIVERSITY AND DIVERSE OUTCOMES

Chinese, South Asians, and blacks are the largest visible minority groups in Canada (table 11.2). Most are foreign-born, although there is a sizeable Canadian-born black population as a result of migration in the aftermath of the American Revolution. Having fought in the British Army, black United Empire Loyalists were given land, with the majority settling in Nova Scotia. More came to Ontario via the Underground Railroad before the Civil War (Milan and Tran 2004; Walker 1980). More recently, black immigrants have come from Caribbean, Latin American, and African countries. Chinese began arriving in the 1840s, although numbers were legislatively suppressed until immigration changes in the 1960s and 1970s. Most came from China, Hong Kong, and Taiwan (Chiu, Tran, and Flanders 2005; Lindsay 2007). Similarly, the South Asian visible-minority group comes from many different countries. Like Chinese, their migration was restricted by immigration laws before the regulatory and legislative changes of the 1960s and 1970s. Today, the largest groups are from India, Sri Lanka, and Pakistan, accounting for almost three-quarters (72.5 percent) of the South Asian immigrant population in Canada (Tran, Kaddatz, and Allard 2005).

These visible minority groups differ from each other and from non-visible minority groups, not just in terms of their histories and geographical origins, but in terms of age, education, and economic characteristics. Table 11.3 provides information on these groups aged 25–64 by sex and by period of arrival from the 1970s on. Canadian-born members of visible minority groups are younger than their foreign-born counterparts, with South Asians being the youngest. Their relatively younger age profile reflects that many are children of immigrants from the 1970s and 1980s. As observed in table 11.1, among the immigrant populations, all groups entering earlier tend to be older than more recent arrivals.

Educational attainments expressed as percentages with a bachelor degree or beyond are highest for those arriving recently. These trends are consistent with their younger age profiles; because education occurs early in the life cycle, increased access to higher levels of schooling usually benefit younger cohorts. But the educational trends also reflect changes in immigration regulations starting in the mid-1990s that give preference to high-skilled and thus highly educated immigrants. However, not all groups are equal in educational attainments. Of the non-immigrant, non-visible minority population, fewer than one out of five (17 percent) has a bachelor degree or higher; among visible minorities, black Canadian-born and select entry cohorts have low percentages compared to Chinese and South Asian groups (table 11.3).

Being in the labour force and being employed signal enhanced access to economic resources, and analysis of the 2001 census shows the following. First, the majority of all groups are in the 2001 labour force, but women are slightly less likely than men to be participants, a pattern thought to reflect their greater domestic responsibilities. Second, labour force participation rates for immigrants are lowest for recent arrivals of both sexes. In particular, Chinese who arrived between 1991 and 2001 have the lowest rates of involvement, with 58 percent of the women and 74 percent of the men working in the labour force. Third, for all groups, the percentages unemployed are highest for arriving in the 1990s, but blacks tend to have higher unemployment rates than others. Explanations of the lower labour-force participation and higher unemployment rates of recent arrivals include the time required to get settled, language difficulties, unfamiliarity with Canada, and employer-based discrimination against those lacking Canadian experience.

Table 11.3
Select Demographic, Social, and Economic Characteristics for Non-immigrant and Immigrant Populations, Age 25–64 by Period of Arrival,[a] Sex, and Visible Minority Group Membership, Canada 2001

	Women					Men				
	Not Visible Minority (1)	Chinese (2)	South Asia (3)	Black (4)	Other Visible Minorities (5)	Not Visible Minority (6)	Chinese (7)	South Asia (8)	Black (9)	Other Visible Minorities (10)
MEAN AGE										
Non-immigrant	43	36	31	37	36	43	37	31	37	37
Immigrant[a]	43	42	41	41	41	43	42	42	41	41
1971–1980	46	45	46	46	45	46	45	47	46	45
1981–1990	42	43	41	40	42	43	43	41	40	41
1991–2001	39	40	39	37	39	39	41	39	38	39
Percent Age 25-34[b]										
Non-immigrant	25	49	81	52	57	25	46	79	52	55
Immigrant[a]	25	26	33	32	29	24	23	29	29	29
1971–1980	17	14	16	17	17	19	15	15	18	20
1981–1990	21	21	27	32	23	21	23	22	30	27
1991–2001	38	33	45	46	39	35	27	39	39	35
PERCENT WITH BACHELORS DEGREE OR HIGHER										
Non-immigrant	18	51	54	19	35	17	48	42	17	37
Immigrant[a]	26	29	27	11	27	30	39	34	19	32
1971–1980	20	25	26	10	23	22	34	33	17	29
1981–1990	24	24	22	11	21	26	32	27	14	25
1991–2001	36	33	30	12	32	42	45	39	25	39

PERCENT IN THE LABOUR FORCE										
Non-immigrant	75	85	82	77	79	87	88	87	86	87
Immigrant[a]	74	65	67	79	71	90	80	88	88	87
1971–1980	75	77	75	83	78	89	87	88	89	89
1981–1990	76	70	74	81	76	91	86	90	89	88
1991–2001	71	58	59	73	65	90	74	88	87	84
PERCENT UNEMPLOYED										
Non-immigrant	6	4	5	9	7	6	4	8	8	5
Immigrant[a]	6	8	11	11	9	5	7	7	10	8
1971–1980	5	4	6	7	5	4	4	5	6	5
1981–1990	5	5	9	11	7	4	5	5	9	7
1991–2001	10	11	16	16	12	8	9	8	13	11

(a) Refers only to the immigrant population arriving from 1970 on.

(b) For example, of those age 25–64 who are non-immigrants and also are not members of visible minority groups, 25 percent are age 25–34.

LABOUR MARKET INEQUALITIES

Judging from labour-force participation rates and unemployment rates, recently arrived immigrants do not seem to be doing as well as those who arrived earlier. However, because census data are a cross-sectional look at one point in time, this conclusion risks confounding age and period effects. We have already seen that persons who came earlier are older, and this might underlie their better economic status. As well, immigrants who entered Canada in the 1970s found a different economic climate that may have influenced the rapidity with which they became economically established. Meanwhile, the recession of the early 1990s may have suppressed the economic integration of those arriving during or shortly after this time.

That said, a number of indicators and studies that compare recent arrivals across censuses confirm that today's arrivals are not doing as well as previous entry cohorts. Immigrants who entered Canada in the 1990s were less likely to be employed in 2000 than the Canadian-born or immigrants who arrived earlier. Additionally, comparisons across censuses show that the employment gap between those arriving within ten years of each specific census and either the Canadian-born or immigrants arriving earlier widens with each successive census, with the gap largest in 2001 (Heisz, LaRochelle-Côté, Bordt, and Das 2005).

Multivariate analyses of immigrant earnings strongly support an image of recent arrivals not doing as well as groups entering Canada in previous decades. Comparisons of the earnings of new arrivals across censuses from 1961 on indicate that the relative entry earnings of those who arrived in the 1990s have declined over time. Immigrant men arriving between 1995 and 1999 had estimated earnings in their first year that were, on average, 24 percent lower than their counterparts arriving between 1965 and 1969 (Aydemir and Skuterud 2005; see Frenette and Morissette 2005 for comparisons of entry cohorts between 1981 and 2001).

The earnings gap between immigrant and Canadian-born men widened from 11 percent in 1980 to 33 percent in 1995, before declining to 22 percent in 2000. Similar trends exist in the Canadian-born/immigrant earnings gap for women. Studies also suggest that the time it takes for the wages of new entry cohorts to catch up to those of the Canadian-born is increasing (Frenette and Morissette 2005).

Table 11.4 provides additional evidence for the deteriorating condition of new arrivals, using 2001 Census data on occupations and earnings for women and men who are Canadian-born or who have arrived since 1970. The first three panels show percentages employed in management and high-skill occupations, using the National Occupational Classification developed by Human Resources and Social Development Canada (no date). The first panel indicates the overall percentages employed in these occupations, regardless of educational attainments. However, high-skill occupations usually require university degrees, and panel 1 partly reflects group differences in higher levels of education. The second panel adjusts for this by providing percentages only for those with a bachelor degree or higher. The third panel expresses these percentages as ratios to the percentage observed for the Canadian-born who are not members of visible minority groups (71 percent of women, 74 percent of men).

Two conclusions emerge from the occupational data in panels 2 and 3 (table 11.4) for the university educated. First, within each non-visible and visible minority group, Canadian-born women and men tend to have the highest percentages employed in managerial or high skill occupations. By comparison, the likelihood of well-educated immigrants finding employment in managerial occupations declines steadily for those arriving between 1970–1980, 1981–1990, and 1991–2001, with the most recent arrivals having the lowest percentages (panel 2, table 11.4).

Second, visible minority immigrants are less likely to have managerial or high-skill occupations, something made evident by expressing the percentages as a ratio to percentages of non-immigrants (Canadian-born) who are not members of visible minority groups (panel 2, table 11.4). Only immigrant Chinese men arriving in the 1970s and non-immigrant Chinese men do as well or better than this reference group. Compared to non-visible, non-immigrant men, recently arrived South Asian and black men with a bachelor degree or higher are substantially less likely to have managerial and high-skill employment, as are recently arrived South Asian women.

A similar analytical approach to the wages and self-employment earnings of the population in 2000 (asked of respondents to the 2001 census) produces similar conclusions. Persons who arrived in 2000 or 2001 are omitted, since they would not have a full year of potential earnings in Canada. Table 11.4 shows the annual wage and self-employment earnings for all earners and then for full-time, full-year workers (panels 4 and 5). This latter designation removes variations that might stem from differences between groups with respect to part-time or part-year work. Compared to the Canadian-born who are not visible minorities, earnings decline for recent arrival cohorts. Even among full-time, full-year workers, those arriving in Canada in 1991–1999 earn far less than immigrants arriving earlier and the non-visible minority Canadian-born. Black men arriving in 1991–1999 earn 58 percent of the average annual earnings of non-visible minority Canadian-born men,

Table 11.4

Percentages in Managerial and High Skill Occupations and Average Wage, Salary and Self-Employment Earnings for Non-Immigrant and Immigrant Populations, Age 25–64 by Sex, Visible Minority Status, and Period of Arrival, Canada 2001

	Women					Men				
	Not Visible Minority (1)	Chinese (2)	South Asia (3)	Black (4)	Other Visible Minorities (5)	Not Visible Minority (6)	Chinese (7)	South Asia (8)	Black (9)	Other Visible Minorities (10)
PERCENT IN MANAGERIAL AND HIGH SKILL OCCUPATIONS										
TOTAL POPULATION										
Non-immigrant	29	46	46	29	36	28	50	43	26	42
Immigrant	31	29	20	19	21	36	42	29	21	28
1971–1980	30	34	27	25	28	35	43	39	23	33
1981–1990	30	29	20	19	20	34	37	25	20	25
1991–2001	33	28	16	13	19	40	44	26	21	28
PERCENT IN MANAGERIAL AND HIGH SKILL OCCUPATIONS										
POPULATION WITH BACHELORS DEGREES AND HIGHER										
Non-immigrant	71	66	66	65	63	74	75	66	68	72
Immigrant[a]	62	56	39	53	39	71	68	53	57	53
1971–1980	69	67	51	67	47	77	75	64	67	61
1981–1990	62	60	41	52	44	73	71	54	60	56
1991–2001	57	50	32	43	34	65	65	48	51	49
RATIO, BACHELORS AND HIGHER										
Non-immigrant	(rg)	93	93	92	90	(rg)	101	89	92	97
Immigrant[a]	87	79	55	75	55	95	92	71	77	72
1971–1980	97	95	72	95	66	104	102	87	91	83
1981–1990	87	84	57	74	63	99	95	72	81	75
1991–2001	80	71	45	61	47	88	88	65	69	66

WAGES & SELF-EMPLOYMENT EARNINGS, 2000[a]

All Workers

Non-immigrant	40,540	42,890	34,010	35,390	36,270	62,930	54,310	44,090	48,630	54,630
Immigrant[a]	36,610	34,460	29,990	32,440	28,620	57,990	46,390	45,590	37,010	41,180
1971–1980	40,990	44,020	37,410	38,260	36,380	68,520	64,000	59,710	45,570	53,790
1981–1990	38,550	40,930	32,760	34,270	33,100	59,320	51,470	46,950	39,140	43,850
1991–2001	31,550	26,770	23,450	24,890	22,810	48,620	35,550	37,170	30,020	33,210

FULL-TIME, FULL-YEAR WORKERS[b]

Non-immigrant	49,370	52,530	42,600	43,780	45,090	69,280	59,420	56,900	54,770	65,140
Immigrant[a]	46,280	44,920	38,370	41,980	35,980	65,610	56,280	53,530	45,480	48,630
1971–1980	49,860	53,110	43,750	45,930	42,540	74,810	68,210	66,510	50,730	59,340
1981–1990	46,670	46,800	41,410	40,180	38,770	65,830	58,660	52,770	46,350	50,160
1991–2001	42,690	38,800	31,650	37,980	29,870	56,940	46,630	45,300	40,050	40,460

RATIO, FULL-TIME, FULL-YEAR WORKERS[b]

Non-immigrant	(rg)	106	86	89	91	(rg)	86	82	79	94
Immigrant[a]	94	91	78	85	73	95	81	77	66	70
1971–1980	101	108	89	93	86	108	98	96	73	86
1981–1990	95	95	84	81	79	95	85	76	67	72
1991–2001	86	79	64	77	61	82	67	65	58	58

(a) Omits persons immigrating in 2000 or 2001 and persons living in the Atlantic provinces, the territories, or Nunavut; persons who did not work at least one week in 2000 also are omitted. For ease of reading, earnings are rounded to the nearest 10 dollars.

(b) Full-time consists of working 30 hours or more per week and full-year consists of working 49 weeks or more.

while South Asian women earn 64 percent of the wages and salaries received by non-visible minority Canadian-born women.

There are several explanations for the declining labour market conditions for immigrants. A recent report concludes that approximately one-third of the deterioration in the earnings of new immigrants is the result of a decline in the value of foreign labour-market experience, a decline occurring almost exclusively among those from Canada's non-traditional source regions, including Eastern Europe, Africa, and Asia. The report finds that immigrants who arrived during the late 1990s came from different nations and spoke different languages than those of the late 1960s. Roughly one-third of the earnings deterioration was associated with these compositional factors (Picot and Sweetman 2005).

Other factors have contributed to the earnings decline. Young Canadian-born workers have not done well in recent years when they enter the labour force, for example, and possibly all new entrants, including immigrants, are having entry-related difficulties (Picot and Sweetman 2005). In addition, immigrants are competing against Canadian-born workers who are much better educated than in the past; as a consequence, the relative educational advantage enjoyed by immigrants has shrunk, arguably affecting their employment opportunities (Reitz 2001). There is also evidence that foreign degrees are discounted by employers (Alboim, Finney, and Ming 2005). Finally, discrimination (treating people with equal skills differently with respect to hiring, promotion, and pay) may be an important factor, particularly for visible minorities (Pendakur and Pendakur 1998; Yoshida and Smith 2008).

THE SECOND GENERATION

If immigrants, particularly recent immigrants, are not doing as well as the Canadian born in the labour market, what about the generation that follows them, the so-called second generation? At the heart of this question are two competing perspectives. One argues that while immigrants bear the transition costs of changing countries, in a receiving society like Canada, which is governed by principles of equal opportunity and fairness, children born in Canada will do much better and be indistinguishable from generations farther removed from the migration experience. The other emphasizes that ethnic and racial diversities can serve as markers of difference and become the basis of discrimination and stratification. According to this second perspective, the offspring of visible minority immigrants will continue to do less well than the white majority precisely because racialization will affect all facets of their lives, including their labour-market experiences.

Chart 11.2

Age and Generation Profile for the Canadian-Born Population, Age 25–64 by Visible and Non-Visible Minority Groups, Canada 2001

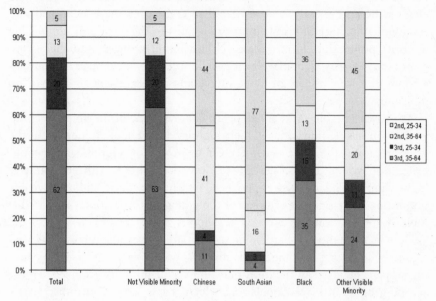

Throughout this chapter, immigrants distinguished by period of arrival are compared with non-immigrants. However, among the Canadian-born, percentages vary substantially by visible and non-visible minority groups with respect to generational composition. The Canadian-born consist of the second generation (Canadian-born with one or both parents foreign born) or third-plus generation (the Canadian-born with Canadian-born parents, including those whose ancestors have been in Canada for generations). Strong age differences accompany these generational differences, reflecting temporal changes in the origins of immigrant parents. For example, substantial numbers from Asian countries began to enter Canada in the 1970s and later. Their children born in Canada are mostly under age 30. By comparison, large numbers of European immigrants arrived in the 1950s and 1960s; their children would be middle-aged by 2001.

Chart 11.2 shows the age and generational status of the non-immigrant population age 25–64 for select visible minority groups. Over 80 percent of the primarily white, non-visible minority population is third-plus generation, most between age 35 and 64; only the black population comes close to this with half being second generation. In contrast, Chinese, South Asian, and other visible minorities are mostly second generation, many between 25 and 34 years of age.

Given the diverse age and generational composition of the Canadian-born population, assessing the well-being of subsequent generations requires age and generational specific analyses. Such assessments could easily be a sole chapter; here, the analysis is restricted to comparing the educational and economic outcomes of visible minority groups to the third-plus non-visible minority population. In most research, this latter group is thought to represent the majority Canadian-born population with advantages accruing as a result of a long history of living in Canada and experiencing little or no discrimination.

As shown in table 11.5, a significant characteristic of the young second-generation visible minorities is their high level of school attendance in the year preceding the 2001 census. Over one-third of South Asian second-generation young adults, age 25–34, attended school, with comparative high-school attendance also experienced by Chinese, black, and other visible minorities. Only one out of seven of the young adult third-plus non-visible minority population was enrolled in school.

How many of those not attending school have university degrees or higher? Again the answer is that the visible minority second-generation groups have higher percentages than the third-plus non-visible minority groups. Even the second-generation black population, which is less likely than other visible minority groups to hold university degrees, exceeds the third-plus generation.

Examining the proportions with managerial and high-skill occupations and the annual earnings of full-time full-year workers confirms that the second generation is very similar to the third-plus non-visible minority group or more likely to be employed in high-skill occupations with higher earnings. To be sure, there are differences among the visible minority second generation, with black males earning less than the non-visible minority third-plus generation. However, some second generation visible minority groups seem to be doing fairly well.

CONCLUSION

As noted above, Canada's immigrants are not a homogenous group. In response to revised immigration policies, immigrants now come from many different countries. Even so, earlier migrants contribute to the diversity of the immigrant population. In its most common Canadian usage, the term "diversity" refers to the kaleidoscope of ethnic and phenotypic characteristics that underlie racial categorization. This chapter demonstrates that immigrants are diverse in other ways – in age composition, family characteristics, geographical location, religion, language, educational attainment, and labour

Table 11.5

Percentages Attending School in the Previous Year, with University Degrees or Holding Managerial and High Skill Occupations and Average Wage, Salary and Self-Employment Earnings for the Second and Third-plus Generations, Age 25–64 by Sex, Visible Minority Status, and Age Group, Canada 2001

	Women					Men				
	Not Visible Minority (1)	Chinese (2)	South Asia (3)	Black (4)	Other Visible Minorities (5)	Not Visible Minority (6)	Chinese (7)	South Asia (8)	Black (9)	Other Visible Minorities (10)
PERCENT ATTENDING										
Age 25–34										
Second Generation	17	24	36	28	30	15	25	34	21	27
Third Plus	15	(c)	(c)	11	(c)	13	(c)	(c)	12	(c)
Age 35–64										
Second Generation	6	7	(c)	15	7	4	7	16	14	4
Third Plus	6	(c)	(c)	9	6	4	(c)	(c)	4	4
PERCENT WITH UNIVERSITY DEGREE OR HIGHER										
TOTAL POPULATION, NOT ATTENDING SCHOOL										
Age 25–34										
Second Generation	31	62	62	24	40	23	52	42	21	38
Third Plus	21	(c)	(c)	11	27	16	(c)	(c)	4	32
Age 35-64										
Second Generation	19	41	26	24	25	21	45	23	25	35
Third Plus	14	(c)	(c)	12	29	15	(c)	(c)	13	35

Table 11.5

Percentages Attending School in the Previous Year, with University Degrees or Holding Managerial and High Skill Occupations and Average Wage, Salary and Self-Employment Earnings for the Second and Third-plus Generations, Age 25–64 by Sex, Visible Minority Status, and Age Group, Canada 2001 (*Continued*)

PERCENT IN MANAGERIAL AND HIGH SKILL OCCUPATIONS

POPULATION WITH BACHELORS DEGREES AND HIGHER

Not Attending School

Age 25–34									
Second Generation	65	66	75	68	62	67	75	66	65
Third Plus	68	(c)	(c)	(c)	(c)	68	(c)	(c)	(c)
Age 35–64									
Second Generation	72	72	(c)	(c)	(c)	78	76	(c)	(c)
Third Plus	74	(c)	(c)	(c)	(c)	78	(c)	(c)	(c)

WAGES & SELF-EMPLOYMENT EARNINGS, 2000[a]

FULL-TIME, FULL-YEAR WORKERS[b]

Age 25–34									
Second Generation	34,630	46,320	39,540	30,500	34,850	43,400	46,230	46,270	36,080	46,250
Third Plus	30,520	(c)	(c)	(c)	(c)	39,950	(c)	(c)	31,150	(c)
Age 35–64									
Second Generation	38,890	47,600	(c)	(c)	(c)	55,330	55,030	53,120	62,880
Third Plus	35,730	(c)	(c)	33,130	47,130	50,800	(c)	41,620	64,990

(a) Omits persons immigrating in 2000 or 2001 and persons living in the Atlantic provinces, the territories, or Nunavut; persons who did not work at least one week in 2000 are also omitted. For ease of reading, earnings are rounded to the nearest 10 dollars.

(b) Full-Time consists of working 30 hours or more per week and full-year consists of working 49 weeks or more.

(c) Fewer than 50 cases in the 2001 Census of Canada Public Use Microdata File.

market characteristics. Such variation is especially evident when we distinguish among immigrants on the basis of when they first arrived in Canada.

The growth in the visible minority immigrant population has coincided with increasing concern that 1990s arrivals are not doing as well economically as earlier cohorts. This chapter confirms this trend of diminishing fortunes by comparing the occupations and earnings of non-immigrant and immigrant groups, defined for both groups by non-visible and visible minority status and for immigrants by period of arrival.

The experiences of recent immigrants direct attention to the fate of their offspring. Here too, Canada's second generation bears the imprint of previous immigration patterns. Most visible minority immigrant offspring are quite young, having been born in the 1970s and beyond. Many are still attending school. But a cursory look at university attainments, employment in managerial and high-skill occupations (for those with university degrees or higher), and earnings of the full-time full-year young adult second generation finds them to be similar to or doing better than the third-plus non-visible minority generation. While more research and other indicators are needed, it appears that the extreme difficulties faced by recent immigrants in the labour market are less likely for many in the next generation.

REFERENCES

Alboim, Naomi, Ross Finnie, and Ronald Ming. 2005. "The Discounting of Immigrants' Skills in Canada: Evidence and Policy Recommendations." *Choices* (Institute for Research on Public Policy) 11 (2): 2–23

Aydemir, Abdurrahman, and Mikal Skuterud. 2005. "Explaining the Deteriorating Entry Earnings of Canada's Immigrant Cohorts, 1966–2000." *Canadian Journal of Economics* 38 (2): 641–72

Boyd, Monica. 1999. "Integrating Gender, Language, and Race." In *Immigrant Canada: Demographic, Economic, and Social Challenges*, eds. Shiva S. Halli and Leo Driedger, 282–386. Toronto: University of Toronto Press

– and Michael Vickers. 2000. "100 Years of Immigration." *Canadian Social Trends* 58 (2):12. Ottawa: Statistics Canada. Cat. no.11–008

Chiswick, Barry R., and Paul W. Miller. 2003. "The Complementarity of Language and Other Human Capital: Immigrant Earnings in Canada." *Economics of Education Review* 22 (5): 469–80

Chui, Tina, Kelly Tran, and John Flanders. 2005. "Chinese Canadians: Enriching the Cultural Mosaic." *Canadian Social Trends* 76: 26–34. Ottawa: Statistics Canada. Cat. no.11–008

Frenette, Marc, and Rene Morissette. 2005. "Will They Ever Converge: Earnings of Immigrant and Canadian-born Workers for the Last Two Decades." *International Migration Review* 39 (1): 229–58

Heisz, Andrew, Sébastien LaRochelle-Côté, Michael Bordt, and Sudip Das. 2005. *Labour Markets, Business Activity, and Population Growth and Mobility in Canadian* CMAs. Analytical Studies Research Paper Series. Ottawa: Statistics Canada, Business and Labour Market Analysis Division. Cat. no.89–613–MIE-No.006

Human Resources and Social Development Canada (no date). National Occupational Classification. www23.hrdc-drhc.gc.ca/92/e/generic/welcome.shtml (Accessed March 2010)

Kelley, Ninette, and Michael Trebilcock. 1998. *The Making of the Mosaic: A History of Canadian Immigration Policy.* Toronto: University of Toronto Press

Knowles, Valerie. 2007. *Strangers at Our Gates: Canadian Immigration and Immigration Policy, 1540–2006.* Revised edition. Toronto: Dundurn

Lindsay, Colin. 2007. *The Chinese Community in Canada.* Ottawa: Statistics Canada. Cat. no.89–621–XIE-No.001

Milan, Anne, and Kelly Tran. 2004. "Blacks in Canada: A Long History." *Canadian Social Trends* 71: 2–5. Ottawa: Statistics Canada. Cat. no.11–008

Paquet, Bernard. 2002. *Low Income Cutoffs from 1992 to 2001 and Low Income Measures from 1991 to 2000.* Ottawa: Statistics Canada, Income Statistics Division. Cat. no.75F0002MIE-No.005

Pendakur, Krishna, and Ravi Pendakur. 1998. "The Colour of Money: Earnings Differentials among Ethnic Groups in Canada." *The Canadian Journal of Economics* 31 (3): 518–48

Picot, Garnett, and Arthur Sweetman. 2005. *The Deteriorating Economic Welfare of Immigrants and Possible Causes: Update 2005.* Ottawa: Statistics Canada, Business and Labour Market Analysis Division. Analytical Studies Research Paper Series no. 262

Porter, John. 1965. *The Vertical Mosaic.* Toronto: University of Toronto Press

Reitz, Jeffrey G. 2001. "Immigrant Success in the Knowledge Economy: Institutional Change and the Immigrant Experience in Canada, 1970–1995." *Journal of Social Issues* 57 (3): 579–613

Schellenberg, Grant. 2004. *Immigrants in Canada's Census Metropolitan Areas.* Ottawa: Statistics Canada, Business and Labour Market Analysis Division. Cat. no.89–613–MIE-No.003

Statistics Canada. 2008. *Report on the Demographic Situation in Canada 2005 and 2006.* Ottawa. Cat. no.91–209–X

Tran, Kelly, Jennifer Kaddatz, and Paul Allard. 2005. "South Asians in Canada: Unity through Diversity." *Canadian Social Trends* 78: 20–5. Ottawa: Statistics Canada. Cat. no.11–008

Walker, James W. St G. 1980. *A History of Blacks in Canada: A Study Guide for Teachers and Students*. Hull, QC: Canadian Government Publishing Centre

Yoshida, Yoko, and Michael R. Smith. 2008. "Measuring and Mismeasuring Discrimination against Visible Minority Immigrants: The Role of Work Experience." *Canadian Studies in Population* 35 (2): 311–38

Zietsma, Danielle. 2007. *The Canadian Immigrant Labour Market in 2006: First Results from Canada's Labour Force Survey*. Immigrant Labour Force Analysis Series. Ottawa: Statistics Canada, Labour Statistics Division. Cat. no. 71-606-XIE. www.statcan.gc.ca/pub/71–606–x/71–606–x2007001–eng.htm

PART FOUR

Families, Children, and the Elderly

12

Changing Canadian Families

ZHENG WU AND CHRISTOPH M. SCHIMMELE

INTRODUCTION

The concept "modern family" refers to any domestic kinship group established through marriage, common-law, birth, consanguinity, or adoption, and represents a primary social institution in Western societies. The popular image Canadians associate with "family" is a household that includes a married heterosexual couple and their dependent children, the nuclear family, even though this designation does not capture the total diversity characterizing numerous Western families. In several respects, the so-called "traditional nuclear family" – i.e., a household containing a husband, wife, their dependent children, and organized around the male breadwinner and female homemaker model – is a highly idealized institution epitomized in television programs such as *Leave it to Beaver* and *Father Knows Best*, but was not the norm for numerous North American families during the 1950s and throughout North American history (Coontz 1991). Among many North Americans, however, there is a strong nostalgia for these 1950s-type nuclear families, and the male-breadwinner model remained entrenched in America's and Canada's social fabric and public policies until recent years (Lewis 2003). Indeed, the popular attitude is that the nuclear family is the "natural" family structure, as evident in social stigma and continuing discrimination surrounding families that deviate from this model, such as single-parent and same-sex households. But the nuclear family's predominance in Western civilization is actually historically brief. As Edward Shorter (1975) argues in his classic treatise, *The Making of the Modern Family*, the nuclear family developed with the Industrial Revolution and market capitalism, which transformed families from extended units built around family economic production, to small, private units defined by domesticity and sentiment, rather than practical concerns.

Families certainly fulfill important functions necessary for society's well-being and survival. The sociologist Talcott Parsons (e.g., Parsons & Bales 1955) regarded the nuclear family as a vital agent for reproducing social and economic order, which was maintained through the gender division of labour in the traditional nuclear family. Families are vital agents in modern societies, especially through child-bearing, child-rearing, and providing children's primary socialization, e.g., teaching children language, behavioral norms, and social values, but many sociologists challenge Parson's structural-functionalist interpretation for its failure to accommodate alternative family forms and its inability to properly rationalize family change (Luxton 2005). Yet the main impetus behind the "family in crisis" rhetoric is premised on the structural-functionalist argument that the traditional nuclear family is the fundamental building block of modern societies, and any changes or deviation from this putative norm are therefore treated as negative incidences. Put differently, against the *Leave it to Beaver* ideal, non-traditional families and family change are frightening prospects that threaten to disrupt social stability. While many sociologists consider structural-functionalism flawed, the basic assumptions guiding this perspective remain very influential within conservative politics, such as the "family values" campaign under the George W. Bush administration. To be sure, family change is a turbulent concern among policy-makers, pundits, and the general population; however, North American society has not destabilized as the male-breadwinner model has declined, but has adapted to the changing social landscape on which families are formed. Rather than considering family change in negative terms, then, it is important to recognize that family change is an inevitable process and that families shift along with broad transitions in socio-cultural attitudes and socio-economic needs.

The following chapter summarizes family change in Canada over the last several decades, a period of major demographic transition defined by declining or delayed marriage, below-replacement fertility, growth in non-marital cohabiting-couple unions and families formed outside of marriage, and increases in divorce, remarriage, and reconstituted families (Cherlin 1992). In addition to some theoretical discussion, the chapter primarily uses Canadian Census data and other data sources to detail changes in household type, marriage and divorce, non-marital cohabitation, fertility, and same-sex unions since 1981.

CANADIAN FAMILIES IN TRANSITION

Family change in Canada has unfolded mainly at the private household-level. A private household refers to a private dwelling, such as a house or

Table 12.1
Private Household Types: Canada, 2001

Household type	Number	Percent
Couple households with children	3,530,180	30.5%
Couple households without children	3,237,620	28.0%
One person household	2,976,875	25.7%
Other household types	1,818,300	15.7%
Total private households	11,562,975	100.0%
Average household size	2.55	–
Population in private households	29,522,305	–

Note: Couple families include married and common-law union families
Source: Canadian Census, 2001

an apartment, in which a couple, a family, or unrelated individuals reside together (Péron 2000a). Statistics Canada (2006) defines a private household as "a person or group of persons other than foreign residents, who occupy a dwelling and do not have a usual place of residence elsewhere in Canada." According to this definition, then, a household does not necessarily represent a family unit, and this signifies an important historical change, for the preponderance of non-family households has grown considerably during the past half-century. The concept "census family" refers to at least two persons sharing a common dwelling, and may feature a married or cohabiting couple, a couple and their unmarried children, a single-parent household, and couple households including stepchildren (Péron 2000a). All other persons are termed "non-family" persons. In other words, Statistics Canada measures families at the household level, thereby excluding wider familial relationships, such as non-resident grandparents, aunts and uncles, and siblings, even though these individuals are indeed family members.

Table 12.1 presents the statistical breakdown of private households by household type for the 2001 Census year. In 2001, there were around 11.6 million private households, containing almost 30 millions persons. By comparison, there were 3.4 millions private households in 1951, which contained 13.6 million persons (Péron 2000a). Between 1951 and 1991, the supply of private housing stocks tripled, mainly because an increase in the number of individuals old enough to establish a private household increased the demand for housing. The population aged 15 years and older doubled over this period, growing at a rate exceeding 10 percent per intercensal period from 1951 to 1981. However, as households became more numerous, the average household size declined from 4.0 persons in 1951 to 2.6 in 2001, which reflected the "baby bust" that came after the "baby boom." The number of single-occupant households also increased. In 1961, around

Table 12.2
Census Family Structure: Canada, 1981–2001

Family type	1981	1986	1991	1996	2001
Total couple families	88.7%	87.3%	87.0%	85.5%	84.3%
Married couples	93.7%	91.8%	88.8%	86.3%	83.6%
Common-law couples	6.3%	8.2%	11.2%	13.7%	16.4%
Total lone-parent families	11.3%	12.7%	13.0%	14.5%	15.7%
Female parent	82.6%	82.2%	82.7%	83.1%	81.3%
Male parent	17.4%	17.8%	17.3%	16.9%	18.7%
TOTAL	100%	100%	100%	100%	100%

Source: Canadian Censuses, 1981–2001

425,000 private households were single-occupant dwellings, accounting for 9 percent of private households (Péron 2000a). As table 12.1 shows, by 2001, almost 3 million households were single-occupant dwellings, representing about 26 percent of private households.

Table 12.1 indicates that the largest household types are couple-family households with children, which account for 30.5 percent of private households, and couple-family households without children, which account for 28 percent of private households, together totaling close to 60 percent of private Canadian households. Most household members belong to an *economic family*, which Statistics Canada defines as "a group of two or more persons who live in the same dwelling and are related by blood, adoption, marriage, or common law" (Péron 2000a, 23). Non-family members account for about 16 percent of private households. Péron (2000a) interprets this pattern as Canadians' continuing preference for the nuclear family, even though many nuclear family households are not organized around the male breadwinner model.

The nuclear family household remains the predominant family structure in Canada, though table 12.2 indicates a decline of married-couple nuclear families over the past two decades. In 1981, married couples accounted for 94 percent of all couple families, whereas common-law couples accounted for the remaining 6 percent. By 2001, married couples' share had declined to 84 percent, while common-law couples' share increased to 16 percent. The number of lone-parent families also grew during this period, increasing from 11 percent of all family households in 1981 to 16 percent in 2001. As table 12.2 suggests, the proportion of male-headed single-parent households increased somewhat during this period, and the proportion of female-headed single-parent households decreased. However, the proportion of male-headed single-parent households remains comparatively small, as lone mothers have accounted for more than 80 percent of single-parent households since 1981.

UNION FORMATION AND DISSOLUTION

Marital Unions

All Western societies practice marriage, and this institution represents the most common form of union formation between men and women today. It has been a legal institution since the 18th century, when the English state codified uniform marriage regulations (Phillips 1988). Before this period, formal marriage was a church domain, and informal marriages were not uncommon because clergymen were often inaccessible in some rural areas and to the peasant class. In general, marriage is defined as a formal union between a man and woman, regulated through behavioural norms and mutual expectations for reciprocity between a husband and a wife, and creating non-consanguine kinship networks, e.g., mothers-in-law. Marriage provides several important functions, including establishing an environment for child-bearing and child-rearing (reproduction of society), economic co-operation and exchange, and companionship and emotional fulfillment. In the 2001 Census, marriage was defined as a legal conjugal union between a man and a woman.

Legal marriage is the primary institution that establishes and organizes most Canadian families (Statistics Canada 2001). Most Canadian marriages are formed through some type of religious ceremony, but a growing proportion of couples are choosing to form their unions through civil ceremonies. Figure 12.1 illustrates the total first marriage rate (TFMR) for men and women between 1986 and 2002. TFMR is defined as the number of never-married males or females aged 15–49 years per 1000 males or females who are expected to enter a marital union by age 50 for a given year. Figure 12.1 shows that 560 of 1000 adult males and 590 of 1000 adult females were expected to get married by age 50 in 1986. The TFMR dropped to an historical low in 2001, with 493 of 1000 males and 518 of 1000 females expected to form a marriage. As noted above, this stands in sharp contrast to the 1950s, when the projected TFMR exceeded the maximum observable for a generation, being over 1000 marriages per 1000 males and females. The crude marriage rate, i.e., marriages per 1000 population, stood at 4.7 in 2002, as 147,000 marriages occurred across Canada, with Prince Edward Island having the highest crude marriage rate and Nunavut the lowest (Statistics Canada 2004). In 1997, moreover, the average age at first marriage was 31 years for brides and 34 years for grooms (Statistics Canada 1997). Compare these ages to the early marriage pattern during the early 1960s, when the average age at first marriage was around 23 years for women and 25 years for men (Wu 1998).

Figure 12.1
Total First Marriage Rates: Canada, 1986–2001

Per 1,000

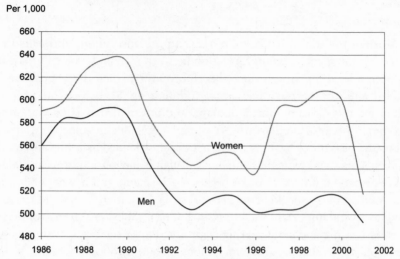

Source: Duchesne, et al., 1999, 8; Belanger, 2003, 21; Statistics Canada, 2004, Annual Demographic
Statistics, 2000–2003, Catelogue no. 91–213. Ottawa: Statistics Canada, 195.

Clearly, Canadians are marrying in the fewest numbers and at the oldest ages since 1940, when World War II increased the average age at first
marriage because many young Canadian men were serving overseas. Many
demographers interpret the rapid decrease in age at first marriage in the
post-war years as a result of recently returned soldiers prospering from economic expansion, giving them the resources to support families at comparatively young ages (Cherlin 1992). Yet conservative family scholars like
David Popenoe (1993) interpret the present trends in marriage formation
as a socio-demographic process that is weakening marriage's institutional
strength, and argue that the so-called "retreat from marriage" amounts to
the deinstitutionalization of marriage. But in Canada and America, marriage
is still the predominant union choice, even though many individuals are delaying marriage formation. By age 35, 87 percent of Canadian women and
83 percent of Canadian men have married (Wu 1998). Similarly, 87 percent
of American women and 82 percent of American men aged 35 to 44 years
reported being married in 2000 (Fields & Casper 2001). In 1970, the average age at first marriage was 23 years for American men and 21 years for
American women, compared with 27 and 25 years, respectively, in 2000.
These older ages at first marriage hardly suggest the deinstitutionalization
of marriage; instead, the very young ages in 1970 ought to be questioned,
giving undue concern to current trends.

Most family demographers agree that the meaning of marriage is changing, but whether this involves a "deinstitutionalization" of marriage is hotly debated (see Waite 2000). In several ways, current marital behaviour represents a decay of oppressive social norms, such as restrictions on non-marital cohabitation, rather than a weakening of marriage. Hence, Popenoe (1993) is correct to observe that marriage is no longer an institution built around economic security and procreation, but a relationship for self-fulfillment; however, this observation cannot properly explain why individuals are choosing to delay-marriage. The most persuasive theories for the delayed marriage pattern focus on the post-industrial economic transformation. The Nobel prize-winning economist, Gary Becker (1981), argues that delayed marriage associates with women's gains in labour markets. Becker perceives potential marriage partners as economic trading partners, with marriage's main benefits accruing from mutual dependence between marital partners, based on a traditional gender division of labour. From Becker's perspective, women's increasing labour market opportunities and financial rewards reduce their economic dependence upon men's wages, thereby reducing their incentive to marry. In short, women delay marriage because delaying marriage reflects their desire to establish careers and financial independence, rather than confining themselves to unpaid domestic labour. In response to Becker, Valerie Oppenheimer (1994) adds that the defunct male breadwinner model is another important factor. Oppenheimer demonstrates that the difficulties men experience in establishing financial security in post-industrial economies slow their ability to earn enough to support a family, thus increasing their socially eligible age at first marriage.

Non-Marital Cohabitations

The spread of non-marital cohabitation is another major reason for delayed marriage (Bumpass, Sweet, & Cherlin 1991). Cohabitation, or common-law union, refers to unmarried heterosexual couples living together in an intimate, but non-contract union (Wu & Schimmele 2003). While sharing similarities with marriage (e.g., sexual exclusivity, common household), cohabitation differs from marriage in several ways, including being more unstable, having weaker social acceptance, and having considerable ambiguity under state legislation. Still, cohabitations have become increasingly popular in Western countries since the 1970s, and this reflects the changes in Western value systems. Most Canadians begin union life in a cohabitation, and most recent marriages are continuations of cohabiting-couple unions (Wu & Schimmele 2005). Although common-law unions were common

Table 12.3
Cohabitation by Age Group, Canada: 1981–2001

Year	15–19 (%)	20–24 (%)	25–29 (%)	30–34 (%)	35–39 (%)	40–44 (%)	45–49 (%)	50–54 (%)
1981	1.7	8.2	7.6	5.7	4.2	3.2	2.4	1.9
1986	1.6	9.5	10.4	7.8	5.9	4.8	3.7	2.1
1991	1.8	11.6	14.0	10.9	8.5	6.8	5.8	4.4
1996	1.6	11.8	16.9	14.1	11.2	9.0	7.3	6.1
2001	1.5	12.5	19.6	16.8	14.2	11.8	9.7	7.9

Source: Canada Censuses 1981–2001.

before the 19th century, the present movement toward cohabitation represents a normative shift vis-à-vis the predominance of legal marriage throughout the 19th and 20th centuries. Until the 1970s, social norms prevented cohabitation from being widely practiced in most Western countries. For many, cohabitation serves as a transitional stage before marriage, and is often considered a "trial marriage." For others, however, cohabitation is an alternative to marriage, and partners no longer anticipate transforming their union into marriage (Manning & Smock 2002).

According to 2001 Census data, the Canadian national cohabitation rate translates into over 16 percent of all couple households, though this figure is elevated by Quebec's high cohabitation rate, where cohabitations account for 30 percent of couple households. In 1981, about 6 percent of Canadian couples were cohabiting, with a low of 3 percent in the Atlantic provinces to a high of 7 percent in British Columbia and Quebec (Le Bourdais & Lapierre-Adamcyk 2004). Recent data indicate that 48 percent of Canadian females and 35 percent of Canadian males form cohabitations by age 25; by age 30, these figures are 65 and 54 percent, respectively (Wu 2000).

Table 12.3 presents figures for cohabitations by age group, covering the period 1981–2001. In 1981, cohabitation remained uncommon, ranging from 1.7 percent of 15–19 year olds to 7.6 percent of 25–29 year olds. Excepting 15–19 year olds, all our selected age groups increased their propensity to cohabit over the next decade. Though the absolute increases were small, the proportion of cohabitors doubled among most age groups. By 2001, there were over 2 million cohabitors aged 15–54 years.

Some observers, such as Popenoe, assume that non-marital cohabitations signal the breakdown of traditional marriages and families. Alternately, Becker and Oppenheimer suggest that cohabitation does not appear to be replacing marriage, but reflects numerous couples' adaptation to the economic changes that have made marital union formation more difficult than in the 1950s, leaving cohabitation as an interim alternative. Most cohabitations are short-term arrangements, lasting around three years, with most of these unions "ending" through the transition to marriage, which implies that most Canadians still prefer marriage over cohabitation for long-term unions (Wu & Schimmele 2003). But the ideational shift is an important factor behind rising cohabitation rates. This normative trans-formation is what separates modern cohabitation from cohabitation before the 19th century. Historically, non-marital unions were formed because of legal ambiguity between marital and non-marital unions, whereas today cohabitation represents a conscious departure from predominant social norms, a decision that expresses the growing tension between the individ-ual desire for self-fulfillment and the normative restrictions associated with persisting, but out-dated social morals. Despite the popularity of this type of union, family experts consider cohabitation an "incomplete institution" because it does not establish well-defined behavioural norms and extended family networks as marriage does, and also because these unions are less than ideal environments for child-bearing and child-rearing (Nock 1995).

Divorce

In 1951, one-in-twenty Canadian marriages ended in divorce, a very low di-vorce rate compared to the all-time high of one-in-two in 1987 (McGovern 1995). Not surprisingly, this massive increase in divorce, called the "di-vorce revolution," is a principal theme in the "family in crisis" literature. Commenting on women's labour market participation, Popenoe (1993, 531) remarks, "at the same time our society has disclaimed the role of wives in the traditional nuclear family, it has also discarded the basic structure of that family type – two natural parents who stay together for life." As a leading figure in the "family in crisis" debate, Popenoe (1988) suggests that family decline parallels high-social acceptance for divorce, claiming that broken homes (single-mother households) increase various social problems, includ-ing juvenile delinquency and substance abuse, teenage pregnancy, school failure and dropout, and child poverty. Judith Stacey (1993, 545) sharply dismisses Popenoe's structural-functionalist interpretation regarding family change, and notes that while women's economic independence is important, "these developments expose the inequity and coercion that always lay at the vortex of the supposedly voluntary companionate marriage of the 'trad-itional nuclear family.' "

Two watershed moments stand behind the Canadian divorce revolution, the 1968 Divorce Act and the 1985 reforms to the Act (Wu & Schimmele 2005). Before 1968, Canada did not have coherent divorce legislation, and divorce regulations varied from province to province. Before reform, divorce was virtually impossible because conservative social legislation and social norms heavily restricted marital dissolution, especially for women. Canadian legal standards reflected the idealized perspective that marriage was a cornerstone of society. Moreover, women's economic dependence on their husbands was another strong disincentive against seeking divorce, even for those in troubled or abusive marriages. Until the 1950s, finding employment was very difficult for women, and most jobs available to them paid a subsistence wage, not enough to support children, which meant that women considering divorce had to choose between remaining in a bad marriage or facing poverty.

The 1968 Divorce Act created uniform divorce legislation for Canada, but still contained the "fault" principle, meaning that a divorce petitioner was obliged to prove his/her spouse guilty of committing a grievous act, such as adultery, rape, or intolerable cruelty. Following the recommendations of the Law Reform Commission, the Divorce Act was amended in 1985 by replacing the "fault" principle with evidence of marital breakdown, defined as separation for one year, adultery, and abuse.

Figure 12.2 illustrates how this reform influenced the total divorce rate (TDR), defined as the number of divorces per 1000 marriages, between 1976 and 2000. Between 1976 and 1983, the TDR steadily rose from 307 to 351 divorces per 1000 marriages, translating into a 30–35 percent divorce rate. The steady increase in divorce marks how the 1968 legislation "uncorked" demand for divorce. Put differently, divorce liberalization did not cause the divorce revolution per se, but simply allowed couples in unhappy marriages to dissolve their unions. In 1984 and 1985, there was a sharp dip in divorce, trailed by a rapid upsurge that came with the 1985 divorce reforms. In 1987, Canada experienced an all-time high divorce rate of 478 divorces per 1000 marriages, meaning that almost one-in-two marriages would end in divorce. After 1987, the Canadian divorce rate slowly tapered, and appears to have stabilized in the 35 to 37 percent range.

The divorce rate is a good barometer for understanding how ideational and economic changes have influenced family change (Wu & Schimmele 2005). In essence, the new divorce legislation was the state's response to growing public demand for divorce. Based on Enlightenment ideals, individuals began perceiving marriage as a private, dissolvable contract, rather than a permanent institution (Basch 1999). The emphasis on individual rights, however, was hampered by gender inequalities. The suffrage movement in the 20th century triggered the final resolution because political enfranchisement would eventually translate into improved educational and labour market opportunities, weakening women's dependence on men's wages. When

Figure 12.2
Total Divorce Rates, Canada, 1976–2000

Per 1,000 marriages

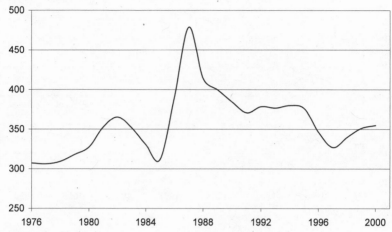

Source: Belanger, 2003, 110–11.

the ideational movement toward individual autonomy intersected with the post-war economic boom, the practical constraints on divorce slackened as women began finding pathways to financial independence. A re-evaluation of the traditional marriage contract followed, with economic security being replaced by personal happiness. "As emotional gratification became the [main criterion] of marriage," observes Furstenberg (1990, 308), "divorce became an indispensable element in the institution of matrimony, permitting couples to rectify poor choices." Although Canadians still have a strong commitment to marriage, most believe that an unhappy marriage justifies divorce.

Remarriage

Before World War II, widowhood represented the most common pathway into remarriage because few Canadians divorced. From the mid-1950s to the mid-1960s, roughly 15 percent of Canadian marriages included at least one previously married spouse (Dumas & Péron 1992). In 1968, the year immediately preceding the divorce revolution, about 44 percent of newly married males and 50 percent of females remarried after widowhood, with divorce accounting for the difference. By comparison, in 1938, widowhood accounted for 83 percent of remarriages among men and 92 percent among women. Today, most remarriages occur through divorce, and between

Figure 12.3
Proportion of Marriages in Which at Least One Spouse Had Previously Married, 1971–2000

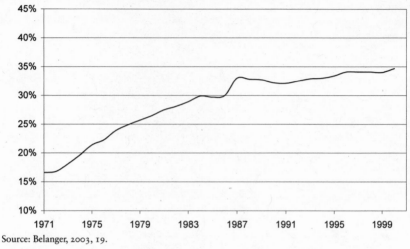

Source: Belanger, 2003, 19.

two-thirds and three-quarters of divorced Canadians remarry (Statistics Canada 1988). Figure 12.3 indicates that over one-third of Canadian marriages include at least one previously married partner. The percentage of marriages with at least one previously married spouse steadily increased between 1971 and 1986, growing from 17 to 30 percent of all marriages, before stabilizing at 33 to 35 percent thereafter. The propensity of remarriage among Canadians indicates that the high divorce rate represents an intolerance for bad marriages, not a rejection of marriage altogether. The remarriage process is more difficult among women than men, because sex-ratio disadvantages (a deficit of eligible men), childcare responsibilities, and socio-cultural norms reduce divorced women's prospects in the marriage market (Wu & Schimmele 2005). For example, four years after marital disruption, the male remarriage rate doubles the female remarriage rate.

HOUSEHOLDS WITH CHILDREN

Below-replacement fertility, or a total fertility rate (TFR) beneath 2.1 children per woman in her lifetime, the minimum live births required to reproduce the existing population, is a central trend within the second demographic transition. The Canadian TFR ranged between 3.4 and 3.9 births per woman in the 1950s, more than enough for population growth. As figure 12.4 presents, between 1986 and 2003, the TFR ranged between a low of 1.5 children per

Figure 12.4
Total Fertility Rates, Canada, 1986–2003

Per 1.000 women

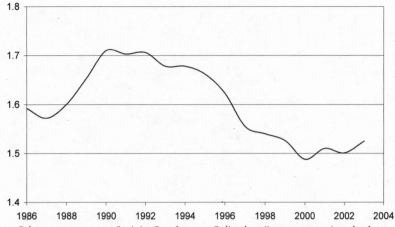

Source: Belanger, 2003, 110–11; Statistics Canada, 2005, Online. http://www.statcan.ca/start.html.

woman in 2002 to a high of 1.7 children in the early 1990s. Fertility changed for various reasons, including improved contraceptive methods, economic shifts, and socio-cultural norms (Hirschman 1994). In Canada, below-replacement fertility largely associates with the opportunity costs of having children (Weeks 1999). That is, many women are delaying motherhood, thus compressing their fecund years and chances for high fertility, to remain in the labour market longer, representing improvements in women's wages and career opportunities since the 1960s. Accordingly, almost one-in-ten Canadian singles expects to remain childless, with little attitudinal difference between men and women aged 20–29 years (Stobert & Kemeny 2003).

These changes have affected household size and child-bearing behaviours. Table 12.4 presents figures for children in Canadian families, 1981–2001. In 1981, about 32 percent of couple households were childless, compared to 37 percent in 2001. Of households with children, the average number of children per household declined from 1.4 to 1.1 during this period. The number of one-child households grew from 37 to 43 percent of couple households, while the number of households with three or more children declined from 25 to 18 percent of couple households. These changes parallel delayed childbearing among Canadian women. Figure 12.5 indicates that the percent of births to mothers aged 30 and older increased from 19 percent in 1975 to 48 percent in 2003.

Table 12.4
Children in Canadian Families: Canada, 1981–2001

Family type	1981 (%)	1986 (%)	1991 (%)	1996 (%)	2001 (%)
Total families without children at home	31.8	32.7	35.0	34.8	36.5
Total families with children at home	68.2	67.3	65.0	65.2	63.5
1 child at home	36.6	39.0	40.6	41.2	43.0
2 children at home	38.4	40.3	40.4	40.1	39.3
3 or more children at home	25.0	20.7	19.0	18.7	17.7
TOTAL	100	100	100	100	100
Average number of children at home per family	1.4	1.3	1.2	1.2	1.1

Source: Canadian Censuses 1981–2001.

Figure 12.5
Percent of Births to Mothers Aged 30 and Over, Canada, 1975–2003

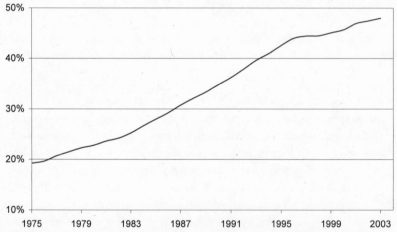

Source: Duchesne, et al., 1999, 25; Statistics Canada, 2005, Online. http://www.statcan.ca/start.html; Statistics Canada, 2000–2003. Annual Demographic Statistics, 2000–2003, Catelogue no. 91–213. Ottawa: Statistics Canada.

Table 12.5 shows an increase of children within cohabiting-couple households. In 1981, 34 percent of cohabitations included children compared to 46 percent in 2001. However, a good portion of this growth involves stepchildren, i.e., one or both cohabitors bringing children into the household from a previous union, rather than just fertility within cohabiting-couple households. Although non-marital union fertility increased from 2 percent of births in 1971–73 to 15 percent in 1997–98, most Canadian cohabitations are childless unions, as most English Canadians consider non-marital unions undesirable unions for child-bearing and parenting (Le Bourdais & Lapierre-Adamcyk 2004). Quebec is an exception to this pattern, however,

Table 12.5
Children in Common-Law Couple Families: Canada, 1981–2001

Family type	1981 (%)	1986 (%)	1991 (%)	1996 (%)	2001 (%)
Total families without children at home	65.9	62.2	58.9	52.8	54.2
Total families with children at home	34.1	37.8	41.1	47.2	45.8
1 child at home	51.6	52.8	54.1	50.4	47.9
2 child at home	30.3	32.5	32.7	35.0	37.3
3 or more children at home	18.2	14.7	13.2	14.6	14.8
Total	100	100	100	100	100
Average number of children at home per family	0.6	0.6	0.7	0.8	0.8

Source: Canadian Censuses, 1981–2001

where 46 percent of births occur in non-marital unions, indicating that cohabitation has become a modal pathway into child-bearing and child-rearing, in correspondence with the institutionalization of non-marital cohabitation within this province.

SAME-SEX UNIONS

Same-sex unions are another important change in the traditional Canadian family. Until recently, it was illegal for same-sex couples to get married, but legislative reforms in 2005 revised the traditional definition of marriage to include homosexual couples. For the first time, the 2001 Census collected information on same-sex unions. Table 12.6 shows the regional breakdown of same-sex cohabitations in 2001. Homosexual cohabitational unions ranged from a low of 0.1 percent of unions in Newfoundland and Labrador to highs of 0.6 percent in British Columbia, Quebec, and the Yukon. The national average is 0.5 percent, representing 34,200 union households, though this number is probably conservative given non-reporting related to fear of social stigma. The number of male same-sex cohabitations outnumbered female same-sex cohabitations somewhat, accounting for 55 percent of homosexual cohabitations (Statistics Canada 2002). About 15 percent of female homosexual cohabitations include children, compared to 3 percent of male homosexual cohabitations. Most same-sex cohabitations are in census metropolitan areas (e.g., Vancouver, Montréal), which is unsurprising because family privacy and tolerance for difference are usually higher in urban areas than rural areas.

SUMMARY

Without question, North American family life has changed considerably during the past several decades. Writing on the so-called "family crisis,"

Table 12.6
Same-Sex Common-Law Couples, Canada, Provinces, and Territories, 2001

Province/Territory	Number	As a percent of all couple families
Newfoundland and Labrador	180	0.1
Prince Edward Island	55	0.2
Nova Scotia	855	0.4
New Brunswick	505	0.3
Quebec	10360	0.6
Ontario	12505	0.5
Manitoba	865	0.3
Saskatchewan	475	0.2
Alberta	2525	0.4
British Columbia	5790	0.6
Yukon	35	0.6
Northwest Territories	30	0.4
Nunavut	15	0.3
Canada	34200	0.5

Source: Canadian Census 2001.

Popenoe (1993, 528) argues that family change represents growth of selfish individualism, under which "people have become less willing to invest time, money, and energy in family life, turning instead to investment in themselves." Such an assessment of social transition contains more hyperbole than substance, for if the conservative interpretation were correct, then today's families would be in chaos. The problem here is that the rhetoric behind nostalgia for the traditional nuclear family is unhelpful to families, particularly women and children, because it represents socio-political resistance to family change (Stacey 1993). This resistance to change, which includes a movement to repeal no-fault divorce legislation, cannot be disassociated from religious dogma and sexist attitudes. In this regard, the main problem with family change is not change per se, but strong socio-political reluctance to accept and accommodate family change. Although divorce, cohabitation, single parenthood, and remarriage present social challenges, clinging to the *Leave it to Beaver* family ideal only exacerbates the adaptation process by refusing to accept and support family diversity.

REFERENCES

Basch, N. 1999. *Framing American Divorce: From the Revolutionary Generation to the Victorians*. Berkeley, CA: University of California Press

Becker, G. 1981. *A Treatise on the Family*. Cambridge, MA: Harvard University Press

Belanger, A. 2003. *Annual Demographic Statistics, 2000–2003*. Ottawa: Statistics Canada

Bumpass, L.L., J.A. Sweet, and A. Cherlin. 1991. "The Role of Cohabitation in Declining Rates of Marriage." *Journal of Marriage and the Family* 53: 913–27

Cherlin, A. J. 1992. *Marriage, Divorce, Remarriage*. Revised Edition. Cambridge, MA: Harvard University Press.

Coontz, S. 1991. *The Way We Never Were: American Families and the Nostalgia Trap*. New York: Basic Books

Duchesne, D., F. Nault, H. Gilmour, and R. Wilkins. 1999. *Vital Statistics Compendium, 1996*. Ottawa: Statistics Canada

Dumas, J., and Y. Péron. 1992. *Marriage and Conjugal Life in Canada*. Ottawa: Statistics Canada

Fields, J., and L.M. Casper. 2001. "America's Families and Living Arrangements." *Current Population Reports*: 20–537. Washington, DC: US Census Bureau

Furstenberg, F.F. 1990. "Divorce and the American Family." *Annual Review of Sociology* 16: 379–403

Hirschman, C. 1994. "Why Fertility Changes." *Annual Review of Sociology* 20: 203–33

Le Bourdais, C., and E. Lapierre-Adamcyk. 2004. "Changes in Conjugal Life in Canada: Is Cohabitation Progressively Replacing Marriage?" *Journal of Marriage and Family* 66: 929–42

Lewis, J. 2003. *Should We Worry About Family Change?* Toronto: University of Toronto Press

Luxton, M. 2005. "Conceptualizing 'Families': Theoretical Frameworks and Family Research." In *Families: Changing Trends in Canada*, ed. M. Baker, 29–51. Toronto: McGraw-Hill Ryerson

Manning, W.D., and P.J. Smock. 2002. "First Comes Cohabitation and then Comes Marriage?" *Journal of Family Issues* 23: 1065–87

McGovern, C. 1995. "The Mirage of Easy Divorce." *Alberta/Western Report* 22: 28

Nock, S.L. 1995. "A Comparison of Marriages and Cohabiting Relationships." *Journal of Family Issues* 16: 53–76

Oppenheimer, V. 1994. "Women's Rising Employment and the Future of the Family in Industrial Societies." *Population and Development Review* 20: 293–342

Parsons, T., and R.F. Bales. 1955. *Family Socialization and Interaction Process*. New York: The Free Press

Péron, Y. 2000a. "Households and Families." In *Canadian Families at the Approach of the Year 2000*, 1–45. Ottawa: Statistics Canada

Phillips, R. 1988. *Putting Asunder: A History of Divorce in Western Society*. Cambridge, UK: Cambridge University Press

Popenoe, D. 1988. *Disturbing the Nest: Family Change and Decline in Modern Societies*. New York: Aldine de Gruyter

– 1993. "American Family Decline, 1960–1990: A Review and Appraisal." *Journal of Marriage and the Family* 55: 527–55

Shorter, E. 1975. *The Making of the Modern Family*. New York: Basic Books

Stacey, J. 1993. "Good Riddance to 'The Family': A Response to David Popenoe." *Journal of Marriage and the Family* 55: 545–7

Statistics Canada. 1988. *Marrying and Divorcing: A Status Report*.

– 1997. "1996 Census: Marital Status, Common-Law Unions, and Families." *The Daily* (14 October): 2–8. Online journal

– 2001. *2001 Canada Yearbook*.

– 2002. "2001 Census: Marital Status, Common-Law Status, Families, Dwellings, and Households." *The Daily* (22 October): 2

– 2004. "Marriages." *The Daily* (21 December): 9

– 2006. 2006 Census Dictionary.

Stobert, S., and A. Kemeny. 2003. "Childfree by Choice." *Canadian Social Trends* 69: 7–10

Waite, L.J., ed. 2000. *The Ties That Bind: Perspectives on Marriage and Cohabitation*. New York: Aldine de Gruyter

Weeks, J.R. 1999. *Population: An Introduction to Concepts and Issues*. 7th edition. Belmont, CA: Wadsworth

Wu, Z. 1998. "Recent Trends in Marriage Patterns in Canada." *Policy Options* 19: 3–6

– 2000. *Cohabitation: An Alternative Form of Family Living*. Don Mills, Ontario: Oxford University Press

– and C.M. Schimmele. 2003. "Cohabitation." In *The International Encyclopedia of Marriage and Family Relationships*, ed. J.J. Ponzetti, 315–23. 2nd edition. New York: Macmillan

– 2005. "Divorce and Repartnering." In *Families: Changing Trends in Canada*, ed. M. Baker, 202–28. Toronto: McGraw-Hill Ryerson

13

Children and Youth

JIANYE LIU, DON KERR, AND RODERIC BEAUJOT

INTRODUCTION

Children have been described as "the ultimate resource" for a society's long term well-being and social and economic development (Simon 1982). The absolute and relative number of young people has a variety of important ramifications for many societal institutions, both over the shorter and longer terms (Preston 1984). The baby bust of the latter 1960s and many years of below-replacement fertility have brought considerable decline in the relative number of children in Canada. As a result, the very fabric of Canadian society and culture has changed. During the baby-boom era, Canada was very youth-oriented and child-centered, whereas by the turn of the century, it has become a society in which the young occupy a much smaller part of the public space. This dramatic shift in our age structure has important consequences for the life experience of the young, whether it be children at the earliest stages of their lives or young adults establishing their independence from the parental home.

This study sets out to document some of the more fundamental trends associated with the life experience of children and youth in Canada. While studies elsewhere have used a variety of definitions, this chapter follows the convention of defining children as persons aged 0 to 14 years, and youth as 15–24 years. We will describe some of the most fundamental demographic and family changes, as well as provide some detail on the economic welfare of children and youth, along with school attendance, and for young adults, labour force participation and commencement of family life (entry into relationships and childbearing). For each of the two broad age categories, we draw systematic comparisons across selected segments of Canadian society and across censuses, with a primary emphasis on the 1981–2001 period.

ABSOLUTE AND RELATIVE
NUMBER OF YOUNG CANADIANS

Canadian fertility has declined to 1.65 in 1981 and 1.5 births per woman in the period 1999–2004 (Statistics Canada 2006, 31). While this presents advantages for children in the competition for parental resources, on a societal level the decline in fertility has lead to a substantial reduction in the relative number of children and youth. While Canada's baby-boom cohort has always drawn a great deal of attention, the contraction at the bottom of the age structure has received far less attention.

Annual births have been steadily falling for well over a decade. Since 1989, this drop has been particularly pronounced, falling by almost 20 percent, from about 403,280 to 327,107 by 2001 (see figure 13.1). Overall, in 2001 there were 32 percent fewer than the 479,275 births at the height of the baby boom in 1959. Both the absolute and relative number of children and youth in Canadian society has declined. A decline in births implies a reduction in the number of infants being born in our hospitals, and with the passage time, this translates into a decline in the number of preschoolers entering into our educational system, and the impact continues over the life course.

In absolute terms, the total number of Canadians under the age of 25 peaked in the 1971 census, before declining somewhat for a decade or so, and then remaining relatively stable. As indicated in table 13.1, the total number of Canadians under 25 was 10.4 million in 1981, which was to drop slightly to about 10.1 million by 2001 (or by about 300,000 over this 20 year period). This relative stability in total population count obscures the real picture in terms of a shift in the relative weight of the young in Canada's age structure. For example, children and youth comprised about 42 percent of Canada's population in 1981, whereas by 2001 they comprised only 32 percent of the total. While there was a slight decline in the number of children and youth (down by about 3 percent over a 20-year period), Canada's overall population size grew at a reasonably robust pace (up by about 25 percent). Overall, Canada is a much older society than it was merely 20 years ago, a generalization that is true across most Western nations.

The size of a birth cohort (infants born in the same year) is a direct function of (i) the relative number of persons at reproductive age, and (ii) their respective fertility behaviour. For example, the number of preschoolers (aged 0–4 years) in the 2001 census can be related to (i) the number of women in Canada of reproductive age over the 1996–2001 period, and (ii) their fertility decisions over this 5-year interval. This in itself explains why the number of births in Canada did not decline further than observed in figure 13.1, as

Figure 13.1
Annual Births in Canada, 1971–2001

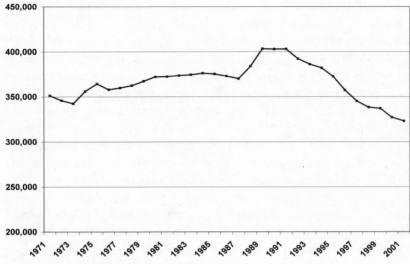

Source: Statistics Canada (2005).

Table 13.1
Children and Youth by Selected Age Group, Canada, 1981–2001

	1981	1986	1991	1996	2001
Children aged 0–4 #	1,803,588	1,840,912	1,958,127	1,961,148	1,759,196
Children aged 0–4 %	7.3	7.1	7.0	6.6	5.7
Children aged 5–14 #	3,728,975	3,643,850	3,831,697	4,024,403	4,095,342
Children aged 5–14 %	15.0	14.0	13.7	13.6	13.2
Youth aged 15–24 #	4,846,366	4,433,978	4,016,221	4,011,848	4,227,228
Youth aged 15–24 %	19.5	17.0	14.3	13.5	13.6
Total children and youth #	10,378,929	9,918,740	9,806,045	9,997,399	10,081,766
Total children and youth %	41.8	38.0	35.0	33.8	32.5
Total population	24,820,393	26,101,155	28,031,394	29,610,757	31,021,251

Note: These population estimates are directly based on the respective Canadian Censuses, with adjustments for census coverage error.
Source: Population Estimates by Age and Sex, Canada, Provinces, and Territories, 1971–2001 (2003 Annual Demographic Statistics).

the fertility rate in Canada has been below replacement since the 1970s. The total annual births increased only slightly in the 1980s and early 1990s, as relatively large cohorts (born during the baby boom) were making their way through their childbearing ages. The much smaller cohorts of the baby bust are now moving through their prime reproductive ages, while continuing with below-replacement fertility. As a result, there has been a major drop in the number of births since the early 1990s and a significant contraction at the bottom of Canada's age structure.

As to exact numbers, the number of preschoolers (0–4 years) in Canada declined slightly over the 1981–2001 period, from about 1.80 million to 1.76 million in 2001 – down by about 2.5 percent (table 13.1). As Canada's overall population grew considerably during this time, the corresponding percentage of Canada's population in this age group declined from 7.3 percent in 1981 to 5.7 percent in 2001. The number of children of elementary school age (5–14 years) went up slightly, from 3.73 million in 1981 to 4.09 million (an increase of almost 10 percent). Yet since this growth was again less than for the Canadian population overall, the relative share of this age group in the total population continued its downward trend, from about 15.0 percent in 1981 to 13.2 percent in 2001. Among the youth (aged 15–24), we have witnessed the most noteworthy drop, from about 4.85 million in 1981 to 4.23 million by 2001. This translated into a decline in population share from about 19.5 percent in 1981 to only 13.6 percent by 2001. In 1981, the tail end of the baby boom cohort was still moving through their later teenage years and early 20s, whereas by the turn of the century, it was the children born during Canada's baby bust era (1970s and 1980s) who were moving through these age groups.

In taking the longer term perspective, it is necessary to return to the situation over half a century ago to find so few children under the age of five in Canada. Even though this country's population has more than doubled since the 1950s, we have roughly the same number of young children at the beginning of the 21st century as 50 years earlier (at roughly 1.7 million). This reduction in the share of Canada's overall population that are children and youth may bring a shift in the focus of social and economic policies from child- and youth-centered priorities to other aspects of our social life.

FAMILY AND LIVING ARRANGEMENTS

Along with this reduction in population share, other demographic changes have had important consequences for the well-being of children. Some of the fundamental demographic trends to influence family life over recent decades include delays in fertility and marriage, further reductions in completed fertility, increases in cohabitation and divorce, increases in maternal employment, as well as a climb in non-marital fertility. Some of these trends can clearly

Table 13.2
Family and Household Types, Canada, 1981 and 2001

| | Number(thousands) | | Change % |
	1981	2001	1981–2001
Total households (private)	8218.50	11563.00	40.7
Family households	6231.50	8155.60	30.9
Non-family households	2050.00	3407.40	66.2
Husband-wife families with children at home*	3599.10	3653.10	1.5
Total married couples with children	3478.90	3132.40	-10.0
Total common-law with children	120.20	520.70	333.2
Lone-parent families	713.80	1311.20	83.7
Husband-wife families without children at home*	2011.40	3406.70	69.4

* includes common-law

Sources: 1981 census, Cat. no. 92–325; Beaujot (1991:244); Statistics Canada, 2003, Cat. no. 97F0005XCB01005.

be thought of as beneficial for children, whereas others suggest potential disadvantages. For example, the tendency for women to delay childbearing has widely been perceived as a plus for children, as parents delay establishing families until they have successfully gained the resources and experience to be successful as parents. On the other hand, it has been argued that divorce and non-marital childbearing can disadvantage children to the extent that they cannot take advantage of the resources and social capital of one of their parents. Since families are the primary socializing agent of most children and youth, these changes are not without their consequences.

As a result of many of the aforementioned trends, the total number of family households in Canada has not been growing quite as rapidly as other types of households, a generalization that is particularly true for families with children. This is represented in table 13.2, which summarizes changes in the number of families and households (by type) on the basis of the 1981 and 2001 censuses. In considering solely dual-parent families with children and youth in the home (disregarding their age), the 1981–2001 period was characterized by very modest growth – of only 1.5 percent over two decades. In comparison, the total number of households (both family and non-family) increased by 40.7 percent. Among families with children, the most rapid growth involved children born in common-law unions (with an increase of over 300 percent), which served to offset somewhat the 10 percent decline in the number of married couples with children. When we compare different types of households, particularly rapid growth is observed for lone-parent families (up by 83.7 percent), as well as families at later stages of their life course. For example, the number of husband-wife families without children at home increased by 69.4 percent.

The demography of families is often presented from the point of view of adults. But the changed patterns of entry and exit from relationships have had important consequences on the family living arrangements of children, and only some of these living arrangements are identifiable via the census. Unfortunately the census does not provide information on the number of stepfamilies (where one of the parents is not the biological or adoptive parent of all the children) and blended families (where at least one child did not have the same biological or adoptive parents as the other children). Table 13.3 summarizes what we know from the census on the living arrangements of children and youth, in distinguishing those living with two parents, living with a lone parent, in a common-law union or a husband wife family.

Consistent with the above discussion, the percentage of children in Canada living with a single parent continues to climb, from 10.7 percent in 1981 to 17.8 percent by 2001. It is difficult to distinguish married couples and common-law couples prior to the 1991 Census in Canada, but since 1991 the percentage living common-law has increased in quite a pronounced manner, from only 7 percent to 12.8 percent in a period of 10 years. In supplementing this census data with information provided by the National Longitudinal Survey of Children and Youth, it has been estimated that just under 10 percent of children live in step families, whereas an additional 6 percent live in blended families (Cheal 1996). While the census indicates that roughly 4 out of every 5 children in 2001 were living with two parents, this does not imply that these children were living with both biological parents. The reality is more complex than the census can document (Juby et al. 2001).

Table 13.3 also provides information on the living arrangements of youth (15–24 years), where changes observed over the 1981–2001 period are distinct from what has characterized children (0–14 years). For example, the percentage of youth living with two parents actually increased over this period rather than decreased, from 53.6 percent in 1981 to 59.8 percent in 2001. The reason for the change rests with delayed home-leaving, a trend that first established itself in the late 1970s (Boyd and Norris 1998). In 1981, fully 36.0 percent of youth were living with neither parent, a percentage which declined to 24.8 percent by 2001. In explanation, economic factors are certainly at play, with considerable evidence suggesting that young adults encountered greater difficulties in establishing themselves in the labour market of the 1980s and 1990s relative to earlier cohorts. Young Canadians are now more likely to spend a longer period at school. Cultural

Table 13.3
Living Arrangements of Children (0–14) and Youth (15–24) by Family Type, Canada, 1981–2001

	1981	1986	1991	1996	2001
Children 0–14					
With two parents	87.1	85.7	84.0	81.5	81.4
Husband-wife			77.0	71.3	68.6
Common-law			7.0	10.2	12.8
With a lone parent	10.7	12.3	13.6	16.5	17.8
With neither parents	14.6	14.4	14.7	13.2	12.4
Youth 15–24					
With two parents	53.6	56.1	57.5	59.7	59.8
Husband-wife			55.2	56.5	55.6
Common-law			2.3	3.2	4.2
With a lone parent	10.3	12.0	12.3	13.9	15.4
With neither parents	36.0	31.9	30.2	26.3	24.8

Note: Husband-wife and common-law could not be distinguished in 1981 and 1986 censuses.
Sources: Based on Census of Canada, 1981–2001, Public Use Microdata File (Individuals File).

factors have also helped to make parental homes more suitable to older children, as the generation gap has narrowed. Parents have developed more flexible and tolerant attitudes toward their adolescent children (Wister, Mitchell, and Gee 1997; Zhao 1994; Boyd and Norris 1995).

FEWER BROTHERS AND SISTERS

Given the delay in marriage and child-bearing, the family circumstances into which children are born have changed. As the percentage of all families that include children and youth has declined, so has the average size of the Canadian family. Children and youth are far less likely than in the past to be raised in a family with a large number of brothers and sisters (see figure 13.2). This is demonstrated in the distribution of children and youth sharing accommodations under the same roof.

The proportion of children and youth with no brothers or sisters at home increased from just over 10 percent in 1971 to about 20 percent by 1991, and 24 percent by 2001 (see figure 13.2). Another 43.5 percent had one brother or sister at home in 2001, relative to just under 40 percent in 1981 and fewer than 1 in 4 in the 1970s. Similarly, whereas almost one in four children lived in a family with 5+ children in 1971, this ratio has plummeted to almost 1 in 40 by 2001. All of this implies that greater proportions of babies are being born to "inexperienced" parents, as fewer brothers and sisters imply fewer older siblings. For instance, half of the generation born

Figure 13.2
Percentage Distribution of Young Canadians Living with Parent(s) by Total Number of
Children and Youth in the Family, Canada, 1971–2001

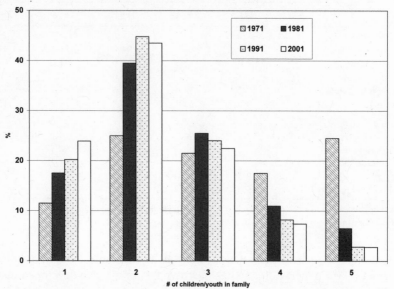

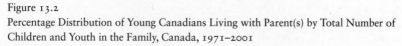

Source: For 1971, Wargon (1979) Children in Canadian Families. Ottawa: Statistics Canada. Cat. no. 98–
810, Table 1. For 1981 and 1991, Kerr et al. (1994) Children and Youth: An Overview. Statistics Canada.
Cat. no. 96–320E. For 2001, the 2001 Census Public Use Microdata File, unpublished tabulation.

in the early 1960s had two older brothers or sisters, compared to less than
one-fifth of those born 30 years later. Fewer births, and their concentration
over a shorter period, not only imply more potential parental resources per
child, but also children having less opportunity to interact with and learn
from siblings.

FAMILY CHANGE AND ECONOMIC WELFARE

Over the latter part of the 20th century, there were some rather noticeable
ups and downs in the Canadian economy. In particular, Canadians experienced two severe recessions, one in the early 1980s and the other in the
early 1990s. In 1982 and 1983, the North American economy witnessed
climbing unemployment, high inflation, and declining real earnings, making
it rather difficult for many parents to meet the needs of their children. After
a period of economic recovery through to the late 1980s, a second recession
took hold in 1991 and 1992, again introducing considerable downward
pressure on incomes. Since this period of economic difficulty during the

early to mid-1990s, labour market conditions in North America have improved noticeably. A concurrent trend throughout this entire period was a noticeable growth in female-labour force participation, particularly among women with children. This has served to increase or at least stabilize family income by increasing the number of earners per family in a context where individual earnings among young adults were often stagnant or even declining (Picot et al. 1998; Baker 2002; Beaujot 2000).

Picot et al. (1998) have emphasized three fundamental institutions in shaping the economic well-being of Canadian children, including (i) the market – especially the labour market, (ii) the state – with direct transfers of both services and payments, and (iii) the family (in explaining how Canadians earn and pool resources). Without downplaying the importance of structural explanations that emphasize the role of labour markets and/or government policy, it is possible to highlight several family changes that obviously hold implications for the economic well-being and societal integration of the young. While obviously changes in labour market conditions are particularly salient, shifts in living arrangements and family structure are also relevant.

Young children are completely dependent upon others for their well-being. The ability to cope with family change varies by age, with childhood clearly a vulnerable stage of the life cycle. Correspondingly, the well-being of children is often jeopardized by the difficulties experienced by the adults in their lives. While this is less the case with youth, many continue to be dependent upon their parents well into adulthood. Family patterns as of late bring considerable diversity to the world of children: from children who experience intact-parental relationships to those who experience episodes of lone parenthood, reconstituted relationships, and stepparenting. All of this diversity brings consequences, frequently unforeseen and unintentional on the part of parents. Family change can have an impact on various dimensions of child well-being, including important changes in the manner in which Canadians earn and pool resources.

There are several obstacles to accurately documenting recent trends in economic well-being, not the least being an absence of consensus among social scientists regarding which threshold might best be chosen to represent a "minimal standard of living" or "poverty." There is currently no consensus among sociologists and economists in Canada regarding the income level that would be appropriate for delineating the poor, or for that matter, how this might differ across families of varying size or across different regions of the country. While Statistics Canada has never claimed to measure poverty (due in part to this lack of consensus), it does regularly produce statistics on the incidence of low income, using alternate LICOs (low-income cutoffs, either before or after tax). These cutoffs provide for some sense as to the proportion of Canadians living under what are considered "strained circumstances. "Table 13.4 provides information on low-income status, by selected family types, for the 1991, 1996, and 2001 censuses. In addition, table 13.4 provides information on median income of Canadian families that include at least one child and/or youth. As the Canadian census gathered no information on income tax paid, all of these statistics refer to income data, prior to tax. While Statistics Canada often highlights low-income statistics using LICOs after tax, table 13.4 is based on their pre-tax (1992 base) LICOs – the only option available when working with census data.

After adjustment for inflation, table 13.4 demonstrates how: (i) family type is particularly important in documenting the incidence of low income and median income (with female lone-parent families particularly disadvantaged), (ii) the recession of the early 1990s had a noticeable impact in terms of worsening the incidence of child poverty and lowering median income (in comparing 1990 with 1995), and (iii) the latter 1990s was a period of economic recovery (in comparing 1995 with 2000). This latter period witnessed significant gains in family income that served to offset the economic downturn of the early 1990s. The overall outcome was that median income was slightly higher in 2000 than in 1990, whereas the incidence of low income did not change significantly. The percentage of children and youth living below Statistics Canada's low-income cut-off (before tax) varied from 15.7 percent in 1991, up to 19.9 percent in 1996, and back down to 17.2 percent by 2001. Both children and youth are less likely to be classified as income-poor when they live with two parents (as opposed to living with a lone parent) and in a married-couple family (as opposed to a common-law family). The incidence of income poverty has been found to be four to five times higher among children in lone-parent families, relative to married families. Moreover, by family type, children have higher poverty rates than youth. This is because the parents of children tend to be younger than those of youth, with less work experience and lower earnings.

Table 13.4 also includes information on the income poverty of young adults who live with neither parent, i.e. youth living apart from their parents in either a married union, a common-law type of arrangement, or as a lone parent. Clearly these young adults face economic difficulties not characteristic of those who continue to live with their parents. For youth apart from parents, the worst case scenario, by far, is to be lone-parent as, for example, about 6 out of 10 young adults raising children alone were classified as low-income in 2001. Younger adults (under 25 years) who are living with

Table 13.4
Incidence of Low Income for Children and Youth, and Median Income by Family Type,
Canada, 1990–2001

	1990	1995	2000
Family type	Incidence of Low Income		
Children (0–14)			
Child in a married couple family	10.9	14.9	12.5
Child in a common-law couple family	21.4	25.4	19.3
Child in a male lone-parent family	25.5	33.1	25.7
Child in a female lone-parent family	62.7	65	54.3
Youth (15–24)			
Youth in a married couple family	6.8	10.3	8.2
Youth in a common-law couple family	10	14	11.4
Youth in a male lone-parent family	15.5	21.9	15.9
Youth in a female lone-parent family	32.7	37.6	31
Youth is married	17.7	27.5	22.4
Youth is living common-law	23.4	32.1	25.3
Youth is lone parent	84.5	88.4	60.1
TOTAL	18.7	19.9	17.2
	1990	1995	2000
Family type	Median Income (2000 dollars)		
Two-parent families with children/youth	63,571	61,110	67,919
One earner	44,638	42,644	43,860
Two earner	63,825	63,879	69,746
Lone-parent families with children/youth	22,065	23,340	30,088
Male lone-parent families	39,366	33,658	43,222
Female lone-parent families	19,868	22,152	27,766

Note: the census collects information on the income for the previous tax year.
Sources: Census of Canada, 1991–2001, Public Use Microdata File (Individuals File).

a partner are clearly better off than those who are caring for a child by
themselves, as 22.4 percent of married youth are classified as low-income, as
are 25.3 percent of young adults living common-law. With this in mind, the
previously mentioned delay of home-leaving serves to reduce the number
of youth classified as low income, as does the level of non-marital fertility
among the young.

The fertility decline that followed the baby boom had a net beneficial
impact on the economic welfare of families. A lowering in the number of
children per family has direct economic ramifications, since it is associated
with fewer dependent children and youth per household, and thus, a decline in the number of claimants on family income (Dooley 1988; Brouillette

et al. 1990). We have also witnessed an upward shift in the age pattern of fertility (Ram 1990; Beaujot et al. 1995; Bélanger 1999). This is associated with a higher level of economic well-being as adults delay having children until later in their reproductive years when economic resources are generally greater (Oppenheimer 1988; Grindstaff et al. 1989) and young adults are much more likely to invest in education and establishing themselves in the labour market. While fertility has declined, non-marital fertility as a proportion of all births has steadily risen. For example, whereas only about 14 percent of all births were to unmarried mothers in 1981, this percentage has approached 40 percent as we moved into the 21st century (Beaujot 2000). This growth in the relative number of non-marital births is not due to an increased incidence of births with no declared father, but to the growing popularity of common-law unions in Canada. While the fertility rate of common-law partners continues to be lower than among married couples (Dumas and Bélanger 1997), this fundamental change in nuptiality is important to the extent that common-law unions tend to be far less stable than legal marriages – even when they include children (Marcil-Gratton 1993; Marcil-Gratton and Le Bourdais 1999; Le Bourdais and Lapierre-Adamcyk 2004).

Recent years have witnessed trends toward higher rates of union dissolution (involving both legal marriages and cohabiting unions). As with births to single parents, there is ample evidence to suggest considerable economic hardship for both women and children following separation and/or divorce (Ross and Shillington 1989; Dooley 1991; Rashid 1994). While the long-term economic repercussions of union dissolution are generally not as difficult as those faced by single women who have births without a partner, in general, children experience considerable economic hardship as a result of their parents' inability to continue their relationship (McQuillan 1991). As a consequence of both lower proportions married and higher rates of union dissolution, the proportion of all families headed by a single parent has increased.

THE EDUCATION OF YOUTH

Canada devotes a considerable share of its public expenditures to education. In international comparisons, it currently ranks sixth among twenty-eight OECD countries in total public investment in education relative to gross domestic product (OECD 2000, 54). In terms of total expenditures from both public and private sources, this rank rises to third, after Denmark and Finland. For a variety of reasons, Canada continues to place priority on public education, resulting in a relatively high proportion of its young continuing its education well into young adulthood.

Table 13.5
School Attendance of Youth, by Gender and Age Groups 15–18 and 19–24, Canada, 1981–2001

		1981			2001			
# number	Total	Not attending	Full-time	Part-time	Total	Not attending	Full-time	Part-time
15–18 T	1,837,695	464,970	1,337,735	34,970	1,646,505	339,865	1,264,225	42,415
M	940,485	243,785	679,485	17,220	851,830	181,750	648,275	21,810
F	897,200	221,195	658,250	17,745	794,680	158,115	615,955	20,605
19–24 T	2,800,300	1,951,120	613,400	235,765	2,341,685	1,132,600	1,011,785	197,320
M	1,401,485	949,710	333,675	118,095	1,182,455	606,165	478,050	98,225
F	1,398,820	1,001,410	279,725	117,675	1,159,230	526,430	533,720	99,090
%								
15–18 T		25.3	72.8	1.9		20.6	76.8	2.6
M		25.9	72.2	1.8		21.3	76.1	2.6
F		24.7	73.4	2		19.9	77.5	2.6
19–24 T		69.7	21.9	8.4		48.4	43.2	8.4
M		67.8	23.8	8.4		51.3	40.4	8.3
F		71.6	20	8.4		45.4	46	8.5

Source: Census of Canada, 1981 and 2001, Statistics Canada Public Use Microdata Files (individual file).

Canada has made very good progress in educating its citizens since the early 1980s. For example, the high-school dropout rate has declined, as graduation has become the minimum requirement for most types of employment (Guppy and Davis 1998; Mori and Burke 1989). Post-secondary education participation rates have also risen quite dramatically, and are currently very high by international standards. Table 13.5 provides information on the school attendance of the young by comparing participation rates in 1981 and 2001. For practical reasons, youth have been divided into two groups, i.e. adolescents aged 15–18 and young adults aged 19–24. This division reflects the common pattern where most youth 18 and under are in high school, with the norm of 12 years of schooling.

For youth aged 15–18, 1 in 4 were not in school in 1981, a number that declined to about 1 in 5 by 2001. While these statistics imply a nontrivial (albeit declining) high-school drop-out rate, many of these youth do eventually return to high-school (through adult education). Among youth aged 19–24, the situation is similar, as participation rates have consistently climbed throughout the 1981–2001 period. Whereas in 1981 about 3 in 10 Canadians aged 19–24 were studying (either full- or part-time), by 2001 this participation rate had risen to just over one-half. In drawing comparisons by gender, young women have clearly made greater gains than young men, as about 55 percent report studying in 2001 relative to about 49 percent of young men. In the early 1980s, the situation was quite different, as

Table 13.6
Population of Youth in Labour Force by Age Group and Sex, Canada, 1981, 1991, and 2001
(in thousands)

Age group and sex	Number			Percentage change	
	1991	2001	1981	1981–1991	1991–2001
15 to 24					
TOTAL	3,036.3	2,564.2	.2,575.1	-15.5	0.4
Male	1,632.1	1,341.2	1,333.5	-17.8	-0.6
Female	1,404.2	1,223.0	1,241.6	-12.9	1.5
15 to 19					
TOTAL	1,074.0	904.4	1,015.8	-15.8	12.3
Male	571.6	471.6	525.1	-17.5	11.3
Female	502.4	432.8	490.8	-13.9	13.4
20 to 24					
TOTAL	1,962.3	1,659.8	1,559.3	-15.4	-6.1
Male	1,060.5	869.7	808.4	-18.0	-7.0
Female	901.8	790.2	750.9	-12.4	-5.0

Source: 1. Census of Canada, 2001, Public Use Microdata File (Individuals File)
      2. Kerr et al., 1994, 39.

young men were more likely to be studying, with about 32 percent reporting
school attendance relative to 28 percent of young women.

THE LABOUR FORCE ACTIVITY OF YOUTH

The absolute number of youth in the Canadian labour force was actually
lower in the 2001 census than two decades earlier in 1981. According to
the 2001 census, about 2.58 million youth were either employed or actively
seeking employment. This was lower than the 3.04 million documented in
1981, although up slightly from 2.56 million in 1991 (table 13.6). Between
1981 and 1991, this number of young people working or looking for work
dropped by about 16 percent, before rebounding moderately by about 7 percent between 1991 and 2001. All persons 15 years and older who are either
employed or seeking employment during the week preceding the census are
included in the labour market (whether they are working full- or part-time).

These shifts in absolute numbers are directly related to changes in age distribution. As the last of the baby boomers moved into mid-adulthood in the
1980s, the number of youth available for employment declined, irrespective
of changes in their propensity to enter the labour force.

Table 13.7 portrays labour-force participation rates of youth by age and
gender, across the 1981, 1991, and 2001 censuses. This participation rate

Table 13.7
Labour-Force Participation Rate of Youth by Age and Sex, Canada,
1981, 1991, and 2001

Age and sex	1981	1991	2001
Both Sexes			
15	14.8	21.9	23.2
16	28.1	34.7	38.5
17	44.1	47.1	51.5
18	64.4	62.6	64.8
19	78.3	75.6	73.5
20	83.5	81.9	77.1
21	84.3	83.9	79.3
22	84.3	85.0	81.0
23	84.4	86.0	82.9
24	83.8	86.5	83.9
All youth (15–24)	65.5	66.9	65.0
Males			
15	16.2	23.1	24.7
16	30.1	35.7	37.9
17	46.2	47.7	51.0
18	66.6	62.9	63.5
19	81.4	76.7	74.6
20	87.8	84.3	77.7
21	89.8	87.1	81.2
22	91.2	88.6	83.2
23	92.5	89.9	86.1
24	93.3	91.3	88.1
Male youth (15–24)	69.7	68.9	65.9
Females			
15	13.5	20.6	21.5
16	26.0	33.8	39.2
17	42.0	46.4	52.0
18	62.1	62.3	66.3
19	75.2	74.5	72.3
20	79.1	79.3	76.4
21	78.8	80.5	77.3
22	77.4	81.4	78.8
23	76.4	82.0	79.7
24	74.4	82.0	79.9
Female youth (15–24)	61.2	64.9	64.1

Source: 1. Census of Canada, 2001, Public Use Microdata File (Individuals File)
    2. Kerr et al., 1994, 40.

has varied from about 67 percent in 1991 to around 65 percent in 1981 and
2001. Table 13.7 demonstrates how some of the most noteworthy changes in labour-force participation have varied by age and sex. The trend for
young women is clearly different from that of young men, as the former
have experienced an upturn in participation rates whereas the latter experienced a decrease. As a result, the participation rates of young men and

women have now reached near parity, at 65.9 percent and 64.1 percent, respectively. A variety of social and cultural factors are responsible for this, including a broad societal shift toward gender equity in employment and other aspects of Canadian life. In 1981, these participation rates were some distance from parity, although since this point in time the participation rates of young men have fallen slightly, just as the participation rates of young women have risen.

In addition, table 13.7 also demonstrates how the trends observed among teenagers are different from those observed among young adults. The general trend for teenagers has been toward increased labour-force participation (typically on a part-time basis) whereas among older youth the trend has been in the opposite direction. In addition, the gender difference in labour-force activity is small if not negligible among high-school aged youth, yet increases among older youth. By age 24, about 88 percent of men are involved in the labour force compared to 80 percent of women. This is consistent with the earlier observation that women have higher participation rates in post-secondary education. In addition, young women are more likely to temporarily leave the labour force due to child-bearing. While the fertility of young adults has declined over past decades, it continues to have a larger impact on the labour-force behaviour of young women than young men.

THE MARITAL CHARACTERISTICS
AND CHILDBEARING OF YOUTH

As the living arrangements of young Canadians have changed over recent censuses, so has their marital behaviour. Observing the marital characteristics of youth by age and sex leads to a fundamental generalization: across most ages, the percentage of youth who are legally married continues to decline, while the percentage living common-law continues to climb (table 13.8). That the former has not been fully offset by change in the latter is consistent with a further generalization – that the percentage of young men and women living together has dropped, whether in legal marriages or common-law unions.

For example, among women 24 years of age, the percentage legally married has declined from more than half (53.1 percent) in 1981 to just about 1 in 4 (25.1 percent) in 2001. During this same period, the percentage living common-law has increased from 9.1 percent in 1981 up to 31.3 percent in 2001. Similarly, among men 24 years of age, the percentage legally married declined from 36.5 percent to only 13.1 percent, while the percentage living common-law rose from 9.2 to 22.4 percent. Again, these numbers suggest

Table 13.8
Marital Status of Youth Age 18–24 by Age Sex, Canada, 1981–2001

	1981			1991			2001		
Age	Single	Married	Common-law	Single	Married	Common-law	Single	Married	Common-law
Female									
18	91.4	4.1	4.5	94.3	1.3	4.4	95.7	0.6	3.6
19	83.1	9.7	7.2	89.2	3.1	7.7	90.8	1.9	7.2
20	73.0	18.0	9.0	82.9	6.3	10.8	83.6	3.9	12.5
21	62.6	27.5	9.9	75.3	11.3	13.4	75.1	6.9	18.0
22	53.2	36.9	9.9	67.1	17.7	15.2	66.1	11.4	22.5
23	44.7	45.7	9.6	58.7	25.1	16.2	54.5	18.9	26.6
24	37.8	53.1	9.1	51.3	32.5	16.2	43.6	25.1	31.3
Male									
18	98.6	0.5	0.9	98.9	0.2	0.9	99.1	0.2	0.7
19	95.7	1.9	2.4	97.1	0.6	2.3	97.5	0.4	2.0
20	90.5	5.1	4.4	94.1	1.5	4.4	94.0	1.0	5.0
21	82.8	10.8	6.4	89.2	3.5	7.1	89.0	2.0	9.0
22	73.4	18.7	7.9	83.4	6.9	9.7	83.3	4.2	12.5
23	63.3	27.9	8.8	76.8	11.4	11.8	73.8	8.2	18.0
24	54.3	36.5	9.2	69.2	17.2	13.6	64.5	13.1	22.4

Note: The difference from 100 comprises the separated, divorced, and widowed.
Sources: 1. Census of Canada, 1981–2001, Public Use Microdata File (Individuals File)
        2. Kerr et al., 1994, 24

a growing inclination among youth to avoid formal marriage, with the option of common-law unions growing in popularity, and a decline in the total proportion in union.

As the fertility of common-law couples is lower than married couples, this change in nuptiality has further contributed to fertility decline. With this change in the marital behaviour of youth, there has been a corresponding decline in the number of children ever born to young women. This is demonstrated in table 13.9, which provides estimates on the number of children ever born for women aged 18 – 24 years (in the absence of a direct fertility question in the 2001 census). Across all ages, the number of children born to women (including those in common-law unions and single women) was lower in 2001 than in earlier censuses. For example, among women 24 years of age, the number of children per 1,000 women was 279 in 2001, down from 578 in 1981. As this is low by historical standards, it is also rather low in international comparisons.

Canada has witnessed a changing age pattern of fertility, with several decades of declining fertility among young adults. More generally, fertility has been declining for all ages 15–29, and especially for ages 20–24. This can be

Table 13.9
Child-Woman Ratio for Women Aged 18–24 by Age, Canada, 1981–2001

Age	18	19	20	21	22	23	24	Total
1981	39	73	138	219	324	435	578	257
1986	21	45	71	151	213	308	426	186
1991	19	36	67	116	160	240	321	140
1996	22	44	71	114	163	214	298	133
2001	21	35	60	102	140	202	279	119

Note: 1. Children at home per 1000 women.
    2. The number of children at home is estimated by author using Number of Persons in Census
    Family and Census Family Status and Living Arrangements.
Sources: Calculation for 1 based on the Census of Canada, 1981–2001, Public Use Microdata File
    (Individuals File).

held in contrast with an upward trend in fertility at ages 30–39. In 1970, the fertility of women in their latter 20s (25–29 years) surpassed the fertility of women in their early 20s, but by 1990, the fertility of women in their early 30s (30–34 years) also surpassed those in their early 20s (Grindstaff 1995). Young men and women are increasingly delaying childbearing in pursuit of alternate priorities, just as they are delaying the establishment of unions (including both marriage and cohabitation).

DISCUSSION AND CONCLUSION

In the 2001 Census, the relative number of children and youth is very low by historical standards. The proportion of all families that include at least one child or youth has declined, as has average family size. The number and proportion of children and youth living with a lone parent has risen, while the proportion living alone has declined. For a variety of reasons, young Canadians are less likely to marry today than in the past, while a substantial number have opted for a common-law union or to live with their parent(s). In addition, the fertility of young adults (youth in their latter teens and early 20s) has fallen to an unprecedented low.

These changes are partly a function of youth facing different circumstances in the labour market and preparing themselves accordingly. In particular, young Canadians are more likely to stay in school than in the past; full-time school attendance is up, and the likelihood of dropping out is down. The participation rate of young women in both post-secondary education and the labour force has risen (almost reaching parity with young men). Significant economic difficulties persist for many children and youth, particularly among those living with a single mother, or living as a lone parent themselves. An income gap persists, across family types, age groups, and by sex. Women with young children but no partner face considerable economic difficulties.

These demographic and socioeconomic changes have had important consequences, both positive and negative, for the young, and these consequences call for a discussion of alternative social and family accommodations. The simple question can be asked, as to whether the society is properly organized to meet the evolving needs of the young. As Canada's population is expected to continue to age into the 21st century, what will be some of the consequences of this change for its youngest citizens? In considering the impact of this transformation on the welfare of children and youth, we can see that they have benefited from the evolution of parental characteristics, in particular parents' higher levels of education and later ages at parenting, as well as smaller family sizes. Economically, they have particularly benefited from the work status of mothers. The main negative is that the young are more likely to be born into unstable relationships, including cohabiting relationships, and that is where the interests of adults and children are most likely to come into conflict. While adults benefit from marital transformations that permit flexibility in the pursuit of stronger satisfaction in relationships, children are more likely to experience the outcome as instability.

In some cases, the greater flexibility in relationships and families can serve to benefit the young, as they can potentially escape environments that are working against their welfare (as for example, in highly conflictive or abusive families). In other cases, children do not experience the absence of a parent from the household in a positive manner, nor do they necessarily experience the addition of a step-parent favourably. These problems are often compounded by the lower labour-force participation and low income of lone mothers. Even in two-parent families, average incomes barely kept pace with the cost of living over the 1981–2001 period, presenting frustrations and hardships for the young in particular.

While children may very well benefit from more stable adult relationships, it is hard to envisage how recent trends in union dissolution could be reversed. Consequently, families need to be supported as they are now, rather than attempting to make them correspond to some ideal. Given the co-existence of various types of families, policies should especially seek to enhance the welfare of the young, regardless of family setting. In developing public policy, we need to know more about the circumstances that lead to the successful adaptation of children under different types of family arrangements. Yet most surveys currently available on the social and economic characteristics of the young are lacking information on the economic links and day-to-day involvement of parents who do not share the child's primary residence. This is certainly true of the census, which has never collected information on family relations beyond the immediate household. The development of policies, supportive of children and youth, lacks this basic information. We know relatively little on the real dynamics underlying many of the changes in familial relationships highlighted in the current chapter.

REFERENCES

Baker, Maureen. 2002. "Child Poverty, Maternal Health and Social Benefits." *Current Sociology* 50 (6): 823–838

Beaujot, Roderic. 1991. *Population Change in Canada: The Challenges of Policy Adaptation.* Toronto: Oxford University Press

– 2000. *Earning and Caring in Canadian Families.* Peterborough, Ont.: Broadview Press Inc

– Ellen Gee, Fernando Rajulton, and Zenaida R. Ravanera. 1995. *Family over the Life Course.* Ottawa: Statistics Canada

Bélanger, Alain. 1999. *Report on the Demographic Situation in Canada 1998–1999.* Ottawa: Statistics Canada. Cat. no. 91–209

Boyd, Monica, and Doug Norris. 1995. "Leaving the Nest? Impact of Family Structure." *Canadian Society Trends* 38: 14–17

– 1998. "Changes in the Nest: Young Canadian Adults Living with Parents, 1981–1996." Paper presented at Canadian Population Society Meetings, Ottawa, June

Brouillette, Liliane, Claude Felteau, Pierre Lefebvre, and Alain Pelletier. 1990. "L'évolution de la situation économique des familles avec enfants au Canada et au Québec depuis 15 ans." *Cahiers Québécois de Démographie* 19 (2): 241–71

Cheal, David. 1996. "Stories about Step-Families." In *Growing Up in Canada.* Ottawa: Statistics Canada. Cat. no. 89–550

Dooley, Martin. 1988. *An Analysis of Changes in Family Income and Family Structure in Canada between 1971 and 1986 with an Emphasis on Poverty Among Children.* McMaster Univeristy, Hamilton: QSFP Research Report, no. 238

– 1991. "The Demography of Child Poverty in Canada: 1973–86." *Canadian Studies in Population* 18 (1): 53–74

Dumas, Jean, and Alain Bélanger. 1997. *Report on the Demographic Situation in Canada 1996.* Ottawa: Statistics Canada. Cat. no. 91–209

Grindstaff, Carl F. 1995. "Canadian Fertility, 1951 to 1993." *Canadian Social Trends* 39: 12–16

– T.R. Balakrishnan, and Paul S. Maxim. 1989. "Life Course Alternatives: Factors Associated with Differential Timing Patterns in Fertility among Women Recently

Completing Childbearing, Canada 1981." *Canadian Journal of Sociology* 14: 443–60

Guppy, Neil, and Scott Davis. 1998. *Education in Canada: Recent Trends and Future Challenges*. Ottawa: Statistics Canada and Nelson Canada

Juby, Heather, Nicole Marcil-Gratton, and Céline Le Bourdais. 2001. "A Step Further in Family Life: The Emergence of the Blended Family." In *Report on the Demographic Situation in Canada 2000*, eds. A. Bélanger, Y. Carrière, and S. Gilbert, 169–203. Ottawa: Statistics Canada. Cat. no. 91–209

Kerr, D, D. Larrivée, and P. Greenhalgh. 1994. *Children and Youth: An Overview*. Ottawa: Statistics Canada; Scarorough, Ont.: Prentice Hall Canada Inc

Le Bourdais, Céline, and Evelyne Lapierre-Adamcyk. 2004. "Changes in Conjugal Life in Canada: Is Cohabitation Progressively Replacing Marriage?" *Journal of Marriage and the Family* 66: 929–42

Marcil-Gratton, Nicole. 1993. "Growing Up with a Single Parent: A Transitional Experience? Some Demographic Measurements from the Children's Point of View." In *Single Parent Families: Perspectives on Research and Policy*, eds. J. Hudson and B. Galaway. Toronto: Thompson Education Publishing

– and Celine Le Bourdais. 1999. *Custody, Access and Child Support: Findings from The National Longitudinal Survey of Children and Youth*. Ottawa: Department of Justice Canada, Child Support Team

McQuillan, Kevin. 1991. "Family Change and Family Income in Ontario." In *Children, Families and Public Policy in the 90s*, eds. L.C. Johnson and D. Barnhorst. Toronto: Thompson Education Publishing

Mori, G.A., and B. Burke. 1989. *Educational Attainment of Canadians*. Ottawa: Statistics Canada. Cat.no. 98–134

OECD (Organization for Economic Co-operation and Development). 2000. *Education at a Glance: Analysis*. Paris: OECD

Oppenheimer, Calerie K. 1988. "A Theory of Marriage Timing." *American Journal of Sociology* 94 (3): 563–91

Picot, Garnet, John Miles, and Wendy Pyper. 1998. "Markets, Families and Social Transfers: Trends in Low-Income among the Young and Old, 1973–1995." In *Labour Markets, Social Institutions, and the Future of Canada's Children*, ed. Miles Corak, 11–30. Ottawa: Statistics Canada. Cat. no. 89–553

Preston, Samuel H. 1984. "Children and the Elderly: Divergent Paths for America's Dependents." *Demography* 21: 435–58

Ram, Bali. 1990. *New Trends in the Family*. Ottawa: Statistics Canada. Cat. no. 91–535

Rashid, Abdul. 1994. *Family Income in Canada*. Ottawa: Statistics Canada. Cat. no. 96–318

Ross, David P., and Richard Shillington. 1989. *The Canadian Fact Book on Poverty, 1989*. Ottawa: Canadian Council on Social Development

Simon, J. 1982. *The Ultimate Resource*. Princeton, NJ: Princeton University Press

Statistics Canada. 2005. *Annual Demographic Statistics*. Cat. no. 91–213–XIB

– 2006. *Report on the Demographic Situation in Canada 2003 and 2004*. Cat. no. 91–209–XIE

Wargon, Sylvia T. 1979. *Children in Canadian Families*. Ottawa: Statistics Canada. Cat. no. 98–810

Wister, Andrew, Barbara A. Mitchell, and Ellen M. Gee. 1997. "Does Money Matter? Parental Income and Living Arrangement Satisfaction Among 'Boomerang' Children during Coresidence." *Canadian Studies in Population* 24: 125–45.

Zhao, John. 1994. Leaving *Parental Homes in Canada*. Ph.D. thesis. University of Western Ontario

14

Canada's Elderly

ZONGLI TANG

The aging of the Canadian population has received increasing attention. Changes in the number and percentage of aging people in a population has numerous implications for societal structures, including family, health care, pensions, political processes, community, consumption, and the labor and housing market. The impact of aging on the Canadian society and economy has been a central issue for policy makers and researchers since the mid-1990s. It also poses challenges and opportunities to society and the economy. The 2001 census data show that as of 15 May 2001 the median age in Canada had reached 37.6 years, increasing by 2.3 years from 35.3 in 1996, and by 4.1 years from 33.6 in 1991. This change was the biggest census-to-census increase and the biggest decade-to-decade increase in a century.

GENERAL SITUATION

In this chapter the terms aging population or seniors refer to Canadians aged sixty-five and over. As of 15 May 2001, there were 3,888,550 Canadians aged 65 and over, accounting for about 13 percent of the national population, an increase of 10 percent from 1996, and 23 percent from 1991. Since the people who became seniors during the decade 1991–2001 were born between 1927 and 1936 – the Great Depression period, which discouraged fertility – this decade saw the lowest increase in seniors during the post-war period. However, the number of seniors still increased more quickly than the overall increase in the Canadian population in the same decade, which went up by only 11 percent. The number of seniors will increase more rapidly in the next two decades, especially when the baby boomers enter retirement age.

The aged dependency ratio, which is the ratio of the population aged 65 and over to the population of intermediate age (between 15 and 64) or working age, reflects the burden that the productive population must bear. While the dependency ratio has increased steadily since 1851·(see table 14.1), it went up noticeably during the recent decades. The ratio was 19.1 percent in 2001, up 2.2 points from 16.9 percent a decade earlier, which was the biggest increase since 1851. The ratio tells us that a senior who was supported by eighteen working-age persons in 1851 is now supported by five.

Meanwhile, the working-age population is becoming older. Before 1981, the median age of this group fluctuated over time, increasing by only one year during the eighty-year period between 1901 and 1981. But it increased dramatically in the 1990s, reaching 41.3 in 2001, up 3.2 years from 38.1 in 1991.

As shown in table 14.2, among seniors, the oldest group (i.e., those aged 80 and over) increased at the fastest pace. In 2001 over 930,000 Canadians reached age 80 and over. They accounted for 3.1 percent of the total population in comparison with 2.4 percent in 1991, increasing by 41.2 percent during the decade 1991–2001. There were more than twice as many in this group as in 1981 and more than twenty times as many as in 1921.

As shown in table 14.1, because of improvements in women's health, the ratio of men to women among Canadian seniors has declined steadily since 1901. As a result, by the 1960s women outnumbered their male counterparts. This trend seemed to reach a turning point in the 1990s, owing to the narrowing of gender mortality differences. In 1981, the death rate of older men was 148.12 per thousand while the rate of older women was only 40.33 per thousand. In 1991, the death rate of older men dropped significantly to 54.37 per thousand while the rate of older women dropped slightly to 39.22 per thousand. In 2001, the death rate of older men dropped further to 49.03 per thousand while the rate of older women went up to 39.84 per thousand. Older men thus regained some ground and the sex ratio began to go up. In the 2001 census, the sex ratio was 75, up from 72 in 1991.

Table 14.3 shows the median age and age group distribution by province and territory. The median age varies among provinces and territories from a low of 22.1 in Nunavut to a high of 38.8 in Nova Scotia and Quebec. Three Atlantic provinces (New Brunswick, Newfoundland and Labrador, Nova Scotia), Quebec, and British Columbia have the oldest populations as their median ages are higher than the national average. In terms of the proportion of seniors in the population, Saskatchewan, Manitoba, and Nova Scotia can be considered the oldest. Among large populations, Alberta is the youngest, with seniors making up 10.4 percent, significantly lower than the national average.

Table 14.4 shows the Canadian population by race with five racial origins considered: white, Asian, African (or black), Latin-American, and

Table 14.1
Canadian Population Trends, 1851 to 2001

Year	Total Population		Elderly Population (aged 65+)			Dependency Ratio (100 times Elderly Population/Total Population)	Sex Ratio of Elderly Population (100 Times Males/Females)
	Number (in 1000s)	Percentage Change in Previous Decade	Number (in 1000s)	Percent of Total Pop	Percentage Change in Previous Decade		
1851	2,436	–	65	2.7	–	5.6	117
1861	3,230	33	98	3.0	51	5.6	123
1871	3,689	14	135	3.7	38	6.7	121
1881	4,325	17	178	4.1	32	7.2	112
1891	4,833	12	220	4.6	24	7.7	110
1901	5,371	11	272	5.1	24	8.3	105
1911	7,207	34	336	4.7	24	7.5	104
1921	8,788	22	421	4.8	25	7.9	104
1931	10,377	18	576	5.6	37	8.8	105
1941	11,507	11	768	6.7	33	10.2	104
1951	14,009	22	1,086	7.8	39	12.5	103
1961	18,238	30	1,391	7.8	28	13.1	94
1971	21,568	18	1,745	8.1	25	13	81
1981	24,340	13	2,361	9.7	35	14.3	75
1991	27,304	12	3,170	11.6	34	16.9	72
2001	30,007	10	3,889	13.0	23	19.1	75

Source: Statistics Canada.

Table 14.2
Canadian Population by Age Group (in 1,000s), 1991–2001

| | Population | | | | |
| | 1991 | | 2001 | | |
Age Group	Counts	Percent	Counts	Percent	Percentage Change 1991–2001
0–4	191	7.0	170	5.7	-11.0
5–12	304	11.1	323	10.8	6.0
13–24	457	16.7	481	16.0	5.3
25–34	487	17.8	399	13.3	-17.9
35–44	437	16.0	510	17.0	16.7
45–64	537	19.7	729	24.3	35.8
65–69	107	3.9	113	3.8	5.6
70–79	144	5.3	182	6.1	26.9
80+	66	2.4	93	3.1	41.2
TOTAL	2,730	100	3,001	100	9.9

Sources: Statistics Canada

Table 14.3
Age Distribution by Province and Territories, 2001

| | | Age Group Distribution (percent) | | |
	Median Age	Age 0–19	Age 20–64	Age 65+
Canada	37.6	25.9	61.1	13.0
Newfoundland and Labrador	38.4	25.0	62.7	12.3
Prince Edward Island	37.7	27.3	59.0	13.7
Nova Scotia	38.8	25.0	61.1	13.9
New Brunswick	38.6	24.8	61.7	13.6
Quebec	38.8	24.2	62.5	13.3
Ontario	37.2	26.3	60.8	12.9
Manitoba	36.8	28.1	58.0	14.0
Saskatchewan	36.7	29.2	55.8	15.1
Alberta	35.0	28.3	61.4	10.4
British Columbia	38.4	25.0	61.4	13.6
Yukon Territory	36.1	29.0	64.9	6.0
Northwest Territories	30.1	35.0	60.7	4.4
Nunavut	22.1	46.5	51.2	2.2

Source: Statistics Canada, the 2001 Census.

Aboriginal. In 2001, whites accounted for 93 percent of seniors while they made up 88 percent of the total population. Asians were the second largest group, followed by Latin-Americans, Aboriginals, and Africans. Whites were also the oldest in terms of both the median age and the senior proportion, which explains why, as just mentioned, their percentage of seniors was higher than their percentage of the total population.

Table 14.4
Canadian Population by Race, 2001

| | All Ages | | Aged 65+ | | |
Race	Counts	Column (%)	Counts	Column (%)	Row (%)
White	25,933,748	87.5	3,366,311	92.9	13.0
Asian	2,488,415	8.4	198,733	5.5	8.0
African	186,597	0.6	5,272	0.15	2.8
Latin-American	470,152	1.6	25,809	0.7	5.5
Aboriginal	554,751	1.9	25,178	0.7	4.6
N/A	5,368	0.02	1,477	0.04	27.5
TOTAL	29,639,031	100	3,622,780	100.0	12.2

Source: Statistics Canada, the 2001 Census.

Table 14.5
Canadian Population by Immigrant Status

| | Total Population | | Old Population | | Mean Age |
Immigrant Status	Counts	Percent	Counts	Percent	
Citizens	24,003,612	81	2,586,814	71	34.8
Landed Immigrants	5,434,253	18	1,026,669	28	45.9
Non-Permanent Residents	195,799	1	7,819	0	29.9
N/A	5,368	0	1,477	0	44.8
TOTAL	29,639,032	100	3,622,780	100	37.6

Source: Statistics Canada, the 2001 Census PUMF (Individual File).

In Table 14.5, Canadians are classified in three groups: citizens by birth, landed immigrants or permanent residents, and non-permanent residents, including those with employment authorizations, student authorizations, or Minister's permit. Of these, Group 2 is the oldest and Group 3 the youngest in terms of the median age. Landed-immigrants account for 28 percent of seniors but only 18 percent of the total population. This finding brings into question the general expectation that immigrants on average will be younger than native-born Canadians.

Whites played a primary role in increasing the age of immigrants. First, whites were the largest immigrant group and accounted for 58.1 percent of the total, followed by Asians (33.7 percent), and Latin-Americans (5.9 percent). Second, Whites were the oldest immigrant group and their mean age reached 50.4, higher than the national average of 37.6.

HEALTH STATUS

The aging society is affected mainly by two factors, fertility and mortality. Canadian total fertility was three children or more per women between the mid-1940s and the 1960s, and then went down rapidly. It has remained below the replacement level since the 1970s. In 2001, it was only 1.5 children per women. As for mortality, it has declined consistently since the 1960s. The national death rate, which was 9.8 per thousand persons between 1941 and 1945, dropped to 7.3 per thousand persons in 1971, and further dropped to 7.1 in 2001. Mortality decline has generated an increase in life expectancy. In 2001, Canadian life expectancy at birth was 77 years for men and 82 for women. Canadian men today can live 18 years and women can live 21 years longer than their compatriots did in 1921.

We should point out that the national death rate did not decrease but increased slightly between 1991 and 2001. The increase cannot be attributed to a deterioration of health conditions but mainly to the growing number of seniors, which has extended the numerator in the death fraction. Elderly death rate on the average has actually dropped year by year since 1981. The rate in 2001 was 43.89 per thousand seniors, while it was 65.26 per thousand seniors in 1981. Canadians generally live their later years in good health, resulting in the senior death rate declining year by year. Of course, their health status was not as good as other age groups. For instance, 19.8 percent of Canadian aged 55–64 reported their health as excellent, and only 18.7 percent as poor. However, when comparing the 2001 cohort of seniors with the cohort between 1994 and 1995, we find a deterioration in health status. Fewer seniors in the 2001 cohort reported their health as excellent and very good, and more reported as poor. We do not know whether the reported deterioration had any impact on deaths. The fact is that the elderly death rate did not rise during that period.

To a large degree, health status is related to how much use is made of health services. In 2000–01, 90.3 percent of Canadian seniors saw at least one medical doctor in the preceding 12 months, higher than any other age group.

The major causes of senior deaths are heart and circulatory disease, cancer, respiratory disease, disease related to the mental health, and diabetes (see chart 1). However, the importance of these diseases to senior deaths changed significantly during the last decade. Heart and circulatory disease still remained as the number 1 cause, but the death rate derived from this disease declined considerably. The death rate caused by respiratory disease declined also. But the death rate caused by cancer and diabetes went up in the last decades. A particularly sharp increase occurred to the death rate related to mental health.

Table 14.6
Marital Status for the Population Aged 40–64 and 65+ Years, 2001

| | Population aged 40–64 | | | | | |
| | Female | | Male | | Total | |
Marital Status	Number	Percent	Number	Percent	Number	Percent
Divorced	718,430	14	570,949	12	1,289,379	13
Married	3,258,445	65	3,328,268	69	6,586,713	67
Separated	223,209	4	190,449	4	413,657	4
Single	551,829	11	672,035	14	1,223,864	12
Widowed	237,087	6	59,219	1	296,306	4
TOTAL	4,989,000	100	4,820,920	100	9,809,920	100
	Population aged 65+					
	Female		Male		Total	
Marital Status	Number	Percent	Number	Percent	Number	Percent
Divorced	121,178	6	92,258	6	213,436	6
Married	890,946	44	1,178,542	74	2,069,488	57
Separated	35,076	2	38,981	2	74,057	2
Single	115,905	6	92,208	6	208,113	6
Widowed	868,431	42	189,255	12	1,057,685	29
TOTAL	2,031,536	100	1,591,244	100	3,622,780	100

EDUCATION AND MARITAL STATUS

As compared with other groups, seniors received less education. In 2001 Canadians aged 20–64 reported 13.6 years of total schooling at elementary, high school, and college or university levels in comparison with 10.3 years for seniors. Canadian females aged 20–64 are more educated than males of the same age group in terms of years of schooling, though the margin is not significant, reflecting a long-term social shift from traditional gender roles toward shared roles and egalitarianism. The documented shift began in the late 1950s, accelerated during the 1960s and early 1970s, and continued through the 1990s in the developed world (Bianchi and Casper 2000; Cherlin and Walters 1981; Thornton and Freedman 1979). However, this shift was not found with seniors, and older men received more education than older women.

14.6 shows comparisons of marital status between seniors and other Canadians. Canadians aged 40–64 were chosen as the reference group. The two groups exhibit significant difference with regard to values. Divorce is more common among younger people: 13 percent of Canadians aged 40–64 are divorced, compared to only 6 percent of seniors. In addition, 12 percent of Canadians aged 40–64 remain single, compared to only 6 percent of seniors. Table 14.6 shows that there are fewer married seniors than in the younger group. Considering the high widowhood rate, the marriage percentage for seniors would be actually higher than that for younger people.

Normative differences in attitudes toward marriage are not found between older men and older women. In such categories as divorce, separation, and singlehood, older men have the same rate as older women. Since women generally live longer, table 14.6 shows a higher percentage of older men who stay married and a higher percentage of older women who are widowed.

ECONOMIC STATUS

According to the 2001 census, Canadian elderly have an average income of $23,698, $7154 lower than other Canadians (aged 20–64) (see table 14.7). The actual financial security of seniors is probably better than what is illustrated by their income, for many seniors have paid their mortgages and are no longer raising children. Unlike other adults, whose income is derived mainly from wages and salaries, seniors incomes come largely from pensions. Government plays a determining role in improving the well-being of seniors. As shown in table 14.7, pensions from government transfers, including the Old Age Security program, the Canada/Quebec Pension, and others, contribute more than 50 percent of the total income for seniors. Pensions from private retirement savings, including the Registered Retirement Income Fund (RRIF), the Employer-Sponsored Registered Pension Plan (RPPs), and the Registered Retirement Saving Plan (RRSP), account for 26 percent of seniors' total income. It is reported that the proportion of income derived from RRSPs and Canada/Quebec Pension Plans has increased in the last two decades, while the proportion of income from Old Age Security has fallen.[1]

An income gap exists between older men and older women. Older women, who make about $10,000 less yearly than older men according to the 2001 census, rely more on government transfer money and less on private employment-related retirement pensions and RRSPs. Transfers from the government account for 58 percent of women's income, compared to 43 percent of men's.

Income level or poverty line is one of the indicators of economic security. In the 2001 census, 17 percent of seniors reported that their before-tax income was below Statistics Canada's Low Income Cut-Offs line (LICOs), as compared

Table 14.7
Income by Major Sources for the Population Aged 20–64 and 65+ Years, 2000

| | Population aged 20–64 | | | | | |
| | Female | | Male | | Total | |
Income	Amount	Percent	Amount	Percent	Amount	Percent
Total	23,530	100	38,391	100	30,852	100
Wages and Salaries	18,547	79	31,353	82	24,951	78
Self-Employment Income	1,017	4	2,727	7	1,859	6
Child Tax Benefit	704	3	118	0	415	1
Old Age Security Pension	55	0	8	0	32	0
Canada or Quebec Pension	329	1	326	1	328	1
Employment Insurance	424	2	538	1	480	1
Others Government Sources	653	3	740	2	696	2
Investment Income	785	3	981	3	882	3
Retirement Pension	643	3	1,254	3	944	3
Other Money Income	373	2	155	0	266	1
Below Low Income Cut-off		17		14		15

| | Population aged 65+ | | | | | |
| | Female | | Male | | Total | |
Income	Amount	Percent	Amount	Percent	Amount	Percent
Total	19,125	100	29,534	100	23,698	100
Wages and Salaries	891	5	3,144	11	1,881	5
Self-Employment Income	891	5	3,144	11	1,881	5
Child Tax Benefit	5	0	17	0	10	0
Old Age Security Pension	6,580	34	5,695	19	6,191	17
Canada or Quebec Pension	3,556	19	5,468	19	4,396	12
Employment Insurance	26	0	77	0	48	0
Others Government Sources	956	5	1,431	5	1,165	3
Investment Income	2,968	16	3,353	11	3,137	9
Retirement Pension	3,774	20	9,146	31	6,134	17
Other Money Income	185	1	185	1	185	1
Below Low Income Cut-off		21		11		17

Source: Statistics Canada. The 2001 Census. PUMFs (Individual Files).

to 15 percent of other adults.[2] However, if tax credits and exemptions for seniors were to be taken into account, their actual level of income would not be as bad.

There are proportionately more older women living in poverty than older men. Their relatively low income and high degree of poverty could be largely attributed to their historically low labor force participation rate and gender inequality in income.

The final topic is housing characteristics of the elderly. According to the 2001 census, 75 percent of seniors own the houses they reside in, compared with 71 percent of other adults. Seniors' dwellings are in better condition than those of other adults. 72 percent of seniors report living in houses that need only regular maintenance while this rate for other adults is 63 percent. The house size of seniors in terms of the number of rooms is slightly smaller than other adults (6.02 versus 6.6 on average). The house value of seniors is about $10,000 lower than that of other adults. Moreover, 65 percent of seniors report living in single houses, close to the 64 percent of other adults. And 9 percent of seniors report living in a condominium, higher than the 5 percent reported by other adults.

Seniors' housing costs relative to their income are measured by the percentage of income occupied by housing payments, including mortgage, electricity, oil, gas, and other fuel, water and other municipal services, property taxes, and condominium fees. Compared with other adults, seniors use less of their income to secure shelter. Therefore, they can spend more of their income on consumer goods and services, thus improving their economic security. Nevertheless, housing costs represent a larger share of income for older women. The cost relative to income is 29.7 percent for older women and 23.9 percent for older men, which widens the financial gap presenting between the two gender groups.

PARTICIPATION IN SOCIETY

Active participation in society is important for seniors to avoid isolation and to have a healthy life. This section deals with two distinct aspects of activities in which seniors participate – paid-work, and non-paid work. 8.4 percent of seniors were employed in 2000, a small decline from 9 percent in 1976. It can be seen in table 14.8 that senior men were more active in the labor force than senior women. The employment rate was 13 percent for senior men and only 5 percent for senior women. Meanwhile, 56.5 percent of employed seniors held full-time jobs. They worked 41 weeks a year and 29 hours a week, less than other adults.

There has been a steady downward trend in the labor force participation rate of older workers in the last three decades.[3] A direct factor in affecting the trend is earlier retirement. Research conducted by an agency of the Federal Government reports that the median age of retirement declined by 3 years for men (from 64.5 to 61) and by 5 years for women (from 65 to 60) between 1976 and 1996.[4] Canadians choose earlier retirement both willingly and unwillingly. Some leave due to the incentives of retirement packages or an increased desire to enjoy life. Others leave due to unemployment, health problems, or mandatory retirement policies. The concentration of

Table 14.8
Labour Force Participation of the Elderly

	Female	Male	Total
Labour force Participation Status			
All Elderly	100.0	100.0	100.0
Employed	4.8	13.0	8.4
Unemployed-Looking for Full time Job	0.1	0.3	0.2
Unemployed-Looking for Part time Job	0.1	0.1	0.1
Unemployed-Not Looking for Job	0.1	0.3	0.2
Not-in-Labour Force	94.9	86.4	91.1
MEAN WEEKS WORKED	N/A	N/A	41.1
MEAN HOURS WORKED	N/A	N/A	28.6

Source: Statistics Canada, the 2001 Census, PUMFs (Individual File).

Table 14.9
Employment Status of the Elderly by Education, 2000

	Elementary or High School	Some College	College	Above College
Labour Force Participation Status (percent)				
All Elderly	100	100	100	100
Employed	6	10	16	22
Unemployed-Looking for Full time Job	0	0	0	0
Unemployed-Looking for Part time Job	0	0	0	0
Unemployed-Not Looking for Job	0	0	0	0
Not-in-Labour Force	93	89	84	77
Employment Status of the Employed (percent)				
All Elderly	100	100	100	100
Full-time	56	53	50	48
Part-time	44	47	50	52

Source: Statistics Canada. The 2001 Census. PUMFs (Individual File)

older workers in declining sectors of the economy could also be a factor as these workers are more likely to be affected by closings and lay-offs.

Labor force participation is closely related to educational attainment. Table 14.9 shows that the employment rate increases with educational attainment. As mentioned previously, seniors are generally less educated than other groups. As the economy has been shifting from traditional or labor-intensive industries to high-tech or knowledge-intensive industries, it would be difficult and costly for seniors, especially those with low-education, to update their skills to meet the challenges of the new information revolution.

Table 14.9 also shows that the proportion of employed seniors who worked full time decreases rather than increases with educational attainment, contradicting with the general connection between education and

employment. There could be a number of explanations. First, a high participation rate by well-educated seniors does not necessarily mean they hold a
high proportion of full-time jobs. Seniors returned to paid work usually following an initial retirement. [5] When making such a decision, financial needs
would be the primary consideration. To meet such needs, a part-time job
would be sufficient for a well-educated senior while a full-time job would
be necessary for a low-class one because of either their distinct economic
statuses before retirement or different pay related to their educational attainment. Second, it would be comparatively easy for a low-class senior to
find a full-time job in his previous area of employment, but it would be more
difficult for a well-educated senior to do so.

Canadian seniors are very active in unpaid work such as housework,
looking after children, and providing care to seniors in one's own household, outside one's own household, and to friends or neighbors. In 2000,
seniors spent 21.5 hours a week on average on the above mentioned work,
although this figure was lower than the 29.2 hours spent by other adults.
Most of the unpaid time was spent on housework. A difference is found in
this area between males and females. Female seniors did more work at home
than male seniors (23.7 vs 18.6 hours), indicating that there have been no
significant changes in gender role within family.

SOCIAL SUPPORTS FROM FAMILY

Social support from family and non-family, including spouses, adult children, relatives, and friends (or non-relatives), is viewed as informal support.
Silverstone describes it as "a rich fabric of informal relationships which en-
velopes the majority of elders in our society along a number of dimensions."
(1985, 156) Marital relationships play a key role in constructing informal
support. Hooyman and Kiyak (1996) state that as parental and employment
responsibilities decline, having a spouse offers built-in companionship. Of
family and non-family members, spouses are most likely to serve as confi-
dents in providing effective support. The presence and degree of informal support can be observed by looking at the living arrangement of seniors in the
2001 census, which show that 58 percent of Canadian seniors live with their
spouses or common-law partner. In other words, a majority of Canadian seniors could enjoy the first degree of informal support. However, senior women,
as compared with men, received less support from spouses. As shown in table
14.14, because of their longer life expectancy and fewer options for remarriage, only 44 percent of older women live with their spouses or common-law
partners as compared with 76 percent of older men.

Table 14.10
Median Age and Age Groups, Canada and Selected Countries, 2000 or 2001

Countries	Median Age (in years)	Age Group Distribution (in percents)			
		All Ages	0–19	20–64	65+
Canada	37.6	100.0	25.9	61.1	13.0
United States	35.5	100.0	28.7	59.0	12.3
Germany	40.1	100.0	21.1	62.5	16.4
France	37.6	100.0	25.3	58.7	16.0
United Kingdom	37.7	100.0	25.2	59.1	15.8
Italy	40.2	100.0	19.6	62.3	18.1
Japan	41.2	100.0	20.6	62.2	17.2
Russia	36.9	100.0	26.1	61.4	12.5
Australia	35.1	100.0	27.6	60.1	12.3
China	30.1	100.0	32.7	60.5	6.8
Mexico	23.3	100.0	43.4	51.9	4.7
World	26.5	100.0	39.1	54.0	6.9
More Developed Countries	37.4	100.0	25.1	60.6	14.3
Less Developed Countries	24.2	100.0	42.5	52.4	5.1
Least Developed Countries	18.1	100.0	53.9	43.0	3.1

Notes: 2001 figures in Canada, 2000 figures in all other countries
Sources: Population Division, Department of Economic and Social Affairs, United Nations

Seniors living with adult children, relatives, or non-relatives or friends are 13.4 percent, 5.5 percent, and 1.7 percent respectively. As compared with older men, older women were more likely to live with children. There is no significant gender difference in living arrangements with relatives and non-relatives. Altogether, more than 70 percent of Canadian seniors had varied degrees of informal support.

TRENDS

The impact of aging is global. As shown in table 14.10, in terms of median age, at the beginning of this new century Japan had the oldest population among major developed countries. The median age in Canada was higher than that of the United States but lower than that of most European countries. Canadian seniors made up 13 percent of the total population, higher than the Unites States, but lower than all other major developed countries. The median age of the Canadian population was 11.1 years higher than the world average, and Canadian seniors were 6.1 percent more of the population than in the overall world population. From this perspective, Canada is without doubt an aging society.

The older population continues to increase. With the coming retirement of the baby-boom generation (i.e., those born between 1946 and 1965), the number of seniors will increase quickly during this decade. The older population is expected to reach about 5 million in 2011, up 28.1 percent in comparison to 22.7 percent between 1991 and 2001. Seniors will make up 14.1 percent of the total population, increasing 1.1 percent from 13 percent in 2001. We need to pay close attention to aging issues, and more research is needed on how age-related changes influence our society and economy.

NOTES

1 See Health Canada in collaboration with the Interdepartmental Committee on Aging and Seniors Issue, *Canada's Aging Population,* Minster of Public Works and Government Services Canada, 2002.

2 On the basis pf the total income of an economic family or an unattached individual, the size of the family and the size of the area of residence, the income status of each unattached individual and economic family is determined in relation to Statistics Canada's low income cut-offs (LICOs).

3 It was also found in other developed countries. Please see National Advising Council on Aging,, *Challenges of An Aging Canadian Society;* and Serow, William J., David. F.Sly and J.Michael Wrigley, *Population Aging in the United States*, New York: Greenwood. Press; Cary S. Kart, The Realities of Aging. Boston: Allyn and Bacon.

4 See Health Canada in collaboration with the Interdepartmental Committee on Aging and Seniors Issue, *Canada's Aging Population.*

5 According to *Canada's Aging Population,* in 1994 13 percent of Canadian retirees reported that they had returned to work following initial retirement. This figure is larger than the employment rate of seniors. Therefore, we concluded that most of employed seniors would be those who returned to paid work following an initial retirement.

REFERENCES

Bianchi, Suzanne M., and Lynne M. Casper. 2000. "American Families." *Population Bulletin* 55 (4): 112–36

Cherlin, Andrew, and Pamela Barnhouse Walters. 1981. "Trends in United States Men's and Women's Sex Role Attitudes: 1972 to 1978." *American Sociological Review* 46: 453–60

Division of Aging and Seniors, Health Canada. 2001. *Healthy Aging and Behavioral Risk Factors: An Overview.* Ottawa: Government of Canada

– 2002. *Canada's Aging Population.* Ottawa: Government of Canada

Grenon, Andre. 2001. "Health Expenditures in Canada by Age and Sex, 1980–81 to 2000–01." Ottawa: Health Canada, Health Policy and Communications Branch

Kart, Gary S. 1998. *The Realities of Aging.* Boston: Allyn and Bacon

Haveman, Robert, Karen Holden, Kathryn Wilson, and Barbara Wolfe. 2003. "Social Security, Age of Retirement, and Economic Well-being: Intertemporal and Demographic Patterns Among Retired-Worker Beneficiaries." *Demography* 40: 369–94

Health System and Policy Division, Health Canada. 1999. *Canada's Health Care System.* Ottawa: Government of Canada

Hogan, Seamus. 2002. "Aging and Financial Pressures on the Health Care System." *Health Policy Research Bulletin* 1 (1): 5–9

Hooyman, Nancy, and H. Asuman Kiyak. 1998. *Social Gerontology.* Boston: Allyn and Bacon

National Advisory Council on Aging. 1999. *Challenges of an Aging Canadian Society.* Ottawa

Myles, John. 2000. *The Maturation of Canada's Retirement Income System: Income Levels, Income Inequality and Low-Income among the Elderly.* A research paper. Ottawa: Statistics Canada. Cat. no. 11F0019MPE No.147

Office of the Superintendent of Financial Institutions Canada. 2003. *Actuarial Report on the Old Age Security Program* (7th). Ottawa: Government of Canada

Organization for Economic Co-operation and Development. 2001. *Aging and Income: Financial Resources and Retirement in Nine OECD Countries.* Paris: OECD

Policy Research Initiative. 2003. *Horizons* 6 (2)

Serow, William J., David F. Sly, and J. Michael Wrigley. 2002. *Population Aging in the United States.* New York: Greenwood Press

Silverstone, B., 1985. "Informal Social Support Systems for the Frail Elderly." In *Aging Social Change,* ed. Institute of Medicine/National Research Council. New York: Academic Press

Statistics Canada. 1984. Vital Statistics. Vol. III. Deaths. Cat. no. 84–206

– 2002. *2001 Census Analysis Series – Profile of the Canadian Population by Age and Sex.* Cat. no. 96F00

– 2002. *Population by Age Group.* www.statcan.ca/English/Pgdb/People/Population/demo31a.htm

– 2005. "Life Expectancy – Abridged Table, 2001." *Health Indicators.* Cat. no. 82–221 (vol. 2005, no.1)

– 2008. Series B51–58. Cat. no. 2008–10–22

Thornton, Arland, and Deborah Freedman. 1979. "Changes in the Sex-Role Attitudes of Women, 1962–1977: Evidence from a Panel Study." *American Sociological Review* 44: 832–42

PART FIVE

Ethnicity, Religion, and Language

15

Ethnic Origins

SHARON M. LEE

INTRODUCTION

Canada has become increasingly diverse since Confederation in 1867. A population dominated by the two Charter or founding populations, English and French, rapidly grew and became more diverse through immigration from other parts of Europe. While the population of European-origin immigrants and their descendants increased, the indigenous population experienced decline from the time of Europeans' arrival, a trend that was not reversed until the early years of the twentieth century.[1] In recent decades, immigrants from Asia, Latin America, the Caribbean, and other regions of the world have added to Canada's population growth and ethnic diversity.

The population characteristics associated with ethnicity have a social significance that reaches into many areas of demographic study. Differences between ethnic groups exist in educational attainment, occupation, income, and other measures of social and economic well-being. The course of Canadian history has also created social systems and attitudes that affect the social position of various ethnic groups and inter-group relations. These historical changes and the effects they have had on ethnic groups contribute to differences in social and economic characteristics between ethnic groups. It is therefore of interest to examine trends in Canada's ethnic composition and compare ethnic groups along social and economic characteristics.

We first review the main concepts and terms used to study ethnicity in Canada. Second, we present a brief trend analysis of Canadians by main ethnic origins to document changes in the ethnic origins of Canadians. We conclude with a more detailed social-demographic portrait of Canadians by ethnic origins, based on analysis of 2001 Census microdata.[2]

Exhibit 15.1 Question 17 on the 2001 Census of Canada requested information about the respondent's ethnic origin (boldface type below was shown in the original 2001 census questionnaire):

*While most people in Canada view themselves as Canadians, information on their ancestral origins has been collected since the 1901 Census to capture the changing composition of Canada's diverse population. Therefore, this question refers to the **origins of the person's ancestors**.*

17. To which ethnic or cultural group(s) did this person's **ancestors** belong? *For example, Canadian, French, English, Chinese, Italian, German, Scottish, Irish, Cree, Micmac, Métis, Inuit (Eskimo), East Indian, Ukrainian, Dutch, Polish, Portuguese, Filipino, Jewish, Greek, Jamaican, Vietnamese, Lebanese, Chilean, Somali, etc.*

Space was provided in the 2001 questionnaire to list as many as 4 ethnic origins.

DEFINING ETHNIC ORIGIN AND RELATED CONCEPTS

The enumeration of ethnic groups in Canada's population census, as in other countries' censuses, is not simple. As Lieberson (1992, 25) noted in his "devilish principles" of ethnic group enumeration in population censuses, the census enumeration of ethnic groups has always been difficult, given different definitions of ethnicity, measurement issues, and the "inherent ambiguities" that may "distort the actual enumeration results." He further notes additional factors that complicate enumeration of ethnic groups, including the fluidity of meaning and membership in ethnic groups and the role of interest groups and politics in census operations.

The Canadian Census, conducted by Statistics Canada, is the primary source for data on Canada's ethnic history and trends (Krotki and Reid 1994). In the 1996 and 2001 censuses, "ethnic origin" referred to the ethnic or cultural group(s) that the respondent's ancestors belong to (see Exhibit 15.1 for the 2001 Census ethnic origin question). Statistics Canada cautions that comparability of data on ethnic origin from different censuses may be affected by various factors. First, changes in the ethnic origin question's format (for example, changing from a closed-ended to an open-ended question) and examples provided on the census questionnaire (such as "Canadian" for the first time in 1996) are likely to affect responses. Second, respondents' knowledge, understanding, and beliefs about ethnic origins may affect responses. For example, people's awareness of their ethnic origins may vary depending on how long they and their families have lived in Canada. Among descendants of immigrants, awareness of ethnic roots is likely to be higher among more recent

Exhibit 15.2 Question 19 on the 2001 Census of Canada requested information about the respondent's identification as a visible minority:
19. Is this person:
Boxes were provided for the respondent to mark one or
more of the following categories:
  White
  Chinese
  South Asian (e.g. East Indian, Pakistani, Sri Lankan, etc.)
  Black
  Filipino
  Latin American
  Southeast Asian (e.g. Cambodian, Indonesian, Laotian, Vietnamese, etc.)
  Arab
  West Asian (e.g. Afghan, Iranian, etc.)
  Japanese
  Korean
  Other (specify):
Question 17 also provided the following explanation:
This information is collected to support programs that promote
equal opportunity for everyone to share in the social, cultural,
and economic life of Canada.

immigrants, compared with those whose families have lived in Canada for several generations. There may also be confusion over the concept of ethnic origin and other concepts such as "visible minority" and nationality. Finally, people's responses to questions about ethnic and racial identity are fluid and are often influenced by personal, social, and situational factors.

Ethnic Origins, Visible Minority Status, and Foreign Birth

A related but distinct concept that provides data on Canada's increasingly diverse population is that of "visible minority," which refers to groups identified under the Employment Equity Act as "persons, other than Aboriginals, who are non-Caucasian in race and non-white in colour." The question on visible minorities was first asked in the 1996 census. Prior to 1996, data on visible minorities were derived from other census questions such as ethnic origin, place of birth, language, and religion (see Krotki and Reid 1994, 18). Exhibit 15.2 shows the 2001 Census question on visible minorities.

Confusion about ethnic origin and visible minority may arise among some respondents because each question may be answered with a similar response, such as "Chinese" or "Arab." Such overlaps between responses to the ethnic origin and visible-minority-status questions may muddy understanding and responses. In addition, as more recent immigrants to Canada originate from Asian countries such as China and India, Latin America, or the Caribbean, nativity also overlaps with ethnic origin and visible minority status since Asians, Latin Americans, and people from the Caribbean are considered visible minorities. For some groups, ethnic origin, visible minority, and foreign birth are highly intertwined. While the focus of this chapter is Canadians' ethnic origins, we will refer to nativity and visible-minority status as appropriate to highlight any overlaps.

MAIN ETHNIC ORIGINS AND TRENDS: TABLE 15.1

The quality of ethnic data collected in the Canadian censuses is generally quite good and provide the primary sources for a trend analysis of Canadians' ethnic origins, but observed changes may be affected by changes in the format of the ethnic origin question. As noted in table 15.1 (see table notes h and i), the introduction of multiple origins reporting in the 1981 Census and the offering of "Canadian" as an example of ethnic origin in the 1996 Census may have contributed to changes in reported ethnic origins during these years.

Prior to large-scale immigration to Canada from Asia, Latin America, and the Caribbean region that began in the 1970s and accelerated in the 1990s, Canada's population consisted of a very large European-origin population and a very small Aboriginal population. Ethnic and cultural diversity mainly referred to language, religion, and other cultural differences across European ethnic groups.

As recently as the 1971 Census, almost all Canadians (95 percent) traced their ethnic origins to Europe, as shown in table 15.1. Close to 45 percent reported origins in the British Isles, almost 30 percent reported French origins, and another 21 percent reported "other European" origins. The Aboriginal population was only 1.3 percent of Canada's 1971 population.

Small but noticeable changes in the main ethnic origins of Canadians began to appear in 1981, with decreases in the proportions reporting single British, French, and "other European" origins, a change that may be related to the introduction of multiple-origin reporting in the 1981 Census when 7 percent reported multiple origins.

Larger changes emerged by the 1991 Census, reflecting the impact of increased immigration from non-European countries during the 1980s and growing proportions of people reporting multiple origins. Canadians

Table 15.1

Main Ethnic Origins of Canada's Population, 1971 to 2001

Ethnic Origin Groups	1971		1981		1991		2001	
	Number[a]	Percent	Number[a]	Percent	Number[a]	Percent	Number[a]	Percent
Total Population	21,402	100.0	24,347	100.0	26,988	100.0	29,634	100.0
Single Origin								
British Isles[b]	9,489	44.3	9,682	39.8	5,619	20.8	2,675	9.0
French	6,157	28.8	6,437	26.4	6,145	22.8	1,087	3.7
Other European[c]	4,443	20.8	4,251	17.5	4,099	15.2	3,744	12.6
Aboriginal	284	1.3	NR	NR	450	1.7	555	1.9
East and Southeast Asian[d]	163	0.8	286	1.2	941	3.5	1,525	5.1
South Asian[e]	NR	NR	NR	NR	420	1.6	801	2.7
West and Other Asian[f]	NR	NR	NR	NR	80	0.3	162	0.5
Arab	NR	NR	NR	NR	142	0.5	235	0.8
African, W. Indian, Caribbean[g]	63	0.2	145	0.6	319	1.2	510	1.7
Latin American	NR	NR	NR	NR	83	0.3	147	0.5
Canadian[h]	NR	NR	NR	NR	758	2.8	6,760	22.8
Other Single Origins	805	3.8	1,622	6.7	51	0.2	108	0.4
Multiple Origins[i]	NR	NR	1,658	6.8	7,881	29.2	11,325	38.2

Notes: NR – Not Reported/Not Available. Percents may not add to 100 because of rounding.

[a] Number rounded to the nearest 1,000. The 1981 total includes 263,000 people in institutions who were not asked their ethnic origins, and 4,000 people who did not report an ethnic origin. An estimated 13,000 people in 1991 and 5,000 people in 2001 did not report an ethnic origin.

[b] Includes English, Irish, Scottish, and other British Isles.

[c] Includes Italian, Polish, Jewish, and other Europeans.

[d] Includes Chinese, Japanese, Korean, Vietnamese, others. In 1971, refers to only Chinese and Japanese, and in 1981, refers to Chinese only. In 2001, about 62 percent of this group were of Chinese ethnicity.

[e] Includes Indian, Pakistani, Sri Lankan, Bangladeshi, and others from the Indian sub-continent.

[f] West Asians include Afghani and other West Asians.

[g] Includes "Negro" in 1971, and Haitian.

[h] "Canadian" was offered as an example of ethnic origin beginning in the 1996 Census.

[i] Respondents could report more than one ethnic origin beginning in the 1981 Census.

reporting multiple origins were the single largest category, at almost 30 percent. The percent of people reporting single British origin was almost halved, between 1981 and 1991, decreasing from almost 40 percent in 1981 to 21 percent in 1991. There were smaller decreases in the proportions reporting single French and "other European" origins. This implies that the multiple-origin population was mostly people reporting British and other origins, with smaller numbers of people reporting French and other origins, and other ethnic combinations. Responses of other ethnic origins became more noticeable, including almost 4 percent reporting East and Southeast Asian origins, almost 2 percent reporting South Asian origins, over 1 percent reporting African origins, and almost 3 percent reporting "Canadian" as their single origin.

The 2001 census revealed that the movement to reporting multiple origins had continued such that almost 40 percent of Canadians reported multiple-ethnic origins. This was again the single largest category, as in the 1991 Census. A new development in 2001 was the large increase in the proportion of people who reported their ethnic origin as "Canadian" only (23 percent, or almost a quarter of Canada's population).[3] Other important trends were the large decreases in percents reporting single British or French origins (just 9 and 4 percent, respectively) and increased percents reporting East and Southeast Asian origins (over 5 percent), South Asian origin (almost 3 percent), and other groups such as Aboriginal (almost 2 percent) and African (almost 2 percent).

Changes in ethnic origin responses between 1991 and 2001 reflected accelerated immigration flows during the 1990s from Asia, Latin America, and the Caribbean; changes in question format and examples provided (specifically, "Canadian" as an example of ethnic origin beginning with the 1996 Census, not shown in table 15.1); and increased propensity to report multiple origins among those with long histories in Canada and high exogamy rates (Kalbach 1983). Immigration, intermarriage, changes in how the census asks and collects data on ethnic origins, changes in how Canadians perceive and report their ethnic origins, and other factors, have produced the most ethnically diverse Canadian population to date.

SOCIAL DEMOGRAPHIC PROFILE OF MAIN ETHNIC GROUPS, 2001

In this section, we focus on 2001 census data to provide a portrait of Canada's current ethnic groups.

Nativity, Visible Minority, and Citizenship: Table 15.2

Immigration's key role in diversifying Canada's ethnic landscape can be seen by comparing the percent foreign-born across the main ethnic groups in 2001 (see table 15.2).

Almost one in five Canadians is foreign-born, but the percent foreign-born ranges from less than 1 percent among those who reported Aboriginal or "Canadian" ethnic origins to over 50 percent among those reporting African, Arab, West Asian, South Asian, East and Southeast Asian, Latin American, and Caribbean. Other ethnic groups that are mainly Canadian-born include the French, with only 6 percent foreign-born, and people reporting multiple origins, with 8 percent foreign-born.

Table 15.2
Percent Foreign-Born, Visible Minority, and Citizen, Main Ethnic Origin Groups, 2001

Ethnic Origin Groups	Percent Foreign-Born	Percent Visible Minority	Percent Citizen
Total Population	19.0	13.4	94.8
British Isles	19.4	1.0	95.9
French	5.5	0.5	98.2
Other European	42.2	1.6	91.3
African	69.1	94.5	70.2
Arab	73.7	73.0	76.3
West Asian	84.4	66.3	66.5
South Asian	73.0	98.6	72.9
East and Southeast Asian	77.7	99.2	76.9
Latin American	80.5	85.5	71.5
Caribbean	67.7	94.2	84.2
Aboriginal	0.6	0.2	99.6
Canadian	0.8	1.2	99.8
Other Single Origins	20.7	6.8	63.4
Multiple Origins	7.5	5.3	97.5

Table 15.2 also shows the large overlap between foreign birth and visible-minority status among Canada's ethnic groups. About 13 percent of Canada's population are members of visible minority groups, but among ethnic groups with high proportions that are foreign-born, such as African, South Asian, East and Southeast Asian, and Latin American, the proportions that are visible minorities are also high.

The percents of ethnic groups that are Canadian citizens are shown in the last column in table 15.2. Not surprisingly, almost all people in ethnic groups with relatively low proportions and that are foreign-born (for example, "Canadian," French, multiple origins) are Canadian citizens, while ethnic groups with higher percents of foreign-born have lower percents reporting Canadian citizenship (for example, West Asian and African). The proportions that are Canadian citizens are quite high among several ethnic groups with high proportions foreign-born. For example, while 73 percent of people of South Asian origins are foreign-born, an equal percent (73 percent) are Canadian citizens.

Age Characteristics: Table 15.3

Age characteristics of a population inform us about the relative "youth" or "age" of the population, with implications for future growth of the population and its changing needs. For example, populations with a higher mean

Table 15.3
Age Characteristics of Main Ethnic Origin Groups, 2001

Ethnic Origin Groups	Percentage 15 Years of Age or Younger	Percentage 65 Years of Age or Older	Mean Age
Total Population	20.8	12.2	36.8
British Isles	8.7	25.5	48.0
French	11.7	17.0	43.4
Other European	11.6	20.8	44.2
African	33.2	2.8	26.5
Arab	26.4	5.6	30.9
West Asian	21.1	6.8	32.9
South Asian	25.1	6.1	31.7
East and Southeast Asian	19.2	9.1	35.2
Latin American	22.5	3.4	30.9
Caribbean	21.7	6.4	33.5
Aboriginal	35.2	4.5	27.2
Canadian	23.5	10.5	35.0
Other Single Origins	11.8	10.6	37.4
Multiple Origins	25.2	8.7	33.7

age and with higher proportions in older age groups imply an aging population that will not be growing as quickly as a more youthful population, and older populations will have greater demand for health care and other services needed by the elderly.

As shown in table 15.3, the mean age of Canada's population is 36.8 years, 12 percent are aged 65 and older, and 21 percent are 15 years or younger. To put this in perspective, the median age for the world's population in 2005 was 26.8 years, much lower than Canada's median age of 36.9, which is about the same as its mean age of 36.8, and almost 30 percent of the world's population in 2005 was aged 15 or younger while only 7 percent were aged 65 and older (Population Reference Bureau 2005; United Nations 2005). In contrast, the median age of Mexico's population was 23.1, 31 percent of its population was 15 and younger and just 5 percent were 65 and older. Thus, Canada's population is older than the world's average and older compared to countries like Mexico because of Canada's lower fertility and longer life expectancies.

Ethnic groups that are heavily foreign-born, such as African and Latin American, have younger age profiles, reflecting higher fertility rates in their countries of origin compared with ethnic groups with longer histories in Canada, such as British, French, and "other European" origin groups. Canadians of British origins have the oldest mean age (48.0 years old), while Canadians of African origins have the youngest mean age, at 26.5. Not surprisingly, ethnic groups with older mean ages have smaller proportions of children aged 15 and younger, and larger proportions aged 65 and older. The different age profiles of various ethnic groups imply faster future growth of ethnic groups with younger age characteristics. Given that most of the younger ethnic groups are recent immigrants and also members of visible minorities, Canada's future population will include more visible minorities from a wider diversity of ethnic origins.

Table 15.3 also shows that people of multiple ethnic origins are relatively youthful, with a mean age of 33.7, almost one-third aged 15 and younger, and less than 10 percent aged 65 and older. This reflects the effects of several factors, including the relative recency of ethnic intermarriage, the shift to permit reporting of multiple origins beginning with the 1981 census, and perhaps greater knowledge and acceptance of multiple origins by younger Canadians.

Geographical Distribution: Table 15.4

The geographical distribution of Canada's population by ethnic origin reflects historical and current patterns of settlement and other social, political, and economic differences by province. For example, while 23 percent of all respondents reported "Canadian" as their only ethnic origin, almost half of Quebec residents, over 40 percent of residents of Newfoundland, and a third of New Brunswick's population chose this option. In contrast, 10 percent or less of residents of Manitoba, British Columbia, and the territories reported "Canadian" ethnic origin.[4]

Reporting multiple-ethnic origins was the modal choice in the 2001 Census, with 38 percent of Canadians reporting more than one ethnic origin. Half of people in Prince Edward Island, Saskatchewan, and Alberta fell in this category. Only two provinces, Newfoundland and Quebec, had lower-than-average proportions reporting multiple-ethnic origins.

Provincial and territorial variations in reporting "Canadian" ethnicity or multiple-ethnic origins reflect factors such as ethnic history, demography and relations, and knowledge and acceptance of these ethnic options. Other geographical variations are mainly related to recent immigrant flows and characteristics. For example, substantial immigration from Asia meant that East and Southeast Asian ethnic origin was among the five main ethnic-origin groups in British Columbia. In contrast, provinces that have not received many immigrants from recent immigrant flows, such as Prince Edward Island and New Brunswick, have mostly European-origin populations.

Table 15.4

Province of Residence for Main Ethnic Origin Groups, 2001

Ethnic Origin Groups	Canada	NFL	PEI	NS	NB	PQ	ON	MB	SK	AB	BC	YK, NW, and NU
Total Population (in 000's)	29,634	507	132	896	719	7,125	11,285	1,104	963	2,941	3,869	92
Total Population (Percent)	100	100	100	100	100	100	100	100	100	100	100	100
British Isles	9	29	19	17	12	2	11	8	7	9	11	7
French	4	1	5	3	8	10	2	2	2	1	1	1
Other European	13	1	2	4	2	6	17	20	19	15	12	5
African	1	0	0	0	0	0	1	0	0	0	0	0
Arab	1	0	0	1	0	1	1	0	0	1	0	0
West Asian	1	0	0	0	0	0	1	0	0	0	1	0
South Asian	3	0	0	0	0	1	4	1	0	2	5	0
East and Southeast Asian	5	0	0	0	0	2	6	4	1	5	12	1
Latin American	0	0	0	0	0	1	1	0	0	0	0	0
Caribbean	1	0	0	0	0	1	2	0	0	0	0	0
Aboriginal	2	2	0	1	1	1	1	8	8	3	2	39
Canadian	23	41	24	28	33	48	14	10	12	13	10	8
Other Single Origins	0	0	0	0	0	1	0	0	0	0	0	0
Multiple Origins	38	25	49	45	43	26	39	45	50	49	45	38

Notes: [a] NFL: Newfoundland and Labrador; PEI: Prince Edward Island; NS: Nova Scotia; NB: New Brunswick; PQ: Quebec; ON: Ontario; MB: Manitoba; SK: Saskatchewan; AB: Alberta; BC: British Columbia; YK, NW, and NU: Yukon, Northwest Territories, and Nunavut.

Metropolitan Residence: Table 15.5

Over 80 percent of Canadians reside in urban areas and 62 percent live in Census Metropolitan Areas or CMAs (see table 15.5, first column), which are defined as urban agglomerations centered on a large urban centre with a population of 100,000 or more. Except for Aboriginals, the majority of most ethnic groups' populations reside in CMAs, and almost all people of African, Arab, Asian, and Caribbean origins live in CMAs.

A comparison of Canada's three largest CMAs, Montreal, Toronto, and Vancouver, reveals interesting differences. Montreal has the highest percent reporting "Canadian" ethnic origin (37 percent), followed by multiple origins (27 percent), "other European" (12 percent), and French (12 percent). These four groups account for almost 90 percent of Montreal's population.

Table 15.5
Census Metropolitan Area (CMA)[a] Residence for Main Ethnic Origin Groups, 2001

		Percentage Residing in		
	All CMAs[b]	Montreal CMA[c]	Toronto CMA[c]	Vancouver CMA[c]
All Ethnic Groups	62	100	100	100
British Isles	54	2	8	10
French	58	9	1	1
Other European	73	12	22	11
African	95	1	2	0
Arab	95	3	1	0
West Asian	97	1	2	1
South Asian	93	2	9	7
East and Southeast Asian	96	3	13	22
Latin American	92	1	1	1
Caribbean	97	2	4	0
Aboriginal	23	0	0	1
Canadian	51	37	8	7
Other Single Origins	67	1	0	0
Multiple Origins	59	27	29	38

Notes: [a] Census Metropolitan Areas (CMAs) are urban agglomerations centred on a large urban centre. The urban centre must have 100,000 or more residents in order to be designated a CMA.
[b] This column refers to the percent of each ethnic group that reside in CMAs. For example, 62 percent of people from all ethnic groups combined (which is the same as the total population) reside in CMAs compared with 54 percent of people of British Isles origins and 95 percent of people of African origin.
[c] These columns provide ethnic group breakdowns of the total population in each CMA. For example, of the total population of Montreal (that is, 100 percent), 2 percent are of British Isles origin, 9 percent are of French origin, and 12 percent are of Other European origin.

In Toronto, the largest ethnic group is multiple origins (29 percent), followed by "other European" (22 percent), East and Southeast Asian (13 percent), South Asian (9 percent), and British and "Canadian" (9 percent each). Together, these six groups make up about 90 percent of Toronto's population. In Vancouver, the largest percent is multiple origins at 38 percent, followed by 22 percent reporting East and Southeast Asian origins, 11 percent reporting "other European", 10 percent reporting British origins, and another 7 percent each reporting South Asian or "Canadian" origins. Together, these six groups account for 95 percent of Vancouver's population. Variations in the ethnic composition of Canada's three largest CMAs reflect historical as well as contemporary demographic processes (including immigration and settlement flows), and other differences such as political, economic, and cultural factors.

Language and Religion: Table 15.6

The definition of ethnic origin as cultural background implies ethnic group variations in language and religion, since language and religion are aspects of culture. Just 1 percent of Canada's population has no knowledge of either English or French.[5] Given this, table 15.6 compares the main ethnic groups by home language if other than English or French, most common home language if other than English or French, and religion.[6]

Twelve percent of all ethnic groups report a home language other than English or French. Zero to less than 5 percent of people reporting British or French or "Canadian" or other single origins or multiple origins report home languages other than the two official languages. In contrast, large percents of some ethnic groups report a home language other than English or French, including West Asian (74 percent), South Asian (58 percent), East and Southeast Asian (68 percent), and Latin American (63 percent). The most common home languages reported by these ethnic groups are Arabic among Arab origin people (51 percent), Spanish among people with Latin American ethnicity (62 percent), Chinese among people of East and Southeast ethnic origin (45 percent), and Punjabi among people of South Asian ethnicity (27 percent).

There is considerable language diversity among people who are grouped into the main ethnic origin groups. While 25 percent of people of "other European" origins speak a home language other than English or French, only 3 percent of these speak Portuguese, the most common home language other than English or French spoken by people in this category. Fifty-eight percent of people reporting South Asian origin speak a home language other than English or French, but the most common home language for this group – Punjabi – is spoken by just 27 percent. Sixty-eight percent of East and Southeast Asians speak a home language other than English or French, but Chinese is spoken by just 45 percent.

The linguistic diversity within some of the broad ethnic-origin categories reminds us that ethnic diversity is greater than implied from examining a limited number of ethnic categories, and it would be incorrect to assume that all people categorized in a particular ethnic category share similar socio-cultural characteristics such as language. At the same time, there is high linguistic homogeneity among some ethnic groups, such as Arabs and Latin Americans; almost all people who report Latin American ethnicity and who speak a home language other than English or French report Spanish as their home language.

Table 15.6
Language and Religion for Main Ethnic Origin Groups, 2001

Ethnic Origin Groups	Language			Religion		
	Percent with Home Language Other than English or French	Most Common Home Language Other than English or French[a]	Percent with Most Common Home Language	Most Common Religion	Percent with Most Common Religion
All Ethnic Groups	12	Other Language[b]	3	Catholic	43.8
British Isles	0	Other Language[b]	0	Protestant	56.4
French	0	Other Language[b]	0	Catholic	85.4
Other European	25	Portuguese	3	Catholic	48.2
African	34	Other Language[b]	31	Protestant	25.1
Arab	54	Arabic	51	Muslim	53.1
West Asian	74	Other Indo-Iranian	50	Muslim	61.7
South Asian	58	Punjabi	27	Sikh	31.1
East and Southeast Asian	68	Chinese	45	No affiliation	42.2
Latin American	63	Spanish	62	Catholic	68.2
Caribbean	7	Other Language[b]	6	Protestant	43.6
Aboriginal	20	Aboriginal	20	Catholic	41.9
Canadian	1	Other Language[b]	0	Catholic	64.9
Other Single Origins	3	Other Indo-Iranian	2	Catholic	60.7
Multiple Origins	3	Other Language[b]	1	Catholic	38.4

Notes: [a] This refers to the most common non-English, non-French language spoken by the ethnic group. For example, for the "Other European" group, the most common home language is Portuguese, spoken by 3 % of this group.

[b] "Other" language refers to languages other than those specified in the table, for example, Thai or Indonesian.

Canada's population is also characterized by considerable religious diversity, which overlaps considerably with ethnicity. The most common religion is Catholicism, reported by 44 percent. Ethnic groups for whom Catholicism is the most common religion include French (85 percent), "other European" (almost 50 percent), Latin American (68 percent), "Canadian" (65 percent), "other" single origins (60 percent), and multiple origins (almost 40 percent). Protestantism is the most common religion for people reporting British (56 percent), African (25 percent), and Caribbean (44 percent) origins.

Ethnic groups associated with recent immigration have added to religious diversity, including Islam (53 percent of people of Arab ethnicity and 62 percent of people of West Asian ethnicity are Muslims) and Sikhism (31 percent of South Asians belong to this religion). Finally, 42 percent of people of East and Southeast origins report no religious affiliation. While Christianity (as represented by Catholicism and Protestantism) remains the most widespread religion of Canadians, there are small minorities of Muslims, Sikhs, and other religions that will further religious diversity in Canada. In addition, recent Latin American immigrants and their descendants, who are primarily Catholic, will increase the proportion of Catholics in Canada in the future.

Socioeconomic Characteristics

Ethnic origin continues to be an important social stratification factor in Canada (Driedger 2003; Kalbach and Kalbach 1999; Reitz and Sklar 1997). We examine ethnic group differences in three socioeconomic characteristics – education, household income, and homeownership.

Education: Table 15.7

The overall mean years of schooling was about 13 years. Most ethnic groups had similar or higher than the national average years of schooling. Four groups – French, "other European," Aboriginal, and "Canadian" – had lower than average mean years of schooling, while Arab, West Asian, and African ethnic groups had the highest mean years of schooling at 14.

For the total population, 29 percent have less than a high-school education while almost 24 percent have college degrees or higher education. Almost half of Aboriginal people, 36 percent of people reporting "Canadian" ethnicity, and 35 percent of people reporting "other European" origins have less than high-school education.

Several ethnic origin groups have high percents with at least a college-level education, including people of Arab origin (over 43 percent), West Asian

Table 15.7
Educational Attainment of Population Aged 25 Years and Older, Main Ethnic Origin Groups,
2001

Ethnic Origin Groups	Mean Years of Schooling	Percent with Less than High School	Percent with College Degree or More
Total Population	12.9	29.1	23.8
British Isles	12.8	31.8	20.0
French	12.6	30.5	24.0
Other European	12.4	34.6	21.5
African	14.0	20.5	31.9
Arab	14.1	23.1	43.3
West Asian	14.0	21.1	41.5
South Asian	13.4	27.9	36.1
East and Southeast Asian	13.6	26.2	40.2
Latin American	13.5	25.5	28.3
Caribbean	13.2	27.4	19.4
Aboriginal	10.6	49.0	8.3
Canadian	12.1	35.9	15.5
Other Single Origins	13.1	27.8	27.9
Multiple Origins	13.6	21.6	27.8

origins (42 percent), and East and Southeast Asian origins (40 percent). In
contrast, less than 10 percent of Aboriginal Canadians have a college education or more. The relatively high proportions who are college graduates or
more among some ethnic groups reflect Canada's immigration policies that
select on education, as most of the ethnic origin groups with high mean
years of schooling and percent with college degrees or more are also heavily
foreign-born, as previously shown in table 15.2.

Household Income and Homeownership: Table 15.8

Mean household income was $35,316 for all households in 2001. Of the
fourteen ethnic origin groups listed in table 15.8 (based on householder's
ethnic origin), just four had mean household incomes that were higher
than the average. These include households of British, "other European,"
East and Southeast Asian, and multiple origins. French-origin households
had mean household incomes similar to the national average. Aboriginal
and African origin households were poorest, with mean household income
about $21,500 and $23,000, respectively.

Ethnic groups are further compared by the percents with mean incomes at
or below the low-income cutoffs (or LICOs) established by the federal government or who had relatively high incomes. Based on an examination of

Table 15.8
Household Income and Homeownership, Main Ethnic Origin Groups, 2001[a]

Ethnic Origin Groups	Mean Household Income ($)	Percent Low Income[b]	Percent High Income[c]	Percent Owning Home	Ratio[d]
Total Population	35,316	20.9	25.8	63.7	100
British Isles	38,764	16.5	28.8	71.9	113
French	35,492	19.7	23.2	62.8	99
Other European	38,492	17.6	32.5	73.1	115
African	23,222	50.4	12.0	20.9	33
Arab	30,075	39.9	18.5	36.6	57
West Asian	27,573	40.9	19.7	40.9	64
South Asian	33,318	27.8	31.2	54.5	86
East and Southeast Asian	37,701	28.4	30.2	59.9	94
Latin American	26,117	34.8	17.9	32.6	51
Caribbean	28,205	33.7	21.3	40.1	63
Aboriginal	21,477	39.6	11.6	38.3	60
Canadian	31,724	22.3	19.9	63.0	99
Other Single Origins	30,654	29.2	18.8	49.6	78
Multiple Origins	38,221	18.5	28.8	63.5	100

Notes: [a] Household-income and home-ownership characteristics of the householder.
[b] Includes households whose mean incomes are at or below the "low income cutoffs" or LICOs. These are income thresholds determined by analyzing family expenditure data, where low-income families devote a larger share of income to the necessities of food, shelter, and clothing than the average family would. For further details, see dissemination.statcan.ca/Daily/English/040309/d040309c.htm.
[c] Defined as households with mean incomes equal to or higher than $75,000.
[d] The ratio refers to the group's percent homeownership relative to the total population's percent home-ownership, which equals 100.

household income distribution, we defined high income as $75,000, which is about twice the national mean household income, or higher. About one-fifth of all households are low-income while one-fourth are high-income. Except for British, French, "other European," and multiple-origin households, all other ethnic groups had higher-than-average percents of low-income households. For example, half of African origin households and about 40 percent of West Asian or Aboriginal households are low-income.

Higher-than-average percents of British, "other European," South Asian, East and Southeast Asian, and multiple-origin households are high income. For example, one-third of households with "other European" householders are high-income. This contrasts with just 12 percent of households where the householder is Aboriginal or African. Finally, there are some ethnic groups with roughly equal percentages of low- and high-income households, including South Asian (28 percent low- and 31 percent high-income), East and Southeast Asian (28 percent low and 30 percent high income) and

"Canadian" (22 percent low- and 20 percent high-income) households, suggesting greater income inequalities in these ethnic groups.

Homeownership

Our final indicator of socioeconomic status is homeownership, an important and unique measure of socioeconomic status. Homeownership reflects the influence of several factors, including sufficient financial resources, life-cycle stage (for example, older and married people are more likely to own their homes), and cultural values and norms about owning homes and real estate. Among immigrants, homeownership may additionally indicate commitment to their new home. However, immigrants' homeownership is also affected by how long immigrants have lived in Canada and knowledge about how to go about buying a home.

Almost two-thirds of Canadians own their homes (about 64 percent), as shown in table 15.8. Two groups have higher-than-average homeownership rates – British and "other European" origin households. French, "Canadian," and multiple-origin households have homeownership rates similar to the national average. Other ethnic groups have below-average rates of homeownership. The lowest homeownership rate is among African origin households at just 21 percent.

Another way of comparing homeownership rates is to calculate the ratio of homeownership relative to the national average rate of 63.7 percent, which equals 100. These ratios are shown in the last column of table 15.8. Ratios above 100 indicate higher-than-average likelihood of homeownership, while ratios below 100 indicate lower-than-average likelihood of homeownership. The lowest ratio, 33, among African-origin households, can be interpreted to mean that African householders have about one-third the homeownership likelihood of all households in Canada. The highest ratio, 115, among households with "other European" householders, implies that such householders are 15 percent more likely than average to be homeowners.

Variations in homeownership rates are quite consistent with variations in household incomes. However, comparisons of table 15.7 on educational attainment with table 15.8 on household income and homeownership reveal some unexpected patterns. Some groups with relatively high educational attainments (for example, African, Arab, and West Asian) have relatively low mean-household incomes and low homeownership rates and ratios, suggesting that education may not translate to other socio-economic achievements for these groups.

CONCLUSION

Canada's reputation as one of the most ethnically and culturally diverse nations is well founded. More than two hundred different ethnic origins were reported in the 2001 Census question on ethnic ancestry. Changing sources of immigrants and their descendants over the years, together with Canada's Aboriginal peoples, have produced the multiethnic and multicultural society that is today's Canada. As immigration continues to be a major factor in Canada's future population change, Canada's ethnic composition will continue to evolve and diversify.

This chapter began with a look at trends in Canada's main ethnic origin groups over the last thirty years and concluded with a comparison of ethnic groups along selected socio-demographic characteristics. There are three main conclusions.

First, there are many more ethnic groups in Canada today, primarily because of immigration from new areas of origins, such as parts of Eastern Europe, Central Asia, the Middle East, Africa, and South America. Second, many of the new ethnic groups are also visible minorities, with important implications for future growth and composition of the visible-minority population. Third, there are substantial variations in age structure, geographical distribution, home language, and socio-economic characteristics across ethnic groups. Such differences have important implications for public policy-making and planning for the future, including policies on immigration, multiculturalism, schools, and housing.

NOTES

1 There is a separate chapter on the Aboriginal population. Canada's Aboriginal population has been growing in recent years, reaching almost 2 percent in 2001, and represents an important and distinct dimension of Canada's ethnic diversity.

2 This chapter's main focus is a sociodemographic profile of ethnic groups in Canada based on 2001 Census data. There are other studies of ethnicity in Canada that provide theoretical overviews and report data from earlier censuses. See, for example, Driedger (2003), Halli et al. (1990), and Kalbach and Kalbach (2000).

3 See Boyd (1999) and Boyd and Norris (2001) on the shift to reporting "Canadian" from 1986 to 1996.

4 See Boyd (1999), Boyd and Norris (2001), and Lee and Edmonston (2009) for further discussions of recent trends and patterns of reporting "Canadian" ethnic origin, including provincial variations.

5 Some groups have relatively high percents without knowledge of either English or French (for example, over 10 percent of East and Southeast Asians), which may have implications for social and economic integration (see Boyd 1990; Boyd and DeVries 1999; and Lee 1999).

6 There is a separate chapter on religion so the comparisons of ethnic groups by religion in this chapter will be brief.

REFERENCES

Boyd, Monica. 1990. "Immigrant Women: Language, Socioeconomic Inequalities, and Policy Issues." In *Ethnic Demography: Canadian Immigrant, Racial, and Cultural Variations*, eds. Shiva S. Halli, Frank Trovato, and Leo Driedger, 275–95. Ottawa: Carleton University Press

– 1999. "Canadian, eh? Ethnic Origin Shifts in the Canadian Census." *Canadian Ethnic Studies* 31 (3): 1–19

– and Doug Norris. 2001. "Who are the 'Canadians' – Changing Census Responses, 1986–1996." *Canadian Ethnic Studies* 33 (1): 1–24

de Vries, John. 1999. "Foreign Born Language Acquisition and Shift." In *Immigrant Canada: Demographic, Economic, and Social Challenges,* eds. Shiva S. Halli and Leo Driedger, 261–81. Toronto: University of Toronto Press

Driedger, Leo. 2003. *Race and Ethnicity: Finding Identities and Inequalities.* 2nd *Edition.* Don Mills: Oxford University Press

Halli, Shiva S., Frank Trovato, and Leo Driedger, eds. 1990. *Ethnic Demography: Canadian Immigrant, Racial, and Cultural Variations.* Ottawa: Carleton University Press

Kalbach, Madeline A., and Warren E. Kalbach. 1999. "Persistence of Ethnicity and Inequality among Canadian Immigrants." *Canadian Studies in Population* 26 (1): 83–105

– eds. 2000. *Race and Ethnicity: A Reader.* Toronto: Harcourt Brace Canada

Kalbach, Warren E. 1983. "Propensities of Intermarriage in Canada, as Reflected in Ethnic Origins of Husbands and their Wives." In *Marriage and Divorce in Canada*, ed. K. Ishwaran, 196–212. Toronto: Methuen

Krotki, Karol J., and Colin Reid. 1994. "Demography of Canadian Population by Ethnic Group." In *Ethnicity and Culture in Canada: The Research Landscape*, eds. J.W. Berry and J.A. Laponce, 17–59. Toronto: University of Toronto Press

Lee, Sharon M. 1999. "Do Foreign Birth and Asian Minority Status Lower Canadian Women's Earnings?" *Canadian Studies in Population* 26 (2): 159–82

– and Barry Edmonston. Forthcoming. "'Canadian' as National Ethnic Origin: Trends and Implications." *Canadian Ethnic Studies*

Lieberson, Stanley. 1992. "The Enumeration of Ethnic and Racial Groups in the Census: Some Devilish Principles." In *Challenges of Measuring an Ethnic World: Science, Politics, and Reality. Proceedings of the Joint Canada–United States Conference on the Measurement of Ethnicity, April 1-3, 1992,* 23-35. Washington, DC: US Census Bureau

Population Reference Bureau. 2005. *2005 World Population Data Sheet.* Washington, DC: Population Reference Bureau

Reitz, Jeffrey G., and Sherrilyn M. Sklar. 1997. "Culture, Race, and the Economic Assimilation of Immigrants." *Sociological Forum* 12 (2): 233–77

United Nations. 2005. *World Population Prospects. The 2004 Revision.* New York: United Nations, Department of Economic and Social Affairs, Population Division

16

Indigenous Peoples

RIMA WILKES

INTRODUCTION

The purpose of this chapter is to provide an overview of the socio-economic characteristics of the Indigenous[1] population of Canada, the provinces, and the territories. I focus on education, income, occupation, and employment patterns and trends as indicators of socio-economic status (see also O'Sullivan 2004). Canadian Census data on many indicators of socio-economic well-being has consistently shown that Indigenous people fare worse than the non-Indigenous population in terms of education, income, and labour force participation (Bernier 1997; Cooke, Beavon, and McHardy 2004; Frideres and Gadacz 2005; Gerber 1990; Tait 1999; O'Donnell and Tait 2004). On average, Status Indians earn $10,000 less than the non-Indigenous population (Beavon and Cooke 2004; Maxim et al. 2001). A large part of this wage gap has been attributed to differentials in education (De Silva 1999), since earnings are similar with comparable levels of education (at least at the higher levels of education) (Wannell and Caron 1994). Furthermore, in recent decades Indigenous people have made enormous gains in educational attainments (O'Donnell and Tait 2004; Tait 1999).

In addition to earning less income, Indigenous people also have higher unemployment rates and lower rates of labour force participation than non-Indigenous people (Kuhn and Sweetman 2002). Typically, the rate of unemployment is about ten percent higher for Indigenous people (Wannell and Caron 1994). While education tends to equalize earnings between the Indigenous and non-Indigenous populations, it has less of an effect with respect to unemployment. Wannell and Caron (1994) find that university education does not translate into equal employment rates between Indigenous and non-Indigenous people. This may however, be gender specific. Drost (1994) finds that while university and trades education reduce the unemployment rates for Indigenous women, it has little effect for Indigenous men.

In this chapter I make three primary contributions to our understanding of the socio-economic status of Indigenous People in Canada. First, by using the 2001 census, I update the existing information. Most research that uses census data on Indigenous people is based on census data from 1996 or even earlier, while research from other sources, such as the Department of Indian and Northern Affairs Departmental Data reports, typically refers to the registered Indian population only. Second, much of the existing research tends to focus on trends for the Indigenous population in Canada as a whole, or on trends comparing the on-and off-reserve or urban and rural populations. In this chapter, I provide detailed information not only for Canada as a whole, but also for the provinces and territories (see also Beavon and Cooke 2004; Wannell and Caron 1994). Third, following several recent studies (Beavon and Cooke 2004; Maxim et al. 2003; Wannell and Caron 1994), I include data on the non-Indigenous population as a reference group, which enables me to consider the *relative* position of Indigenous to non-Indigenous people in Canada.

The data for this chapter refers to those individuals who selected the 'Aboriginal identity'[2] question in the 2001 census. According to Statistics Canada, Aboriginal identity "refers to those persons who reported identifying with at least one Aboriginal group (i.e. North American Indian, Métis, or Inuit)" or "who did not report an Aboriginal identity, but did report themselves as a Registered or Treaty Indian, and/or Band or First Nation membership." I have elected to focus on the Aboriginal identity question in order to be able to include the population who live in the Northern Territories (this group would not be included in the Registered Indian counts) without being so broad as to include those who no longer identify as Indigenous.[3]

According to the census data, 976,305 people, just over 3 percent of the Canadian population, identified as Aboriginal/Indigenous (see table 16.1). Of the sub-groups of Indigenous people, a majority are North American Indian, followed by Métis, and then Inuit. There is considerable variation in terms of the regional distribution of the Indigenous population in Canada. In the East (Ontario to Atlantic Canada), Indigenous people typically make up somewhere between 1 and 3 percent of the provincial populations; in the Prairies (both Manitoba and Saskatchewan) Indigenous people comprise about 13 percent of the population; in the West they comprise about 4 to 5 percent of the population; and in the North their share of the total ranges from 22 percent in the Yukon to 85 percent in Nunavut. Between 49 to 56 percent of the Indigenous population of Canada lives in an urban

Table 16.1
2001 Counts for Canada, Provinces, and the Territories, Indigenous/Aboriginal Identity Population

	North American Indian	Metis	Inuit	Indigenous population total	Non Indigenous/ Non-Aboriginal	Total
Canada	608,850	292,305	45,070	976,305	28,662,725	29,639,030
% of Canadian population	2.10	1.00	0.20	3.30	96.70	
Newfoundland	7,040	5,480	4,560	18,775	489,300	508,080
% of Nfld. population	1.40	1.10	0.90	3.70	96.30	
Prince Edward Island	1,035	220	20	1,345	132,040	133,385
% of P.E.I. population	0.80	0.20	0.00	1.00	99.00	
Nova Scotia	12,920	3,135	350	17,010	880,560	897,565
% of N.S. population	1.40	0.30	0.00	1.90	98.10	
New Brunswick	11,495	4,290	155	16,990	702,725	719,710
% of N.B. population	1.60	0.60	0.00	2.40	97.60	
Quebec	51,125	15,855	9,530	79,400	7,046,180	7,125,580
% of Quebec population	0.70	0.20	0.10	1.10	98.90	
Ontario	131,560	48,340	1,375	188,315	11,097,235	11,285,545
% of Ontario population	1.20	0.40	0.00	1.70	98.30	
Manitoba	90,340	56,800	340	150,045	953,655	1,103,700
% of Manitoba population	8.20	5.10	0.00	13.60	86.40	
Saskatchewan	83,745	43,695	235	130,185	832,960	963,155
% of Sask. population	8.70	4.50	0.00	13.50	86.50	
Alberta	84,995	66,060	1,090	156,225	2,784,925	2,941,150
% of Alberta population	2.90	2.20	0.00	5.30	94.70	
British Columbia	118,295	44,265	800	170,025	3,698,850	3,868,875
% of B.C. population	3.10	1.10	0.00	4.40	95.60	
Yukon	5,600	535	140	6,540	21,975	28,520
% of Yukon population	19.60	1.90	0.50	22.90	77.10	
Northwest Territories	10,615	3,580	3,910	18,730	18,370	37,100
% of N.W.T. population	28.60	9.60	10.50	50.50	49.50	
Nunavut	95	55	22,560	22,720	3,945	26,665
% of Nunavut population	0.40	0.20	84.60	85.20	14.80	

Source: Adapted from Census of Canada, 2001 Topic Based Tabulations Table 197F0011XCB2001001.

area (Siggner 2003), and as shown in table 16.2, Winnipeg, Edmonton, Vancouver, Calgary, Toronto, Saskatoon, Regina, Ottawa-Hull, Prince Albert, and Montreal have the largest Indigenous populations.

FINDINGS

Education

Table 16.3 provides the educational attainment levels for both the Indigenous and non-Indigenous populations in different parts of Canada

Table 16.2
Ten Canadian Cities with Largest Indigenous Populations

	North American Indian	Metis	Inuit	Indigenous	Non Indigenous	Total	Percent Indigenous
Winnipeg	22,955	31,390	190	55,760	605,970	661,730	8.43
Edmonton	18	21,060	460	40,930	886,090	927,020	4.42
Vancouver	22,700	12,505	255	36,855	1,930,620	1,967,480	1.87
Calgary	10,155	10,580	195	21,915	921,400	943,310	2.32
Toronto	13,780	5,100	355	20,300	4,647,660	4,647,955	0.44
Saskatoon	11,290	8,305	125	20,280	202,355	222,630	9.11
Regina	9,200	5,995	35	15,685	174,335	190,015	8.25
Ottawa-Hull	7,555	4,690	450	13,485	1,037,270	1,050,755	1.28
Prince Albert	5,375	5,950	10	11,640	28,250	39,885	29.18
Montreal	6,100	3,670	435	11,085	3,369,560	3,380,640	0.33

Source: Adapted from Census of Canada, 2001 Topic Based Tabulations Table 97F0011XCB2001002.

for 2001. Canada-wide, at both the lowest (less than high school) and highest (university degree) levels, there is a significant discrepancy between the education levels of Indigenous and non-Indigenous people. Whereas 30 percent of the non-Indigenous population has less than high school, the figure is 48 percent for the Indigenous population. In contrast, while 15 percent of the non-Indigenous population has a completed university degree, only 4 percent of the Indigenous population has one[4]. At the 'some university completed' category, the rates between Indigenous and non-Indigenous people are very similar – typically from 1 to 3 percent. It is also worth noting that Indigenous people in all parts of the country (except Manitoba) have higher levels of trades education than the non-Indigenous population. In most provinces the college-graduate rates are similar for both groups.

There are also some notable provincial differences in terms of the educational attainments of Canada's Indigenous and non-Indigenous populations. Nova Scotia has the highest level of university completion for Indigenous people (6.42 percent) and Nunavut has the lowest (1.01 percent). Nunavut also has the largest gaps between the Indigenous and non-Indigenous populations in terms of university completion (33 percent for the non-Indigenous population and 1 percent for the Indigenous population). It also has the largest gap in terms of less than high school (9 percent for non-Indigenous and 60 percent for Indigenous) and is one of five regions (also Quebec, Manitoba, Saskatchewan, and Northwest Territories) where over 50 percent of the Indigenous population has not completed a high school education. By contrast the rates for the other regions are typically around 40 percent. In

Table 16.3

Educational Attainment Rates (%) for Indigenous and Non-Indigenous Populations, 2001

	Less Than High School	High School	Some Post-Secondary	Trades	College	Some University	University
Canada							
Indigenous	48.03	9.87	12.56	12.14	11.57	1.40	4.42
Non-Indigenous	30.81	14.21	10.79	10.84	15.07	2.55	15.74
Newfoundland							
Indigenous	43.61	8.59	10.48	19.15	12.67	1.42	4.08
Non-Indigenous	42.32	9.44	9.17	16.75	10.81	1.79	9.72
Prince Edward Island							
Indigenous	41.76	9.34	8.24	19.23	14.29	2.20	4.95
Non-Indigenous	37.36	11.59	9.93	12.53	14.86	2.24	11.48
Nova Scotia							
Indigenous	40.80	7.93	13.05	16.85	12.67	2.28	6.42
Non-Indigenous	35.28	9.77	9.59	14.05	14.69	2.49	14.14
New Brunswick							
Indigenous	43.06	11.03	12.56	14.50	12.73	1.28	4.83
Non-Indigenous	37.18	14.87	9.50	11.24	13.86	1.92	11.44
Quebec							
Indigenous	51.57	11.17	9.78	11.45	9.64	1.66	4.72
Non-Indigenous	31.51	17.19	8.64	10.78	14.58	3.25	14.05
Ontario							
Indigenous	42.30	12.12	12.16	12.07	14.76	1.11	5.48
Non-Indigenous	29.47	14.45	11.22	9.33	15.72	2.09	17.72
Manitoba							
Indigenous	55.96	8.35	11.17	9.94	9.36	1.18	4.04
Non-Indigenous	35.96	11.71	11.43	10.86	13.54	2.37	14.14
Saskatchewan							
Indigenous	52.63	8.16	13.08	11.06	8.76	1.75	4.56
Non-Indigenous	37.84	11.14	10.95	12.72	12.62	2.92	11.82
Alberta							
Indigenous	47.65	9.16	14.20	12.78	11.00	1.27	3.94
Non-Indigenous	29.77	11.87	12.30	12.80	15.64	2.04	15.59
British Columbia							
Indigenous	43.59	11.14	13.64	12.99	12.79	1.73	4.12
Non-Indigenous	27.43	12.57	13.08	11.76	15.44	3.12	16.59
Yukon							
Indigenous	37.53	7.11	16.96	16.63	16.30	1.53	3.94
Non-Indigenous	21.38	10.66	12.75	15.29	17.95	3.07	18.89
Northwest Territories							
Indigenous	55.70	5.95	12.01	12.34	10.88	0.69	2.43
Non-Indigenous	17.82	11.38	12.06	15.39	17.99	2.36	23.00
Nunavut							
Indigenous	60.40	3.93	13.98	10.00	10.08	0.60	1.01
Non-Indigenous	9.77	10.23	11.28	10.23	21.95	2.71	33.83

Source: Adapted from Census of Canada, 2001 Topic Based Tabulations Table 97F0011XCB2001042.

terms of educational disparity between the Indigenous and non-Indigenous populations, Newfoundland has the least and Nunavut ranks the highest.

Income

Table 16.4 provides the income characteristics for Indigenous and Non-Indigenous people in different parts of Canada. The first five columns of the table show the low-income percent, the average income if working full-time, the average income if working part-time, the average income from all sources, and the median income from all sources. The remaining columns provide the percentages of people with income who fall into specific income categories (e.g. under $5,000, $5000–9,999 etc).

The data indicate that there are gross income disparities between Indigenous and non-Indigenous Canadians. In every region, over 50 percent of Indigenous people are low income, whereas the rates are between high-30 to mid-40 percent for non-Indigenous people. When Indigenous people work full-time, they earn on average $10,000 less than non Indigenous people, with a mean income of $33,416 compared to $43,486 for non-Indigenous people. The gap between Indigenous ($13,795) and non-Indigenous ($19,383) part-time workers is $5,588. The largest income gap is found for average income from all sources: Indigenous people have a mean income of $19,132, whereas non-Indigenous people have a mean income of $30,062 (a $10,930 difference). These pay gaps are especially significant because additional income provides greater benefits for those living at the low-income level. An additional $1,000 per year means more for someone with an annual income of $19,000 than it does for someone with an annual income of $60,000.

Although there is considerable variation, these pay gaps continue to persist when we look at the figures for individual provinces and territories. In Nunavut, the pay gap is $32,988, whereas in Newfoundland it is $5,406. Nevertheless, the overall trends in terms of relative income distribution between regions do not appear significantly different for Indigenous and non-Indigenous people – noting, of course, that non-Indigenous poverty is more concentrated in the Maritimes. Overall, both Indigenous and non-Indigenous peoples have the highest income in the north – Yukon, Northwest Territories, and Nunavut. Nevertheless, it is of particular concern that although Nunavut has the highest percent of the paid workforce earning over 60,000 per year for non-Indigenous (40 percent), only 5.85 percent of Indigenous people in Nunavut earn this amount. With the creation of the new territory, many of the 'good' jobs have gone to non-Indigenous people (see also Kuhn and Sweetman 2002, 343 on this gap).

Table 16.4
Indigenous and Non-Indigenous Income for Canada, Provinces, and Territories

	Low income (%)	Avg.ft income ($)	Avg.pt income ($)	Avg. income ($)	Median income ($)	Under $5,000	5,000–9,999	10,000–19,999	20,000–29,999	30,000–39,999	40,000–49,999	50,000–59,999	60,000 and over
Canada													
Indigenous	55.9	33,416	13,795	19,132	13,525	23.28	15.53	24.81	14.05	9.67	5.49	3.14	4.03
Non-Indigenous	37.6	43,486	19,383	30,062	22,431	12.68	10.77	21.96	15.74	13.18	8.99	5.97	10.70
Newfoundland													
Indigenous	57.9	30,690	11,917	17,383	13,034	22.91	15.32	29.52	14.41	8.05	4.95	2.39	2.44
Non-Indigenous	46.3	38,076	14,721	22,789	16,167	16.01	14.10	27.39	15.85	10.41	6.90	3.83	5.51
P.E.I.													
Indigenous	53.1	28,482	10,714	16,565	13,702	25.73	13.45	26.32	16.96	8.77	5.85	1.75	1.17
Non-Indigenous	37.3	33,538	13,787	23,769	18,931	12.39	11.46	28.55	19.81	12.64	6.66	3.48	5.02
Nova Scotia													
Indigenous	61.2	30,947	12,097	16,646	11,392	26.96	18.28	25.01	12.73	7.41	4.49	2.54	2.58
Non-Indigenous	38.3	37,942	15,631	25,427	18,902	14.49	12.41	24.96	16.40	11.66	8.31	4.98	6.79
New Brunswick													
Indigenous	57.5	28,669	11,763	15,867	11,426	26.57	18.11	26.85	13.70	6.57	4.00	1.89	2.30
Non-Indigenous	38.3	36,183	14,894	24,254	18,419	14.07	12.64	26.21	17.37	11.82	7.63	4.21	6.05
Quebec													
Indigenous	56.7	32,396	13,919	20,050	15,330	15.38	17.86	27.21	16.61	11.21	5.64	2.78	3.30
Non-Indigenous	43.7	39,264	19,115	27,192	20,731	12.21	12.20	23.78	16.82	13.25	8.33	5.33	8.09
Ontario													
Indigenous	50	36,163	14,453	21,822	16,023	20.40	13.15	23.68	14.39	12.13	6.85	4.08	5.32
Non-Indigenous	33.8	47,426	20,382	33,027	24,981	12.54	9.75	19.89	14.95	13.55	9.55	6.54	13.23
Manitoba													
Indigenous	60.9	29,079	11,916	16,970	12,459	24.95	15.97	26.44	14.79	8.87	4.31	2.29	2.38
Non-Indigenous	38.7	37,350	16,225	27,560	21,634	11.39	10.54	24.43	18.08	13.82	8.58	5.54	7.62

Table 16.4

Indigenous and Non-Indigenous Income for Canada, Provinces, and Territories (*Continued*)

Saskatchewan													
Indigenous	60.8	30,141	12,287	15,961	11,366	28.82	16.60	24.96	13.36	7.46	4.06	2.33	2.41
Non-Indigenous	34.5	35,783	16,130	26,914	20,653	11.67	11.29	25.37	17.14	12.93	8.08	5.75	7.78
Alberta													
Indigenous	50.8	33,775	15,057	19,398	13,437	26.22	13.82	23.54	13.77	9.28	5.44	3.09	4.83
Non-Indigenous	32.6	44,441	20,367	31,898	23,650	13.92	9.39	20.65	15.08	13.05	9.20	6.10	12.61
British Columbia													
Indigenous	59.5	34,696	14,801	19,424	13,242	22.20	17.47	24.11	13.10	9.46	5.85	3.37	4.43
Non-Indigenous	37.4	44,552	20,375	29,999	22,535	12.52	10.93	21.87	14.97	12.99	9.52	6.43	10.77
Yukon													
Indigenous	n.a.	35,100	15,960	21,842	16,223	18.45	13.69	25.41	13.23	10.56	7.77	6.38	4.52
Non-Indigenous	n.a.	46,032	21,665	34,406	30,040	10.44	7.68	16.51	14.70	13.41	11.45	9.18	16.63
NW Territories													
Indigenous	n.a.	42,376	15,057	23,344	16,141	21.79	12.62	22.57	11.59	9.77	7.65	5.53	8.47
Non-Indigenous	n.a.	55,717	25,383	44,522	40,303	8.17	5.60	11.19	11.05	12.35	11.30	10.17	30.17
Nunavut													
Indigenous	n.a.	38,505	11,542	19,876	13,190	23.89	16.10	24.59	12.36	8.07	5.31	3.83	5.85
Non-Indigenous	n.a.	61,939	33,132	52,864	50,128	4.24	4.09	7.58	9.39	11.36	10.91	11.97	40.45

Source: Adapted from Census of Canada, 2001 Topic Based Tabulations Table 97F0011XCB2001044.

Occupation

Table 16.5 presents the distributions of groups by region for the following occupations: management, business, natural science, health, social science, arts, sales, trades, primary industries, and processing/manufacturing. The most common occupations (for both Indigenous and non-Indigenous people) are those related to sales and service. In Canada as a whole, a greater percentage of the Indigenous population works in sales (28 vs. 23 percent), trades (19 vs. 14 percent) and primary industries (7 vs. 4 percent) than the percentage for non-Indigenous people. Compared to the Indigenous population, a greater percentage of the non-Indigenous population works in management (10 vs. 6 percent), business (17 vs. 13 percent) and sciences (6 vs. 3 percent). There is little difference in terms of the distribution of the Indigenous and Non-Indigenous workforce in the arts, culture, and sports, or processing occupations.

These patterns change when we consider individual provinces and territories. In the Atlantic Provinces (Newfoundland, Prince Edward Island, Nova Scotia, and New Brunswick) the rates of involvement in trade occupations are very close. In contrast, Indigenous people in the northern territories (Yukon, Northwest Territories, and Nunavut) are twice as likely to work in trade as the non-Indigenous population. When we consider employment in primary industries, Saskatchewan is the only region where the non-Indigenous population has a higher involvement in primary industries than Indigenous people (16 vs. 8 percent). The other large gap in occupational distribution worth noting is the large discrepancy between Indigenous and non-Indigenous employment in management occupations in the North, especially Nunavut (5 vs. 21 percent).

Labor Force Participation

Table 16.6 shows three indicators of labour force involvement: the participation, employment, and unemployment rates. Canada-wide, there is only a very small difference in the labour force participation of Indigenous and non-Indigenous people (61 vs. 66 percent). However, there is an enormous gap in the employment and especially in the unemployment rates. In 2001, 7 percent of the non-Indigenous workforce was unemployed, whereas 19 percent of the Indigenous workforce was unemployed.

In terms of regional differences, there are large disparities in the labour force participation rate between the Indigenous and non-Indigenous populations in the Prairies (Manitoba and Saskatchewan), Alberta (about a

Table 16.5
Percentage of Workforce by Occupational Area

	Management	Business	Science	Health	Social Science, Educ., Govt.	Art, Culture, Sport	Sales, Service	Trades	Prim. Industry	Manufacturing
Canada										
Indigenous	6.68	13.74	3.13	3.37	9.73	2.28	28.44	19.56	7.04	6.02
Non-Indigenous	10.50	17.87	6.53	5.26	7.69	2.81	23.49	14.61	4.22	7.03
Newfoundland										
Indigenous	5.47	12.40	4.83	3.56	8.71	2.23	27.15	18.82	10.49	6.36
Non-Indigenous	8.29	14.08	5.16	5.97	7.68	1.97	25.50	17.14	7.70	6.51
P. E. I.										
Indigenous	6.31	15.32	5.41	1.80	11.71	0.00	17.12	14.41	20.72	6.31
Non-Indigenous	8.30	15.75	4.28	5.24	6.40	2.20	23.30	15.05	13.08	6.40
Nova Scotia										
Indigenous	6.76	13.52	3.38	3.08	10.82	1.80	30.13	16.30	9.32	4.88
Non-Indigenous	9.60	16.03	5.13	6.11	7.49	2.53	27.14	14.92	5.55	5.49
New Brunswick										
Indigenous	5.27	12.36	3.72	2.67	8.99	0.98	26.69	17.56	12.64	9.13
Non-Indigenous	8.49	16.76	4.95	5.59	6.68	1.90	26.23	16.78	5.57	7.05
Quebec										
Indigenous	6.82	15.45	3.57	3.57	11.09	3.94	26.43	18.07	5.39	5.67
Non-Indigenous	9.45	18.29	6.46	5.66	8.20	3.03	22.87	14.54	2.90	8.60
Ontario										
Indigenous	7.66	13.67	3.90	3.85	8.63	2.16	28.19	19.65	4.23	8.04
Non-Indigenous	11.49	18.38	7.09	4.79	7.59	2.88	22.81	14.03	2.72	8.22
Manitoba										
Indigenous	6.07	14.54	2.26	4.50	10.00	1.69	29.54	19.05	5.54	6.77
Non-Indigenous	9.09	17.97	4.86	6.54	7.74	2.15	23.70	14.41	7.18	6.36

Saskatchewan										
Indigenous	6.37	11.98	1.98	3.38	12.58	1.75	30.81	18.99	8.11	4.07
Non-Indigenous	8.63	15.06	4.03	6.13	7.29	2.05	22.84	14.44	16.52	3.00
Alberta										
Indigenous	6.37	13.87	2.77	2.73	8.31	1.62	28.34	24.01	7.52	4.46
Non-Indigenous	10.62	17.41	7.18	4.95	6.94	2.26	23.27	16.55	6.91	3.92
B.C.										
Indigenous	6.52	13.21	3.36	2.91	9.50	2.59	27.95	16.91	10.44	6.60
Non-Indigenous	11.00	17.71	6.24	5.33	7.92	3.37	25.48	14.25	3.97	4.73
Yukon										
Indigenous	7.47	14.31	4.45	1.59	12.40	3.34	26.07	21.78	6.20	2.38
Non-Indigenous	13.91	18.49	6.71	4.55	12.05	3.68	22.18	14.81	2.31	1.27
NW Territories										
Indigenous	8.52	16.65	3.61	2.19	10.06	2.13	26.32	21.68	7.55	1.29
Non-Indigenous	15.90	17.71	9.39	4.93	12.43	2.72	19.96	13.41	2.49	0.95
Nunavut										
Indigenous	5.97	14.62	2.36	1.64	12.79	7.61	30.03	20.98	1.97	1.97
Non-Indigenous	21.42	15.30	7.57	5.64	19.00	2.25	16.59	10.63	1.13	0.32

Source: Adapted from Census of Canada, 2001 Topic Based Tabulations Table 97F0011XCB2001044.

Table 16.6
Labor Force Characteristics (%) in 2001

	Participation Rate	Employment Rate	Unemployment Rate
Canada			
Indigenous	61.4	49.7	19.1
Non-Indigenous	66.5	61.8	7.1
Newfoundland			
Indigenous	60.4	40.2	33.5
Non-Indigenous	57.5	45.2	21.4
Prince Edward Island			
Indigenous	63.3	48.3	24.6
Non-Indigenous	69.1	60	13.1
Nova Scotia			
Indigenous	60.6	47.4	21.9
Non-Indigenous	61.6	55.1	10.7
New Brunswick			
Indigenous	62.1	44.6	28.1
Non-Indigenous	63.1	55.4	12.2
Quebec			
Indigenous	57.7	47.1	18.5
Non-Indigenous	64.2	59	8.1
Ontario			
Indigenous	64.6	55.1	14.7
Non-Indigenous	67.3	63.3	6
Manitoba			
Indigenous	59	47.8	19
Non-Indigenous	68.4	65.2	4.7
Saskatchewan			
Indigenous	54.5	42	23
Non-Indigenous	69.3	66	4.8
Alberta			
Indigenous	64.2	54.6	14.9
Non-Indigenous	73.5	70	4.8
British Columbia			
Indigenous	62.9	48.7	22.5
Non-Indigenous	65.3	60	8
Yukon			
Indigenous	72	52.7	26.8
Non-Indigenous	81.8	75.1	75.1
Northwest Territories			
Indigenous	65	53.2	18.2
Non-Indigenous	87.4	83.9	4
Nunavut			
Indigenous	61.8	47.6	22.9
Non-Indigenous	93.3	90.6	2.7

Source: Adapted from Census of Canada, 2001 Topic Based Tabulations Table 97F0011XCB2001044.

10 percent gap), and also in the North. Interestingly, the gap in the North is primarily a result of the relatively higher rate of labour force participation (compared to the national average) of the non-Indigenous population rather than due to especially low labour force participation by the Indigenous population (see also Kuhn and Sweetman 2002). In terms of differences in unemployment rates, Ontario has the lowest gap (8.7 percent) and Nunavut has the highest (20.2 percent).

CONCLUSION

In the following section, I review the general findings for Canada as a whole and for the provinces and territories. Data from the 2001 census indicate that there continues to be a gap in the socio-economic status of the Indigenous and non-Indigenous populations. This disparity is especially pronounced at the extremes of each indicator considered, be it education, income, occupation, or labour force participation. The Indigenous population has lower rates of university completion, higher rates of less-than-high-school completion, lower average incomes, higher rates of poverty, lower rates of high-income earners, and higher rates of unemployment. The indigenous population is also more likely to be employed in trades and primary industries than the non-Indigenous population, which is more likely to be involved in management and business occupations than the Indigenous population.

However, there is evidence that gains are being made. Based on the data from the 2001 Census, at some of the middle levels of each of these indicators, a measure of parity has been achieved. At the middle levels of education (trades and college), the rates are very close for the two populations. Indeed, in most parts of Canada, Indigenous people have higher levels of trades education than the non-Indigenous population. Given that there is an increasing shortage of skilled trade workers in Canada, this bodes well for the future employment and income opportunities for Indigenous people. Similarly, when income comparisons are made between the Indigenous and non-Indigenous populations, there appears to be relative parity between the two groups at the $10,000 to $50,000 range. The labour force participation rates between Indigenous and non-Indigenous peoples are also essentially the same.

There are a variety of policy and research implications that follow from the above conclusions about Canada as a whole.[5] From a research point of view, it is important to note that statistical significance testing needs to be conducted in order to ascertain whether, controlling for the differences in population size of the two groups, percentage differences of 2–3 points are in fact meaningful. Multivariate analyses such as that provided by Maxim,

White, and Beavon (2003) in their study of the factors (e.g. age, weeks worked, sex, education, work status, skill level, industrial sector, and region) that affect the income earned by Indigenous and non-Indigenous Canadians would also prove fruitful.

From a policy perspective, policy needs to be developed to enable people to move out of the bottom as well as into the top socio-economic categories. One possibility that may aid in this endeavor is to revisit existing policies such as Employment Equity. Employment Equity policies affect those work-places that receive federal contracts in excess of $200,000 and that have more than 100 employees. Between 1987 and 1998, Indigenous people in-creased their representation in these workplaces from .7 percent to 1.3 per-cent against a labour market share of 2.1 percent (Dib 2002). By 2002 the representation of Indigenous peoples had increased to 1.7 percent (Human Resources and Skills Development Canada 2003). Clearly, there is improve-ment in those workplaces to which the Act is applicable, although some of these improvements may have taken place regardless, given the enormous gains Indigenous people made in educational attainments during this period. However, Employment Equity only applies to about two million employees across Canada. Another 17 million are employed in workplaces that are not governed under the Act. Policy that affects the representation of Indigenous peoples among these 17 million "others" may provide a means to reducing the wage and employment gaps that currently exist.

In this chapter, I have also sought to draw attention to the importance of making inter-provincial comparisons. In doing so, one can identify par-ticular challenges for specific regions of Canada. The greatest discrepancies between the Indigenous and non-Indigenous populations are found in the northern territories where there are significant gaps in education, income, and employment rates. Part of the explanation for this discrepancy lies in the fact that non-Indigenous people with specific skills and education levels are recruited to live in this region. However, this does not explain the very high rates of unemployment found among Indigenous peoples in these areas. The regional comparisons also show considerable variation in the income gap between the Indigenous and non-Indigenous populations. Although the income gap Canada-wide is approximately $10,000, in Newfoundland it is about $5,400 and in Nunavut it is almost $33,000. This may reflect a larger reliance on government transfer payments in Newfoundland than in Nunavut, a process that would be less likely to discriminate than the marketplace. Further research is needed on the variations in socio-economic status across regions of Canada. Can these differences be explained as mere-ly reflecting differences in human capital available to the Indigenous and

non-Indigenous populations? If so, then research is clearly needed to identify means of rectifying these regional discrepancies in human capital.

NOTES

1 In this chapter I use the terms Aboriginal and Indigenous interchangeably to
   refer to people of Indian, Métis, and Inuit ancestry. The government agencies that
   collected the statistics upon which this chapter is based routinely use the term
   Aboriginal as opposed to Indigenous. However, where possible, I use the term
   Indigenous in order to recognize the fact that the members of this group exist irrespective of (and prior to), their official recognition as 'Aboriginal' by the federal
   government and in the Canadian Constitution (see Alfred and Corntassel 2005 on
   this point). The reader should bear in mind that both the text and the tables refer
   to the same group(s) of people.
2 It is important to note that there are several other questions in the census that ask
   about Indigenous/Aboriginal origins, one broader and the other more specific.
   The Aboriginal ancestry/origin question "refers to those persons who reported
   at least one Aboriginal origin (North American Indian, Metis, or Inuit) on the
   ethnic origin question in the census. The question asks about the ethnic or cultural group(s) to which the respondent's ancestors belong" (Natural Resources
   Canada 2009). 1,319,890 Canadians reported having Aboriginal origins. On the
   other hand, a more specific question asks whether a respondent is a registered,
   status, or treaty Indian, which "refers to those respondents registered under the
   Indian Act of Canada. Treaty Indians are persons who are registered under the
   Indian Act of Canada and can prove descent from a band that signed a treaty."
   558,175 Canadians reported registered Indian status according to the 2001 Census
   (Statistics Canada 2003).
3 It should also be noted that the 2001 census data is missing information on the
   population of 30 reserves and settlements (slightly over 30,000 people) that
   were incompletely enumerated. Most of this population is located in Quebec and
   Ontario, and, to a lesser extent, Alberta. As a result of this missing data, figures for
   these regions should be interpreted with caution.
4 These figures are lower than those in other studies (e.g. O'Donnell and Tait 2004,
   likely because of different data sets used – the Census versus the Aboriginal Peoples
   Survey/APS). Given that the APS is sampled from the Census, I would expect that
   the former is providing a slightly more accurate estimate of the true population
   value.
5 I wish to acknowledge the following limitation to the research presented in this
   chapter: it is situated within a human-capital framework that assumes that all

groups of people within a society have the same goals. As noted by and in the critical work of scholar Gerald Taiaiake Alfred, to focus solely on the socio-economic status of Indigenous peoples is to perpetuate an assimilationist model whereby Indigenous peoples are slotted into the capitalist wage economy. This model does nothing to address other areas such as language and culture, which also matter and which may be more important to Indigenous Peoples' overall social and psychological well-being. Thus, this caveat should be kept in mind in reference to all the results and conclusions of this chapter.

REFERENCES

Alfred, Taiaiake, and Jeff Corntassel. 2005. "Being Indigenous: Resurgences against Contemporary Colonialism." *Government and Opposition: An International Journal of Comparative Politics* 40 (4)

Beavon, Daniel, and Martin Cooke. 2004. "An Application of the United Nations Human Development Index to Registered Indians in Canada, 1996." In *Indigenous Conditions: Research as a Foundation for Public Policy*, eds. Jerry White, Paul Maxim, and Dan Beavon, 201–21. Vancouver: University of British Columbia Press

Bernier, Rachel. 1997. "The Dimensions of Wage Inequality among Indigenous Peoples." Ottawa: Statistics Canada. Paper no. 109

Cooke, Martin, Daniel Beavon, and Mindy McHardy. 2004. "Measuring the Well-Being of Indigenous People: An Application of the United Nations Human Development Index to Registered Indians in Canada, 1981–2001." In *Aboriginal Policy Research: Setting the Agenda for Change*, eds. Jerry White, Paul Maxim, and Dan Beavon, 47–69. *Vol. 1*. Toronto: University of Toronto Press

De Silva, Arnold. 1999. "Wage Discrimination Against Natives." *Canadian Public Policy* 15: 65–85

Dib, Kamal. 2002. "Employment Equity in Canada: Women and Minority Groups in the Canadian Labour Market." Appendix G in the *Employment Equity Act Review*. Ottawa: Government of Canada

Drost, Helmar. 1994. "Schooling, Vocational Training and Unemployment: The Case of Canadian Indigenouss." *Canadian Public Policy* 10: 52–65

Frideres, James S., and Rene R. Gadacz. 2005. *Indigenous Peoples in Canada*. Toronto: Prentice-Hall

Gerber, Linda. 1990. "Multiple Jeopardy: A Socio-Economic Comparison of Men and Women among the Indian, Metis and Inuit People of Canada." *Canadian Review of Sociology and Anthropology* 22: 69–84

Human Resources and Skills Development Canada. 2003. "Employment Equity Annual Report – Employers' Reports – Aboriginal Peoples." Ottawa: Human

Resources and Skills Development Canada. www.hrsdc.gc.ca/eng/lp/lo/lswe/we/ee_tools/reports/annual/2003/Chapter5-3-EmployersReports-Aboriginals.shtml (Accessed March 2010)

Kuhn, Peter, and Arthur Sweetman. 2002. "Indigenous as Unwilling Immigrants: Contact, Assimilation and Labour Market Outcomes." *Journal of Population Economics* 15: 331–55

Maxim, Paul, Jerry White, and Dan Beavon. 2001. "Dispersion and Polarization of Income among Indigenous and Non-Indigenous Canadians." *Canadian Review of Sociology and Anthropology* 38: 465–76

– 2003. "Dispersion and Polarization of Income among Indigenous and Non-Indigenous Canadians." In *Indigenous Conditions: Research as a Foundation for Public Policy*, eds. Jerry White, Paul Maxim, and Dan Beavon, 222–47. Vancouver: University of British Columbia Press

Natural Resources Canada. 2009. "The Atlas of Canada: Data and Mapping Notes." Ottawa: Natural Resources of Canada. www.atlas.nrcan.gc.ca/auth/english/maps/peopleandsociety/dataandmappingnotes_2001.html (Accessed March 2010)

O'Donnell, Vivian, and Heather Tait. 2004. "Well-being of the Non-reserve Aboriginal Population." *Canadian Social Trends* 19–23

O'Sullivan, Erin. 2004. "Indigenous Language Retention and Socio-Economic Development: Theory and Practice." In *Indigenous Conditions: Research as a Foundation for Public Policy*, eds. Jerry White, Paul Maxim, and Dan Beavon, 136–63. Vancouver: University of British Columbia Press

Siggner, Andrew J. 2003. "Urban Aboriginal Populations: An Update Using the 2001 Census Results." In *Not Stranger in These Parts: Urban Aboriginal Peoples*, eds. David Newhouse and Evelyn Peters, 15–21. Ottawa: Government of Canada Policy Research Initiative

Statistics Canada. 2003. "2001 Census: Analysis Series Aboriginal peoples of Canada: A Demographic Profile." Ottawa: Minister of Industry. Cat. no. 96F0030XIE2001007.

Tait, Heather. 1999. "Educational Achievement of Young Indigenous Adults." *Canadian Social Trends* (Spring): 6–10

Wannell, Ted, and Nathalie Caron. 1994. "A Look at Employment-Equity Groups among Recent Postsecondary Graduates: Visible Minorities, Indigenous Peoples and the Activity Limited." Ottawa: Statistics Canada. Paper no. 69

17

Religion in Canada

MADELINE A. KALBACH

INTRODUCTION

A question about the religious affiliation of preference of Canadians has been asked at every decennial census since 1871. According to the 2001 Census user guide, the intent of the question has been to count the numbers who indicate that they adhere to, belong to, or favour a specific religious denomination or body or otherwise defined community. The question has never measured church attendance or membership per se.

Religion as defined by the 2001 Census Dictionary (Statistics Canada 2002) refers to specific religious denominations, groups, or bodies, as well as to sects, cults, or other religiously defined communities or systems of belief. Respondents were instructed to report a specific group or denomination even if they were not practicing members of their group. Adults with children were instructed to report the denomination or group the children would be raised under. Individuals who had no affiliation with a religious group or denomination were instructed to mark the provided category, No Religion. Those who thought of themselves as being agnostic or atheists were asked to specify in the write-in area of the question.

The purpose of this chapter is to present a portrait of Canada's religious mosaic at the time of the 2001 Census. In so doing, characteristics such as age, sex, language, ethnicity, nativity, and intermarriage will be examined. The importance of this chapter lies in its contribution to the understanding of the ethnocultural profile of Canadians.

Changes in the relative share of the major religious groups in Canada since 1871 are shown in figure 17.1. It can be seen that the Roman Catholic Church has been dominant since 1871 and has maintained its dominance over the past 130 years. The growth curves for the other denominations

Figure 17.1
Religious Composition, Canada: 1871–2001

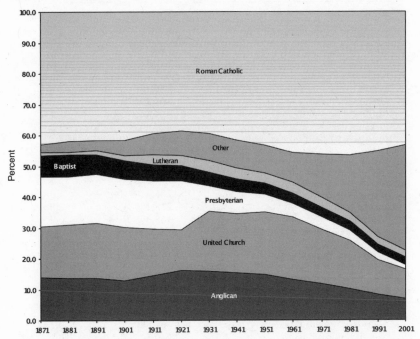

Source: 1951 Census of Canada, Volume 1, Table 37; 1971 Census of Canada, Volume 1, Part 3, Table 9; 1991 Census of Canada, Catalogue no. 93–319, Table 3; 2001 Census, Special Tabulations, PCH.
Note: United Church refers to Methodists from 1871 to 1921.

have been rather uneven over the course of time, particularly for the United Church and the Presbyterians. The latter have been affected by the formation of the United Church in 1925 as a result of the merger between the Congregationalists, Methodists, and Presbyterians. The relative increases in the Roman Catholic Church and the Other religious groups clearly reflect the change in the ethnocultural characteristics of the immigrant stream. This change was due to the establishment of a non-discriminatory immigration policy in the late 1960s that resulted in a large influx of non-European immigrants, most of whom are either Roman Catholic or of other religions such as Muslim and Hindu.

The percent distribution of Canada's population by religious denominations at the time of the 2001 Census is presented in table 17.1. As can be seen, Roman Catholics at nearly 46 percent of the population were dominant, followed by No Religion at 17 percent, United Church at 10 percent and Anglicans at 7 percent. Eastern Non-Christians, as a whole, represented

Table 17.1
Population by Religious Denominations, Canada, 2001

Religion	Number	Percent
Roman Catholic	12,793,125	45.8
No Religion	4,796,325	17.2
United Church	2,839,125	10.2
Anglican	2,035,500	7.3
Baptist	729,475	2.6
Lutheran	606,595	2.2
Muslim	579,640	2.1
Presbyterian	409,830	1.5
Pentecostal	369,475	1.3
Jewish	329,995	1.2
Buddhist	300,350	1.1
Hindu	297,200	1.1
Sikh	278,410	1.0
Greek Orthodox	215,170	0.8
Mennonite	188,395	0.7
Jehovah's Witness	154,750	0.6
Ukrainian Catholic	126,200	0.5
Reformed Bodies	115,735	0.4
Methodist Bodies	106,540	0.4
Latter Day Saints	104,750	0.4
Salvation Army	87,790	0.3
Christian and Missionary Alliance	66,285	0.2
Adventist, Seventh Day	62,880	0.2
Non-denominational	40,545	0.1
Ukrainian Orthodox	32,715	0.1
Aboriginal Spirituality	29,825	0.1
Hutterite	26,300	0.1
Brethren in Christ	20,590	0.1
Serbian Orthodox	20,525	0.1
Atheist	18,605	0.1
Baha'i	18,020	0.1
Agnostic	17,815	0.1
Unitarian	17,480	0.1
Russian Orthodox	15,610	0.1
Church of Christ (Disciples)	15,335	0.1
Church of the Nazarene	13,960	0.0
Wesleyan	11,630	0.0
Pagan	11,505	0.0
Church of God, n.o.s.	11,215	0.0
Armenian Orthodox	10,955	0.0
Coptic Orthodox	10,280	0.0
Zoroastrian	4,955	0.0
Doukhobor	3,800	0.0
Taoist	3,440	0.0
Jain	2,460	0.0
Rastafari	1,135	0.0
Total	27,952,240	100.0

Source: Statistics Canada, 2001 Census, Special Tabulations, PCH.

about 5 percent of Canada's population, followed by Baptists and Lutherans at around 2 percent of the population at the time of the 2001 Census. Of the Eastern Non-Christians, the largest sub-group at the time of the 2001 Census was the Muslim group at around 2 percent of the Canadian population.

REGIONAL DISTRIBUTION

Religion is an important dimension for many of Canada's ethnic and cultural groups. Thus, it is not surprising that some religious denominations have regional patterns similar to Canada's ethnic populations. Table 17.2 presents the percentage distribution of the population by selected religious denominations for Canada and provinces in 2001. Figure 17.2 presents a visual portrait of percentage distributions by province and territory for selected religious denominations. The most obvious concentration is that of the Roman Catholics in Quebec who accounted for 46 percent of all Roman Catholics in Canada and who constituted 85 percent of the provincial population at the time of the 2001 Census. Another 20 percent were residing in Ontario in 2001, but this only represented 34 percent of the province's population. Roman Catholics were overrepresented in two other areas, namely New Brunswick, where they comprised 55 percent of the population, and in the Northwest Territories, where they comprised 48 percent of the population. Ukrainian Catholics, Ukrainian Orthodox, and Greek Orthodox were concentrated in the Prairies.

The second largest denomination in 2001, i.e., No Religion, was concentrated in Ontario, where they accounted for 38 percent of all Canadian respondents indicating No Religion. However, they represented only 17 percent of the province's population. Another 28 percent were residing in British Columbia and represented 38 percent of that province's population. Nearly, one quarter of Alberta's population reported No Religion.

Relative to provincial populations, Anglicans had their highest proportions in Nunavat, Newfoundland, Northwest Territories, the Yukon, and Nova Scotia. United Church adherents had their highest relative concentrations in Ontario, the Prairies, and the Maritimes. Presbyterians who did not become a part of the United Church were concentrated in Prince Edward Island. Eastern non-Christians, relative to provincial populations, had their highest concentrations in British Columbia, Ontario, and Alberta.

"Newfoundland and Labrador was the only province in which Protestant denominations formed the majority of the population in 2001" (Statistics Canada 2003). Moreover, Ontario was only one-third Protestant, while Protestants were no longer in the majority in Saskatchewan in 2001 (Ibid.).

Table 17.2

Percentage Distribution of the Population by Selected Religious Denominations, Canada, Provinces, and Territories, 2001

	Canada	Newfound-land	PEI	Nova Scotia	New Brunswick	Quebec	Ontario	Manitoba	Saskatch-ewan	Alberta	British Columbia	Yukon	NWT	Nuna-vut
Roman Catholic	45.8	37.4	50.8	37.8	55.1	85.4	36.7	28.5	31.5	28.0	18.9	22.5	48.0	24.5
No Religion	17.2	2.5	7.0	12.0	8.1	5.8	17.2	19.7	16.3	25.1	38.4	40.1	18.3	6.3
United Church	10.2	17.2	21.3	16.4	9.9	0.8	12.7	17.2	20.6	14.7	10.2	7.9	6.3	1.4
Anglican	7.3	26.5	5.2	13.9	8.3	1.2	9.3	8.4	7.2	6.4	8.4	14.3	15.6	60.9
Baptist	2.6	0.2	4.8	10.9	11.5	0.5	2.7	2.2	1.8	2.7	3.0	3.4	1.8	0.3
Lutheran	2.2	0.1	0.1	1.3	1.3	0.1	2.0	4.9	8.6	5.3	2.9	2.2	1.2	0.3
Muslim	2.1	0.1	0.2	0.4	0.2	1.6	3.3	0.5	0.2	1.8	1.6	0.2	0.5	0.1
Presbyterian	1.5	0.3	6.3	2.6	1.0	0.1	2.6	0.9	0.8	1.1	1.0	0.7	0.4	0.2
Pentecostal	1.3	6.7	0.8	1.1	2.9	0.3	1.5	1.6	1.6	1.6	1.3	2.3	3.0	4.6
Jewish.	1.2	0.0	0.0	0.2	0.1	1.3	1.8	1.3	0.1	0.4	0.6	0.1	0.1	0.0
Buddhist	1.1	0.0	0.1	0.2	0.1	0.6	1.2	0.6	0.3	1.2	2.4	0.5	0.4	0.1
Hindu	1.1	0.1	0.0	0.1	0.1	0.4	2.1	0.4	0.2	0.6	0.9	0.0	0.2	0.0
Sikh	1.0	0.0	0.0	0.0	0.0	0.1	1.0	0.5	0.1	0.9	3.8	0.4	0.1	0.0
Greek Orthodox	0.8	0.0	0.0	0.2	0.2	0.7	1.1	0.7	0.7	0.8	0.4	0.4	0.2	0.0
Mennonite	0.7	0.0	0.0	0.1	0.0	0.0	0.5	5.0	2.1	0.8	1.0	0.2	0.1	0.0
Jehovah's Witness	0.6	0.3	0.4	0.5	0.3	0.4	0.5	0.4	0.7	0.7	0.9	0.5	0.4	0.0
Ukrainian Catholic/ Orthodox	0.6	0.0	0.0	0.0	0.0	0.1	0.5	3.3	2.5	1.4	0.3	0.2	0.2	0.0
Reformed Bodies	0.4	0.0	0.2	0.1	0.0	0.0	0.7	0.3	0.1	0.8	0.5	0.0	0.1	0.1
Methodist Bodies	0.4	0.0	0.0	0.1	0.0	0.1	0.5	0.7	0.8	0.7	0.4	0.3	0.2	0.1
Latter Day Saints	0.4	0.0	0.2	0.3	0.2	0.1	0.2	0.2	0.3	1.9	0.5	0.5	0.3	0.0
Salvation Army	0.3	8.0	0.3	0.5	0.2	0.0	0.3	0.1	0.2	0.2	0.2	0.1	0.6	0.1
Other Orthodox	0.2	0.0	0.0	0.4	0.0	0.1	0.4	0.1	0.0	0.1	0.1	0.1	0.0	0.0
Christian & Missionary Alliance	0.2	0.0	0.0	0.0	0.0	0.0	0.1	0.3	1.0	0.9	0.4	0.0	0.2	0.4
Adventist, Seventh Day	0.2	0.1	0.0	0.2	0.1	0.1	0.3	0.1	0.2	0.3	0.3	0.2	0.3	0.0
All Other	1.0	0.3	2.1	1.0	1.6	0.2	0.9	2.2	2.1	1.6	1.4	3.0	1.6	0.5
TOTAL														
Number	27,952,240	501,480	124,560	867,490	699,890	6,945,990	10,549,260	1,026,875	911,145	2,701,180	3,537,110	26,575	35,310	25,365
Percent	100.0	100.0	100.0	100.0	100.0	100.0	100.0	100.0	100.0	100.0	100.0	100.0	100.0	100.0

Source: Statistics Canada 2001 Census, Special Tabulations, PCH.

Note: "All Other" includes: Protestant Non-denominational, Aboriginal Spirituality, Hutterite, Bretheren in Christ, Atheist, Baha'i, Agnostic, Unitarian, Church of Christ (Disciples), Church of the Nazarene, Wesleyan, Pagan, Church of God, Zorastrian, Doukhobor, Taoist, Jain, and Rastafari.

Figure 17.2

Anglican

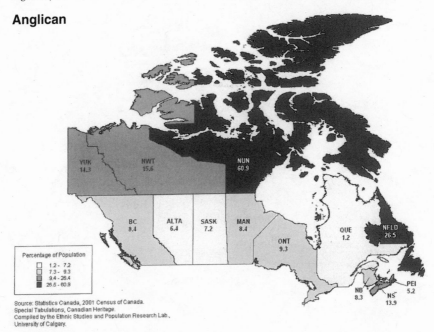

Source: Statistics Canada, 2001 Census of Canada.
Special Tabulations, Canadian Heritage.
Compiled by the Ethnic Studies and Population Research Lab.,
University of Calgary.

Eastern Non-Christian

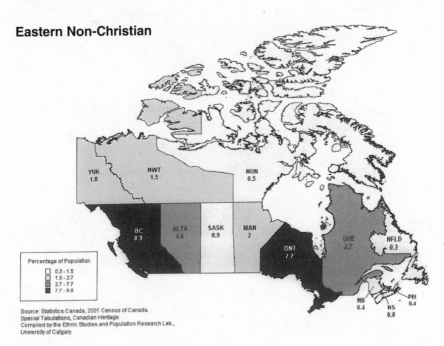

Source: Statistics Canada, 2001 Census of Canada.
Special Tabulations, Canadian Heritage.
Compiled by the Ethnic Studies and Population Research Lab.,
University of Calgary.

No Religion

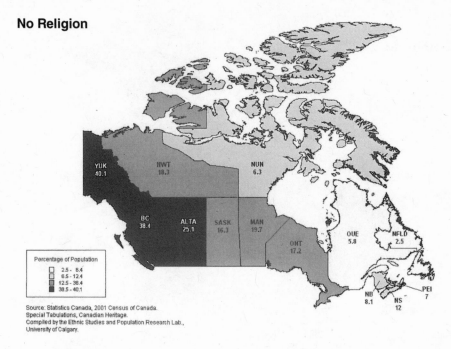

YUK
40.1

NWT
18.3

NUN
6.3

BC
38.4

ALTA
25.1

SASK
16.3

MAN
19.7

ONT
17.2

QUE
5.8

NFLD
2.5

PEI
7

NB
8.1

NS
12

Percentage of Population

☐ 2.5 - 6.4
☐ 6.5 - 12.4
▨ 12.5 - 38.4
■ 38.5 - 40.1

Source: Statistics Canada, 2001 Census of Canada.
Special Tabulations, Canadian Heritage.
Compiled by the Ethnic Studies and Population Research Lab.,
University of Calgary.

Roman Catholic

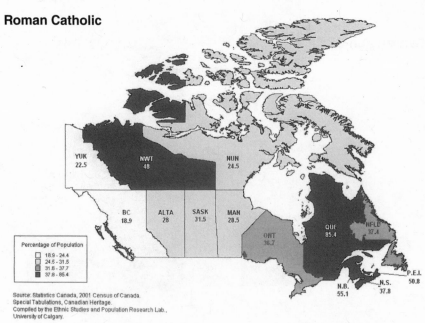

YUK
22.5

NWT
48

NUN
24.5

BC
18.9

ALTA
28

SASK
31.5

MAN
28.5

ONT
36.7

QUE
85.4

NFLD
37.4

P.E.I.
50.8

N.B.
55.1

N.S.
37.8

Percentage of Population

☐ 18.9 - 24.4
☐ 24.5 - 31.5
▨ 31.6 - 37.7
■ 37.8 - 85.4

Source: Statistics Canada, 2001 Census of Canada.
Special Tabulations, Canadian Heritage.
Compiled by the Ethnic Studies and Population Research Lab.,
University of Calgary.

United Church

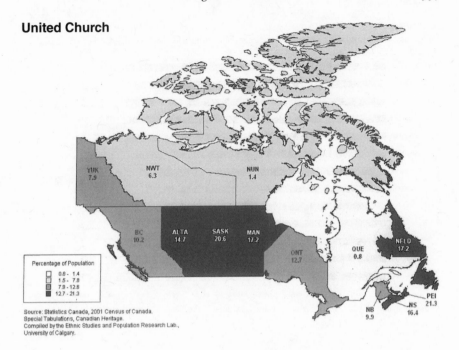

Percentage of Population

☐ 0.8 - 1.4
☐ 1.5 - 7.8
▨ 7.9 - 12.6
■ 12.7 - 21.3

Source: Statistics Canada, 2001 Census of Canada.
Special Tabulations, Canadian Heritage.
Compiled by the Ethnic Studies and Population Research Lab.,
University of Calgary.

NATIVITY

Religious denominations are made up of native- and foreign-born components. Fertility of the native-born, and their ability to retain offspring within their denominations is the most important influence on the size of their denominations. Kalbach and McVey (1971, 231) indicate that growth for the foreign-born will only occur if "the number of migrants exceeds the numbers dying plus those dropping out of the church." This of course can't be tested due to the absence of reliable data. However, as revealed in figure 17.3, the religious groups (e.g., Hindu, Sikh, and Muslim) with the highest proportions of foreign-born in 2001 tended to be members of Canada's most recent immigrant groups. Older religious groups such as the Jewish, Anglican, Lutheran, and United Church have significantly smaller proportions of foreign-born. These groups have witnessed a decrease in their proportion over the past 34 years due to lower levels of immigration for many of the immigrant groups associated with these denominations (See Kalbach and McVey 1971).

Table 17.3 presents data for religious groups by generation for Canada in 2001, except for the Maritimes and the territories. The data in this table reflect changes in religious affiliation. There is a general shift in the relative

Figure 17.3

Percentage Distribution of Selected Religious Denominations by Nativity, Canada, 2001

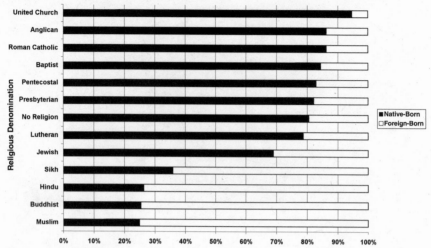

Source: Statistics Canada, 2001 Census of Canada, Special Tabulations, Canadian Heritage.

size of Catholics and Protestants from 33.0 and 20.3 percent respectively to 51.8 and 29.1 percent. This is evidence of a generational strengthening for both groups. Other groups such as the Jewish experienced a general shift in their relative size from 1.9 percent of the foreign-born to only 0.6 percent of the native-born. Similar declines are found for the Christian Orthodox and No Religion.

RELIGIOUS EXOGAMY

Religious marital patterns tend to be favourable to the continuance of a religion's status quo, particularly since husbands and wives tend to rarely cross religious lines when they marry (Kalbach 2000, 2002; Richard 1991). At the time of the 2001 Census, as indicated in figure 17.4, 20.5 percent of all husbands married someone of a different religious faith. In general, then, all husbands, regardless of religious affiliation, were overwhelmingly endogamous with respect to religion. A similar pattern can be seen for total husbands of the selected religious denominations shown in figure 17.4. Foreign-born husbands also tended to be overwhelmingly endogamous with respect to religion, as were native-born husbands, except for husbands who were Eastern Orthodox or Buddhist. The latter two are small in number, so their marriage pools with respect to religion are much smaller than most. It

Table 17.3
Percentage Distribution of the Population by Selected Religious Denominations for
Generations, Canada: 2001

| | Generation | | | | |
	First	Second	Third +	Total Percent	Number
Catholic	33.0	33.0	51.8	44.1	9,685,771
Protestant	20.3	38.0	29.1	28.6	6,277,892
Christian Orthodox	4.7	3.0	0.3	1.8	401,150
Christian not identified elsewhere	3.9	2.7	2.1	2.6	574,739
Muslim	7.1	0.8	0.0	1.8	406,584
Jewish	1.9	2.4	0.6	1.2	267,190
Buddhist	4.1	0.6	0.1	1.1	249,228
Hindu	3.9	0.5	0.0	1.0	225,813
Sikh	3.3	0.8	0.0	0.9	202,899
Eastern religions	0.4	0.1	0.1	0.1	31,553
All other religions	0.1	0.2	0.3	0.2	47,660
No religious affiliation	17.4	17.8	15.7	16.4	3,616,667
Percent	100.0	100.0	100.0	100.0	21,987,146
Number	5,256,151	3,776,326	12,954,669		21,987,146

Source: Statistics Canada 2001 Census Public Use Microdata File.
Note: More specific religious denominations by generation unavailable for 2001.

Figure 17.4
Percentage of Husbands of Selected Religious Denominations with Wives of a Different
Religious Denomination, Canada 2001

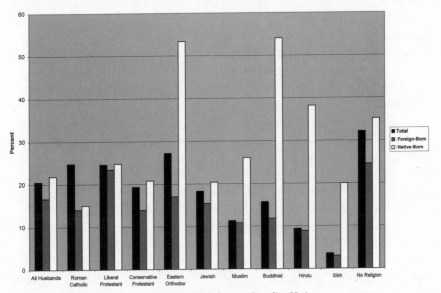

Source: Statistics Canada. 2001 Census. Special Tabulations. Canadian Heritage.

is clear from figure 17.4 that husbands who are native-born tended to religiously intermarry to a greater extent than their foreign-born counterparts. This is in keeping with patterns of ethnic exogamy by nativity in Canada (Kalbach 2000, 2002; Richard 1991).

More specifically, husbands affiliated with the Roman Catholic, Protestant, No Religion, and Eastern Orthodox religions were among the highest proportions of husbands who married wives of a different religion. Roman Catholic and Protestant husbands were numerically dominant at the time of the 2001 Census and would therefore be more likely to be selected as marriage mates by wives of other, smaller religious affiliations. Husbands who were Eastern Orthodox were relatively small in number and as such would have a smaller marriage pool from which to choose a spouse of the same religion, so it is likely that not every male could find a wife of the same religion as himself. Overall, Sikh, Hindu, and Muslim husbands had the lowest percentages of religious exogamy with 3.6, 9.4, and 11.3 percent respectively. These religious affiliations are associated with Canada's most recent ethnic or cultural origin groups. These husbands, then, were mainly foreign-born in 2001, so it is not surprising that their rates of religious exogamy are among the lowest. The native-born component of these more recent immigrant groups is still very small, and therefore the results for the native-born must be viewed with caution.

It is interesting to note that husbands reporting a liberal Protestant affiliation were significantly more exogamous with respect to religion than their conservative counterparts. This, of course, is not surprising since one would expect individuals with liberal views to be more likely to intermarry than those with more conservative religious views. Foreign-born husbands who claimed no religious affiliation in 2001 showed higher percentages of religious exogamy than husbands of any of their counterparts from the other religious groups presented in figure 17.4.

In summary, religious marital patterns in Canada in 2001 did contribute to the maintenance of Canada's religious denominations, particularly among foreign-born husbands because they are most likely to have married someone of the same religion as themselves before they came to Canada, or the husbands (and wives) might have had an arranged marriage, which would ensure that their wives (husbands) would be of the same religious affiliation. In addition, overall, rates of religious exogamy are relatively low for most groups.

Figure 17.5 presents the percentage of husbands of selected ethnic origins who were married to wives of a different religion than themselves by nativity of husband at the time of the 2001 Census. It can be seen that overall about 20 percent of all husbands were exogamous with respect to religion.

Figure 17.5
Percentage of Husbands of Selected Ethnic Origins with Wives of a Different Religion,
Canada 2001

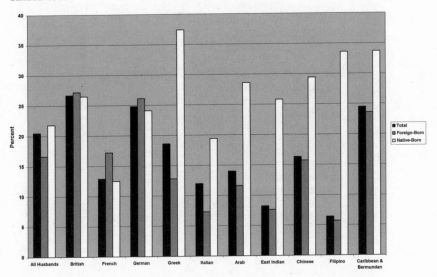

Source: See Figure 17.3.

married with respect to religion. Overall, husbands of Canada's more recent ethnic populations, such as the Chinese and East Indians, tend to be
overwhelmingly endogamous with respect to ethnic intermarriage (Kalbach
2000). It would stand to reason, then, that they would also be overwhelmingly endogamous with respect to religion since many would have been
married upon their arrival or might have had an arranged marriage, which
would tend to ensure that they married within the same religious group.
Figure 17.5 reveals that this is the case for most Asian husbands. Native-
born husbands of the more recent immigrant groups shown in figure 17.5 are
more exogamous with respect to religion than their foreign-born counterparts. The "older" immigrant groups, i.e., British, French, and German, did
not exhibit the same pattern. This may reflect the fact that many of the
husbands with these ethnic ancestries belong to denominations such as the
Catholic Church, which does not encourage religious intermarriage. Thus,
such individuals are less likely to cross religious lines when they marry.

In summary, husbands belonging to denominations that encourage their
adherents to marry within the same religion are the most likely to do so.
Previous research points out that while many husbands may be willing to
cross ethnic lines with respect to marriage, they are not as likely to cross
religious lines (Kalbach 1991).

Figure 17.6

Religious Composition by Broad Age Groups, Canada 2001

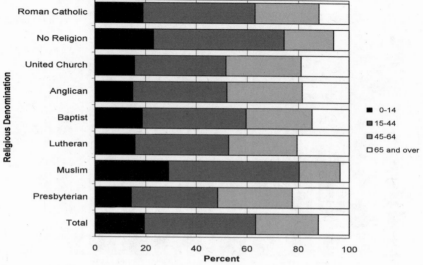

Source: 2001 Census of Canada, PUMF Individual File, Statistics Canada.

FERTILITY

Changes in patterns of natural increase and immigration certainly affect the number of adherents of a religious denomination. An older population will produce more deaths relative to births than a young population. Thus, denominations with most of their members beyond the childbearing ages will tend to have lower rates of increase than religious groups with younger populations. Groups with high proportions in the population under 15 years of age and low proportions 65 years of age and over reflect a high fertility population, while those with relatively high proportions in the group 65 and over and low proportions under 15 years of age tend to reflect a population with low fertility.

Figure 17.6 reveals variations by broad age groups for selected denominations at the time of the 2001 Census. Muslim and No Religion are examples of groups with relatively high fertility, while Presbyterians, United Church, Lutheran, and Anglicans are examples of groups with relatively low fertility, as their populations tend to be older.

Population pyramids tell the story of varying levels of fertility, mortality, and immigration on a population's age-sex structure. Figure 17.7 presents population pyramids for selected religious populations. Again, it is evident

Figure 17.7
Age and Sex Composition Selected Religious Denominations, Canada 2001

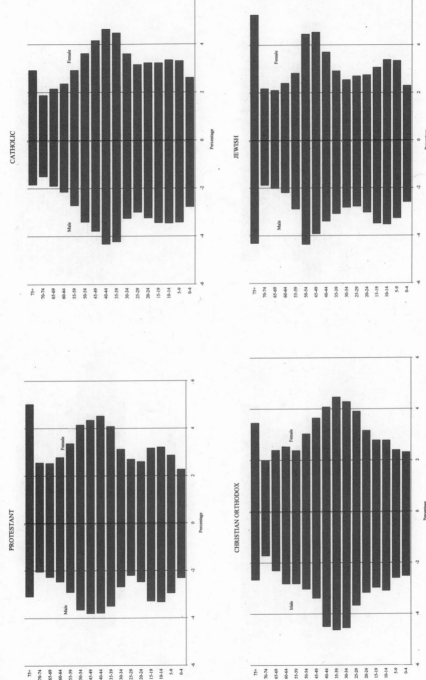

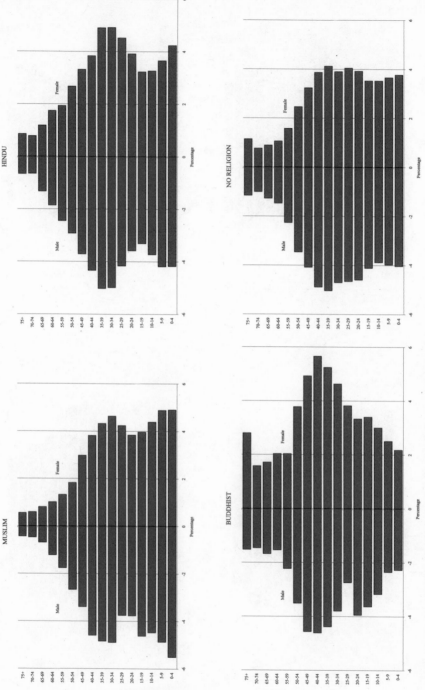

Source: Statistics Canada, 2001 Census. Public Use Microdata File, Individual File.

that Muslims were one of the most fertile and youngest religious groups, followed by the Hindus and No Religion. It is also evident that the Catholics, Protestants, Jews, and Christian Orthodox reflect a decline in fertility and have relatively elderly populations.

Increased immigration of non-Europeans since the late 1960s has also had an effect on the growth of Canada's religious populations. The relatively high fertility of Canada's recent immigrants compared to the older European immigrant populations has been an increasingly important factor contributing to the relative increase of the Roman Catholic, Muslim, Hindu, and other Eastern Non-Christian populations. Conversely, the decline in immigration and levels of fertility for the older European populations has contributed to the relative decline in the major Protestant populations.

SUMMARY

Canada's major religious groups all appear to have experienced declines in population compared to their proportions in the mid-twentieth century with the exception of Roman Catholics. Changes in immigration source countries, natural increase, conversion, church attendance, and increased secularization of society all appear to have contributed to the population declines experienced by many of Canada's major religious denominations. McVey and Kalbach (1995) indicates that low fertility has been one of the most important factors in the decline of the major Protestant religions. This appears to have continued to be the case at the time of the 2001 Census, and it appears likely to continue for some time in the future.

Kalbach and Kalbach's (1995, 2000) research indicates that there have been some conversions of both the foreign-born and native-born away from their ethnic church. Changing religions is clearly a pathway to assimilation because becoming less ethnically connected vis-à-vis religion tends to result in increased economic integration for some ethnic groups, especially for the first generation or foreign-born (ibid.). This conversion from the more ethnically oriented churches to the major Canadian churches, such as the Anglican, United Church, and Roman Catholic churches, as well as declines in church attendance, are among the factors contributing to changes in Canada's religious mosaic.

One of the most interesting aspects of the changing religious mosaic has been the increase in the number of respondents indicating No Religion. Only 4 percent of Canada's population indicated they were No Religion at the time of the 1971 Census. This proportion increased to 7 percent by 1981, 13 percent by 1991, and 16.5 percent by 2001. This trend is consistent with what one would expect in an increasingly secular society, but it is difficult to interpret exactly what this trend means. The question "What is this person's religion?" is somewhat ambiguous, even though the accompanying explanation asks respondents to indicate a specific denomination or religion, even if he/she is not a practicing member of the group (McVey and Kalbach 1995). Nonetheless, it can be argued that the trend has contributed to changes in Canada's religious mosaic.

Canada's religious mosaic is undergoing change. Immigration, fertility, intermarriage, and conversion are all important factors in this change. Change is likely to continue throughout the twenty-first century, and as a result Canada's ethnocultural profile will continue to be affected throughout most of the new millennium.

REFERENCES

Kalbach, Madeline A.. 2000. "Ethnicity and the Altar." In *Perspectives on Ethnicity in Canada: A Reader*, eds. M.A. Kalbach and W.E. Kalbach, 111–20. Toronto: Harcourt Brace Inc
– 2002. "Ethnic Intermarriage in Canada". *Canadian Ethnic Studies* 34(2): 25–39
– and Warren E. Kalbach 1995. "The Importance of Ethnic-Connectedness for Recent Immigrants to Canada." *Canadian Ethnic Studies* 37(2): 16–33
– 2000. "The Importance of Ethnic-Connectedness for Canada's Post-War Immigrants." In *Perspectives on Ethnicity in Canada: A Reader*, eds. M.A. Kalbach and W.E. Kalbach, 182–202. Toronto: Harcourt Brace Inc
Kalbach, Warren E., and Wayne W. McVey Jr. 1971. *The Demographic Bases of Canadian Society*. Toronto: McGraw-Hill
McVey, Wayne. W. Jr, and Warren E. Kalbach. 1995. *Canada's Population*. Toronto: Nelson Canada
Richard, Madeline A. 1991. *Ethnic Groups and Marital Choices*. Vancouver: University of British Columbia Press
Statistics Canada. 2002. *2001 Census Dictionary*. Ottawa: Minister of Industry
– 2003. *Religions in Canada*. 2001 Census: Analysis Series. Cat. no. 96F003 XIE2001015. www.statcan.ca/cgi-bin/downpub/freepub.cgi.

18

Language and Demography

RÉJEAN LACHAPELLE AND GUSTAVE GOLDMANN

INTRODUCTION

Linguistic duality sets Canada apart. Like the United States and Australia, it includes Aboriginal languages as well as languages that are associated with immigration (i.e. heritage languages). But French and English hold a special place. They have equal status at the federal level, as well as in New Brunswick, under the *Canadian Charter of Rights and Freedoms* (incorporated into the *Constitution* in 1982), sections 16 to 20. Section 23 recognizes also that the official-language-minority communities of a province have a right to primary and secondary instruction in their language. In Quebec, French is the sole official language according to the provincial legislation – the Charter of the French Language enacted in 1977. However, except in some situations or places in Quebec, the proportion of people who use English exceeds the proportion of Anglophones because of the country's history and the areas that surround Quebec.

The first section of this chapter will address the demographic aspects of linguistic duality. The "Francophone, Anglophone, and Allophone" triplet will be used often. There will be many references to mother tongue,[1] a feature inherited from parents. In addition, reference will be made to attributes that correspond to the actual language behaviour in families[2] and to the language abilities of the individual.

Clearly, the term "allophone" does not designate a specific demolinguistic entity. It is a residual category, as indicated by its Greek roots (*allos*, which means "other" and *phônê*, which means "voice, sound"). Strictly speaking, there is no third language group. Allophones often have to use one of the two official languages to communicate among themselves.[3] Moreover, allophones include people who speak the Aboriginal languages and those who speak non-official languages that were introduced through immigration: their situations are quite different and deserve to be treated separately.

The country's linguistic duality is rooted in its history. In the 1871 Census, conducted a few years after the country's Constitution was enacted, linguistic duality remained connected to ethnic duality, because at the time, people of British origin made up 61 percent of the population, and those of French origin made up 31 percent (Lachapelle 1999). Thus, more than nine out of ten Canadians belonged to one of these two ethnic groups. Yet, ethnic duality disappeared during the first half of the twentieth century. After the Second World War, in the 1951 Census, the proportion of people of French origin remained at 31 percent, whereas those of British origin fell to 48 percent. The stability of the former is attributed to the high fertility rate of French Canadian women (Lachapelle 1988); the decrease in the latter stems from the large numbers of non-British international immigrants in the years before and after the First World War. Canada had become polyethnic. Nonetheless, in 1951 it had retained its linguistic duality, as six out of ten Canadians had English as their mother tongue, and three of the remaining ten reported French; the latter were highly concentrated in Quebec. In the first section, we focus mainly on the evolution of linguistic duality and of territorial concentration in the second half of the twentieth century.

The demolinguistic situation of Aboriginal languages and their current and potential users will be addressed in the second section. Without overlooking the general change in numbers, our attention will focus on the persistence and revitalization of these languages.

The third section will address the changes in the groups whose defining non-official language originated from non-English and non-French speaking countries. This is what we mean by the expression "heritage languages." While the major groups from the earlier waves of immigration – e.g. German, Ukrainian, and Italian – are declining, there is a strong demographic upswing among the more recent immigrant groups – e.g. Chinese, Punjabi, and Arab (Marmen and Corbeil 2004). Does the use of these languages extend beyond respondents declaring them as their mother tongue? Do they survive beyond the second or third generation as the main language spoken at home, in contrast to what is observed in the United States, even with Spanish (Rumbaut, Massey, and Bean 2006; Veltman 1983)?

LINGUISTIC DUALITY AND TERRITORIAL CONCENTRATION

The demographic evolution of a language group is based on the phenomena (mortality, fertility, international migration, and internal migration) that are the source of the different components of demographic growth. There is an additional phenomenon in demolinguistics – linguistic mobility – which results in language shifts or language transfers. The mobility is intergenerational when the focus is on non-transmission to a child of the mother's or father's mother tongue. It is intragenerational when the study addresses changes in a lifetime of the dominant language in the family domain, particularly the adoption of a language that differs from the mother tongue, this being considered the predominant language in early childhood.

We will first consider the official language minorities, which is to say Francophones in Canada as a whole, Anglophones in Quebec, and Francophones in the other provinces and territories. For half a century, between 1951 and 2001, the proportion of these minorities, whether defined by mother tongue or home language, has fallen everywhere (table 18.1). In Canada, the proportion of the population whose mother tongue was French fell from 29 percent in 1951 to 27 percent in 1971 and to 23 percent in 2001; the same trend was observed for French as home language between 1971 (26 percent) and 2001 (22 percent). The one percentage point difference between the two variables is due to intragenerational language mobility, in this case the net anglicization of Francophones, since the population with French as a home language is smaller than the population whose mother tongue is French. A larger difference in absolute and relative terms has been observed among Francophones living outside Quebec. This does not apply to Quebec's Anglophone population, which has benefited from the significant anglicization of the Allophone population.

The percentage of Quebec's Anglophone minority, however, fell from 13.1 percent in 1971 to 8.3 percent in 2001, based on mother tongue, and from 14.7 percent to 10.5 percent for home language. These marked decreases in proportion were compounded by a significant decrease in numbers, as the population whose mother tongue was English fell from 790,000 people in 1971 to 590,000 in 2001.

Outside Quebec, slightly more than one-half of the population whose mother tongue was French lived in Ontario. However, this only represented 4.5 percent of Ontario's population in 2001, a marked decrease from 1951 (7.4 percent). In New Brunswick, one-third of the population's mother tongue was French, and this province had one-quarter of all the Francophones living in minority situations at provincial level.

The proportion of the official language majority groups is not rising everywhere, especially since 1971. This applies even for language spoken at home. While the proportion of people speaking French at home increased in Quebec (83.1 percent in 2001 compared to 80.8 percent in 1971), as did, although to a lesser degree, the proportion speaking English across the

Table 18.1

Population by Mother Tongue, Home Language, and Knowledge of Official Languages, Canada, Quebec, Canada outside Quebec, New Brunswick, Ontario and the Rest of Canada, 1951 to 2001

| Region and language | Mother Tongue | | | | | | Home Language | | Speakers | | | Speakers as a Second Language among Those Who Do Not Have It as Mother Tongue | | |
| | 1951 | | 1971 | | 2001 | | 1971 | 2001 | 1951 | 1971 | 2001 | 1951 | 1971 | 2001 |
	N	%	N	%	N	%	%	%	%	%	%	%	%	%
Canada														
Total	14,009,429	100.0	21,568,310	100.0	29,639,035	100.0	100.0	100.0						
English	8,280,809	59.1	12,967,445	60.1	17,521,897	59.1	67.0	67.5	79.3	80.5	85.2	49.5	51.2	63.7
French	4,068,850	29.0	5,792,710	26.9	6,782,294	22.9	25.7	22.0	31.9	31.4	31.0	4.0	6.3	10.5
Other	1,659,770	11.8	2,808,155	13.0	5,334,849	18.0	7.3	10.4						
Quebec														
Total	4,055,681	100.0	6,027,765	100.0	7,125,575	100.0	100.0	100.0						
English	558,256	13.8	788,830	13.1	591,378	8.3	14.7	10.5	37.0	38.1	45.4	27.0	28.8	40.5
French	3,347,030	82.5	4,866,410	80.7	5,802,022	81.4	80.8	83.1	88.1	88.5	94.6	31.8	40.1	70.8
Other	150,395	3.7	372,525	6.2	732,175	10.3	4.5	6.5						
Canada outside Quebec														
Total	9,953,748	100.0	15,540,545	100.0	22,513,465	100.0	100.0	100.0						
English	7,722,553	77.6	12,178,615	78.4	16,930,519	75.2	87.2	85.6	96.6	97.0	97.8	84.8	86.1	91.0
French	721,820	7.3	926,300	6.0	980,272	4.4	4.3	2.7	9.0	9.3	10.8	1.9	3.6	6.8

Other	1,509,375	15.2	2,435,630	15.7	4,602,674	20.4	8.4	11.7						
New Brunswick														
Total	515,697	100.0	634,560	100.0	719,710	100.0	100.0	100.0						
English	325,412	63.1	411,275	64.8	468,084	65.0	67.9	69.0	80.4	84.0	90.7	46.9	54.5	73.4
French	185,110	35.9	214,720	33.8	239,357	33.3	31.4	30.3	38.2	37.4	43.4	3.5	5.3	15.2
Other	5,175	1.0	8,565	1.3	12,274	1.7	0.8	0.7						
Ontario														
Total	4,597,542	100.0	7,703,110	100.0	11,285,550	100.0	100.0	100.0						
English	3,755,442	81.7	5,967,725	77.5	8,041,997	71.3	85.1	82.7	97.3	96.6	97.6	85.5	84.8	91.5
French	341,502	7.4	482,350	6.3	509,264	4.5	4.6	2.7	9.5	10.5	12.1	2.3	4.5	7.9
Other	500,598	10.9	1,253,035	16.3	2,734,289	24.2	10.3	14.5						
Rest of the Country														
Total	4,840,509	100.0	7,202,875	100.0	10,508,200	100.0	100.0	100.0						
English	3,641,699	75.2	5,799,615	80.5	8,420,438	80.1	91.2	89.7	97.6	98.6	98.5	90.3	92.7	92.3
French	195,208	4.0	229,230	3.2	231,651	2.2	1.7	0.8	5.4	5.6	7.3	1.4	2.5	5.2
Other	1,003,602	20.7	1,174,030	16.3	1,856,111	17.7	7.1	9.4						

Note. The home language corresponds to the language spoken most often at home. In 2001, for mother tongue and home language, multiple answers were distributed equally among the languages reported.

Sources: Census of Canada, 1951, 1971, and 2001. Authors' calculations.

country (67.5 percent in 2001 compared to 67.0 percent in 1971), the proportion of people speaking English at home outside Quebec fell, except in New Brunswick. These changes are due to the marked rise in the relative size of the Allophone population across the country. When this trend overtakes the decrease in the proportion of official-language-minority population, the result is a drop in the relative size of the official-language majority.

The rapid rise in the proportion of Allophones is attributable to the immigrants who have landed in the country since the mid-1980s and to the increased proportion of the heritage mother tongues among immigrants (Marmen and Corbeil 2004). In fact, there was an increase in the proportion of Allophones among immigrants (69 percent in 2001, compared to 51 percent in 1971), and a decrease in the proportion of Anglophones (28 percent in 2001, compared to 45 percent in 1971); the proportion of Francophones remained very small (between 3 percent and 4 percent).

The decrease in the proportion and numbers of Anglophones in Quebec was essentially due to its strong net losses on migratory exchanges with the rest of the country. Between 1971 and 2001, these net losses were just over 275,000 (Marmen and Corbeil 2004). As a side effect, it increased the proportion of Francophones in Quebec.

The decline in the proportion of Francophones in the country as a whole has been essentially the result of the drop in their fertility rates since the 1950s in Quebec as well as in the rest of the country. Their fertility has remained below that of the rest of the population since the 1970s (Lachapelle 1988).

Women do not always transmit their mother tongue to their children. The ratio of the number of children with a given mother tongue to the number of children whose mothers have that mother tongue defines the index of linguistic continuity (Lachapelle and Henripin 1982). A language group benefits from intergenerational mobility when the index is higher than one and is at a disadvantage when the opposite applies. We calculated this index for children less than 18 years of age who, in 2001, lived in two-parent families (table 18.2).

This index shows that continuity is high among the Anglophone population. The index of continuity is also relatively high for Francophones in Quebec, although it is still lower than for Anglophones. This is due to the language preferences of Allophone women when they transmit French or English to their children. In 58 percent of cases, they transmit French, and in 42 percent, English, which is much higher than the proportion of the English mother tongue in Quebec. Outside Quebec, the phenomenon penalizes the Francophones, since in almost 30 percent of cases women do not transmit their French mother tongue.[4] As for Allophone women, 40 percent of them do not transmit their mother tongue to their children. These values

Table 18.2
Index of Linguistic Continuity Among Children Under 18 Years of Age Living in Two-Parent
Families, Canada, Quebec, Canada Outside Quebec, New Brunswick, Ontario, and the Rest
of Canada, 2001

	English	French	Other
Canada	1.16	0.98	0.60
Quebec	1.19	1.03	0.69
Canada outside Quebec	1.16	0.71	0.59
New Brunswick	1.05	0.94	0.43
Ontario	1.19	0.72	0.60
Rest of Canada	1.13	0.49	0.58

Source: 2001 Census, Catalogue no. 97F0007XCB2001011 and authors' calculations.

are not comparable other than for our specific goal, because Francophone women have been much more exposed to the risk of non-transmission of their mother tongue since they were almost all born in Canada, which is not the case with Allophone women.

The number of children by mother tongue is determined by the number of women of childbearing age by mother tongue, the differential fertility and the index of continuity. The small proportion of Allophones under 20 years of age in 2001 (19 percent nationally) is essentially a result of the low linguistic continuity of the non-official languages (table 18.3). The same situation exists for Francophones outside Quebec, which explains the lower proportion of Francophones under 20 years of age (18 percent) when compared to Anglophones (30 percent); as a side effect, the proportion of Francophones aged 65 and over is higher (15 percent) than that of Anglophones (11 percent).

In general, the proportion of Allophones aged 20 to 64 is higher because of the incidence of immigration within this population. This proportion is also higher within the Francophone population than among Anglophones, especially outside Quebec, because of the high fertility of Francophones in the past. This situation will reverse in the coming decades when the baby boomers are replaced by the baby busters who came after them.

The proportions of French speakers and English speakers are on the rise almost everywhere.[5] In Quebec, the proportion of French speakers[6] reached 95 percent in 2001, compared to 88 percent in 1951 (table 18.1). This marked increase has mainly been evident since 1971 for both French and English. The same applies outside Quebec, in spite of the decrease in the proportion of French as a mother tongue. However, there is a noteworthy exception: the proportion of French speakers has been slowly falling for the country as a whole, from 31.9 percent in 1951 to 31.0 percent in 2001.

Table 18.3

Distribution by Major Age Groups (in %) of the Population by Mother Tongue, Canada, Quebec, and Canada Outside Quebec, 2001

	Total	English	French	Other
Canada				
0–19 years	26.3	29.5	23.8	18.8
20–64 years	61.5	59.6	63.7	65.0
65 years and over	12.2	10.9	12.5	16.2
Total	100.0	100.0	100.0	100.0
Quebec				
0–19 years	24.6	27.4	24.7	21.3
20–64 years	63.1	59.0	63.2	65.3
65 years and over	12.3	13.6	12.1	13.4
Total	100.0	100.0	100.0	100.0
Canada outside Quebec				
0–19 years	26.8	29.5	18.4	18.4
20–64 years	61.0	59.6	66.6	65.0
65 years and over	12.2	10.8	15.0	16.6
Total	100.0	100.0	100.0	100.0

Source: 2001 Census, Catalogue no. 97F0007XCB2001001 and authors' calculations.

If we assume that people who report a mother tongue are always able to carry on a conversation in that language, a distinction can be made between people who speak it as a mother tongue from those who speak it as a second language. Therefore we can estimate the proportion of people who speak it as a second language among the people who do not have it as a mother tongue. Both the knowledge of French among non-Francophones and the knowledge of English among non-Anglophones are on the rise everywhere. Thus, in Quebec, the proportion of non-Francophones who speak French as a second language rose from 40 percent in 1971 to 71 percent in 2001. There is also a marked increase in the prevalence of English speakers among non-Anglophones (40 percent in 2001 compared to slightly fewer than 30 percent in 1971). Outside Quebec, the prevalence of knowledge of French among non-Francophones has not yet surpassed the 10 percent mark, except in New Brunswick.

In addition to linguistic duality, there is the phenomenon of territorial duality, with Francophones concentrated in Quebec, and Anglophones in the rest of the country. This is a somewhat simplified view, because Francophones represent one-third of the population of New Brunswick. Furthermore, in New Brunswick, Francophones are heavily concentrated in areas to the north and east, where they make up a majority of the population. To the west of Quebec, in Ontario, Francophones also comprise large minorities in the eastern and north-eastern parts of this province, areas bordering on Quebec. Quebec's Anglophone minority is mostly concentrated in Montréal and in the areas bordering on the United States (the Eastern Townships) or Ontario (the Outaouais). These areas of contact between the two official language groups, in Quebec, Ontario, and New Brunswick are known as the "bilingual belt," the areas that surround the essentially Francophone territory of Quebec (Castonguay 1998; Joy 1967; Lachapelle and Henripin 1982). Hence, there are considerable disparities in language distribution by region. Overall there are very few opportunities for contact between Francophones and Anglophones, except for the minorities. In fact, the population with French as mother tongue living in Quebec is increasing (86 percent in 2006 and 2001, compared with 84 percent en 1971 and 82 percent in 1951), as is the population speaking mostly French at home (91 percent in 2001, compared with 88 percent in 1971).

However, the concentration of French speakers in Quebec is declining (73 percent in 2006 and 2001 compared with 79 percent in 1971). This shift is the result of two factors: the decrease in Quebec's share of the Canadian population (24 percent in 2001 compared with 29 percent in 1966 and 1951) and the increased percentage of French speakers in Canada outside Quebec (11 percent in 2001 compared with 9 percent in 1971). The increase is proportionately lower in Quebec (95 percent in 2001 compared with 88 percent in 1971).

ABORIGINAL LANGUAGES

The preservation of any language requires that the incentive, the means, and the context exist to pass the language on from one generation to the next. The context is defined as the places where people live and the fora for interaction. While it is possible for Aboriginal people to function in their traditional languages within their own communities, this is not necessarily the case outside of their communities. Economic activity outside Aboriginal communities generally requires knowledge and competence in either English or French. Similarly, access to social services and other government services also requires communication in either English or French. Therefore, the context when dealing with the non-Aboriginal segments of Canadian society is not conducive to language retention.

The means to preserve languages are not uniformly available in all Aboriginal communities. Some communities have the necessary infrastructure, such as access to television programs in Aboriginal languages (through the Aboriginal Peoples Television Network), radio broadcasts through local stations, and print media in their respective languages (David 2004; Minore and Hill 1990).

Table 18.4
Distribution of Aboriginal Languages for Those Declaring Aboriginal Identity

			Degree of Language Use at Home			
Language	Ability to Speak N	Mother Tongue N	Only %	Mostly %	Equally %	Regularly %	Occasionally or Never %
Algonquian languages	171,600	142,090	29	25	8	27	11
Inuktitut (Eskimo)	32,775	29,695	49	32	1	18	0
Athapaskan languages	22,705	18,530	30	23	10	25	11
Siouan languages	4,950	4,310	43	9	14	17	17
Salish languages	5,000	3,210	5	3	12	42	38
Tsimshian languages	2,745	2,030	12	7	8	40	34
Wakashan languages	1,775	1,445	5	3	6	39	47
Iroquoian languages	1,225	670	2	2	3	46	46
Haida	275	165	0	6	0	55	39
Kutenai	220	170	6	6	18	21	50
Tlingit	230	105	0	0	0	62	38

Source: Statistics Canada – 2001 Census and calculations by the authors.

Other communities implemented programs to teach Aboriginal languages in their primary and secondary schools. The key to preserving a language is that a large proportion of the population in the community has some understanding and ability to speak the language, especially in the home. Concerns have been expressed over the loss of Aboriginal languages in Canada (Norris 1998).

More than thirty Aboriginal languages are separately tabulated in the census data. This analysis focuses on those declaring an Aboriginal identity and aggregates the languages into their major groups. Table 18.4[7] shows the distribution of the knowledge of Aboriginal languages, mother tongues, and the degree to which the language is spoken at home for the major groups. The data are sorted in descending order of number of people having a given mother tongue. The degree to which the language is spoken at home is divided into four categories according to the frequency of use.

Previous work on this topic highlights some of the factors that may contribute to language retention. For instance, Norris (1998) and Beaujot and Kerr (2004) comment on the importance of age in maintaining a language. It is often the elderly who are most proficient. The middle-aged generation is often less proficient since they were the group that experienced the Residential School system – a system that emphasised non-aboriginal languages in its programs. Geography is also important. Aboriginal people who live in communities in which there is a larger concentration of indigenous speakers "appear to find it easier to retain their language" (Beaujot and Kerr 2004).

Table 18.5

Population by Aboriginal Identity Who Know an Aboriginal language, Who Declare an Aboriginal Mother Tongue and Who Declare That They Speak an Aboriginal Language Most Often or Equally with English or French in the Home

Aboriginal Identity (single response)	Median Age	Knowledge		Mother Tongue		Home Language	
		Proportion of the Population	Median Age	Proportion of the Population	Median Age	Proportion of the Population	Median Age
		%		%		%	
North American Indian	23.5	30.9	32.0	24.5	33.0	15.0	29.0
Métis	27.0	5.7	40.0	3.4	40.5	1.5	31.0
Inuit	20.6	70.0	22.0	63.3	23.0	51.2	20.0

Source: 2001 Public Use Microdata File and calculations by the authors.

Language retention can be measured by calculating the degree to which the language is used in the home for those who declared that language as their mother tongue. One can assume that if a language is spoken in the home it is likely that all members of the household are exposed to it, thereby improving the likelihood of retention.

Members of households in the Algonquian, Inuktitut, Athapaskan, and Siouan language groups are frequently exposed to their respective languages since more than 50 percent speak it predominantly (labelled as only and mostly in table 18.4) and well over 80 percent speak it at least regularly in the home. The people declaring their mother tongues in the remaining language groups tend to use it less often than either English or French in the home.

As stated earlier, age has a bearing on whether the language is transmitted to subsequent generations. For example, a language group may suffer substantial loss over time as a result of normal demographic processes if it is mostly the elderly who speak it at home or in any other context.

Table 18.5 shows the distribution of people declaring Aboriginal identity by median age and language characteristics. The first pair of substantive columns (columns 3 and 4) shows the percentage and median age of the population who declared that they were able to conduct a conversation in an Aboriginal language. The next pair of columns provides comparable statistics for those who declared an Aboriginal mother tongue. The final pair of columns shows the percentage and median age for those who declared an Aboriginal mother tongue and who also speak that language most often or equally with English or French in the home.

The Métis are least likely to either declare an Aboriginal mother tongue (3.4 percent) or to be able to conduct a conversation in an Aboriginal language (5.7 percent). Furthermore, a small fraction of the Métis who declared an Aboriginal mother tongue also speaks it in the home. We also note that the median age of the Métis who either speak an Aboriginal language or who declare it as their mother tongue is 40 (compared to 27 for the total Métis population), indicating that it is generally the older members of the community who have any connection with that language.

About one quarter of North American Indians declared an Aboriginal mother tongue in 2001 and just over 30 percent indicated that they were able to conduct a conversation in an Aboriginal language. It must be noted that their median age is about ten years older than the total North American Indian population, indicating that fewer young people are either speaking the language or have it as their mother tongue. The combined effect of age and language use in the home suggests that transmission and preservation may be at risk for this population.

The median ages of the Inuit who either speak it (22) or declare Inuktitut as their mother tongue (23) and that of the total Inuit population (20.6) are similar. We also see in table 18.5 that relatively high proportions of the Inuit speak an Aboriginal language (70 percent), declare it as their mother tongue (63.3 percent) and speak it most often or at least equally with English or French in the home (51.2 percent). Over 80 percent of the Inuit population lives in Nunavut, northern parts of Québec, and in Newfoundland and Labrador (Statistics Canada 2003). The geographic context in which they live, the relative youth of the population having some direct association with the language, and the high proportions who speak the language suggest that conditions exist to preserve Inuktitut and to transmit it to subsequent generations (Dorais 1995).

We need to consider the population who know an Aboriginal language but who do not declare it as their mother tongue in order to complete this analysis. The data show us that the proportion of Aboriginal people who know an Aboriginal language among those who did not declare it as their mother tongue is 8.5 percent for North American Indians and 18.3 percent for the Inuit. While these proportions are relatively small, they add to the capacity of the respective Aboriginal groups to preserve their languages. Furthermore, an analysis of the respective median ages for this subgroup of the population shows that North American Indians and the Inuit who are able to conduct a conversation in an Aboriginal language are substantially younger than those whose mother tongue is an Aboriginal language (26 years compared to 34 years for the North American Indians and 16 compared to 23 years for the Inuit). This suggests that some Aboriginal languages are transmitted to the young people as a second language. These points notwithstanding, criteria beyond those presented in this section need to be considered when looking at the future of Aboriginal languages in Canada.

HERITAGE LANGUAGES IN CANADA

The methodology used in this section is similar to that used in the previous section. The means to preserve a language and the context in which the language is to be preserved take on a different significance for heritage languages (when compared to Aboriginal languages). Most of these languages (other than English, French, and Aboriginal languages) are the lingua franca for a society living in the source country from which the immigrants to Canada arrived. Therefore, we are not discussing the disappearance or preservation of a language but rather the change over time in its use in Canadian society. In addition to the factors discussed earlier in this chapter, the preservation of a heritage language depends on whether or not the individual is an immigrant or direct descendent of immigrants. This is a measure of both the potential cultural distance from the source country and the period during which the individual was at risk of shifting to either English or French. The literature suggests that cultural distance from one's roots may contribute substantially to the reduction in the use of the language (Rumbaut, Massey, and Bean 2006).

It is possible to associate a heritage language with a given ethnic group in most instances.[8] Furthermore, it is helpful to classify ethnic groups on the basis of the proportion who are immigrants in order to examine the retention of heritage languages.[9] The first category consists of the groups in which less than 20 percent of those declaring that origin are immigrant. It includes the Dutch, German, and Ukrainian, all of which have a long settlement history in Canada. The second category (Greek, Italian, Polish, and Portuguese) includes the groups in which between 20 percent and 60 percent are immigrants. The final group are those in which more than 60 percent are immigrants. It includes the more recent arrivals to Canada – notably the Chinese, South Asians, and Vietnamese.[10]

Language retention will be examined in two stages in this section. We begin by exploring the basic language characteristics of people declaring one of the aforementioned ethnic origins. The results in table 18.6 show that an inverse relationship exists between the proportion of people who declare a heritage mother tongue and the proportion of immigrants in the group. People who declare their origins to be one of the groups in the first category are less likely to report a heritage mother tongue. Furthermore, their median ages are higher than that of the total population of Canada (37.6 years) – a

Table 18.6

Proportion of People Declaring a Heritage Mother Tongue and Home Language for Selected Ethnic Origins

	Mother Tongue Is a Heritage Language		Heritage Home Language for Those Having a Heritage Mother Tongue	
Ethnic origin	%	Median Age (years)	%	Median Age (years)
Dutch	18.9	56	13.7	50
German	16.2	55	25.6	42
Ukrainian	17.9	60	27.3	46
Greek	63.1	45	57.1	54
Italian	41.8	50	43.0	62
Polish	30.9	46	50.5	42
Portuguese	62.9	40	54.7	48
Chinese	83.3	38	79.8	39
South Asian	69.2	33	75.0	33
Vietnamese	84.8	33	81.6	35

Source: 2001 Public Use Microdata File and calculations by the authors.

result that is consistent with literature dealing with linguistic retention over time (see Rumbaut, Massey, and Bean 2006).

The results in table 18.6 show that people belonging to the second group are younger than those in the first category. A greater proportion of immigrants suggests that the ties to the source country are more recent. Hence, exposure to the language through relatives living in the source country is more likely. Not surprisingly, the people belonging to the final category of ethnic group are most likely to declare a heritage mother tongue. This result is to be expected, given that most of the people belonging to one of these groups are immigrants and had acquired their mother tongue before coming to Canada.

The second set of columns in table 18.6 show, among the people who declared a heritage mother tongue, the proportion who speak it at least on a regular basis at home. These results indicate that the proportion of people who use a heritage language in the home is consistent with the pattern we saw for mother tongue.

The next stage of this analysis explores the patterns of language retention by generation status.[11] The order of presentation of the ethnic groups in table 18.6 will be used for all charts in this section.

In general, the results shown in figure 18.1 are consistent with the theory of linguistic assimilation (Gordon 1964; Rumbaut, Massey, and Bean 2006). The proportion of people declaring a heritage mother tongue declines over the generations. In fact, fewer than 10 percent of the people in these ethnic

Figure 18.1
Proportion of People Declaring a Heritage Mother Tongue by Generation Status for Selected Ethnic Origins[14]

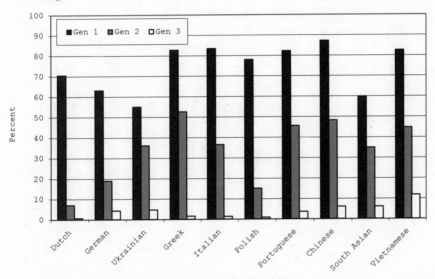

Source: 2001 Public Use Microdata File and calculations by the authors.

groups declare a heritage mother tongue by the third generation. It is clear from these results that the socialisation processes, both through formal education and through the labour force and social contact, have an impact on the transmission of mother tongue across generations. However, the effect is not uniform across all ethnic groups. Relatively high proportions of people declare a heritage mother tongue in the second generation, indicating that the transmission process continues for a longer period for those with European origins belonging to the second group[12] and for those with Asian origins. Cultural distance may explain this result. Other research on the acculturation of immigrant groups has shown that these ethnic communities tend be more institutionally complete with respect to cultural opportunities (including heritage language education) and that people belonging to these ethnic groups tend to retain attachment to their origins and to their language (Goldmann 2000).

Figure 18.2 shows the proportion of people with a heritage mother tongue who declare that they speak it most often in the home by generation status. No values are shown for the third generation for people of Greek, Portuguese, and Vietnamese ancestry since the sample size is too small to provide reliable estimates. There is a general decline in the proportion of

Figure 18.2

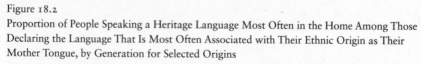

Proportion of People Speaking a Heritage Language Most Often in the Home Among Those Declaring the Language That Is Most Often Associated with Their Ethnic Origin as Their Mother Tongue, by Generation for Selected Origins

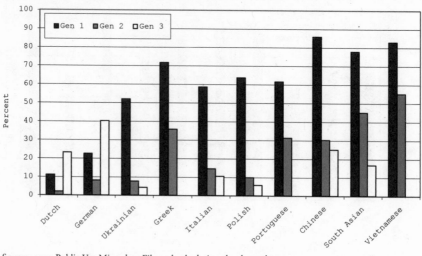

Source: 2001 Public Use Microdata File and calculations by the authors.

people speaking a heritage language most often in the home over the generations for most ethnic groups. Factors such as exogamy, the socialisation process, and the geographic context in which the people live contribute to this decline.

People of Dutch and German ancestry are notable exceptions. The data from the 2001 Census indicate that 87 percent of the first-generation Dutch and 75 percent of the first-generation German speak English most often in the home. This can be explained in part by how long they have been living in Canada. Approximately 80 percent of Dutch immigrants and 75 percent of the German immigrants have been living in Canada more than 30 years.[13]

The results that we see in this section suggest that the effect of linguistic preservation, when measured by the proportion of people who declare a heritage language as their mother tongue and who speak a heritage language in the home, tends to diminish substantially by the third generation. In fact, we have seen that the use of some languages vanishes entirely by the third generation. However, one must also consider the number of people who can carry on a conversation in the language.

Figure 18.3 shows the proportion of people who do not declare a heritage language as their mother tongue but are able to speak that language by generation. The obvious pattern that emerges is the sharp decline in the proportion

Figure 18.3
The Proportion of People Who Are Able to Speak a Heritage Language Associated with
Their Ethnic Origin and Who Do Not Declare It as Their Mother Tongue, by Generation
for Selected Origins

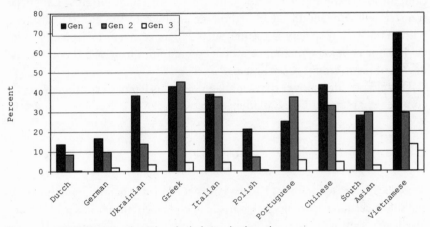

Source: 2001 Public Use Microdata File and calculations by the authors.

of people in the third generation who are able to speak the language. This
result suggests that linguistic assimilation is likely to occur by the third generation regardless of the strength of language retention in the second generation. It should be noted that Rumbaut, Massey, et al. (2006) found similar
results in their analysis of immigrant populations in California.

CONCLUSION

During the twentieth century the characteristics of the Canadian population were transformed as a result of the number of immigrants and their
changing composition. Canada has thus become a multi-ethnic society
that still retains its language duality. According to the 2001 Census, about
90 percent of the population spoke English or French most often at home
and a little more than 98 percent used either or both official languages most
often at work. The proportion of Francophones is decreasing at the national
level, and they are increasingly concentrated in Quebec.

With respect to Aboriginal languages, the conditions for some transmission
appear to be present for the larger language groups (Algonquian, Inuktitut,
Athapaskan, and Siouan). Furthermore, the number of people who can speak
an Aboriginal language exceeds the number who declares it as their mother
tongue. If we consider the number who knows an Aboriginal language, it
is reasonable to conclude that the capacity for some language retention is

present. In fact, the data show that a small proportion of Aboriginal languages are being transmitted to the young as a second language.

The analysis of heritage languages shows evidence of linguistic assimilation, although the impact is not uniform for all ethnic origins. Language transfer is less pronounced for ethnic groups where the cultural distance with main stream society is greater. Also, language retention appears to be evident for people belonging to ethnic communities in which there is some degree of institutional completeness.

This chapter has shown that language is, and is likely to continue to be, a complex characteristic of Canadian society.

NOTES

1 According to the census, this is the first language learned at home during childhood and still understood, a definition that has remained practically unchanged for more than half a century.

2 Since 1971, the census asks a question on the language spoken most often at home. In the 2001 Census, a sub-question was added to determine the other languages spoken "on a regular basis" at home.

3 If one considers the 120 or so mother tongues other than French or English identified in the 2001 Census, there is a probability of 0.042 that two allophones taken at random in the country will have the same mother tongue.

4 This proportion has had minor changes over the previous three decades.

5 The question asked in the census on the knowledge of official languages is used to distinguish between people who can carry on a conversation either in English only or in French only, or in English and French, or in neither of the two official languages. This question has hardly changed since at least the 1971 Census. It was worded as follows in the 2001 Census: "Can this person speak English or French well enough to conduct a conversation?"

6 These are people who reported that they could conduct a conversation in French but not in English, as well as those who reported that they could do so in English and in French.

7 One must be careful in interpreting the results in this table since the number of people who declared an Aboriginal mother tongue or home language is extremely small for some of the language groups. Furthermore, a number of Aboriginal communities did not participate in the Census.

8 Spanish is a notable exception since many people with Caribbean and South and Central America heritage have Spanish as their mother tongue. Therefore, it will not be included in the analysis.

9 The number of individual ethnic origins listed in the Census Public Use Microdata Files is limited. Therefore, the empirical analysis in this section is restricted to the following ethnic origins: Chinese, Dutch, German, Greek, Italian, Polish, Portuguese, South Asian, Ukrainian, and Vietnamese.

10 The respective mean ages of the immigrants in the three categories of ethnic groups mirrors their immigration history. Group 1 is between 50 and 60, Group 2 is between 40 and 50, and group 3 is less than 40.

11 The first generation is defined as persons who are born outside of Canada. The second generation is those individuals who have at least one foreign-born parent. The third generation consists of individuals whose parents were born in Canada.

12 The Polish are the exception. Their language patterns in the second generation tend to be similar to the Germans.

13 The unusual distributions that exist in Figure 18.2 for immigrants of Dutch and German origins are not fully explained by the observations in this paragraph. The higher value for language retention at home in the third generation for these origins is surprising. This may be explained by a selective process. The few who declared a heritage mother tongue in the third generation are probably quite different from the main-stream population declaring these origins.

14 The data represented in this figure are for the population 15 years of age and older. Data on the birth place of parents were not collected for the population under the age of 15.

REFERENCES

Beaujot, Roderic, and Don Kerr. 2004. *Population Change in Canada*. Toronto: Oxford University Press

Castonguay, Charles. 1998. "The Fading Canadian Duality." In *Language in Canada*, ed. J.R. Edwards, 36–60. Cambridge: Cambridge University Press

David, Jennifer. 2004. "Aboriginal Language Broadcasting in Canada: An Overview and Recommendations to the Task Force on Aboriginal Languages and Cultures." Aboriginal Peoples Television Network

Dorais, Louis-Jacques. 1995. "Language, Culture and Identity: Some Inuit Examples." *Canadian Journal of Native Studies* 15: 293–308

Goldmann, Gustave J. 2000. "The Determinants of Acculturation: How Immigrants Adapt." Department of Sociology and Anthropology, Carleton University, Ottawa

Gordon, Milton. 1964. *Assimilation in American Life: The Role of Race, Religion and National Origins*. New York: Oxford University Press

Joy, Richard J. 1967. *Languages in Conflict: The Canadian Experience*. Ottawa: Richard J. Joy

Lachapelle, Réjean. 1988. "Changes in Fertility among Canada's Linguistic Groups." *Canadian Social Trends* (Fall): 2–8

– 1999. "Preface." In L. Marmen and J.P. Corbeil, eds. *Language in Canada: 1996 Census, New Canadian Perspectives.* Ottawa: Minister of Public Works and Government Services Canada

– and Jacques Henripin. 1982. *The Demolinguistic Situation in Canada: Past Trends and Future Prospects*, trans. by D.A. Mark. Montreal: Institute for Research on Public Policy

Marmen, Louise, and Jean-Pierre Corbeil. 2004. *Language in Canada: 2001 Census.* Ed. by C. Heritage. Ottawa: Minister of Public Works and Government Services Canada

Minore, J.B., and M.E. Hill. 1990. "Native Language Broadcasting: An Experiment in Empowerment." *The Canadian Journal of Native Studies* 10: 97–119

Norris, Mary Jane. 1998. "Canada's Aboriginal Languages." *Canadian Social Trends* 51: 36

Rumbaut, Rubén, Douglas S. Massey, and Frank S. Bean. 2006. "Linguistic Life Expectancies: Immigrant Language Retention in Southern California." *Population and Development* 32: 447–60

Statistics Canada. 2003. *Aboriginal Peoples of Canada: A Demographic Profile.* 2001 Census. Ottawa. Cat.no. 96F0030XIE2001007

Veltman, Calvin. 1983. *Language Shift in the United States.* New York: Mouton Publishers

Index

spatial distribution. *See* regional distribution
Statistics Canada: census 3, 16–17; data productions, 17; microdata, 17–18
suburbs. *See* urbanization

urban: definition, 176; growth of, 177–9; reasons for growth, 181
urbanization: and ethnic-origin, 160–9, 302–3; general, 11; and immigration, 183–5; internal differentiation of metropolitan area populations, 186; metropolitan centres, emergence of, 175–6; recent migration, 181–6

unions. *See* cohabitation; marriage; same-sex unions

visible minorities: ethnic-origin, 163–7, 295–6; growth of, 213–16; immigrants, 213–16; inequalities, 217–24; regional distribution, 163–7
vital statistics, 4

women: age composition of, 41–6; educational attainment, 85–6, 88–92
world population: elderly, 287; trends, 33–4